DEFENSE MANAGEMENT

Prentice-Hall, Inc., *Englewood Cliffs, New Jersey*

Edited by

Stephen Enke

Manager, Special Projects,
General Electric TEMPO

recently
Deputy Assistant Secretary, Economics,
Department of Defense

DEFENSE MANAGEMENT

DEFENSE MANAGEMENT
Edited by Stephen Enke

Library of Congress Catalog Card Number: 67-10540

Printed in the United States of America—C

Current Printing (last digit):
10   9   8   7   6   5   4   3   2   1

Prentice-Hall International, Inc., *London*
Prentice-Hall of Australia, Pty. Ltd., *Sydney*
Prentice-Hall of Canada, Ltd., *Toronto*
Prentice-Hall of India (Private) Ltd., *New Delhi*
Prentice-Hall of Japan, Inc., *Tokyo*

Defense Management describes a revolution that still is little understood on the "outside." Each of its chapters appraises or describes some aspect of cost-benefit analysis of the kind now widely practiced within the U.S. Department of Defense. It is the first major work on this subject since Secretary Robert S. McNamara came to the Pentagon in January, 1961, and changed defense planning forever.

EVOLUTION OF COST-BENEFIT ANALYSIS BY ECONOMISTS

Any revolutionary idea is evolved slowly and applied painfully. It was in 1948 that a few economists in RAND's old Broadway Building in Santa Monica—notably Hitch, Alchian, and this writer—first evolved and applied cost-benefit principles to the prescription of strategic-bombing systems.[1] In late December, 1960, Secretary McNamara selected Charles J. Hitch as his future Comptroller. During 1961–62 most of what is novel and important about the present Pentagon instruments of management came into operation. Among these innovations, ably described for the first time by Dr. William A. Niskanen in the opening chapter, are the interacting Presidential Memos, Joint Strategic Objectives Plan, Program Change Proposals, Program Packaging, and the Five-Year Force Structure and Financial Plan.

Accompanying these changes was an important accounting innovation. The military establishment of the United States had long recorded and estimated disbursements by such *objects* as pay and allowances, construction, and fuel—as most foreign nations still do. Arranging costs in such a way defines rational management by a Secretary or Minister of Defense, which is perhaps why the military services in most countries favor it.

Previously it was not readily possible to "cost" a B-52 wing or a Polaris submarine. The many types of costs incurred in developing, acquiring, and operating such weapons systems could not be collected into relevant totals and without knowing the total costs of rival B-52 and Polaris systems, the *cost* part of cost-benefit analysis is clearly impossible.

One of the great achievements of Comptroller Hitch, based on the pioneer work while at RAND of

Preface

[1] See "Using Costs to Select Weapons," *American Economic Review, Papers and Proceedings* (May, 1965), by the editor.

Mr. David Novick, Dr. Harold Asher, and Dr. Robert Grosse, was to establish each major weapons system and certain military activities as program *elements* and to "cost" them. The result was a kind of accounting column-and-row matrix with yearly costs available by object, as before, but also now by element. Programming by such elements is one of several essential instruments of defense management.

Cost-benefit analysis also requires that the "benefits," or "outputs," of services performed by different weapons systems be studied. In the Comptroller's office in the early months of 1961 was the youthful, energetic, and brilliant Dr. Alian C. Enthoven, directly in charge of an expanding staff analyzing rival weapons systems. In 1965 this "whizziest" of all the McNamara "whiz kids" was elevated to the position of Assistant Secretary of Defense for Systems Analysis.

Institutionally, besides confirming the role of systems analysis in the defense establishment, this marked the "coming of age" of military cost-benefit analysis.

The military departments initially did not favor the managerial innovations that assisted Mr. McNamara in functioning as the first effective Secretary of Defense in the nation's history. The generals and admirals were most hostile to the cost-benefit analysts, who often recommended against some prized weapons system of their own service. It was incredible to them that these youngsters, many being Ph.D.'s in Economics of all things, could have anything to contribute compared with their own combat or military-command experience.

During the years, these attitudes have softened. Many senior military officers have come to realize that operations analysts, together with scientists and economists, are qualified to evaluate *future* weapons systems. The reason for this is explained below.

When it comes to preparing for a possible thermonuclear war between the Soviet Union and the United States, military personnel have little more experience than do operations analysts, and it is worth remembering that no commander of SAC has yet conducted an intercontinental ballistic missile exercise or campaign. Conversely, when it comes to ground-force engagements or antisubmarine warfare, only the most arrogant of defense economists would deny the value of direct-command experience. Indeed, one purpose of this book is to explain through an examination of different problems how interdependent military, scientific, and cost-benefit analysts are when recommending future force structures.

Since early 1965, the cost-benefit revolution in defense has spread to other agencies of government. The Bureau of the Budget, notably under the efforts of Henry S. Rowen, has been promoting the establishment of program-budgeting units. Thus in HEW, the Post Office, and elsewhere, operations analysis and economics are being consciously applied.[2]

---

[2] It is interesting that this extension of cost-benefit analysis into government decision making owes almost nothing directly to our universities' economics departments. Indeed, during the early days of The RAND Corporation, leading professors at major institutions advised their new Ph.D.'s not to apply themselves to military problems. And yet the DoD was and is responsible for determining how half the federal budget is spent and how almost 10 per cent, in some years, of the resources of the U.S. economy are used!

WHAT COST-BENEFIT ANALYSIS IS

Essentially, cost-benefit analysis is operations analysis at one higher level of optimization, with the various physical inputs to the operation being variables rather than "givens." The overall constraint on the system's "output" basically is generalized resources, expressed perhaps as a money budget. Military cost-benefit analysis often compares and selects from among alternative weapons systems that are sufficiently in the future to allow time to translate available land, labor, and capital into not yet existing antiballistic missiles, orbiting atomic satellites, or some other imaginary weapons system.

Today's military cost-benefit analysis has its immediate origins in the operations analysis of World War II. The latter's methodology was developed greatly by Professor P. M. S. Blackett in Great Britain and such academicians as Phillip Morse and Bernard Koopman in the United States. But all these analyses concentrated on the best use of currently available equipment. There was no need to consider the cost or worth of physical "inputs" to the operations being examined. They stopped just short of applied economics.

Consider the commander of a convoy who has at his disposal a certain number of destroyer escorts—a carriers with aircraft, helicopters, and depth charges. His mission perhaps is to protect the convoy on the way to some destination with minimum tons of shipping lost. How he can best deploy and use his protective forces is a problem for operations analysts. If the commander follows their tactical doctrine, he should theoretically achieve the maximum "output" (e.g., take minimum losses) on an average per any single "input" (i.e., destroyers, helicopters, etc.) at his disposal. But what *kind* of forces he commands and what *quantities* of each are already given.

Cost-benefit analysis begins when the composition of the convoy-commander's forces becomes the question. What is the "trade-off" or substitution between ship-based helicopters and destroyer escorts, for example? The same operations analyses as employed before indicate perhaps, with no change in expected ship losses, that three more helicopters would be needed if one more destroyer were subtracted and cost analysts indicate that the cost or alternative employment worth of one more destroyer is far more than that of three helicopters. Thus, cost-benefit analysis would indicate that helicopters should be substituted for destroyers until their rate of substitution or "trade-off" is the reciprocal of their respective "worths" or costs. Then, the job, here supposed to be expected ship losses of no more than a given tonnage, will theoretically be done at least cost.

Where there is time to produce enough of some input, its "worth" is likely to be its cost of acquisition and operation, and this could be true of helicopters if the planning horizon were one or two years. However, new destroyers cannot be constructed and commissioned so rapidly, and they have alternative uses. In the interim their value, because of other employments, may be greater than their cost of acquisition, so they have a special but temporary scarcity value or "worth." The interim "worth" of such destroyers should be the cost of purchasing some other "input" to the rival operation that would be needed if one or more destroyers were subtracted from it. It is this intermediate period analysis, where only some inputs to an operation can be produced but others have to be taken from competing uses, that is the most difficult (because several operations have to be analyzed simultaneously).

Simpler is the case of a planning period so long that everything can be acquired in such quantities that the value of each input in the operation under analysis approximates its cost of acquisition and maintenance. Then the only constraint is money, used as an alias for generalized economic resources, and the object is to perform some "job" at least-money cost (or conversely, to maximize output for a given budget). The analyst is then in the fortunate position of being able to consider how best to do each job, on the supply or cost side at least, independently of other military missions.

Clearly, the more modest the scale of one or more "jobs," the more likely that all inputs will be available within the planning horizon without a scarcity value in excess of their money costs.

Cost-benefit analysis also is often used to select from among rival weapons systems. Reverting to the convoy example, perhaps destroyers using conventional depth charges constitute the present system and helicopters using nuclear depth charges comprise a possible rival system in the future. (They are *rival* rather than *complementary* systems if a given "output" can be obtained more economically using one system or the other but not some parts of both.)

It is important to understand that cost-benefit analyses, unlike simple operations analysis alone, does not try to maximize output in terms of a single input. All military jobs employ more than one input that is not a *free* good or service but costs something to use or acquire. The object then is to minimize the cost of these inputs *collectively* (or to maximize output for a limited budget) and not to use the lest possible quantity of some one input (or maximize output in terms of that particular input).

Thus, in a strategic-offense problem, two nonfree inputs are: (1) the nuclear materials and (2) the delivery vehicles used. The nuclear materials can be packaged in various ways to obtain more smaller-yield weapons or fewer larger-yield bombs or warheads. If the analyst ignored the costs and risks of delivery as free, his problem would mistakenly seem to be how to package nuclear materials in such a way as to maximize targets destroyed per unit-quantity of such materials. His resultant recommendation would be too many weapons of too low yield. This is what happened in the early years of planning for nuclear strategic bombing.

Had the physicists and operations analysts responsible ever taken an elementary economics course, they should have known better. Even a farmer, in deciding how to combine land, labor, fertilizer, and so on, does not add more and more fertilizer, regardless of cost, for instance, in an attempt to maximize his output per acre of land. Most cost-benefit analyses are actually applications of the most simple economic principles.

In almost any R&D problem involving a choice among rival weapons systems of the future, only the scientists and engineers can describe the *performance* (e.g., speed, endurance, rate of turn) and the engineering *characteristics* (e.g., materials, turbine inlet temperatures, type of fuel) of the major items in the system. The operations analysts need these performance estimates to calculate trade-offs among different hardware items in the total weapons system. The cost analysis need these engineering characteristics to estimate costs of construction, maintenance, and so on. The economists tend to be the integrators, defining the appropriate output of the system and being largely responsible for the overall analytic model that is to determine the most efficient combination. (For example, in the convoy illustration above, the economist attempting a still larger optimization might ascertain that the commander's prime "job" should be to kill submarines attacking his convoy rather than to thwart their attempts to sink his merchant ships.)

The role of the experienced military officer is also important. He alone may have a good sense of what operations can really be executed by military personnel and the amount of training exercises needed to acquire and to maintain the necessary proficiency. Thus, operations analysts, cost analysts, and hardware designers certainly need to consult the military.[3]

SELECTION OF AUTHORS

The author of each of the twenty chapters that follow was selected with only one constraint. It was decided that no one should contribute who, on date of publication, was serving in the Office of the Secretary of Defense (OSD). In retrospect, this decision now seems more of an advantage than a handicap, for it has resulted in more freely expressed views by people who are almost as well informed through either close association or former employment with OSD.

Today, almost twenty years since modern defense cost-benefit analysis was born, there are many competent and experienced analysts from whom an editor can choose. They are to be found mostly within a small family of organizations, all closely linked to OSD, the Joint Staff, or one of the military services. Among these are the Institute for Defense Analyses (OSD and Joint Staff), The RAND Corporation (USAF and OSD), the Center for Naval Analyses (USN), and the Research Analysis Corporation (USA). Mention should also be made of the Hudson Institute and General Electric TEMPO. Each chapter has been written by men who have gained their experience at one or more of these institutions.

Because of this expanding group of experienced analysts, it has been possible in Parts II and III to present a variety of chapters by acknowledged experts in their fields. Not only have a broad range of subjects been covered, but the method of treatment also varies considerably. So does the language of the authors—ranging from ordinary prose in some chapters to extensive use of mathematical symbols in others.

Part I, Pentagon Decision Making, is designed for *everyone* who is interested in the management of the DOD. Its five chapters describe the basic concepts and/or main instruments of management as introduced in 1961 and since. Some

---

[3] Nothing is new. Because cost-benefit analysis is a kind of common-sense planning, it is not surprising that some military leaders of history seem to have used its concepts. Among these are Julius Caesar and Napoleon Bonapart; von Clausewitz' writings hint at it, too. But any such applications were quite unsystemmatic.

of the authors also assess these new procedures candidly—free of editorial consorship and without our necessary agreement.

Finally, before turning the reader over to the authors, it is well recognized that the present set of Pentagon procedures can stand some further improvement, this is always true in any large organization. Cost-benefit analysis is less easy to apply to general-purpose forces than to strategic forces—RAND tackled the easier problems in the early days. No system of analysis or of management is better than the men performing it. Much of the reason for the fantastic advance in defense management starting in 1961 is attributable to Secretary McNamara and the able men he recruited into OSD. Nevertheless, many of the authors are perfectionists, and they tend to dwell more on what remains to be done than on what has been accomplished. Their criticisms may be eagerly quoted by persons and interests hostile to the present management within the Pentagon. In many ways this would be regrettable, ironic, and even perverse, for almost each one of the twenty-four authors concerned would readily acknowledge that Secretary McNamara is the most effective "manager of defense" yet to serve the United States.

Stephen Enke

Preface

I

PENTAGON DECISION MAKING

1

II

COST EFFECTIVENESS APPLICATIONS

88

Contents

III

SPECIAL DEFENSE PROBLEMS
267

17 Defense Expenditures and the Domestic Economy

18 Defense Decentralization Through Internal Prices

19 NATO Defense Planning: The Political and Bureaucratic Constraints

20 Military Assistance Programs

1
PENTAGON DECISION MAKING

WILLIAM A. NISKANEN

Institute for Defense Analyses

William A. Niskanen, Jr., is presently the Director of the Economic and Political Studies Division of the Institute for Defense Analyses. This division is engaged in contract research for the Department of Defense and other federal agencies. His recent independent research has been focused on the organization of the overall federal resource-management process. Dr. Niskanen previously served as the Director of Special Studies in the Office of the Secretary of Defense and as an economist at The RAND Corporation; he has also worked for short periods with the Bureau of Mines, the Treasury Department, The University of Chicago, and the University of California at Los Angeles. The author received his undergraduate education at Harvard and his Ph.D. in economics from The University of Chicago.

1

The Defense
Resource Allocation Process

INTRODUCTION

Department of Defense budgets were approximately $50 billion a year from fiscal year 1962 through fiscal year 1965—an amount representing 8 to 10 per cent of the U.S. gross national product. This chapter summarizes and evaluates the process of determining the total Defense budget and the allocation of funds among the major defense activities. The gross characteristics of the present Defense program are outlined, the program-change process is described, and several general problems of defense management are identified. Later chapters describe the resource-allocation problems in some of the major mission areas and support activities.

It is important to recognize that the focus of both this chapter and the book is upon the decisions to provide military forces, not upon the decisions to use these forces as an instrument of U.S. policy—upon resource allocation, not upon resource utilization. The complex decision process by which U.S. military forces are controlled, operated, deployed, and committed interacts, over a period, with the resource-allocation process, involving some of the same people and component organizations. But it is beyond the scope of this book to describe and evaluate the short-run resource-utilization process.

THE DEFENSE PROGRAM

U.S. military forces are now more powerful and flexible than at any time in our peacetime history, and a major share of the credit for the improved capabilities of these forces must be granted to the eighth Secretary of Defense, Robert S. McNamara. The Defense program—representing the aggregate of existing and planned military forces, support activities, and funding—is also subject to greater control by McNamara than was the case with any of his predecessors. What are the primary instruments that McNamara and his principal assistants have used to shape and control the defense program? What are the historical and institutional reasons for the use of these instruments? Most importantly, perhaps, what part of the substantial recent improvement in the capabilities of U.S. military forces represents the personal contribution of McNamara and his assistants, and what part is attributable to the use of these new instruments of program control?

The basic directive governing the Defense program defines clearly and forcefully the primary instrument of program control:

The "Five Year Force Structure and Financial Program" is the official program for the Department of Defense. The programming system, outlined herein, will provide the means for submission, review, record keeping, and decision making on the DoD program. The planning, programming, resource, materiel, and financial management systems of all DoD components will be correlated with the programming system set forth herein."[1]

[1] The Department of Defense Directive Number 7045.1, October 30, 1964. Subject: DoD Programming System Section I.C.

The Five-Year Program is a set of tables, updated quarterly, which presents the officially approved level of military forces and support activities, manpower, and funding. These characteristics of the defense program are displayed and controlled in two critical dimensions:

Output—related information by major mission and activity, and
Time—related information for several prior years, the current fiscal year, and a subsequent five-year period.

These two dimensions of control represent the major changes from the type of program control that existed prior to 1961. Until that time, Congress and the Department of Defense had exercised program control through appropriations by military service and by input category for a single fiscal year. Although Congress still exercises its primary control of the defense program in this way, the Department of Defense analyzes, formulates, and controls the defense program by the mission and activity categories for a five-year planning period: Funding by service and input categories is a by-product of the present Defense program rather than its basic building block.

The Historical Basis

Some lessons from recent history will better explain the reason for this fundamental change in the dimensions of defense-program control. If these new concepts of program control are now so important, how did the U.S. until 1961 (and other nations up to the present) manage defense programs with any effectiveness? In retrospect, the reason is clear: *Resource control by component organizations provides an adequate basis for program control only if there is a strong separation of missions by organization.* This condition prevailed through the end of World War II, but considerable interservice mission competition developed in the postwar period.

Through the end of World War II, the Army, Navy, and (Army) Air Force each had a single primary mission. The primary Army mission was that of sustained land combat in the European and Pacific theaters. In addition, at the start of the war the Army had maintained a small coast artillery force (which rapidly lost importance) and also operated the troopships throughout the war. The primary Navy mission was that of sea combat against other naval forces; the Navy also provided the coastal defense against submarines and supported the movement of troops and cargo to the theaters. Even the Marines and the carrier air forces presented less competition to the similar Army and Air Force forces than that which developed in the postwar period; the Marines were used primarily as navy-supported assault forces and only in the Pacific theater; and the carrier air forces were used primarily against other naval forces and for support of assault operations beyond the reach of land-based tactical air forces. The primary Air Force mission was tactical air support of land combat in both theaters; during the course of the war the Air Force also developed forces for the strategic air mission against the German and Japanese heartlands and also operated a small air-transport force. For the most part, the services had different types of forces and, even for similar forces, noncompetitive mission responsibilities.

After World War II, this separation of mission responsibilities broke down as a consequence of the rapid development of military technology and the different character of the potential military opposition. Each of the services developed forces in new mission areas as a hedge against changes in strategic concepts and military technology. An attempt to limit interservice competition was made in the Key West Agreement of 1947, but this agreement was rapidly—and understandably—undermined.

The Army, until recently, had been least successful in broadening its mission base; and, as a consequence, its existence as a major force was threatened by the "massive retaliation" strategy following the Korean War. During the late 1950's, they based an unsuccessful case for operation of the strategic missile force upon their development of the intermediate-range Jupiter missile and upon the doctrinal argument that "missiles are artillery." The Army did develop effective surface-to-air missile systems for continental defense, a substantial force of light aircraft and helicopters, and a forward stockage posture to complement the airlift and sealift forces. Sustained land combat is still the primary Army mission, however, and at present this service is the only one characterized by a single dominant mission.

The Navy, whose position was threatened by the absence of a significant Soviet surface navy, was most successful in broadening its mission base. They developed an effective contribution to the strategic offense forces, first with the carrier air forces and subsequently with the POLARIS missile submarines; they also developed substantial antisubmarine forces to defend coastal waters and to protect sealift to the theaters where the large Soviet submarine force would be a threat. The Marines have been partly transformed from a navy-supported assault force to a more independent, sustained land-combat force. The carrier air forces have been reoriented to provide tactical air support for land combat in all theaters.

The Air Force, believing that the dominance of the strategic offense had been proved by the World War II strikes against the German and Japanese heartlands, concentrated for a long time after World War II on long-range delivery vehicles and nuclear weapons. During the last 1950's, however, the Air Force developed a substantial continental air-defense force and, more recently, a substantial tactical air force and airlift force.

At present, antisubmarine warfare is the only mission which is the single responsibility of one service (the Navy, in this case). The separate service contributions to each of the other missions are sufficient to present effective competition for a larger part of the mission resources.

The Administration and Congress recognized the major operational problems raised by interservice competition for a given mission and passed the Defense Reorganization Act of 1958. This Act established Unified Commands on a mission and theater basis with the primary responsibility for operational control of associated forces. It did not, however, address the major problems presented by this competition regarding the planning and control of the defense program. During the late 1950's, there was a growing recognition that the civilian administration of the Department of Defense had been losing control of the central political element of the defense program—the allocation of resources among missions. The traditional role of the political and management processes had been inverted: The allocation of resources among missions, properly a political decision, was being made primarily by the services; the allocation of resources within missions, properly a management decision, was often being made in the political arena. Several major controversies among the services on how to perform a given mission became public issues that were resolved only by bargaining and fiat.

Two substantially different solutions were developed during the late 1950's to correct this situation. The first proposed solution, linked with some of the most distinguished names in the eastern business and legal community, would have eliminated service competition by creating a single service or by reorganizing the services along clearly defined mission lines. (The Soviet military establishment, incidentally, is organized along these lines.) This proposal would have maintained program control by component organization through a significant restructuring of the component organizations.

The second proposed solution, developed primarily by a group of economists at The RAND Corporation, involved a change in program control from a service to a mission base; the services would maintain their present form and would continue to compete with each other for each of the major missions. This proposal was outlined in publications by David Novick[2] in 1954 and 1956 and by Charles Hitch and Roland McKean[3] in 1960. The proposed program format presented military forces and funding by mission aggregations and funding for major groups of support activities. The mission aggregations were designed to focus the political choices primarily upon the allocation of resources among missions and the management choices primarily upon the allocation within missions. The proposal also presented both forces and funding for a five-year planning period, in order to identify the long-range commitments inherent in the decisions of any one fiscal year.

The Experience Since 1961

After the Presidential campaign of 1960, in which the Defense program was a major issue, John F. Kennedy appointed Robert McNamara as Secretary of Defense and Charles J. Hitch as the Defense Comptroller. Before

[2] David Novick, "Efficiency and Economy in Government through New Budgeting and Accounting Procedures," R-254; and "A New Approach to the Military Budget," RM-1759, RM-1956, The RAND Corporation, 1954.

[3] Charles J. Hitch, and Roland N. McKean, *The Economics of Defense in the Nuclear Age* (Cambridge: 1960) Harvard University Press.

TABLE 1–1   The Defense Program: Financial Summary by Fiscal Year

	FY61	FY62 Orig.	FY62 Final	FY63	FY64	FY65	FY66 Prop.
Strategic Forces			(total obligational authority, in billions)				
Offense	—	7.6	9.0	8.4	7.3	5.3	4.5
Air and Missile Defense	—	2.2	2.0	1.9	2.0	1.7	1.6
Civil Defense	—	—	0.3	0.1	0.1	0.1	0.2
Total	—	9.8	11.3	10.4	9.4	7.1	6.3
Tactical Forces							
General Purpose	—	14.5	17.4	17.6	17.7	18.1	19.0
Airlift and Sealift	—	.9	1.2	1.4	1.3	1.5	1.6
Reserves	—	1.7	1.8	1.8	2.0	2.1	2.0
Military Assistance	—	1.8	1.8	1.6	1.2	1.2	1.3
Total	—	18.9	22.2	22.4	22.2	22.9	23.9
Support Activities							
General Support	—	11.4	12.1	13.0	13.7	14.3	14.6
Research and Development	—	3.9	4.2	5.1	5.3	5.1	5.4
Retired Pay	—	0.9	0.9	1.0	1.2	1.4	1.5
Total	—	16.2	17.2	19.1	20.2	20.8	21.5
Total Obligational Authority	46.1	44.9	50.7	51.9	51.9	50.9	51.7

six months had passed, the program format proposed by the RAND economists became the Five-Year Force Structure and Financial Program, with few changes. This set of tables, originally considered "the Secretary's book," became the only official program statement and was soon recognized, with some concern, as a powerful instrument for control of the defense program. From 1961 to the Viet Nam buildup, total defense expenditures increased by about 10 per cent, and the defense program was substantially strengthened in most major areas. Because these changes to the Defense program and the use of new management techniques are both associated with McNamara's administration of the Department of Defense, it is understandable that the program changes are generally attributed to the management changes. A careful examination of the published information, however, raises the serious question of whether the major changes to date *are*, in any fundamental way, attributable to the new management techniques.

The nature, magnitude, and timing of the major program changes can be adequately identified from the annual unclassified statements on the Defense program by the Secretary of Defense. Table 1–1 presents a financial summary of the Defense program for the fiscal years 1961 through 1966. The financial summary itself suggests many of the major changes. The funding information is not conclusive, of course, because the component funding levels are large and major changes could be implemented within a constant mission funding. The detailed force tables that accompany the financial summary are classified, but the published information is sufficient to identify the major force levels and the timing of the force-level decisions.

The major changes suggested by Table 1–1 are the consequence of two major concerns about the U.S. defense program—the survivability of the U.S. strategic offensive forces and the adequacy and mobility of U.S. tactical forces—which were raised, beginning in 1956, primarily by informed civilians outside the federal government. The first concern stemmed from the spectacular Soviet missile and space developments beginning in 1956 and the "intelligence gap" following the May, 1960, U-2 incident, which raised serious questions about the survivability of our own strategic offense forces (at that time consisting primarily of a warning-dependent bomber force). The second concern stemmed from the Suez and Hungary crises of 1956 and the Lebanon and Quemoy crises of 1958. These events raised serious doubts whether the U.S. had sufficient tactical forces and mobility to counter military threats that our strategic forces did not deter and for which the use of these forces was clearly purposeless. The Kennedy Administration came into office in 1961 with a commitment to correct these problems and already well developed ideas for changing the Defense program.

It is surprising how quickly these ideas were translated into the Defense program and how few subsequent changes have been made. In late 1960 the Eisenhower Administration had prepared a FY 1962 defense budget of $44.9 billion and had left office with a somber warning about the size of the U.S. military-industrial establishment. During the first few months of 1961, before the existence of the new program format or a formal programming system, the Office of the Secretary of Defense (OSD) prepared a revised FY 1962 defense budget of $50.7 billion, incorporating many of the force-level decisions still effective. During the remainder of 1961, with the programming system in a formative stage and with service contributions only nominal, OSD prepared a FY 1963 Defense budget of $51.9 billion, incorporating most of the major force-level decisions that remained in effect until the 1965 Vietnam buildup.

A review of the FY 1963 defense program submitted to Congress in January, 1962, illustrates how few major changes postdate this program. Although the Department of Defense, unlike other federal agencies, does not formally develop its program from a tentative budget estimate, the total Defense budget prior to the Vietnam buildup did not change by more than $1 billion (or 2 per cent) from the budgets prepared in 1961. Improvements in the efficiency of defense management, of course, have increased the "real output" of the defense program, but the growth of "output" since 1961 has been essentially constrained by the rate at which economies derived from an improved combination of forces and the cost reduction program could be realized. Basic decisions on the size of the strategic offense and defense forces reflected in the FY 1963 program are still effective. The quality of the strategic offense force has been improved, for example, by the recent decisions to procure the FB-111 and the MINUTEMAN II and

POSEIDON missile systems, but the total numbers of both bombers and missiles are essentially those programmed in 1961. The strategic defense force reflects the still current decision to thin out the air-defense force and strengthen civil defense. The FY 1963 program includes the aggregate Army, Navy, and Marine general-purpose forces that were effective until the recent Vietnam buildup and only a slightly smaller land-based tactical air force; this program also reflects the basic decisions to strengthen the airlift, sealift, and reserve forces and thin out the military-assistance program. Within a constant number of divisions and tactical air wings, of course, some improvements were made, such as the organization of the air-cavalry division and the development of the A-7 fighter bomber. The growth of the general-support program (primarily for improved command and control) and the research and development program were also largely planned at this time.

Since 1961, within a constant total budget, approximately $5 billion has been transferred from the strategic forces to various support activities, and the decisions reflected by this transfer were largely made in this first program. None of this discussion questions the correctness of the decisions, but it does suggest that the major program decisions were made on the basis of objectives defined, ideas developed, and analysis performed before the effective use of the new management techniques and, largely, outside the government.

During 1962, the first full year of the programming system, the services responded with enthusiasm to McNamara's open-ended invitation to submit program-change proposals based on their perceived requirements; the resulting FY 1964 program differed hardly at all from the FY 1963 program in either force levels or funding. The services had a direct confrontation with McNamara's analysts for the first time in 1962, and the result was a nearly wholesale rejection of the service proposals. From that year, unfortunately, the analytic process has often been associated with the refutation of service arguments rather than with the initiation and channeling of continued change.

Partly as a consequence of the use of the new program format and supporting analysis, two major opportunities for substantial improvement in the defense program have been identified in the last few years: The characteristics of a balanced defense against nuclear attack are now better understood; and the cost of achieving high survival levels is less than that previously estimated. The level and characteristics of an effective nonnuclear defense against a Soviet attack on Europe are also better understood, and the costs are much less than previously estimated. The President and Congress have the basic responsibility for the political choice of whether or not the Department of Defense should provide these capabilities. Both issues are complex and involve other parties, but it is disturbing that the two major program issues that have developed since 1961 are not yet resolved one way or another. The Defense programming system has proved to be an effective instrument of program control; only some period of external pressure, such as the Vietnam war, will prove whether or not it can be an effective instrument of program change.

THE DEFENSE PROGRAM-CHANGE PROCESS

The program-change process used on the Department of Defense since 1962 merits serious study—whatever one's interpretation of its effectiveness during this period. This is true because similar processes will be adopted by other federal agencies, and there are important lessons to be gleaned from the Defense experience by both the advocate and critic. A summary of the program-budget cycle serves as the best introduction to the characteristics of this process and the role of the component organizations. Table 1–2 presents a schema of this cycle in 1965 for preparation of the FY 1967 program and budget. A number of important features of this process should be recognized at the outset: First, the annual budget cycle is about eighteen months long (in this case, from August, 1964, through January, 1966). As a result, the component organizations, for some period, must begin preparation of the following program before the final decisions on the present program are made. Second, this process has been changed in some respect every year and will probably be subject to continued periodic change.[4]

Planning

The program-budget cycle begins in effect in August, eighteen months before the Defense program is presented to Congress and about two years before funds are appropriated. At this time the services and unified commands begin to prepare force recommendations to be reviewed by the Joint Chiefs of Staff (JCS) and presented in the Joint Strategic Objectives Plan (JSOP), Part VI. These recommendations are presumably based on a review of the world situation, an interpretation of U.S. national security policy, and an agreement on the mission responsibilities of the component organizations. This background work is completed in the prior March–June period and presented in the JSOP, Parts I–V; it reflects the traditional military approach that desired force levels can somehow be derived from the military threat and national policy statements; according to this approach, the costs of military forces determine only the difference between the desired and budgeted force levels. At present, the JSOP, Parts I–V, which include some incisive political analysis, are largely unread and almost totally ignored. The services and unified commands each propose a single array of forces, rather than a menu of alternatives with estimates of the respective military capabilities and costs; the language of these submissions suggests that a specific force level is either "required" or it is not. The service force recommendations usually reflect an estimate of "reasonably attainable" budget levels (often around 20 per cent more than the present budget), but it is

---

[4] Robert Anthony, Hitch's successor as Defense Comptroller, initiated a set of changes in the summer of 1966 which are expected to be fully implemented by July, 1967.

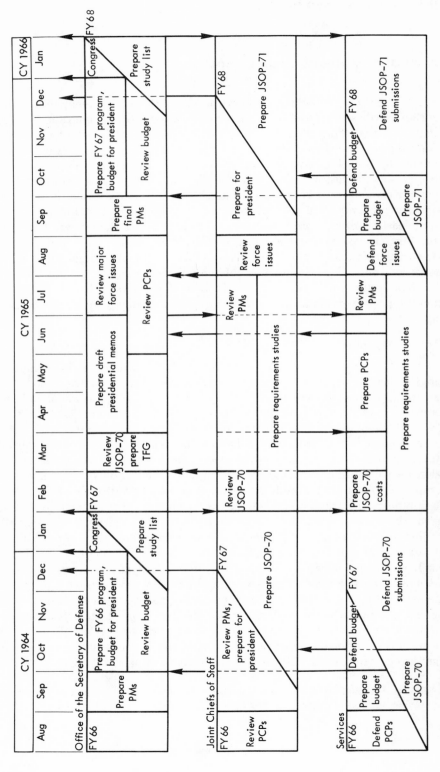

TABLE 1-2 Department of Defense Program—Budget Process for Preparation of FY 1967 Budget

not clear that force costs enter the determination of the composition of forces. Force recommendations of the unified commands are almost completely unaffected by economic considerations and, as such, are of little value; these submissions to the JSOP (which the Office of the Secretary of Defense does not usually see) are the only formal contribution by the unified commands to the Defense program-change process, with the exception, oddly enough, of their major role in planning the military-assistance program.

About September 15 the Joint Staff begins a review of the recent requirements studies and the service and unified command force recommendations as the basis for preparing the JSOP proposed forces. The force levels are now reviewed in three major groups: the strategic offense and defense forces, the general-purpose forces, and the airlift and sealift forces. This review includes a good deal of continued discussion with the military components as well as, in recent years, formal analysis of increasing quality. (This exercise is always hectic, as most of the analysis has to be completed before the final decisions on the present program are made.) The Chiefs review the force levels and associated costs proposed by the Joint Staff in February and on March 1 transmit their force-level recommendations to OSD in the format of the official Defense program. In some cases, the analysis presented in the JSOP may indicate the relationship of capability and cost for several force levels; the JSOP recommends a single array of force levels, however, unless one service has recommended an alternative level for some forces. In recent years, the aggregate cost of the JSOP recommended forces has been about 20 per cent higher than the present budget.

Programming

The Office of the Secretary of Defense reviews the JSOP in March. In 1965, this review was translated into a set of Tentative Force Guidance (TFG) tables, which provided initial guidance to the services in preparing their Program Change Proposals (PCP's). The services are directed not to appeal this initial guidance, and they are discouraged from submitting a PCP not in accord with this guidance. Formally, PCP's are used only to review the detailed costs and to update the official program, not to review the basic force level. In fact, the TFG tables are usually incomplete and subject to change, and many small issues are resolved during the PCP review.[5]

After transmitting the TFG to the Services on April 1, McNamara and his staff begin preparation of the draft memoranda to the President (PM's) on each major mission area and support activity. These memoranda, of which there are now twelve, cover such topics as the strategic offense and defense forces, the antisubmarine warfare forces, and the research and development program; they summarize the major force levels proposed, the rationale for choice among these alternatives, and the recommended force levels and funding. These memo-

---

[5] The Tentative Force Guidance has proved to be both cumbersome and unpopular and is presently being modified.

randa, which are the basic statement on the Defense program by the Secretary of Defense to the military components and to the President, are explicit, critical, surprisingly honest, and based on analysis of generally high quality. McNamara now sends these memoranda to the JCS and services in June for review of the recommended forces; these reviews are sent to OSD during July, and the major remaining issues are resolved by the end of August. The draft memoranda and the military reviews are now the primary decision documents of the Defense-programming system, and the exchange among the contesting parties is usually spirited. McNamara has often overruled a majority of the JCS, but seldom has he overruled all the Chiefs on a force-level issue; this places a high premium on consensus with all the consequent bargaining. Although the force-level decisions made through this process are sometimes substantially different from the initial guidance, the services do not prepare new PCP's to implement the change; the decisions are merely transmitted to the services in the standard format for replying to a PCP.

The services and other defense components currently submit Program Change Proposals for all force and support changes above a specified threshold by June 15. About three hundred PCP's are now submitted, most of which involve program elements not covered by the Tentative Force Guidance; all but a few of the PCP's are submitted by the services. The PCP's present the presently approved and proposed force structure, manpower, and funding by program element, and some supporting analysis is usually attached; the PCP submissions, unfortunately, seldom convey any sense of priority either among submissions or in relation to the base program. These PCP's are reviewed during the June–August period by the OSD office of primary interest—most of the proposed force changes by Systems Analysis, the logistics changes by Installations and Logistics, the development changes by Research and Engineering, and so on. Decisions on these PCP's are issued by the end of August, and there is no formal procedure for appealing the outcome.

Preparation and review of the PCP's is a considerable and, possibly, unnecessary chore; most of the PCP's involve such minor issues that they could be incorporated in the budget review later in the year. During this same period the major force issues must be resolved by the same offices through the preparation and review of the draft memoranda to the President. This was not always so. During 1962 and 1963, without any Tentative Force Guidance, the PCP's were the primary decision documents, and the draft memoranda to the President were used mostly to summarize the decisions of the PCP review. In order to reduce the number of "unrealistic" PCP's, OSD initiated the use of the Tentative Force Guidance and greatly increased its role in the program-change process.

Budgeting

In September, on the basis of the program decisions made during the parallel review of the draft memoranda to the President and the PCP's, the services prepare the budget for the next fiscal year in the traditional budget categories. OSD and the Bureau of the Budget review the budget submissions during October and November. Presumably, all major decisions should be resolved by this time, but these budget offices initiate about six hundred Subject Issues, identifying areas of potential saving. The Subject Issues are not intended to change the earlier force-level decisions, but they have sometimes undermined the effectiveness of these forces by reducing support resources. Budget-review decisions have a different time horizon than the program review discussed earlier: The program decisions generally have a long-term cost basis, whereas budget decisions are based on a single fiscal year. It is often difficult to make a case (in the budget review) for spending resources now to save funds in the future. In any case, this final budget review, reflecting a remarkably detailed understanding of defense expenditures, usually reduces the total Defense budget by several billion dollars.

During this same period, the OSD staff is also completing the final draft memoranda to the President based on the August decisions; the statement to Congress by the Secretary of Defense, in turn, is based on these memoranda, including the basic organization, style, and analysis of these internal documents. The Joint Chiefs of Staff have one more court of appeals—their December visit with the President—at which a number of major programs have been decided. Such last-minute changes are incorporated in the new budget for transmittal to the President in late December. The Secretary's statement to Congress is usually prepared for presentation late in January.

The last step of a defense program-budget cycle is, of course, the first step of the next cycle. This step is characteristic of the best features of the present defense-management techniques. On the basis of the problems identified during the cycle just completed, OSD and, more recently, the services, draw up lists of important studies that should be completed to assist the forthcoming program reviews. The Secretary's project list is received by the JCS and the services in late January, and a six-month study cycle begins. The resulting studies, in turn, form the basis for both support and review of the proposed Defense-program changes. The study process is more subtle and less hurried than the formal program-change process; and the integration of these two processes may be the most important feature of the new defense-management techniques.

SOME PROBLEMS AND PROPOSED SOLUTIONS

A review of the five-year history of the new defense resource-allocation process reveals three major problem areas:

(1) Military components do not effectively express their priorities.
(2) The resource-management process is highly centralized.
(3) Some of the major Defense resources are substantially underpriced and, thus, require special management.

The Problem of Priorities

A recommended defense program reflects two kinds of judgments: the professional judgment (based on experience or analysis) that a given mission budget should be allocated for certain forces and the political judgment that so much capability is desired and so much should be spent in each mission area. The Defense programs proposed by the military components, through the JSOP and PCP's, seldom separate these two kinds of judgment; these documents, which propose a single force level or an array of force levels, do not identify the effect of higher or lower mission budgets on the proposed force composition. The JCS and service force recommendations for a given mission budget merit respect on the basis of the professional judgment of the senior officers of the U.S. military establishment; the force levels and budgets by mission areas proposed by the JCS merit respect on the basis of their political judgment as informed citizens, an issue on which their vote is important but not decisive. There is now no formal mechanism that the military components can use to explicitly state their estimates of the efficient force composition for a given mission budget; as a consequence, the Secretary of Defense has assumed the primary responsibility for these management decisions.

A part of this problem is attributable to McNamara's ambivalent guidance. Without establishing an explicit budget guidance, he has invited the JCS and services to submit force recommendations based on their perceived requirements—but his decisions have implied that these "requirements" had better not increase the Defense budget. The Department of Defense has operated under a strong implicit budget constraint without making effective use of this constraint as a planning instrument. The military components, however, must bear most of the responsibility for this problem. At present, the only military components whose responsibility spans the major mission areas are the unified commands and the Joint Chiefs of Staff. Most of the force-structure planning outside OSD, however, is performed by the services, which provide only part of the forces in each major mission area (except the antisubmarine warfare forces). The unified commands have no budgets and no planning responsibility for their own forces; a weak attempt by OSD to permit the unified commands to comment on the PCP's was vigorously opposed by the services. With no budgets or planning responsibility, the submissions by the unified command to JSOP (their only formal contributions to the defense program-change process) have little value.

The JCS have no budget, but they do have a fundamental planning responsibility. The basic limitation on the potential contribution of the JCS is its role as a legislative body, rather than an independent review and analysis group.[6]

---

[6] This does not suggest a generic superiority of the analytic process over the bargaining process, rather that the JCS do not represent the appropriate constituency for the resolution of political problems.

It consists, after all, of the service Chiefs of Staff, and it should not be surprising that the officers on the Joint Staff are often chosen to represent service positions. In this situation, faced by a strong Secretary of Defense, consensus is more important than objectivity; and consensus is much easier to achieve by proposing larger defense programs that do not threaten the present position of any component. The consensus usually breaks down under explicit budget constraints in which an improved position of one component clearly threatens the position of other components. In fact, the JCS contribution is greater than this situation implies, but only because individual officers bring to their task considerable energy and devotion to broad national objectives.

The military contribution to the force-planning process would be greatly improved by reorganizing the JSOP to present alternative recommended forces for several mission budgets. For each major mission, a group from the Joint Staff, working with officers from the relevant unified commands and services, would prepare what they believed to be the most efficient combination of forces for three mission budgets—10 per cent below the current level, equal to the current level, and 10 per cent above. The mission budgets should probably be defined in terms of the five-year program costs with future costs discounted at a positive rate to discourage transfer of funds to the early years. This mission review group would also evaluate the capabilities of the forces at each budget level, given the programmed level of complementary U.S. and allied forces. This group would present, in the language of economics, a part of the "supply curve" of the military forces in this mission area. If one service objected to the combination of forces proposed by this group, it would be obliged to prepare alternative combinations for each budget level, evaluate the capabilities, and explain the basis for proposing forces other than those outlined by the mission review group. The recommended forces for three budget levels for each major mission, as modified and approved by the majority of the JCS, would be the primary output of the JSOP. It would also be valuable, but less important, for the JCS to recommend a single array of forces for all missions and the total defense budget that they, as informed citizens, believe the nation should support. The military components include many officers both capable of and interested in making such a contribution, but the nature of the system is such that OSD initiative would probably be necessary to effect this change.[7]

The Problem of Centralization

The substantial centralization of Defense management since 1961 is indicated by the grumbling of lower-level managers, the substantial increase in the OSD staff, the small problems for which OSD approval is routinely required, and by the increasing concern about who could succeed McNamara in the role

[7] The present incentive structure within the services, unfortunately, does not reinforce this proposed role of the Joint Staff mission review group. Creation of a special career pattern (or a separate "purple suit" service) may be necessary for officers who have been assigned to the Joint Staff.

that he has created as Secretary of Defense. The costs of this centralization are suggested by comparing Defense management with that of the most efficient (and much smaller) private industrial firms. The primary indictment of the present centralized process, however, is its failure to be an effective instrument of continued change.[8]

The centralization of political decisions regarding the total defense budget and its allocation among missions is the key element of the present decision process and is probably necessary for effective civilian control of the U.S. military establishment. But the centralization of the management decisions regarding the allocation of resources within each mission area is a matter of style. In the short run, this style may not be detrimental so long as the Secretary of Defense and his staff are as capable and hard working as is now the case and so long as the morale and judgment of the lower-level managers are not eroded. The sluggishness of continued program change, however, suggests that the increased centralization of defense management may already be having a detrimental effect upon national security interests. What important first steps should be considered to reverse the centralization of resource management?

The primary requisite of effective decentralized management is that the objectives of the lower-level managers promote actions that are generally consistent with the objectives of the organization. In a profit-maximizing organization a lower-level manager can be rewarded for efficiency by higher pay or a share of the profits, whether or not his actions lead to an increase or decrease in the resources under his control; in a bureaucratic organization, a lower-level manager is rewarded primarily on the basis of the size of the activity under his control. If the demand for the output of his activity is highly elastic, the manager can maximize the size of his activity, and his own objectives, by efficient management. But if the demand for the output of his activity is highly inelastic, he can garner these rewards through inefficient management. Because the demands for the output of many aggregate defense activities are inherently inelastic, the only way to provide an incentive for efficiency is to divide the aggregate activity among several component organizations and to present each resource

---

[8] The concern expressed by Hitch and McKean is still most relevant:

"Decentralization of the decision-making function is an extremely attractive administrative objective—in the military as elsewhere. The man on the spot can act quickly and flexibly. He has intimate first-hand knowledge of many factors relevant to his decisions. Large hierarchical organizations, by contrast, tend to be sluggish and hidebound by rules and regulations. Much of the time and energies are consumed in attempting to assemble, at the center, the information so readily available 'on the firing line'; and since these efforts are never successful, their decisions have to be made on the basis of information both incomplete and stale. Decentralization of decision-making responsibility has the further advantage of providing training, experience, and a testing ground for junior officers. The best way to develop qualities of responsibility, ingenuity, judgment, and so on, and to identify them is to provide genuine opportunities for their exercise . . . . Unfortunately the superficial illogicalities of decentralization are more strikingly obvious than the deadening consequences of extreme centralization." Hitch and McKean, pp. 236–37, 238.

manager with competition whose supply curve is highly elastic. Paradoxically, the situation that led to control of the defense program by missions—the competition among the services in the major mission areas—is the primary requisite for decentralization of the management decisions within each mission area. It is not surprising that there is collusion among component organizations in both industry and government in an attempt to restrict competition among themselves—but such agreements should not be reinforced by public policy. Many of our present tactical concepts and weapons systems are the products of interservice competition. Perhaps the Key West Agreement should be rewritten to encourage each of the services to develop both concepts and weapons systems in any mission area.

The first step toward increasing the management responsibility at lower organizational levels would proceed from the proposed changes in the JSOP outlined above. On the basis of the alternative force levels and budgets for each mission area presented in the revised JSOP, OSD should issue a Tentative *Budget* Guidance for each mission area. In most cases, this Tentative Budget Guidance should be accompanied by a statement of marginal objectives, such as the value of systems that are less dependent on warning relative to those that are more dependent, or the value of present capability relative to future capability. The primary concern about issuing budget guidance by service—that is, that they would reallocate resources among missions—would thus be avoided.

The services would then prepare PCP's that they were prepared to support within the Tentative Budget Guidance for the overall mission. These PCP's would first be transmitted to the Joint Staff mission review group that was responsible for preparing the JSOP forces in this area. This group would evaluate the competing service proposals and again prepare what they believe to be the most efficient combination of forces for this mission, in this case, within the Tentative Budget Guidance; this combination might not be the same as that recommended in JSOP, since the budget level might be different, new information might have developed, or one service might be able to make a better case for its forces in this mission. The program recommended by this mission review group and the service PCP's would be sent as a package to OSD for review of the competing proposals, the cost estimates, and consistency with the earlier guidance on marginal objectives. All the PCP's in each mission area would be reviewed at the same time, first by the Joint Staff and then by OSD. The OSD review should be greatly assisted by the prior Joint Staff review of the mission program. During the OSD review, the services would have the opportunity to defend PCP's that the Joint Staff group recommends for disapproval. This procedure would substantially change the responsibilities for program planning—the services and JCS, not OSD, would have the primary responsibility for preparing balanced forces in each mission area, within the political guidance on mission budgets and marginal objectives.

After OSD has completed its review of the programs recommended by the Joint Staff mission review group and the service PCP's, the services would prepare budgets based on the force-level decisions. Since a final budget review would probably still be valuable, all proposed expenditures not considered by the mission reviews could be incorporated in the budget submission. The memoranda to the President would merely summarize the major decisions and the rationale for choice rather than serve as the primary decision document.

The effectiveness of this procedure depends on the ability of the Joint Staff to serve as a professional, independent review and force-planning group. Some skepticism on this point is justified; but it is characteristic of the U.S. military establishment that capability follows real responsibility, and the challenge and excitement of an important role in the force-planning process should attract the best talent in the system. If this procedure should not work out, the only other obvious way to decentralize the major management decisions would be more radical: to issue the Tentative Budget Guidance to the unified commands and permit them to "buy" forces from the services. Full exploitation of the "buyer-seller" device to induce efficient management may, at some time, involve this next step, but institutions that survive do not take giant steps in the dark.

The Problem of Resource Pricing

No organization, however the management responsibilities are divided, can efficiently allocate resources if the prices faced by the decision maker do not reflect the full value of these resources. The Department of Defense, however, acquires and uses several major resources at prices considerably below their full value. The most important examples are military manpower, land, and nuclear materials; other minor examples include the electronic frequency spectrum and the airspace. It is not surprising that each of these resources requires special management. In the aggregate, the annual cost of resources used by the Department of Defense, but not entering its expenditure accounts, is probably about $10 billion.

Since 1948, with the enactment of the Selective Service Act, the Department of Defense has chosen to draft some military manpower rather than pay salaries high enough to maintain the desired force levels. As a consequence, the total resource cost of military manpower may be $5 billion a year higher than the explicit expenditures. (McNamara has stated that the additional salaries necessary to eliminate the draft would total $20 billion a year; this total is grossly inconsistent with other evidence but, in any case, reinforces the case for reform of the military-pay structure.) The existence of the draft, by reducing the explicit manpower cost and by selecting personnel without regard for the individual's choice of alternative occupations, distorts both the level and composition of military manpower. A system of selective manpower controls has partially compensated for these distortions, but these controls cannot meaningfully be applied below the service level.

Defense landholdings total about 30 million acres, over 50 per cent of which has been transferred from the public domain. Public land can be acquired by administrative transfer at no cost and private land, at the market value exclusive of the value to local governments as a property-tax base. Once acquired, the lease value of the land never enters the expenditure accounts, nor does a service receive credit to its accounts if land is returned to other public use or sold. The acquisition and use of foreign land is particularly distorted; the pertinent activity pays nothing for such land, but the military and economic-aid accounts often bear the high cost of this resource. The Department of Defense usually treats its enormous landholdings as a free good, except during periodic special campaigns (often under congressional pressure) to dispose of particular parcels.

The Department of Defense pays nothing for the development and production of nuclear weapons. Until recently, all parties (except the Bureau of the Budget) were happy with this arrangement; Defense ordered all the weapons that could be produced, and the Atomic Energy Commission managed to produce all the weapons that were ordered. Defense activities are not charged for weapons acquired or in stockpile and are not credited for nuclear material returned. The resulting escalation of Defense "requirements" and AEC capabilities was halted only by the direct intervention of the President and some rather awkward management controls.

One major support activity—military air transport—is seriously underpriced within Defense, although the resources used by this activity (except manpower) are correctly priced on transfer from the private sector. This underpricing has led to a substantially greater reliance on airlift for wartime mobility rather than on substitute activities for which the services pay nearly full cost. A few other activities, such as basic training and the Defense communications system, are subject to similar problems.

In some cases, the Department of Defense pays considerably more for resources than their value. The most striking examples in recent years are the high premiums for U.S. flag shipping and other U.S. substitutes for goods and services available at a lower price abroad. Such overpricing, usually the result of using the Defense budget to support balance-of-payments policy or a domestic-employment objective, also distorts the resource-allocation process.

Ideally, all resources acquired or released by the Department of Defense should be transferred at their full value. Fortunately, improved resource management need not be dependent on this condition. The manpower draft, however undesirable, looks like a permanent feature of our military establishment, and there are many pressures against an explicit accounting for such resources as public land and the frequency spectrum. A satisfactory interim solution for the misallocation resulting from distorted resource prices would be the establishment of annual "shadow charges" (or credits) for the use of these resources. These shadow charges would be used for all resource-allocation decisions within the Department of Defense, although they would not be included in the formal budget. For example, the manpower costs for each defense activity should be estimated at the level of pay and perquisites that would be necessary in the absence of the draft. All land, both public and private, should be valued at the market value plus the public value as a property tax base, and the land-using activities should be charged an annual lease based on this total value. All defense activities "using" nuclear weapons should be charged an annual lease on the value of the nuclear materials in the present stockpile, and the fabrication cost plus an annual lease on all new weapons. The component defense organizations should be able to make a case to OSD for an increase in their explicit budgets if they can demonstrate a more than offsetting reduction in these shadow charges; the Department of Defense, of course, should be able to make a similar case to the Bureau of the Budget. The case for such arrangements is not widely appreciated, but the annual value of these "lost resources" is larger than the cost of any major mission, and the potential savings from good management of these resources would compare with those from the present cost-reduction program.

CONCLUSION

The substantial improvements in the capabilities of the U.S. military establishment since 1961 should be recognized. The decisions leading to the major improvements, however, were largely made in 1961 and cannot be attributed to the use of the new defense-management techniques. Without questioning the major force-level decisions, certain features of the Defense resource-allocation process are subject to criticism. The principal defects are the failure of the military components to state priorities meaningfully, overcentralization at the level of the Secretary of Defense, and unrealistic resource pricing.

This chapter has outlined the major strengths and weaknesses in the Defense resource-allocation process with the conviction that both the Defense program and the Defense-management process should be subject to continued improvement.

BIBLIOGRAPHY

1. Committee for Economic Development, *Budgeting for National Objectives.* A Statement by the Research and Policy Committee, New York, January, 1966.

2. Hitch, Charles J., *Decision Making for Defense.* Berkeley: University of California Press, 1965.

3. ———— and Roland N. McKean, *The Economics of Defense in the Nuclear Age.* Cambridge: Harvard University Press, 1960.

4. Novick, David, ed., *Program Budgeting; Program Analysis and the Federal Budget.* Cambridge: Harvard University Press, 1965.

5. Seligman, Daniel, "McNamara's Management Revolution," *Fortune*, LXXII, No. 1 (July, 1965).

ROBERT N. GROSSE

Research Analysis Corporation

Robert N. Grosse was Head of the Economics and Costing Department of the U.S. Department of Health, Education and Welfare from 1963 to 1966, when he left to become Deputy Assistant Secretary for Program Coordination in the Department of Health, Education and Welfare. He has also been a lecturer on defense economics at the Industrial College of the Armed Forces, the Armed Forces Staff College, the Army War College, and the National War College.

From 1954–61 he was Chief of the Factors and Estimates Branch, Cost Analysis Department, of The RAND Corporation. As Director of the Bethesda Office from 1961 to 1963 he assisted the Assistant Secretary of Defense (Comptroller) in developing the Defense program-budgeting system.

From 1949–1951 he served as an economist on the Harvard University Research Project on the Structure of the American Economy and from 1951–53 worked in the Bureau of the Budget, Office of Statistical Standards.

Dr. Grosse received his Ph.D. in Economics from Harvard (1948) and has taught at Bowdoin, Bates College, and Rutgers University.

He is the author of reports and papers on military cost analysis and interindustry economics and of cost-effectiveness studies.

ARNOLD PROSCHAN

Research Analysis Corporation

Arnold Proschan, Head of the Economics and Costing Department since 1966, joined the Research Analysis Corporation in June, 1963, as an analyst. At RAC he has headed studies pertaining to military-force-development analysis system, correlation of management systems, manpower planning, development of models for research and development planning, and planning-programming-budgeting systems.

As a consultant in the Cost Analysis Department of The RAND Corporation (1961–63) he assisted in the inauguration of a program-budgeting system for the Assistant Secretary of Defense (Comptroller). He is also the author of several RAND research memoranda on program budgeting and cost modeling.

Mr. Proschan has worked as a teacher in the New York City high schools (1937–40); as an Information Specialist in the Army Air Force (1941–43), as a management analyst for the War Assets Administration (1946–49), Air Force, 1949–50, and Munitions Board, 1950; as Budget Analyst, ASD (Comptroller), 1950–55; as Controller, Government Products Group, American Machine and Foundry Company, 1955–58; and has been self-employed in the investment field (1958–61).

He received his M.S. in Education and Accounting from The City College of New York (1939), his M.A. in Statistics from George Washington University (1942), and his M.A. in Public Administration from American University (1954). He is the author or coauthor of reports and papers in various journals.

2

The Annual Cycle:

Planning-Programming-Budgeting

The unified planning-programming-budgeting system installed in the Department of Defense in 1961 has been widely recognized as a major management innovation in the allocation of resources. So apparent are its benefits that the President has adopted the approach for installation throughout the government.

In essence, the system establishes a formal five-year planning structure and process to guide the formulation of annual budgets. The structure classifies the entire scope of Defense activity into individual program elements, such as the Minuteman missile and the infantry division, grouped into major programs such as strategic forces and general-purpose forces. For each program element the pertinent military department or agency proposes force- manpower- and dollar-planning levels for the Secretary of Defense's approval as ingredients of the five-year program. An important aspect of the planning process is the performance of systems analyses; these are studies in which alternative ways of achieving desired objectives are generated and evaluated and in which the basic objectives themselves are subjected to searching examination.[1]

The administrative association of planning, programming, and budgeting, as elements of a resource-allocation process, reflects a decade's work by economists and other nonmilitary professionals in assisting the military in the analysis of alternative weapon systems and programs. The growing complexity of weapon systems and the proliferation of possible configurations and combinations of weapons in this period of technological advancement led military planners to seek the help of physical and social scientists in systematically developing the consequences of alternative choices; in this work RAND played a leading role. While participating in these studies, economists became more and more aware of the deficiencies in the existing resource-allocation process; thus the ideas and approaches underlying the Defense planning-programming-budgeting system were developed.

Before discussing the new system, we will consider the Defense budgetary process before 1961 and the resource-allocation problems it presented.

THE DEFENSE BUDGETARY PROCESS BEFORE 1961

The ideal budgetary process as envisioned in the later 1940's was well described by Mr. Ferdinand Eberstadt, a close associate of James Forrestal and a principal influence in the unification movement:

> The process starts with the National Security Council upon which the statute lays the obligation of striking a balance between our foreign risks and commitments and the size of our armed forces, so that our military establishment shall be neither too large nor too small, weighed in the light of our national security needs and resources. . . .
>
> Possessed of the views of the National Security Council and of such other advice as he desires, it is contemplated that the President should lay down, in general outline, the initial

[1] See E. S. Quade, ed., *Analysis for Military Decisions* (Chicago: Rand McNally & Co., 1964).

dimensions of the military budget, which then passes through the Secretary of Defense to the Joint Chiefs of Staff. Their functions in this connection are threefold: (1) to prepare strategic plans; (2) to assign logistic responsibilities in accordance with such strategic plans to the three military services which thereupon translate their military responsibilities into terms of personnel and material; and finally (3) to review the major material and personnel requirements of the military forces in accordance with such strategic plans and logistic assignments.

At this point strategic plans, translated into personnel and end-item requirements, are in turn converted into monetary terms grouped under the individual programs and objectives which we call the performance budget. Here is a particularly favorable opportunity to spot and to eradicate excessive duplications and expenditures.

Here, too, occurs the preliminary pricing of these detailed plans in order to reflect the dollar cost of the proposed military programs. If this cost is in excess of the amount deemed by the President to be necessary or available for military defense, the Joint Chiefs of Staff must develop alternative and less expensive programs.

● ● ●

When the strategic plans of the Joint Chiefs of Staff have been brought within the prescribed fiscal limitations, final budget estimates within the military departments are made. Thereupon, they are ready for submission to the Secretary of Defense for final analysis, review, and integration.[2]

The responsibilities intended for the Joint Chiefs in the budget process were not effectively assumed, particularly in regard to the review of the major material and personnel requirements of the military forces in accordance with JCS strategic plans and logistical assignments. For example, the House Appropriations Committee concluded that the Joint Chiefs did not discuss, specifically in connection with the fiscal-year 1960 budget, whether the Army should be maintained at 870,000 or 900,000, whether funds should be sought for a Navy carrier, or what should be done about the B-52 program.[3]

In practice, Defense budget making evolved into (1) a JCS review of major force levels and (2) negotiations on the size and composition of annual budgets by the Bureau of the Budget and the Defense Comptroller's staffs with the staffs (military and civilian) of the military departments. In these negotiations "stated military requirements" (some sanctioned at JCS level, others bearing only military-service approval) were subjected to relatively modest questioning in the budget reviews at the level of the military department or of the Office of the Secretary of Defense; the areas of concern were rather production feasibility, achievable rates of manpower buildup, price tags, extent of mobilization reserves, "standard of living" at military bases, depth of supporting programs, and so on.

Military requirements were often developed from an assumed objective; an example is taken from the testimony of General Maxwell D. Taylor in congressional hearings on the Defense appropriations:

The basic question in all cases is to decide how much is enough. What are we shooting for? What is the level which is our objective? Having once determined that, it becomes pretty

[2] U. S. Congress, Senate Committee on Armed Services, *National Security Act Amendments of 1949*, 81st Cong., 1st sess. (Washington: GPO, March–May, 1949), Hearings on S 1269 and S 1843, pp. 210–11.

[3] U. S. Congress, *Department of Defense Appropriation Bill, 1960*, House Report No. 408, 86th Cong., 1st sess. (Washington: GPO, May 28, 1959), p. 11.

much a technical, semimechanical procedure for the military experts to translate objectives into divisions, planes, aircraft carriers, submarines, and the like.[4]

It was obviously difficult under this approach to relate incremental effectiveness and costs, a key aspect of the programming system to be installed in 1961.

Target budget ceilings (sometimes unkindly called "arbitrary") were used extensively as a means of constraining military requirements to levels acceptable to the Administration. Several budgets might be required simultaneously at a base dollar level and at fixed amount or percentage increases or decreases from the base. The procedure followed on the fiscal-year 1961 budget, for example, consisted of the establishment of a "basic budget" at a level somewhat lower than that of the previous year and the submission of an "addendum" of up to $500 million above the previous-year level. Such a test-budget procedure was described by Mr. Maurice H. Stans, Director of the Bureau of the Budget from 1958 to 1961, as a flotation process to force older items into competition with the new. Although not always effectively carried out, the use of sets of budgets did, nevertheless, inject some marginal thinking into budget formulation.

The culmination of budget negotiations was a set of annual budgets drawn up by each military department. The proportion of the total defense budget going to each military department was a widely accepted index of success in budget negotiation (it probably still is).

Program objectives of budgets were stated in terms of force levels, major-equipment inventory objectives, and military manpower levels. No price tags were available for particular elements of the service program, such as for either tactical forces of the Air Force or for Army forces in Europe. The primary categories within the departmental totals were the congressional appropriations. These in recent years have been principally as follows: research, development, test, and evaluation; procurement; military construction; military personnel; and operation and maintenance. Civil defense and military assistance are managed separately from the other five categories.

The establishment of appropriations of this kind was generally regarded as fulfilling the recommendation of the first Hoover Commission (1947–1949) for the adoption of a budget based upon functions, activities, and projects, which it designated as a performance budget. Under performance budgeting,

attention is centered on the function or activity—on the accomplishment of the purpose—instead of on lists of employees or authorizations of purchases. . . . It places both accomplishment and cost in a clear light before the Congress and the public.[5]

It would later be questioned whether these appropriations adequately revealed the purposes of Defense activity. The growing need for a more in-

---

[4] U. S. Congress, House Committee on Appropriations, *Department of Defense Appropriations for 1960*, 86th Cong., 1st sess. (Washington: GPO, 1959), Part 1, Hearings, p. 337.

[5] The Commission on Organization of the Executive Branch of the Government, *Budgeting and Accounting, A Report to the Congress* (Washington: GPO, February, 1949), pp. 8–9.

formative classification would be a principal motivation of the programming system.

Although not revealing in terms of major purposes, the appropriations in terms of research, development, test and evaluation, procurement, military construction, military personnel, and operation and maintenance (1) helped to establish centralized fiscal control within the Army and Navy (by eliminating appropriations in terms of technical-service'and bureau designations); (2) distinguished dollars benefiting forces of the future from those of the present; (3) provided a convenient breakdown for congressional examination of procurement and military manpower; and (4) made interdepartmental comparisons easier. By fiscal year 1960, the budget presentation to Congress was emphasizing appropriation category (such as military personnel) rather than service; and the congressional appropriation bills were being arranged on the same basis, first by appropriation category and then by service. Congressional appropriation hearings were also being reported on an appropriation-category basis.

The budget system as an element of financial management deserves a few more words. In the 1949 amendments to the National Security Act of 1947, Title IV provided for the appointment of a Comptroller in the Office of the Secretary of Defense (described by Congressman Carl Vinson[6] as a "business manager for the entire military organization"), the appointment of comptrollers in the military departments, budgetary control, bases for budgetary and fund accounting, financial accounting for property, and use of revolving funds to finance and manage inventories of materiel and operations of industrial- and commercial-type activities.

Reviewing accomplishment in 1958, the first Defense Comptroller, Mr. Wilfred J. McNeil, was able to report that financial-management organizations existed in the military departments at levels from headquarters down to major field installations, under the ultimate supervision of assistant secretaries for financial management in OSD and in each military department; he also stated that budgeting and budgetary control had become indispensable parts of total management.[7]

Lately the virtues of this pre-1961 budget system have not been extolled; there are, however, several points to be made in its favor. It provided a mechanism, however limited, for translation of military planning into the requisite materiel, manpower, and other resources. It was an effective instrument of unification and the primary medium through which the Secretary of Defense could exercise control, particularly in the early 1950's. The appropriation structure of this system was simpler and more uniform than that which existed earlier. Compared with the budget process that prevailed prior to defense unification, the budget system of the 1950's was a significant advance.

[6] U. S. Congress, House Committee on Armed Services, *Full Committee Hearings on H.R. 5632*, 81st Cong., 1st sess. (Washington: GPO, July 14, 1949, No. 94), p. 2655.

[7] W. J. McNeil, "Financial Management in the Department of Defense," *The Federal Accountant*, Vol. VII (March, 1958), p. 39.

THE BUDGET SYSTEM AND RESOURCE ALLOCATION

Whatever the virtues of the budget system of the 1950's, it was limited in effectiveness as a mechanism for resource allocation. It did not associate funds with major missions or functions of the military departments, such as strategic forces in the Air Force, antisubmarine warfare in the Navy, or defense of Europe in the Army. Within a military department some insight into how much was going into each mission could be gained from an analysis of force structure or from a knowledge of internal distribution of funds to the operating commands, such as the Strategic Air Command (these often paralleled missions). But the administration of procurement, construction, and military pay on a centralized basis for a military department as a whole made it difficult to aggregate all resources going into a mission area. For missions involving more than one military department, it was difficult to develop consistent and comparable costing. For this and other reasons, military planning tended toward a unilateral service basis in the ordering of priorities of forces, weapon systems, and activities.

Recognition of these difficulties led some students of budgeting to propose changes. A well-defined proposal for a mission-oriented fiscal structure was developed within RAND by David Novick.[8] Frederick C. Mosher in his important book on Defense budgeting[9] advanced a proposal for a program budget that would aid in the development, appraisal, and authorization of future policies and programs at top levels. The major programs Mosher suggested, using the Army as an example, were these: combat operations (if any), overseas noncombat operations, active defense of the United States, operation and support of active forces in the United States, training, mobilization reserve, research and development, construction, and services (not directly allocable). Mosher visualized this upward-oriented budget as operating in synchronization with an administrative budget, structured organizationally, which would furnish the primary vehicle for internal planning and control. The administrative budget would lag a year behind the program budget and would start only after the President's budget was known. This proposal recognized that budgets serve different purposes, for which different arrangements and timing might be appropriate. Arthur Smithies suggested the costing of military programs and a program budget; he did not recommend a change in the appropriation structure, however.[10]

[8] D. Novick, "Efficiency and Economy in Government through New Budgeting and Accounting Procedures," R-254, The RAND Corporation, February 1, 1954.

[9] F. C. Mosher, *Program Budgeting: Theory and Practice with Particular Reference to the U. S. Department of the Army* (Chicago: Public Administration Service, 1954), pp. 237–43.

[10] A. Smithies, *The Budgetary Process in the United States* (New York: McGraw-Hill Book Company, 1955), pp. 257–77.

Efforts by those in authority to achieve insight on resource allocations by mission did not aim at upsetting the established budget system. In 1954 General Decker, Comptroller of the Army, suggested a mission-program structure as an alternate means of reviewing the Army's resource requirements. In 1956 the National Security Council, in its efforts to match policy and resource allocations, levied a requirement on the Defense Department for mission-cost breakdowns. The results were not too useful.[11]

Concern with resource allocations by mission intensified in the late 1950's, as the Navy sought a greater role in strategic retaliation and as the Army sought a reassessment of the balance between resource allocations for strategic retaliation and for limited warfare.

The success of the Navy's development of the Polaris submarine-launched missile raised a threat of diversion of resources from established Navy programs if the Navy's overall funding level remained essentially unchanged, as was likely. A congressional subcommittee report suggested a solution:

> A Polaris-launching submarine is thus treated fiscally like any other naval vessel. In terms of its military mission, however, it is radically different from other ships in the fleet. Actually, the Polaris system is part of our national military deterrent against all-out war. It is an instrument of strategic reprisal. It is more analogous to a SAC bomber or a land-based IRBM or ICBM than to other ships of our Navy. . . .
> From the standpoint of national deterrent strategy, the Polaris system should therefore not be treated as part of our regular shipbuilding program. In assigning money and priority to it, this system should be compared, not with other naval ships, but with the manned aircraft and land-based strategic missiles of our national deterrent force.[12]

Concerned that disproportionate defense resources were going into the strategic retaliatory forces and not enough into preparation for limited war, General Taylor proposed a mission-oriented budget review. In his testimony before the House Appropriations Subcommittee, he stated:

> . . . the meaningful way of looking at our armed services, the fighting forces of all three services, is not to look first at the Army from top to bottom, then the Navy, then the Air Force, but rather is to consider the military functions which the various components of these services must perform.[13]

He proposed a budget review oriented around these missions: atomic retaliation, continental air defense, general war deterrent, general strategic reserve, antisubmarine warfare, and reserves.

[11] See W. R. Kintner, *Forging a New Sword* (New York: Harper & Row, Publishers, 1958), pp. 130–31. Kintner gives these as the reasons: the complexities of the operation, the assignment of more than one mission to some types of forces, and the opposition of the services.

[12] U. S. Congress, Joint Committee on Atomic Energy, *Report of the Underseas Warfare Advisory Panel to the Subcommittee on Military Applications*, Joint Committee print, 85th Cong., 2d sess. (Washington: GPO, August, 1958), pp. 12–13.

[13] U. S. Congress, House Committee on Appropriations, *Department of Defense Appropriations for 1960*, 86th Cong., 1st sess., Part 1, Hearings (Washington: GPO, 1959), pp. 336–37.

After the congressional hearings, Mr. George Mahon, Chairman of the House Appropriations Subcommittee, requested that the fiscal-year 1961 defense budget be analyzed in functional categories. Responding to this request, the Secretary of Defense had the services submit budgetary information on the basis of five force groupings: atomic retaliatory forces, continental air defense, general-purpose forces, support forces, and unallocated.

In addition to the growing interest in resource allocations by mission, there was another influence at work that pointed up the limitations of the existing budget system. This was the increasing scope of decision making and even management on a weapon-system basis. With the growth of technology the means by which missions are performed have become more complex and costly, and in many cases more specialized. Under the existing budget system it was difficult to pull together all the costs that would eventually result from a decision to undertake a major weapon system; the costs were scattered among many appropriations, and the budget projected fiscal requirements only for a period of a year. Operating costs in particular tended to be obscured because of the variety of fund pockets; over a period of years such costs may for some systems be more significant than development and procurement costs.

Despite the difficulties, total cost estimates were sometimes generated for major systems as an aid to program decisions. This was done, for example, for the B-52. There was, however, no formal system for developing such estimates and keeping them up to date as programs moved along.

This lack of forward visibility encouraged the services to propose, or at least did not deter them from proposing that more weapon systems be undertaken than could in all likelihood be funded to completion. In the absence of substantial increases in overall Defense funding levels, the lack of foresight brought about excessive cancellation of ongoing projects (technological factors and changing military requirements were also major causes of cancellation). The need to plan by weapon system for more than a year in advance was clearly set forth in a House report:

> Steps must be taken at once to eliminate the waste so obviously inherent in the current system. . . . In furtherance of this policy the services will be expected to project a total estimated cost for each major weapon system under procurement and/or development to a final program fulfillment. It is to be emphasized that weapon-systems expenditures cannot be isolated for one-year budget consideration.[14]

If lifetime cost estimates by weapon system could not easily be generated in the established budget system, it was certainly difficult to make systematic comparisons of the costs and effectiveness of alternative possibilities for weapon

---

[14] U. S. Congress, *Department of Defense Appropriation Bill, 1961*, House Report No. 1561, 86th Cong., 2d sess. (Washington: GPO, April 29, 1960), p. 26.

systems, an increasing necessity as the rapid growth of technology multiplied the alternatives available. Such systematic comparisons were being employed in RAND and other organizations to aid decision makers in the evaluation of alternative program choices.

A new art of systems or cost-effectiveness analysis was being developed to deal with complex questions of choice in the face of great uncertainty, such as occur in problems of national defense. Such analyses involve studies in depth in which it is necessary to define objectives, lay out alternative ways of accomplishing each objective, calculate how effectively each alternative accomplishes an objective, and compute how much each alternative costs. Lest too mechanical an impression of systems analyses be conveyed by this description, it is necessary to add the qualifications that Charles J. Hitch, a leading practitioner of the art and later Comptroller of the Defense Department, viewed as distinguishing the useful and productive analyst: ability to formulate (or design) the problem; to choose appropriate objectives; to define the relevant, important environments or situations in which to test the alternatives; to judge the reliability of cost and other data; and to invent new systems or alternatives to evaluate.[15] Analysis of programs in terms of marginal products and costs is a major emphasis, reflecting the key contribution of economists to the development of systems analysis.

A distinctive approach to costing was developed in support of systems analysis. Costing for systems analysis aims at the collection of all costs pertaining to the force or weapon for an extended period of time (as against costing for budget categories for a period of a year) and places emphasis on costs of relative rather than absolute accuracy for comparisons among alternatives. Costing of this kind requires a thorough understanding of the structuring of systems analyses, the use of appropriate cost categories (unconstrained in many cases by budget categories), discrimination between relevant and irrelevant cost elements, consideration of uncertainties, and application of cost-sensitivity techniques.[16]

The budget structure and system, with its short-range outlook and with appropriations in such categories as procurement, military personnel, and operation and maintenance, did not provide a good framework for the performance of systems analyses.

In summary, the financial-management system was proving inadequate as an instrument for resource allocation because of the growing concern with missions transcending service lines and the rapid innovation of enormously expensive weapon systems—both demanding the application of analytical tools for which the existing system was poorly suited: in terms of its structure, its time horizon, and its separation of military planning and costing.

---

[15] C. J. Hitch, *Decision-Making for Defense* (Berkeley: University of California Press, 1965).

[16] See R. N. Grosse and A. Proschan, "Military Cost Analysis," *The American Economic Review*, Vol. LV (May, 1965), pp. 427–33.

DEPARTMENT OF DEFENSE PROGRAMMING SYSTEM:
1961–1965

Although deficiencies in the budget system regarding mission analysis and planning of weapon systems had been recognized for some years, the idea of major reform of the budget system had not really been seriously entertained by those in authority prior to Secretary Robert S. McNamara. This reluctance indicated a recognition of the long and arduous effort involved in introducing changes acceptable to both the executive and legislative branches. It is to the credit of both Secretary McNamara and his first Comptroller, C. J. Hitch, that they found a practicable road to reform—not by direct change of the existing budget system, but by establishing a programming process to precede the budget formulation stage. This programming process essentially consisted in the maintenance of a five-year program, subdivided into output-oriented program elements, to provide a firm basis for budget formulation and other resource-connected management activities.

The programming system as it evolved during Hitch's tenure as Comptroller (1961–1965) is at the time of writing undergoing extensive changes by his successor, Robert N. Anthony. Because these changes have not as yet assumed a fully definitive form and because of the widespread interest which the programming system in its earlier form has aroused, the outlines of the programming system as it took shape during the Hitch tenure are described in the following paragraphs. The changes to the programming system being made by Anthony are treated in a subsequent section.

The major elements of programming in 1961–1965 were these:[17]

1. *A Department of Defense Five-Year Force Structure and Financial Program consisting of projections of force, manpower, and dollar requirements for approved programs on weapon and support systems and other program elements.* These elements were grouped into eight major programs: strategic retaliatory forces, continental defense forces (including civil defense), general-purpose forces, airlift and sealift, Reserve and Guard forces, research and development, general support, and military assistance. In addition, there is separate funding of retired pay. The forces of the first two programs were actually treated simultaneously in Defense analyses concerned with a general nuclear war, in recognition that the strategic forces also make a contribution to the "damage limiting" mission of the continental defense forces. Elements of the Reserve and Guard program were reviewed in the mission packages that they support as well as in the Reserve and Guard program as a separate entity.

---

[17] This system is treated in many sources. A summary of the system and testimony on it by Mr. C. J. Hitch are contained in: U. S. Congress, House Committee on Government Operations, *Systems Development and Management*, 87th Cong., 2d sess., Part 2, Hearings (Washington: GPO, 1962), pp. 513–47 and 642–804.

The program elements (nearly 1,000 in all) represented the alternative or complementary means that should logically be evaluated in conjunction with one another, regardless of the particular military department involved. Some program elements were these: Titan, F-111, infantry division, destroyers, Army port terminals, exploratory development on materials, procurement and supply operations, and recruiting and examining. Within a major program, program elements were grouped into several aggregations. For the strategic retaliatory forces these were: aircraft forces, missile forces, and command, control, and communications systems and support.

2. *A process for review and approval by the Secretary of Defense and his military and civilian advisers of program-change proposals (PCPs) by the military departments.* These were to be submitted at any time during the year when changes to the official five-year program were desired or anticipated which exceeded threshold levels according to a multiplicity of criteria established for program-element dollar levels, force units, and manpower. One threshold criterion, for example, was the addition of a new-equipment item exceeding in investment cost the amount of $10 million in the first program year or $25 million over the entire duration of the program. The use of threshold criteria is an obvious application of management by exception.

Anticipation of changes exceeding threshold levels required the military departments to review their programs frequently.

Simplified PCPs were used to record the five-year program decisions already made by the Secretary of Defense or to note certain minor changes. Budget- and manpower-decision documents that were in use before the inauguration of the programming system continued to be used when only the current and budget years were affected.

The emphasis on functional reviews in such fields as intelligence, command and control, transportation, medical services, and procurement and supply programs further reduced the use of PCPs.

3. *Preceding annual budget formulation, a method for reviewing and changing the five-year program.* This method included (a) an annual review of changes in the military-force structure proposed in the Joint Strategic Objectives Plan of the Joint Chiefs of Staff (the format of this plan was modified to bring it into harmony with the new program structure), (b) Secretary of Defense force guidance to the military departments at about the beginning of April based on this review, (c) formal PCPs by the military departments in April, May, and June, predicated on the Secretary's tentatively approved force structure, and (d) review and approval of the PCPs by the Secretary of Defense and his military and civilian advisers. The aim was to complete this phase by the end of August, in order to provide the military departments with an approved program upon which to base their budgets. Budget estimates are submitted by the military departments in early October, and a Defense budget is generally prepared by mid-December.

4. *Emphasis in the annual reviews and in PCP submissions on supporting*

studies in the form of systems analyses. These studies were prepared by study groups located in the Joint Staff, the military departments, and various contractor organizations. Some study subjects have been: the number of strategic bombers and missiles needed in the next decade for priority targets, the requirements for airlift and sealift, and the comparative advantages and costs of refurbishing existing items of ground equipment, replacing them with new equipment, or pushing ahead on development of better equipment.

An indication of the importance accorded to systems analysis was the 1965 creation in OSD of an Assistant Secretary for Systems Analysis, charged with review of studies prepared by other elements of the defense establishment, improvement in their quality, and performance of studies in a few important cases in which studies would not otherwise be available. Appropriately enough, the office was organized into teams of analysts by major program.

5. *For approved programs, submission of force- and manpower-level forecasts and cost projections by the military department after each calendar quarter.* These reflected decisions on program changes, current-year reprogramming, and various minor changes. The update for the December quarter picked up budget-review decisions.

Forces were projected for eight years, manpower and costs for five years. To reflect the major phases of the weapon cycle, costs were categorized as research and development, investment, and operating. This categorization plainly displayed the costs involved in a decision to produce and deploy a weapon system, as contrasted with the cost of its development. Costs were also stated in terms relatable to budget-appropriation accounts, thus making it easier to translate programming to budgeting decisions.

Programming-budgeting correlation was enhanced by the use in programming of the same financial measure as in budgeting—total obligational authority; budgeting requires in addition the determination of requirements for new obligational authority to augment prior-year funds already available. Although the use of obligation rather than cost figures was not in accord with the second Hoover Commission recommendations on cost-based budgeting and accrual accounting, subsequently adopted in Public Law 84-863, the feasibility of a programming operation was increased by conforming to budget usage.

6. *Progress reporting by the military departments in both physical and financial terms as a basis for control of actual performance in accordance with the program.* This was the least developed part of the programming system.

The major differences between programming and pre-1961 budgeting were these:

1. Programming emphasized the products of defense activity, such as an armored division, whereas budgeting was in terms of appropriations, such as procurement, military personnel, and operation and maintenance.

2. The structure in programming permitted analysis of competitive or complementary programs (for example, Minuteman and Polaris missile systems)

without direct concern with service roles and missions. Competition was engendered on a program-by-program basis within broad mission areas rather than on a service share-of-the-budget basis.

3. In programming there was a longer-term view than in budgeting. The objective in programming was to determine the total cost implications of current approvals; this is particularly significant for missile systems and other major hardware programs involving research and development, investment, and operating costs over a period of five to ten or more years.

4. Central to the programming approach was the encouragement of thinking on alternative program possibilities; new programs competed with the old. In budgeting there tended to be a concentration on the justification for change—established programs and levels were carried along from year to year with relatively little justification required. From time to time there were efforts made in budgeting to get to a "zero base," in which it was assumed that past expenditure of funds did not create a justification for future expenditures. The complexities of budgetary costing generally defeated such efforts.

5. In programming, physical and financial data were secured and maintained on a program-by-program basis, thus facilitating the application of systems analysis; in budgeting, military requirements were generally developed by military planners for the force as a whole and then translated into dollars. This budgeting practice made especially difficult the marginal analysis by program, a principal feature of systems analysis.

6. Programming emphasized the rational aspects of decision making; budgeting, the tactical aspects of obtaining funds.

7. Programming decisions were made over a longer period of time than were budget decisions. The periodicity of budget formulation, however, led to a similar periodicity in programming submissions and reviews, though not to the hectic rush characteristic of the final weeks of budget review.

The programming system, with its attendant emphasis on systems analysis, provided the factors that C. J. Hitch and its other protagonists considered necessary for the making of the crucial decisions, particularly decisions on forces and weapons. These factors include knowledge about the availability of alternatives in terms of their military worth in relation to their cost, projections of costs over a period of years, and data organized in terms of programs. The process proved especially effective in regard to the planning and control of advanced-technology weapon systems (missiles, aircraft, command and control systems, and so on).

Through this system, "budgets are balanced with programs, programs with force requirements, force requirements with military missions, and military missions with national security objectives."[18] Although budgets may have been in balance with Defense programs as approved by the Secretary of Defense, they

[18] C. J. Hitch, *Decision-Making for Defense* (Berkeley: University of California Press, 1965).

did not cover all the programs advanced by the services; thus differences of opinion as to the adequacy of budget levels remained significant. This discrepancy is indicated by comparing figures on the President's budget with service requests (expressed in terms of new obligational authority) :[19]

(in billions of dollars)

Fiscal Year	Service Requests	President's Budget
1952	94.4	60.7
1955	37.6	30.9
1958	45.2	37.9
1960	48.4	40.8
1964	63.9	51.3
1966	56.3	47.4

The benefits provided by the programming system were widely recognized, in the Defense Department, elsewhere in government, in Congress, in industry, and even among foreign governments (for example, in the United Kingdom, Germany and Canada).

A prime indication of the degree of acceptance of the programming system was its influence on the establishment of such a system on a government-wide basis. In August, 1965, the President launched a program for installing a new planning-programming-budgeting system, to be monitored by the Bureau of the Budget. In his initial presentation to heads of departments and agencies, the Budget Director cited deficiencies of the same nature as those motivating the establishment of the new system in Defense; he further stated an objective of having the system operational for the fiscal-year 1968 budget. He described the new system as relating national needs to specific goals, goals to alternative government programs, programs to specific resources, and specific resources to budget dollars—all projected several years ahead.

A further indication of the Defense origin of the program was the designation of Henry S. Rowen, who had previously been with RAND and the Defense Department, as the Assistant Director of the Bureau of the Budget with primary responsibility in the establishment of the new planning-programming-budgeting system.[20] In an early speech in connection with this effort, Rowen presented the needs in terms similar to those previously applied to the Defense Department and drew on the Defense programming system for several illustrations.

---

[19] U. S. Congress, *Department of Defense Appropriation Bill, 1966*, House Report No. 528, 89th Cong., 1st sess. (Washington: GPO, June 17, 1965), p. 8. These figures do not include military assistance.

[20] With Alain Enthoven, who later became Assistant Secretary of Defense for Systems Analysis, Rowen had earlier written an important paper: A. Enthoven and H. Rowen, "Defense Planning and Organization," P-1640, The RAND Corporation, July 28, 1959.

Although thus markedly successful, the Defense programming system as it evolved under C. J. Hitch had some shortcomings:

1. Data generation and review and approval procedures of the combined programming-budgeting process were excessively burdensome. A complex programming process had been superimposed on a budgeting process that itself has long been in need of major improvements.

2. The translation of program decisions to budget terms, and budget decisions to program terms, was in some areas difficult to accomplish either quickly or accurately because of structural differences and data limitations. A related problem existed in the follow-through on programming decisions at the several stages of implementation.

3. Cost estimates for some program elements were limited in accuracy, involving many prorations and redistributions. There was an exhortation in Department of Defense Directive No. 7045.1 on the programming system that "calculations of resource requirements should, to the maximum extent possible, be done by program element, minimizing those calculations performed other than by program element which require redistribution to program elements"; this became especially difficult for the Army to accomplish, in view of the multiplicity of major-equipment items required for most force units and the planning of procurement on a service-wide basis.

4. The programming structure, little changed from the form in which it had originally been introduced, was proving less than fully suitable.

DEPARTMENT OF DEFENSE PROGRAM/BUDGET SYSTEM: 1966–

Shortly after Robert N. Anthony became Comptroller (in September, 1965), he started on the development of a comprehensive resource management system, to serve the needs of management at all levels within the Department of Defense. These are the principal subsystems which he envisioned: programming and budgeting, management of resources for operating activities, management of inventory and similar assets, and management of the acquisition, utilization and disposition of capital assets. The entire system was to be operational by July 1, 1967.

Insight into Anthony's thinking is afforded by a proposal for programming-budgeting correlation which he made some years prior to his becoming Defense Comptroller.[21] His approach, based on the concept of responsibility-center accounting, involved these elements in the operating expense area:

1. Classification of units as mission or service;

[21] Unpublished working paper prepared in December, 1961, in connection with a study of Defense financial and nonfinancial information systems. See also R. N. Anthony, "New Frontiers in Defense Financial Management," *The Federal Accountant*, Vol. XI (June, 1962), pp. 13–32.

2. Distribution of costs incurred by service units to the mission units served by them;

3. Fund allotments to the mission units to cover all their estimated expenses, including the charges of the service units (a buyer-seller relationship is sought); and

4. Financing of service units by a working-capital fund.

Thus operating costs would be provided by mission unit, thereby reflecting in organizational terms the purposes to be accomplished.

While all of the subsystems of the comprehensive resource management system are interrelated, it is the programming and budgeting subsystem which is our primary concern here. Directly affecting the programming system are changes which have been proposed in the programming structure, and interim operating procedures which have been adopted for programming submission and review.

A revised set of major programs has been proposed:

Program 1. Strategic Forces. Major subdivisions would be Strategic Offensive (former Program I) and Strategic Defensive and Civil Defense (former Program II). This program would include the command organizations associated with these forces.

Program 2. General Purpose Forces. Substantially the same as former Program III.

Program 3. Specialized Forces. This would consist of missions and activities directly related to combat forces, but not a part of any of the forces of Programs I or II, on which independent decisions could be made. Included would be resources for primarily national or centrally directed DoD objectives for intelligence and security, specialized missions such as weather service, aerospace rescue/recovery, and oceanography. Also includes military assistance (this may later be given separate program status).

Program 4. Transportation.

Program 5. Guard and Reserve Forces.

Program 6. Research and Development.

Program 7. Logistics. One of three programs whose size and resource consumption are considered to be dependent on the size and composition of the independent activities contained in the first six programs.

Program 8. Personnel Support. As another of the dependent programs, it would not include training and other kinds of costs specifically identified with other program elements.

Program 9. Administration. A dependent program consisting of Department-wide administration and miscellaneous activities.

In conjunction with this structure, ground rules for costing are being developed to charge *mission* program elements with the costs of services which are relatable and measurable. *Service* program elements are to reflect those costs which are not charged to mission elements as paying customers. The proration of costs is to be kept to a minimum.

We now turn to the interim operating procedures which have been adopted. Designed to simplify program formulation and speed up major decision-making, the procedures center on a distinction between major force-oriented issues and other issues. Major force-oriented issues are defined as issues concerning proposals which, if approved, would have a major quantitative or qualitative effect on forces. Such issues are to be identified early in the programming process by interchange between the Secretary of Defense and Department of Defense components.

For each major force-oriented issue a primary action office is to be designated, with a responsibility for arriving at recommendations for decision by the Secretary of Defense. Recast into the form of a Draft Presidential Memorandum, the recommendations are then to be reviewed by appropriate Department of Defense components, after which revised Draft Presidential Memoranda containing Secretary of Defense decisions are to be issued.

Issues other than those which are major force-oriented would in the main be acted on from both a program and budget point of view as part of the overall budget submission. The specifics of the decision process on such issues are still to be issued.

So that the programming and budgeting system can provide a means for making decisions out of phase with the annual cycle, a program adjustment procedure has been established based on the submission of the Program Adjustment Request (PAR), a very much simplified version of the program change proposal.

The Five Year Defense Program (the renamed Five-Year Force Structure and Financial Program) data files are to be updated on a bi-weekly cycle, to reflect the latest decisions of the Secretary of Defense.

It is apparent that while many of the details remain to be worked out, an important aspect of the Anthony efforts to devise a comprehensive resource management control system will be an improved integration and simplification of the programming and budgeting processes.

PROSPECTS

Although the programming system as introduced by Hitch is being modified in many respects, it retains its major features: an output-oriented five-year program, the thorough review of major issues prior to budget preparation, the widespread participation in the reviews by the Joint Chiefs of Staff, the Office of the Secretary of Defense, and the other components of the Department of Defense, and a program adjustment procedure to keep the five-year program reasonably current throughout the year. Pervading the entire process is the continued emphasis on the use of systems analysis to aid decision-makers.

The programming concept has thus survived a change in Defense comptrollers. Will it survive a change in Defense secretaries? To those who argue that the programming system has been a device for the centralization of authority in the Department of Defense,[22] its future would seem assured. A Secretary of Defense would presumably be reluctant to relinquish power. It might well be the case, however, that some future Secretary of Defense would be disinclined to get involved in program-by-program decision making to the same extent as the Secretary of Defense who installed the system. The programming system might then require change to reflect another management style. Also a future Secretary might be less concerned about conforming budget decisions to a previously established five-year program. Enthusiasm for planning varies widely among executives. It is conceivable, however, that the programming system may become so firmly entrenched in the legislative and executive establishments that lack of full support at the secretarial level will be compensated for.

Congressional support might be a strong influence toward the continued maintenance of the programming system. Programming embodies several features that had earlier been urged by the House Appropriations Subcommittee. Many Congressmen have joined in praise of the knowledge of the Defense program displayed by Secretary McNamara in comprehensive summaries and in related testimony; and they have developed a respect for the system that aided him in achieving this command of the program.

The installation of a planning-programming-budgeting system throughout the government will in turn gain support for the Defense Department system.

There is another influence that in the long run is perhaps the strongest. This is the degree of acceptance of the planning-programming-budgeting system by military planners and programmers, systems analysts, and financial managers at many levels in the Defense Department and their willingness to work together. A productive partnership on the part of these professionals is the best assurance that the aims of the planning-programming-budgeting system will continue to be realized. This partnership could be enhanced by more cross-training. A broadening of comptroller training, for example, is desirable to give comptrollers a better understanding of the possibilities and limitations of planning, a greater appreciation for systems analysis, and more insight into the similarities and differences between budgetary costing and costing for programming and systems analysis.

BIBLIOGRAPHY

1. Hitch, C. J., *Decision-Making for Defense*. Berkeley: University of California Press, 1965.

2. Mosher, F. C., *Program Budgeting: Theory and Practice with Particular Reference to the U. S. Department of the Army*. Chicago: Public Administration Service, 1954.

[22] Such as A. Wildavsky in *The Politics of the Budgetary Process* (Boston: Little, Brown and Company, 1964) p. 140.

3. Quade, E. S., ed., *Analysis for Military Decisions*. Chicago: Rand McNally & Company, 1964.

4. Smithies, A., *The Budgetary Process in the United States*. New York: McGraw-Hill Book Company, 1955.

5. U. S. Congress, Senate Committee on Government Operations, *Financial Management in the Federal Government*, Staff Report, 87th Cong., 1st sess. Washington: GPO, February 13, 1961.

6. U. S. Congress, Senate Committee on Government Operations, *Organizing for National Security, The Budget and the Policy Process*, 87th Cong., 1st sess., Part VIII, Hearings. Washington: GPO, July–August 1961.

7. U. S. Congress, House Committee on Government Operations, *Systems Development and Management*, 87th Cong., 2d sess., Part 2, Hearings. Washington: GPO, 1962. See testimony of C. J. Hitch, Comptroller of the Department of Defense.

8. Wildavsky, A., *The Politics of the Budgetary Process*. Boston: Little, Brown and Company, 1964.

NORMAN V. BRECKNER

Center for Naval Analyses

Norman V. Breckner is Director, Economic Analysis Division of the Institute of Naval Studies, Center for Naval Analyses. After military service he completed the B.A. and M.A. at the University of Washington, Seattle, Washington and received the Ph.D. in Economics from the University of Chicago in 1956. From 1952 to 1960 he taught Economics at Northwestern University and the University of California, Los Angeles. He was a consultant to the RAND Corporation from 1958–61 and a member of the RAND cost analysis staff thereafter, until joining the Center for Naval Analyses in 1962. In his principal area of research, government expenditures, he is the author of "Government Efficiency and the Military 'Buyer-Seller' Device," *Journal of Political Economy*, 1960, and "The Search for an Appropriations Basis," *National Tax Journal*, 1960.

JOSEPH W. NOAH

Planning Research Corporation

Joseph W. Noah received his undergraduate degree in industrial engineering from North Carolina State University in 1951 and was immediately recalled to active military duty. He received the M.S. from Stanford University in 1955 and remained with the Air Force as a procurement officer until 1958. He then joined The RAND Corporation where he participated in studies of ballistic missile systems, space booster systems, and space propulsion systems under examination by DoD and NASA. He joined the Center for Naval Analyses in 1963 and was Head of the Cost Analysis Division. In 1966 he joined Litton Industries, FDL Project, as Head of the Cost-Effectiveness Department, and is currently Manager, Cost Analysis Department, Planning Research Corporation.

3

Costing of Systems

A systems analysis compares alternative system proposals for the achievement of a mission and attempts to discover which is preferred on quantitative grounds. Less ambitiously, it reveals those variations that are decidedly inferior and assists in avoiding gross inefficiencies. A systems analysis typically examines only a part of the defense forces. A partial study cannot, by itself, determine the appropriate *level* of mission achievement; however, by evaluating force-mixes at each of several plausible levels within the mission, it assists the "higher-order" comparison among program levels of alternative missions.

THE ROLE OF COST

In assessing alternatives, the procedure may take either one of two fundamental forms: A desired level of effectiveness may be specified, and the analysis seeks the most economical way to achieve it; or a level of expenditure may be specified, and the analysis explores the effectiveness offered by system variations.

In most cases there are several meaningful elements of achievement in the objective. In a nonmarket activity, such as defense, the level of these positive achievements within a mission are not readily represented by dollar magnitudes or by any other single denominator. For this reason, the specified cost (fixed-budget) procedure is often employed. This does not provide a means of evaluating the relative desirability of the several elements of achievement in the mission; it merely permits translation from the measurement of resources to the measurement of effectiveness elements, for *each* system examined, in order to advance sensible comparisons and selections.

Why should the compared force-mixes be structured deliberately to be equal in cost (or effectiveness)? The answer is straightforward. If system or Force I is demonstrably more effective than II and also costs more than II, we cannot determine from this information whether I's greater effectiveness results simply from a larger scale of expenditure or from a more productive mixture of resources and operational methods, or both. But if their cost is equal, the more effective alternative is clearly preferred. In terms of economic analysis, this comparison attempts to locate a single point on the function that relates total cost to "output" (effectiveness) for the mission.

It is often appropriate to define a bench-mark force for the postulated budget. In a study to assist future procurements for a current mission, one bench mark may be taken as a current financial program with systematic extrapolation. Variations may then be generated by diverting expenditures on one subsystem—for example, attack aircraft—and applying the amount to other subsystems, such as interceptor and reconnaisance aircraft. If the quantitative change in effectiveness associated with each decrement or increment is computed separately, we have estimated portions of the subsystem marginal productivity functions.[1]

The reconstruction and analysis of forces in this fashion shows that in a comparative evaluation of such proposals it is their *differences* in resource drains that count. Errors and omissions in estimating costs that are invariant among structural variations do not bias a comparison. But these costs must be estimated if the result is to contribute to "higher-order" allocations between force levels for different missions in the military sector.

Thus a partial or comparative systems analysis usually demands substantially more than the bare-minimum cost analysis needed for comparison alone. Program decisions and budgetary implementation within the Department of Defense require exposure of the full incremental cost of a candidate system as programmed over time. Further, the wider the scope of alternatives evaluated in a particular systems analysis (for example, Navy vs Air Force systems), the larger will be the fraction of costs that differ among systems, and the more extensive is the minimal cost analysis directly required for the partial analysis.

Selection of a system affects the flow of only a portion of defense resources. The cost estimates for a systems analysis should identify incremental resource costs for each system proposal. A proposal should be charged with all the costs that are required to achieve the measured mission effectiveness but exempted from charges that attach to effectiveness in an unevaluated mission or in another era. By this principle, an attempt to attach costs to effectiveness can succeed in practice only if the cost analysis is intimately governed by the type and time-profile of effectiveness that is evaluated. This is now conventional knowledge in defense analysis. The difficulty lies in measuring additional resource claims.

Cost measurements employ monetary prices, and for most issues there is no better way. An exception occurs in a tightly constrained operational analysis of a task in which the physical quantities of certain resources are absolutely fixed. If resources can be employed only in the analyzed task, with no additional quantities available from other uses, monetary prices observed in exchange transactions elsewhere are irrelevant. Without substitutability of resources among tasks, the suboptimization is a purely internal maximization.

With this exception (ignoring imputed costs for the moment), system and cost analysts in practice employ actual money prices observed in exchange transactions. Resources claimed by a selected project must be paid dollar prices sufficient to attract them to defense from other employments. Prices thus express fundamental economic costs of defense in our economy as well as constraints on a decision maker's ability to achieve objectives. (At the end of this chapter is cited the situation in which observed prices are imperfect reflectors of true, alternative costs.)

---

[1] Alain Enthoven, "Systems Analysis and the Navy", *Naval Review 1965* (Annapolis, Maryland: United States Naval Institute, 1964), pp. 99–117.

The cost analysis of systems studies may be given two dimensions: (1) synthesis and summary of full system costs for the comparison of alternative force-mixes; (2) research on component, subsystem, and associated costs—work involving specific development and application of cost-estimating data and techniques.

In a systems study analysts find themselves simultaneously resolving issues in both dimensions. For each force variant the analyst estimates the resource combinations and associated cost of the structure providing the capability. The cost analyst should not simply transmit cost data; rather, he must work closely with those system analysts who structure and compare the effectiveness of candidate alternatives. Only then can the cost of each system be properly estimated and summarized in relation to the effectiveness that results.

SYNTHESIS OF SYSTEM COSTS

There are many ways of splitting and then summarizing a system's total cost. The process ought to be inspired by a simple theoretical guideline. If we had the power to make good estimates of all the necessary variables and parameters, and the time to do so, we would determine for each course of action the time pattern of mission effectiveness and the time pattern of associated costs that achieve it. Further, if we could demonstrate the appropriateness of some rate of discount with which to reduce magnitudes in different years to equivalence, we could discount future terms in calculating present values of cost. Then we could seek the preferred effectiveness for a given present value of cost, or the minimum present value of cost for any given stream of effectiveness.

In practice, the application of this model is not easy. Various expedients and rules of thumb are used. The authors have at some time used many of these and been tempted by most. We will highlight some problems and practices in cost analysis with an example.

An Example of Force Costs

Both ground systems and air systems contribute to the same mission capability. Currently there are forty ground units and twelve air units in the force structure. Expansion of the capability to a higher level is considered, including either improved ground or air units, or both. For simplicity we construct three alternative incremental mixes only. The example illustrates the problem of comparing costs if the forces are estimated to have equal effectiveness and suggests the necessity of reconstructing the illustrated incremental forces if they are to be made equal-cost in some acceptable sense.

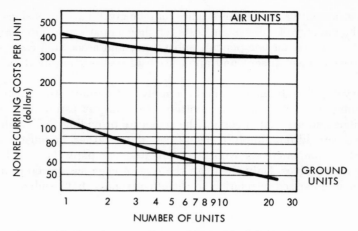

Figure 3–1   *Cumulative Average Costs of New Units*

Each mix is an increment to the current force of forty ground and twelve air units. Mix I is a pure ground increment, mix II includes both ground and air units, and mix III is a pure air increment. They are as follows:

	I	II	III
Ground Units	60 (+20)	50 (+10)	40 (+0)
Air Units	12 (+0)	14 (+2)	17 (+5)

The "effective" life is estimated to be fifteen years for new air units and five years for new ground units. Nonrecurring costs per unit of air and ground are estimated as functions of the volume produced. As shown in Fig. 3–1, per-unit initial investment costs decline when production efficiencies are achieved at increased volume. The recurring cost is estimated to be a constant $50/unit/year for air and $10/unit/year for ground.

Expenditures are then summed to get a total cost for each force-mix shown in Table 3–1.

TABLE 3–1   *Total Costs*

Mix No. of Years	I $\begin{bmatrix} 20\ Ground \\ 0\ Air \end{bmatrix}$	II $\begin{bmatrix} 10\ Ground \\ 2\ Air \end{bmatrix}$	III $\begin{bmatrix} 0\ Ground \\ 5\ Air \end{bmatrix}$
5	1975	2311	2900
10	3950	3886	4150
15	5925	5461	5400

If effectiveness is desired over five years only and total costs are compared only for that interval, the pure ground system has the lowest cost. If the three forces promise equal effectiveness over five years, the air units cannot compete because of their high nonrecurring costs.

Suppose effectiveness is wanted beyond five years, but the cost comparison is limited to the short interval. If air units are selected now rather than ground units, at the end of five years such air units would then provide a remaining effectiveness that permits the avoidance of later expenditures that otherwise would be necessary for replacements of any ground units had they been selected now. A side calculation may take into account this end-of-study "remaining value" of durable systems.

It can be shown that the remaining value of *air units* actually in the inventory five years hence equals subsequent expenditures (beyond five years) that would have been incurred on *ground units* (if selected initially) *minus* subsequent expenditures on *air units* that were selected initially (given that either selection can provide a specified effectiveness). This excess is the net expenditure that can be avoided in the period after five years if *air units*, rather than ground units, are selected initially to provide effectiveness over the entire longer interval.

If remaining value is properly accounted for, the time horizon must be extended as a side calculation and the remaining value then quoted separately, accompanying the five-year total costs. It is simpler to extend the time horizon for the main study to include future procurement and operation of ground units

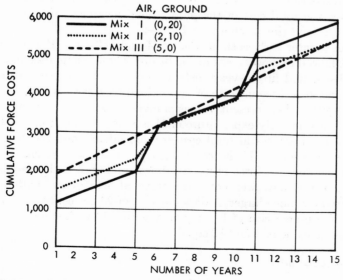

Figure 3–2   *Cumulative Force Costs, High Air System Operating Cost*

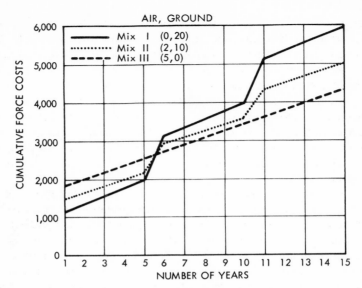

Figure 3–3   *Cumulative Force Costs, Low Air System*
                   Operating Cost

as replacements. As the study interval lengthens, the remaining value of air units is deferred and reduced. It vanishes if an interval is constructed so that across all three structures the end of every chain-of-assets coincides. This interval in the illustration is 15 years. For this horizon, total costs of II and III are about equal and below the total cost of the pure ground increment. The relationship between total cost and time is shown in Fig. 3–2.

Clearly the greater early costs in Forces II and III above Force I are more than counterbalanced by lower costs in the future. These are undiscounted costs. Perhaps the discounted fifteen-year costs are desired. The present values of I and III are equal at a discount rate of approximately 8 per cent. For I and II, the rate that equates their present values is higher, approximately 13 per cent, because the penalty in early expenditure of II is much smaller than that of III.

Quantitative differences in total cost are dependent upon the estimates in the various cost categories. If the recurring cost of the air system is smaller, \$35/unit/year, cumulative force costs are shown in Fig. 3–3. Force-mix I still has a significant but narrower cost advantage at five years. Differences at fifteen years are now much larger. A discount rate of 20 per cent is now required to reduce the fifteen-year cost of I to equality with that of III; and 25 per cent makes the present value of I and II equal.

Cost Categories

A useful step in cost analysis is the preparation of appropriate categories of relevant costs. Cost categories assist in separating expenditures into

TABLE 3–2   *Typical Classification of Weapon System Cost Elements*

A. Nonrecurring

    I. Research and Development
       1. Preliminary Research and Design Studies
       2. Design and Development (Of Subsystems)
       3. System Test (Of Complete System)

   II. Initial Investment
       1. Prime Mission Equipment
       2. Support Equipment
       3. Initial Spares, Spare Parts and Stocks
       4. Initial Training
       5. Initial Travel, Transportation, and Miscellaneous
       6. Military Installations

B. Recurring

  III. Annual Operations
       1. Pay and Allowance
       2. Equipment and Installations Replacement
       3. Equipment and Installations Maintenance
       4. Replacement Training
       5. Consumables (e.g., fuel, oil, etc.)
       6. Recurring Travel, Transportation, and Miscellaneous

quasi-homogeneous types that are distinguished by particular resources, activities, and by the causes that determine their amount. Usually costs will divide according to whether they are nonrecurring or recurring and into major categories such as R&D, investment, and operations and maintenance.[2]

Elements similar to those listed in Table 3–1 are usually included in a weapon-system cost analysis. The three major categories follow a chronological order, but there is usually some time overlap. Investment expenditures occur before the completion of research and development; and operations expenditures begin before the delivery of all items of prime mission equipment.

The systems analysis should reveal what the costs are and whether an item is an investment or an operating cost. A routine categorization, exactly as shown in Table 3–2, can be misleading. An example is a study of alternative means of placing payloads into orbit around the earth. In most military systems the cost of launching rockets would be considered an initial investment; however, if earth satellites are to be kept continuously in orbit, boosters must be launched periodically. If they are nonrecoverable, their costs should be treated as operations costs similar to other recurring costs.

   [2] J. P. Large, ed., *Concepts and Procedures of Cost Analysis*, RM-3589-PR, The RAND Corporation, June, 1963; and Martin V. Jones, *System Cost Analysis: A Management Tool for Decision Making*, TM-04063, The MITRE Corp., July, 1964.

The cost of altering ships and their weapons and electronic systems for the purpose of improving capability involves a problem of categorization. During her lifetime, a ship may be altered several times but at irregular intervals, because frequent major alterations are not physically necessary to achieve the major capability of the ship. Cost models that include an estimate for alterations averaged as a periodic expense over a ship's lifetime will be inappropriate for a course of action involving ultimate retirement of existing ships without further alteration. Cost categories should depend upon the application, and each analysis should assess its special needs.

Time-Patterning the Estimates

Another virtue of cost categories is that they assist an analyst in focusing his estimates over a series of future years. It is useful to disaggregate considerably in order to make credible estimates of the annual pattern of costs. When similar costs are more remote and uncertain, in the case of advanced proposals, this detail is less useful.

Estimates of cost time-streams serve several purposes: (1) Some elements of cost are typically deferred and sometimes inadvertently omitted from analysis unless the procedure calls specifically for time-patterning costs; examples are infrequent ship modernizations or aircraft model improvements. (2) Decision makers must anticipate when and what types of expenditures will occur, because the budgetary process authorizes expenditures annually and by specific types. (3) Decision makers are not indifferent to the timing of expenditures, even if the arithmetic total of expenditure over a period of years is given. Some of the most important substitution possibilities within defense are substitutions over time—for example, maintaining existing forces longer and developing replacements later.

Time Horizon and Remaining Value

The study interval is appropriately determined within the individual analysis. No general convention or rule of thumb, apart from the purpose of the analysis, can specify it except arbitrarily. Within the analysis, considerations of cost and production feasibility alone cannot specify it. Analysts should confront the questions of what the characteristic threat is, what types of capability may meet it, how long each operational system may be expected to provide effectiveness, what the prospective future equipments and methods may be, and when development may provide them.

As illustrated earlier in the example, some systems may promise further effectiveness beyond a chosen time horizon. This may be credited to the air units at a five-year horizon by estimating expenditures in the still-further future that may be avoided if those units are then in the inventory. If assets are not expected to be very effective in the primary mission, there may be a credit to be derived from a secondary role in which their availability will permit the avoidance of certain expenditures.

Even when longer time-horizons, such as fifteen years, are employed we may expect assets of some forces to be effective beyond the study interval. We usually lack reliable evidence or techniques for estimating remote effectiveness and the remote avoidable expenditure the assets permit. Cost analyses sometimes employ the arithmetic of amortization as an implicit predictor, but care must always be taken to avoid substituting simple arithmetic—because it is simple—for attempts at estimation or analysis. Even an arbitrary accounting method, however, will frequently give a far better estimate of remaining value at the end of a study interval than if the question had been evaded and the value set at zero. One cannot avoid making an implicit estimate—and it may be a bad one.

A related issue involves existing assets proposed for use in a system under evaluation. Is such equipment to be treated as free when "inherited" by a system, or not? Almost any comparison of alternative systems involves existing assets, although many will be specific to a particular purpose with no meaningful alternative use. Nevertheless, rather than assume this, the analysis should question whether the asset is useful for another objective, and what would be the maximum expenditure that could be avoided by its application elsewhere. This is the (alternative) cost of "assigning" it to a system in the analysis. If this factor becomes important, the study may consider a widening of scope in an attempt to include more types of effectiveness.

Current alternative values and future remaining values are imputations. Estimates of net costs involving imputations appear less straightforward, and therefore less reliable, than estimates of most explicit costs. To be convincing, an estimate of remaining value must demonstrate that the asset structure promises a desired effectiveness in some mission in the further future. It is little wonder that cost analysts are unenthusiastic about imputations that rest on effectiveness measures. Yet these imputations do not introduce, but merely underscore, an analytic difficulty of effectiveness measures.

Time Preference

Economists differ in their interpretation of what economic analysis implies about applying a discount rate in comparing nonmarketable projects such as defense. One opinion recommends discounting at the rate of interest on "comparable" types of investment in the market economy. The rationale is that when we extract resources for the nonmarketable sector from other uses we cannot compare validly unless we only direct resources to defense systems that are as productive as successful investments in the private sector.

Another opinion says that such comparisons cannot be extended to demonstrate efficiency by testing nonmarketable investments against the market rate of interest as experienced by private investors. This opinion can be quite unsparing in criticizing unevaluated nonmarketable projects. But it rejects the direct relevancy of a market rate of interest for evaluating such activities.[3]

Another question concerns discounting cost streams "to take account of risk." Loading the discount rate with a factor "for risk" is quite perverse if it is intended to act as a corrective for doubts about the relative *cost* estimates in the systems studied.

This is shown by considering two estimated cost streams for producing a given effectiveness. Suppose we know from empirical evidence that cost estimates for the further-future are less reliable. Applying a discount rate to streams of single-valued, annual cost estimates clearly reduces remote costs more than early costs. The discounting operation thereby biases choice toward projects with relatively large and more uncertain later cost estimates. This bias would be still stronger if less reliable cost estimates were discounted at higher rates.

Adding a risk factor to a discount rate is sometimes suggested for a different reason: the inability to anticipate options that might later seem attractive. There are many cases in which options that were initially unanticipated, because of either ignorance or myopia concerning the real nature of the threat or technology, were later discovered to be most attractive. Future evidence, if not examined too late to influence a selection, will cause us to reevaluate an initial selection and perhaps to abandon it.

Will loading comparisons with a discount rate aid such sequential decision-making? In a sense, yes, because choice is thereby shifted away from projects with relatively heavy early costs, thus dampening early commitments. It is, however, hard to imagine anything more arbitrary than loading a discount rate as a device to promote incremental spending in search of reliable information on obscure benefits and costs.

Cost-Summarizing Techniques

A number of conventions for summarizing costs may be found. Several that have been employed in studies are defined here.[4]

Five-Year System Cost. This convention arithmetically sums the R&D, initial investment, and five times the annual cost of operating the system at a specified level. Remaining values at the end of five years of level operations (which may be seven to fifteen years after the initiation of R&D) are excluded. Also excluded are "build-up costs," that is, the operating costs incurred during the phase-in period before the system reaches its full force.

Period Outlay. Build-up costs are included and outlays are time-phased, either by year of obligation or expenditure. In some studies, remaining value has been referenced simply by listing the age structure of assets as of the study's cut-off date.

[3] Vartkes L. Broussalian, *The Evaluation of Non-Marketable Investments*, RC-15, Center for Naval Analyses, June, 1965.

[4] J. W. Noah, *Concepts and Techniques for Summarizing Defense System Costs*, SEG RC-1, Center for Naval Analyses, September, 1965.

Net Cost. This technique attempts a measurement of remaining values. Specifically, it gives effect to unequal useful lifetimes among the principal assets both within and across force-mixes. The time pattern of costs is estimated, including a remaining value of assets at the cut-off date. This is then subtracted from the estimated expenditures to get a "net cost."

Equal Life-Lengths Cost. An approximate time period is computed so that across all force-mixes the end of each estimated chain-of-assets roughly coincides. A special case occurs when in each chain the replacement equipments are expected to have the same useful lifetime as initial equipments in the chain. This is illustrated by the five-year replications of ground units in the example above.

There has been overemphasis of the five-year system cost technique in the past. Because of its exclusions, it can be misleading in some cases. But this is not meant to suggest that the five-year cost has no place in cost analysis. The five-year system cost estimate is useful in a predevelopment analysis of systems that rely upon technological advances far in the future. An aerospace plane or a nuclear-powered missile imposes requirements and associated costs that cannot now be estimated with an accuracy sufficient to warrant the use of detailed cost summaries.

For less advanced systems nearing procurement, whose specifications can be estimated with more accuracy, one should not ignore the time pattern of costs, unequal lifetimes of alternatives, build-up costs, and so on. Feasible production, construction, and introduction schedules should be examined more carefully. A satisfactory resolution should be found for the question: "Are we examining optional mixes having a useful capability over the same time period?" At this stage, reliance on a short study interval and effectiveness measurements for only one nominal future date can obscure real issues involved in selection of a production program.

TOPICS IN COST ESTIMATION

Broadly, there are two types of decisions in which systems analyses assist: force-structure procurement and development planning. The following topics relate to both.

Use of Historical Data

Although sunk costs are irrelevant to evaluations of future options, records of past costs are indispensable as a base upon which to project estimates of future costs and system characteristics. Prospective systems usually involve components and operations that have close analogs in the past or present. Past or current experience also warns us of pitfalls, delays, and improvisations having substantial cost consequences.

It takes years to build a good library of data on both procurement and operational aspects of defense programs. The task is riddled with frustrations. Government record-keeping has always been adapted primarily to assuring fidelity to financial authorizations. These records are not ordinarily useful in relating means to ends—in evaluating activities by their claims on resources and their contributions to some agreed objective.[5] Enormous effort is required to adapt them to this function.

Defense-related cost data are often treated as sensitive information by government agencies and as privileged information by industrial contractors. (Neither treatment is necessarily related to military security.) One effect is to reduce the information available to defense cost analysts outside the government proper. Although certain information is rightly privileged to private enterprise, impediments here are gradually eroding. The military services have instituted publication of general program-planning and cost factors. Contractors are required to submit certain cost reports depending upon the type of contract. These are very useful sources of data but require much evaluation. There is often inconsistency across sources. An investigator who wants detail usually must probe beyond the reports.

Cost-Quantity Relationships

Hardware procurement costs have received more attention than operating costs. The chief relationship established for major items of military hardware is the dependency of total production cost per unit upon volume of output. Cost per unit is observed to decline with increased production over an extended range of output. This has been observed in the airframe industry and has found application elsewhere among major equipments produced in quantity.[6] Marked reductions in man-hours used in production of successive lots are observed. One explanation is "learning." In the course of operations, workers and supervisors learn the process and how to do it better. Data on other inputs also indicate a similar effect for materials. Cost analysts have by now fitted a number of functions relating cumulative cost to cumulative quantity.

Another influence of total volume on cost is difficult in practice to separate from the first. In planning production, there is an initial choice of how much investment in plant, equipment, and special tooling to undertake. For a planned cumulative volume, trade-offs are possible between initial investment costs and subsequent operating costs. As the intended volume (for which initial plans are made) increases over a significant range, a firm can plan the production method to select more diverse and durable equipment and tooling, thereby lowering

---

[5] David Novick, *Efficiency and Economy in Government Through New Budgeting and Accounting Procedures*, R-254, The RAND Corporation, February 1, 1954.

[6] Harold Asher, *Cost-Quantity Relationships in the Airframe Industry*, Report R-291, The RAND Corporation, July, 1956.

per-unit costs of production.[7] This proposition has received less empirical testing than has "learning," but it is familiar to defense contractors who produce specific equipments to order. It may warrant more investigation as a planning device for the volume production of such items as ships or the huge new C5A transport aircraft. Cost analysis in this context strives to determine the most efficient (economical) technology to employ in major defense production.

Estimating Procedures

For an operational (or retired) aircraft an analyst may find production costs on, for example, four to eight delivered lots produced by a specific firm. In estimating future costs of a proposed aircraft with different attributes, this information represents *one* observation only. The objective may be to estimate the future research and development, procurement, and operating costs of a proposed aircraft that flies faster, lands more slowly, carries more payload and has an all-weather capability. Such an aircraft will attempt aerodynamic advances. It will weigh more, have bigger and perhaps more efficient engines, use different alloys, mount advanced sensors and weapons. Its configuration may imply different maintenance practices. Perhaps its operational mode will imply different attrition. The cost analyst enumerates the delivered aircraft that differ in these distinctive factors but are in other respects sufficiently homogeneous so that their recorded costs may have direct bearing on estimation for the new vehicle. In a predicament that appalls most statisticians, if the cost analyst finds four to eight observations on other "similar but different" vehicles, he feels an embarrassment of riches.

In fact, there is perhaps now more good information available on aircraft and their components than on any other type of major vehicle or equipment. There is now enough data in some areas to warrant use of multiple regressions. Estimated regression relationships for airframes, engines, ships, and certain aspects of aircraft and ship maintenance have now appeared.[8]

These must be tested by their fruitfulness—can better cost estimates be made with them than without them? Few, if any, of the "samples" can be said to exhibit the statistical properties for which regression has been derived in statistical theory. The application of statistical estimating relationships to an estimating problem must be made with caution, particularly when forecasting beyond the limits of the data. If the subject forecast is for an item that differs in important attributes from the events used in estimating the regression, an experienced researcher will also employ judgment based on information "outside" the regression.

---

[7] Armen Alchian, "Costs and Outputs," in Moses Abramovitz and others, *The Allocation of Economic Resources* (Stanford, Calif.: Stanford University Press, 1959), pp. 23–40.

[8] R. P. Caldarone, a classified paper prepared for the Center for Naval Analyses, February, 1966; and A. Frank Watts, a classified paper prepared for The RAND Corporation, July 1965.

Most cost estimates must be accomplished with too few observations on particular subsystems or components to permit regression estimation of relationships. When data are sparse, the estimator may use two types of procedures.

First, he may look for one or more close analogs for which information is available. For example, in estimating the cost of a new reentry subsystem, he will examine in some detail the cost of the one or two recent vehicles resembling the candidate design. In such procedures, it is common to try to account for systematic effects of different components on the total cost of the vehicle and to treat cost elements such as labor, material, and engineering-hours separately. Experience has shown, however, that detailed estimates can still be bad estimates. For advanced proposals, ill effects are more likely if an analyst attempts to relate estimates exclusively to forecasted component weights rather than to prescribed performance. Detail frequently implies credibility to the uninformed. Perhaps this accounts to some extent for the detail one often finds in cost estimates. If the estimation exhibits are very detailed, it can be difficult to distinguish a paucity from a plenty of reliable and independent observations.

By contrast with the specific analog, a second approach, when independent observations are sparse, is to use cost information that is aggregated to a higher level. Where information has not been disaggregated to relate it to characteristics of individual units, it is often available from budgetary exhibits on an overall basis. This type of information has been employed in estimating costs of operation and support. Here, too, cost factors are frequently constructed, such as cost per military man. This factor is derived from an aggregate budgetary expenditure for pay and allowances and from an aggregate manpower figure.

If applied to quasi-homogeneous categories of manpower or materials, simple cost factors provide satisfactory estimates for most comparative purposes. It should be emphasized that this is a procedure solely for estimating costs of given, specified methods of employing these resources. It says nothing about the efficient ways of combining manpower and equipments in defense activities. This is a different and more penetrating question. If analysis is to provide findings on this question, it must attempt experiments or simulations that actually vary amounts and qualities of manpower in combination with materials and equipments.

Early Estimates for Advanced Systems

Defense cost analysis is now old enough to have a history. A review of the record of approximately the first decade of cost estimating, a period corresponding closely to the fifties, shows a variable performance. There is a bias toward underestimation.[9] The degree of underestimation, and the variance of

---

[9] Robert Summers, a classified paper prepared for The RAND Corporation, April, 1962; and A. W. Marshall and W. H. Meckling, "Predictability of the Costs, Time, and Success of Development," *The Rate and Direction of Inventive Activity: Economic and Social Factors*, National Bureau of Economic Research (Princeton, N. J.: Princeton University Press, 1962), pp. 461–475.

estimation errors, both seem to be related to the earliness of the estimate and the type of proposal. Differences between early estimates and ultimately realized costs have been small for systems where attempted advances were modest. These include, for example, noncombatant ships and cargo aircraft. Errors in early estimates are systematically larger for new combat aircraft with advanced radars, communications, and weapons, and for advanced rocket engines and guidance systems.

Systematic early underestimation of costs is substantially explained by the advocacy that affects many forecasters, particularly under "cost-plus" contracts lacking both carefully specified performance characteristics and penalties for inability to meet them at "estimated" costs. Further, there are two major areas of uncertainty that account for the variance of estimation errors. One is uncertainty concerning the time and difficulty required to develop for procurement a design and configuration that ultimately achieves a promised performance. The other is pure estimating uncertainty concerning the costs of delivering any specified physical configuration. For proposals where attempted technological advances are great, the development-and-cost estimating record can probably be improved by focusing early estimation on information that relates cost to advances in performance instead of costing someone's early design specifications.

Why do we want early cost estimates for proposals "promising" great advances? At this stage the problem is far different from procurement selection, in which both contractor and proposal must be selected for large production runs. By contrast, research and development is a process of securing information about the real capability of proposers to *deliver* performance—how, when, and at what cost. It is a process that buys this information incrementally, year by year. It would be foolish early in predevelopment to proceed as though each proposal's cost could be estimated sufficiently reliably to allow a single, terminal selection to be made without component- and subsystem-development yielding test data.

Early estimates are wanted because development resources are also constrained. Even if the intention is to buy partial or sequential development on similar proposals, these must be selected from a range of aspirants. The cost estimate is one aid in preliminary evaluation of development proposals. As estimates are revised when confronted with experience, they become credible for force-structure analyses leading to production decisions.

Sensitivity

All studies include doubtful features that cannot be satisfactorily specified or quantitatively resolved within the study.[10] The character of the threat, the detection range of a sensor, the effectiveness of an aircraft against a target, the cost of the needed support activities may all be examples. Each can

[10] G. H. Fisher, *A Discussion of Uncertainty in Cost Analysis*, RM-3071-PR, The RAND Corporation, April, 1962.

be varied in magnitude to see how the final quantitative results are influenced by, or are "sensitive" to, possible variability in the doubtful factor.

This exercise can be very revealing. In a complicated analysis, it can greatly reduce the obscurity between assumptions and findings by showing separately the features to which results are and are not responsive. We can thereby indicate where the more costly "mistakes" may be, even if we cannot estimate a strict statistical reliability. Uncertainties bearing heavily on results become options for further research and experiment. This must be the path of progress in systems analyses. Most formal studies are more synthesis than analysis. Each synthesizes much existing knowledge, adds a bit to the fund, or helps to identify efforts that will be instructive.

SOME AVENUES FOR FURTHER WORK

The broad and pervasive area called "support" presents difficult problems in measuring resource claims. Apart from the question of management efficiency, and how it may be improved, it is difficult simply to identify the incremental (decremental) physical quantities of many resource services associated with incremental (decremental) achievements in system effectiveness. Looking behind the warfare system "identifiers,"—that is, the hardware items— one finds substantial investment and operating costs for "support" activities required to sustain capability. Specific and necessary services are partially obscured in the supporting military structure. Although the current Department of Defense programming system has made a contribution to unraveling this structure, the format does not automatically answer questions that are raised by a systems analysis about which portions of support activities are incrementally linked to possible changes in a system or force structure.

Another difficulty in specifying relevant costs occurs when a system directed to one objective would, if selected, increase effectiveness or reduce costs of another mission. In economic analysis these are external economies or spillovers. Spillovers within the market-and-price system, as a result of one decision maker's choices, consist of items of benefit or costs that are experienced, without charge or compensation, by other participants within the economy. Although in different form, similar phenomena are found in government, including the defense sector. The narrower the effectiveness concept that defines the scope of a systems analysis, the greater will be the range of excluded activities that employ similar or identical systems and provide effectiveness related to that of the analysis; hence, the systems analysis either requires arbitrary cost allocations to be made among narrow missions or it excludes types of effectiveness provided by some of the resources whose costs are charged in the analysis. Thus it is often desirable to attempt to broaden a study to include more types of effectiveness and reduce the allocation of costs among narrow missions.

For some resources employed in defense, including categories of manpower, there are ceilings on prices paid. These and other resources are rationed or assigned among alternative users in defense on some basis other than price-expressed valuations. Assigned users do not have to pay as much as would be required to secure them from other abortive claimants through open bidding. If prices are fixed or nonexistent, neither the external-acquisition nor the internal-allocation process yields good information on relative productivities in different uses and, thus, on true alternative cost. In this environment, further exploration of technological possibilities for substitution among manpower and equipments in defense programs will very likely reduce costs or improve capabilities. There is a growing awareness of possible payoffs in efforts to analyze manpower utilization and to improve the quantification of system claims on manpower.

ROLAND N. McKEAN*

University of California at Los Angeles

Roland N. McKean is coauthor, with Charles J. Hitch, of *The Economics of Defense in the Nuclear Age* (which also includes contributions by five other authors). Now a Professor of Economics at UCLA, McKean worked in the Economics Department at The RAND Corporation from 1951 to 1964 on a variety of defense problems. He has served as chairman of the program-planning committee for the Universities-National Bureau Conference on the economics of defense (1966), as a member of the Board of Editors of the American Economic Review (1961–64), and on various government committees, including the 1964 legislative task force on natural resources. In World War II, he was a fighter pilot with the Eighth Air Force. He received his Ph.D. in Economics at The University of Chicago (1948) and taught Economics at Vanderbilt University from 1948 to 1951.

* I am especially indebted to The RAND Corporation for an opportunity to study program budgeting and to James R. Schlesinger for exchanges of ideas about these issues when I was with RAND. For related materials, see the volume, *Program Budgeting*, David Novick, ed., Cambridge: Harvard University Press, 1965.

4

Remaining Difficulties in Program Budgeting

To say that program budgeting would aid decision makers is almost like saying that better budgeting procedures would be better. Those who advocate program budgeting rarely have in mind a specific budgeting system for a specific governmental unit; they simply feel that it must be possible to design a system that would be more helpful. With that general proposition almost everyone would agree. Disagreement and difficulties arise when the question gets down to "brass tacks" and there is an attempt to design specific improvements in particular budgetary systems. Then it becomes clear that there are difficulties with each alternative proposal—that complete dominance and free lunches are rare, even in designing new administrative aids.

This paper, after part of the background has been briefly reviewed, will focus upon some of the difficulties encountered in the major experiment with program budgeting to date. This emphasis on difficulties and disadvantages does *not* imply that past budgetary reforms should never have been undertaken or that further improvements cannot be effected. Similarly, to say that lunch costs something does not imply that one should never eat. The gains may well outweigh the costs. It does suggest, however, that program budgeting is no panacea, that tremendous and unalloyed benefits should not be expected from budgetary reforms alone, and that the costs as well as prospective gains should be taken into account in choosing the design and scope of budgetary arrangements.

BACKGROUND

Even in general terms, program budgeting means different things to different people. Some use the term to mean the use of revised budgetary exhibits, for example, a revised version of part or all of the U.S. budget. The revised exhibits would present proposed costs for "programs" producing services that were more nearly end-products than the services yielded by the old categories; and those costs would be projected over longer time periods. Others doubt that such exhibits would be very useful unless supplemented by special cost-effectiveness or cost-benefit analyses to improve particular program decisions; and they define program budgeting to include the use of such *ad hoc* analyses. Still others feel that both these tools would be relatively useless unless some official were given clear-cut effective authority to make the program trade-offs (that is, to chop some and increase others); and they may define program budgeting to include organizational or other reforms to implement decisions based on the new budget format and the *ad hoc* cost-effectiveness analyses.

To reduce the overlap with other chapters, program budgeting will be discussed mainly as a revised budgetary exhibit, although possible implications regarding cost-benefit analysis and the centralization of authority will also be commented upon.

The notion of performance or program budgeting is an old one, but the most dramatic experiment along these lines began in the U.S. Defense Department in 1961. The defense budget was recast in terms of categories that were more nearly like end-services or programs, such as the strategic retaliatory forces; these categories were broken down into sub-missions or "program elements," such as Minuteman or The Fleet Ballistic Missile System; and costs were projected five years ahead. The resulting exhibits were summarized in the "Blue Book," which consisted of several blue books (all having a security classification); the official title was the *Five Year Force-Structure and Financial Plan.* There remain numerous difficulties in preparing and using these exhibits, but on balance they are apparently regarded as being quite successful; for the Defense Department experience has excited renewed interest in program budgeting—in the U.S. federal government, in other governments, and in such nongovernmental organizations as universities.

One of the main virtues of program budgeting is simply the fact that it calls attention to relatively important trade-offs that might otherwise be neglected. After all, the main purpose of any budgeting system is to show officials the categories that make up total proposed outlays and the possibilities of shifting resources from some of these categories to others. Conventional government budgeting has often reminded officials that proposed outlays are for personnel, travel, construction, and other input categories; and they have been confronted with such substitution possibilities as shifting resources from travel to type-writers. The program budget reminds them that resources can be shifted from strategic deterrence to continental defense or, within broad programs, that trade-offs can be considered between Polaris and Minuteman or between air transport and sea transport.

Program budgeting in the Defense Department has called attention to these trade-offs in another way—not because of the format but because of an altered emphasis accompanying the introduction and (so far) the use of the plan. The revised procedures have explicitly stressed that budget ceilings are not to be regarded as unalterable and that particular forces are not to be regarded as absolute requirements. Choices are supposed to be made by weighing the gains from each proposal against the costs (that is, whatever would have to be given up). The mechanism set up for changing the five-year financial plan is intended to shout, "Consider the trade-offs!" to all participants in the planning process.

The old system was one in which physical "requirements" were often selected prior to cost estimation and budget ceilings were often set prior to adequate consideration of the value of various forces. To be sure, some kind of cost constraints were recognized, since the lists of "requirements" or "needs" were not infinitely long, and, in later stages, explicit budget constraints were introduced. Also, on the budget side, the constraints were of course not wholly independent of notions concerning the value of alternative forces. Moreover, a bargaining process ensued in which the "need-firsters" (those who tried to figure out what was needed regardless of cost) compromised concerning their "indispensable" requirements and the "budget-firsters" (those who tried to estimate how much could be spent regardless of payoff) compromised regarding their absolute budget ceilings. Thus, in actual fact, tacit and explicit bargaining pressures forced planners to consider some trade-offs. Nonetheless, many choices became embedded in the budget at an early stage, and other choices were made in haste at later stages—without conscious or careful weighing of needs or benefits against the costs, that is, against competing benefits.

Another virtue, or at least aim, of program budgeting is to *facilitate* the consideration of those trade-offs. This is supposed to be accomplished by (a) presenting full-cost estimates that are more pertinent to choices than partial-cost estimates would be, and (b) focusing attention on those trade-offs about which planners and others can make better judgments. Conventional budget formats usually show costs (proposed outlays or obligational authority) for only one year in advance. For many choices this projection represents merely the down payment and fails to indicate substantial future costs that are implied by the proposed activities, if carried to completion. As in constructing a factory, those future costs are not always inevitable; for work could be halted and the project cancelled. But the future costs are implied to the extent that the probability of completion is high. And, once a substantial investment has been made, it is frequently economical to complete the program and incur the additional costs. The probable full costs, not just the down payment, should be recognized at the outset, just as the full costs should be considered when a firm decides to build another factory.

Conventional budgets have often shown, in another sense, only part of the relevant costs—namely, the costs incurred in one branch or service (for example, the Navy) or those invested in particular components (such as missiles), without regard for related costs incurred in another branch (for example, the Air Force) or for other system components (such as transportation, personnel, or servicing activities). Again the full-cost implications of the alternatives have more relevance to the choice among alternatives than do partial-cost implications; and program budgeting is intended to provide a more complete picture of costs throughout the system as well as costs over time.

Program budgeting may facilitate consideration of important tradeoffs for another reason: Better intuitive judgments can be made about trades of end-services or program elements than about trades of across-the-board inputs to numerous end-services. Thinking in terms of amounts budgeted for conventional input categories may obscure the connection between the inputs and the end-purposes of the various activities. A determination of the number of people or air transports or typewriters to employ certainly depends upon the purposes that are to be carried out. A budget in terms of typewriters, personnel, and air transports, for all activities lumped together, makes it difficult to relate these ingredients to the desired outputs and therefore to reach sound judgments regarding the trade-offs. Lower-level programmers no doubt relate the inputs to tasks, but they cannot compare the cost and worth of increments to alternative tasks. And, to repeat, bulky exhibits of across-the-board inputs are of little aid to higher-level officials in making judgments about these trade-offs. Similarly, if a bakery operator tried to decide how much flour, sugar, and butter to buy without linking these items to the amounts of bread and pastries to be produced, he would be handicapped in considering the trade-offs. Program budgeting is intended to reduce this sort of handicap.

Another aim of program budgeting has been to improve incentives. Officials in the public as well as the private sectors presumably maximize utility in view of whatever constraints they face. This does not mean that they are intensely selfish—good deeds, aid to the unfortunate, and the national interest (as each individual sees it) are elements in most people's utility functions. But it does mean that if one item in an official's utility function becomes more expensive (that is, entails greater sacrifice of other items), he will take less of that item. And if one item becomes more valuable in relation to others, he will take more of that item. Institutional changes such as the introduction of program budgeting should be examined in this framework. The question should be asked: Which activities of various officials and employees become more rewarding to them, and which ones are made more expensive to them, than formerly was the case?

In the Defense Department, program budgeting was partly an attempt to make certain undesirable behavior more expensive to decision makers. In government, officials often find it rewarding to seek increased staffs and budgets—rewarding from both a personal career standpoint and from the standpoint of increasing their ability to carry out the mission that is their particular responsibility. They tend to make choices in such a way as to achieve increased budgets. They are sometimes quite candid about it, pointing out that, in the economist's jargon, the marginal productivity of effort devoted to expanding next year's budget is often greater, from their standpoint, than the marginal productivity of effort devoted to increasing the efficiency with which a given budget is used. They tend to use "foot-in-the-door" techniques, that is, to get something started without calling attention to the full costs. Later, when part of the costs have been sunk and the incremental costs are correspondingly lower, completion of the new venture may be efficient from everyone's viewpoint. Such behavior may be rendered comparatively rewarding or inexpensive to officials under conventional budgeting, with only part of the costs emphasized and with the budget organized in terms of input categories. But program budgeting stresses the full implications of choices when they are reached, making such behavior more difficult (expensive) for officials.

It might be noted that we sometimes exaggerate the ill effects of the conventional budgeting process. Adherence to fixed requirements or ceilings, neglect of full-cost implications, use of the "foot-in-the-door" tactic—all these phenomena are kept in check to some extent by (a) the trade-offs within officials' utility functions (for example, concern about the national interest prevents parochial interests from having unlimited influence on one's decisions) and (b) bargaining pressures from other officials who have conflicting aims. Gross neglect (either deliberate or inadvertent) of substitution possibilities or of future costs, or flagrant use of the "foot-in-door" tactic would bring harsh criticism and costs for the erring decision maker. Consequently, use of the conventional budget is not totally devoid of desirable influences. But program budgeting aims to go further in making desirable behavior less costly and undesirable behavior more costly to the individual officials.

SHORTCOMINGS OF PROGRAM BUDGETING

When advocating or considering the adoption of program budgeting, we should be realistic and fully recognize its limitations. In other words, we should look at *its* full-cost and full-effectiveness implications too.

Limited Value of the Information That Can Be Provided

First of all, there is nothing to be gained by exaggerating the worth of the information provided by program budgeting. The value of the trade-off and cost information yielded by such budgeting systems may be relatively modest.

Inability to direct attention to all important trade-offs. It has been stated above that one major virtue of program budgeting is that it calls attention to important trade-offs. At the same time, a little reflection indicates that *no* set of programs and program elements can focus attention on *all* the trade-offs that should be considered. The pre-1961 Defense budget, it was said, directed attention to trade-offs between across-the-board inputs within each military service or among Army, Navy, and Air Force outlays *in total* but obscured tradeoffs between rival missions—and within, for example, the deterrent-mission, rival systems. The new budget set up such packages as Program I, Strategic Retaliatory Forces, calling attention to the possibilities of substitutions among Minuteman, Polaris, and manned bomber systems. It was apparently felt, however, that this obscured trade-offs between such elements in Program I and those in Program II, Continental Air and Missile Defense Forces; and those two program packages were later combined. Now some feel that the new budget, by putting general-purpose forces into a separate compartment (monitored by different individuals from those who monitor the other Programs), obscures such trade-offs as those between limited-war forces and elements of the strategic forces. If the budgetary format were adjusted in response to all such arguments, of course, all defense activities might be combined into one gigantic program-package. But there is no use pretending that this would highlight all important trade-offs; indeed it would take us back to Square One, for we would face anew the question: which compartments (categories, programs, program elements, or whatever they might be called) within the covers of the budget would be most helpful?

It is also contended that the present (1965) format, though highlighting trade-offs among certain close substitutes (such as different strategic deterrent systems or different air transports), obscures substitution possibilities among systems that are not obvious substitutes, such as air transport and infantry divisions, or aircraft for guerilla warfare and aircraft for continental defenses. (Even close substitutes, for example, alternative locations for weapon systems, are not necessarily shown as adjacent parts of the budget structure or indeed shown at all.) Multipurpose systems, it is argued, are especially handicapped by the new compartmentalization, for their function is not neatly confined to any one mission or package. New systems emerging from Research and Development, or systems that should be further explored in R&D, may also be discriminated against—as far as focusing attention on relevant trade-offs is concerned.

The point that should be stressed, though, is that *no* set of compartments can illuminate *all* the relevant trade-offs. Focusing attention on one set of substitution possibilities "defocuses" attention from others. One way of combining activities precludes other combinations, at least in the same exhibit. And if multiple or extremely detailed exhibits are used, it becomes increasingly costly to high-level decision makers to review and employ the mass of information; at the same time, it is difficult to avoid having a multiplicity of lower-level officials prepare and monitor separate pieces of the budget. Action in any direction—more programs or fewer programs, more program elements or fewer program elements, more detail or less detail, more individuals monitoring separate pieces or fewer individuals monitoring broader programs—involves cost as well as gain. Changes in format and procedure that yield *net* gains can be sought, but changes that yield all gain and no cost will not often be found. Some believe that the best approach is to shake up the budget structure periodically to avoid the "bureaucratic blindness" that can develop with any given structure.

Inability to direct attention to all important interdependencies. A point closely related to the above argument is that no budget format or process can throw a spotlight on all the other relevant interdependencies. It would be desirable if the structure reminded us not only of the question, "Should we buy more fallout shelters or more Polaris?" but also of such facts as: "An extra purchase of deep shelters may increase the effectiveness of our strategic retaliation forces in deterring minor aggressions (with possibilities of escalation) but decrease their effectiveness in deterring thermonuclear attack," or "A decrease in the B-52 force may reduce the costs of expanding interceptor capabilities (since extra airbases and installations would thereby be made available)." Collecting interrelated inputs into weapon systems or program elements and collecting interrelated elements as adjacent parts of Programs can increase our awareness of certain interdependencies; but these procedures do not illuminate *all* the significant interrelationships. This deficiency becomes particularly evident in preparing and considering program-change proposals (PCP's)—in other words, proposed alterations in the Blue Book—because each PCP may affect the desirability of several other PCP's. The new budgeting process has often been plagued with what are sometimes called "ricochet effects."

Again the point is that *no* set of program elements would eliminate the complications caused by interdependencies. They exist because life is complicated, not because either the old or the new budget format creates them. Again, therefore, we should anticipate perpetual difficulties as officials struggle to spotlight the most important interrelationships.

Costs shown in the budget are not necessarily close to the relevant costs. The cost estimates for the various program elements are less accurate and more variable in accuracy than many outsiders may imagine. Allocating "overhead" or "common" costs among program elements can yield only a crude approximation of each element's total cost. The expenses of administrative staffs that serve a whole agency, the costs of repair shops and facilities that serve numerous program elements, and indeed all O and M (Operations and Maintenance) expenses are likely to be allocated on an almost arbitrary basis. Inputs such as petroleum and lubricants can probably be managed better on an aggregate basis with the allocation among program elements left flexible; therefore, any specific allocation is likely to be (and should be) off the mark.

Furthermore, the accuracy of the estimates probably varies from program element to program element. The Army, Navy, and Air Force each have different difficulties in cost allocation. Different elements within each program or within each service—Army divisions, Army surface-to-surface missile battalions, antisubmarine warfare carriers, or nuclear attack submarines—pose cost-allocation issues having varying degrees of difficulty. Again it means that one cannot know precisely how to interpret the cost figures in the budget.

Even more fundamental, however, is the fact that there is no unique cost of a program element that is pertinent to all decisions about that element. The incremental cost of each choice is the pertinent figure, and it changes with circumstances. Even if the budgetary exhibits showed the correct total cost of a program element or average cost per unit (for example, cost per Minuteman squadron), it would still be only a crude approximation of incremental cost (that is, the cost of the particular increment or decrement under consideration). Incremental costs of defense activities depend upon the particular circumstances: Would administrative or servicing facilities really have to be expanded proportionately? Would some other aircraft or activity be phased out so that part of the installations would be inherited? Would this particular increment in the activity be located in the arctic, the tropics, the mountains, or downtown San Francisco?

Budget exhibits shed little light on effectiveness. By posing some of the right questions (that is, by spotlighting some of the more important trade-offs among missions), program budgeting should facilitate making better judgments about the effectiveness of alternative choices; but the preparation and presentation of the exhibits cannot do *much* to indicate the effectiveness or worth of the alternatives. To know more about costs alone is better than nothing. In choosing between alternative automobiles, a prospective buyer would certainly rather have information about their costs alone than have no clues about either costs or effectiveness. Yet, at the same time, sufficient ignorance about effectiveness can make the value of the cost information relatively low. For any great improvement in decisions, officials would have to sharpen their judgments about both the gains and costs of the alternatives; and revised budget formats by themselves are not likely to do this.

For several reasons, program budgeting does not ordinarily provide information about gains or effectiveness. The exhibits are bulky enough if they simply present costs. Still, if simple indexes of effectiveness could be prepared, the exhibits would surely be expanded to include them. The basic difficulty is that of generating unique, simple, helpful measures of effectiveness. First, for numerous weapon systems and program elements, there are no satisfactory metrics of effectiveness. Consider infantry divisions. A frequently used proxy for effectiveness is firepower; yet most persons would be uneasy about putting such a metric in the budget for fear that some readers might apply it mechanically. In addition to firepower, the worth of an incremental division depends upon many other factors, such as type of firepower, mobility, auxiliary equipment, morale, terrain, and so on. And of course many program elements, such as communications and support activities, or intelligence and security activities, have no measure of effectiveness that is anywhere near as satisfactory a yardstick as firepower is for infantry units.

Moreover, as is true of incremental costs, incremental effectiveness can differ greatly from average effectiveness, for in military activities there are not constant costs or gains.[1] The worth of another unit of firepower, for instance, depends upon what other forces are available, what the enemy has, and how he reacts. If one's firepower begins to surpass that of the enemy, one's effectiveness suddenly increases more than proportionately. Similar complexities affect the incremental worth of Honest John Battalions, ASW Aircraft Carriers, Frigates, TFX Squadrons, and almost all program elements.

Second, though actually a point closely related to the preceding discussion, many program elements yield multiple and incommensurable achievements. Cruisers, destroyers, and certain long-range aircraft can serve multiple purposes. Even forces for which there seems to be a relatively clear-cut metric of effectiveness usually turn out to have several incommensurable capabilities. Manned bombers, Polaris, and land-based missile systems all yield several different capabilities—for city destruction, for tactical-target destruction, and for announcement of intentions—and each yields different combinations of these capabilities. These achievements cannot be made commensurable by putting them in terms of a common denominator. To show an indicator of one achievement and omit the others could be highly misleading. To show indicators of all such achievements could generate a clumsy budgetary exhibit that would be very costly in use.

Third, there is another vital aspect of effectiveness (or of costs) that a program budget cannot costlessly show—namely, the uncertainties. There is

---

[1] Malcolm W. Hoag, "Some Complexities in Military Planning," *World Politics* (July, 1959), pp. 553–76.

inherent uncertainty about the effectiveness of weapons systems and other program elements, because there is doubt about enemy reactions, other nations' reactions, future strategic contexts, technological developments, and other contingencies. As just one example, there is usually uncertainty about the vulnerability of our systems, such as command and control, and therefore doubt exists about the value of countermeasure systems.

Thus program budgets can at best provide only modest assistance. For these several reasons the information provided by program budgets, even if that information is fully utilized, can lead to only moderate improvements in decisions. This is true because the information is still rather poor, even though it may be twice as good as it had been. A program budget can highlight some, but not all, important trade-offs and interdependencies. It can generate and display better, but by no means perfect, cost estimates. It can facilitate the making of some better judgments about effectiveness but cannot display highly useful indicators of effectiveness or of the inherent uncertainties. As has been suggested elsewhere, a new tool such as program budgeting is like a dramatically improved means of cleaning one trouser leg of a pair of pants or a much better method of appraising the rabbit in a horse-and-rabbit stew.[2] Program budgeting can be of some help, but there are plenty of remaining difficulties. We should probably seek better ways of appraising the horse, but in the meantime we cannot count on a vastly tastier stew.

To repeat, the exhibits in the Five-Year Force Structure and Financial Program provide information that may help officials make broad allocative decisions, but this help is quite limited, and it gives still less assistance in reaching detailed management decisions. For these reasons, as mentioned earlier, many persons believe that specific *ad hoc* cost-effectiveness analyses are an essential complement to a program budget—that the latter without the former would be of little use. Here too, however, people should expect no miracles. For *ad hoc* cost-effectiveness analyses are bedeviled with difficulties similar to those outlined above. Weighing the costs and gains attributable to each alternative is unquestionably the right approach to problems of choice, yet actual analyses should be used with caution. Effects that are incommensurable or even non-quantifiable in any generally valid way (for example, impacts of alternative systems on the probability of war) abound; uncertainties about future contingencies are pervasive; heroic judgments have to be made; and the quality of analyses varies but is costly to appraise.

Limited Impact on Incentive to Provide and Use Information

Over and above the limitations on the kind of information that budgeting systems can provide are the limitations on the kind that will in fact

---

[2] See the remarks of Anthony Downs in *Measuring Benefits of Government Investment*, ed. by Robert Dorfman (Washington, D. C.: The Brookings Institution, 1965), pp. 350–51.

be provided and on the use that will be made of it. As stressed before, each individual in the Defense Department seeks to maximize his utility. If actions that he believes to be in the national interest entail smaller sacrifices in other things, he will take more such actions; if they entail greater sacrifices of other desirable things, he will take fewer such actions.

With the advent of program budgeting in the Defense Department, personnel within the services gradually found it more rewarding than before to prepare better program data and improved analyses to accompany PCP's. Or, on the other side of the coin, it became more costly for the services to withhold information or to submit irrelevant data. Even so, the shift in cost-reward structures in such a bureaucracy was not prompt or sufficient to eliminate persistent foot-dragging. Still more importantly, that shift in the cost-reward structures confronting lower-level personnel depended mainly on the imagination and decisiveness of the Secretary of Defense and his staff. With different officials in OSD (the Office of the Secretary of Defense), the cost-reward structures facing lower-level personnel can change again, and the quality of the information contained in the Blue Book can alter greatly. Although this matter deserves detailed inquiry, the main point here is simply that the data that are in fact provided will always be less useful than the data that could in principle (that is, in a world free of cost) be generated.

A more interesting question is: What happens to the cost-reward structures confronting those who use the information? If program budgets (and cost-effectiveness analyses) are no more than informational aids, very little happens to the costs and rewards felt by various officials. If OSD had not strengthened its authority beginning in 1961, the services would have ignored most of the information that they had helped to generate for the program budget. Sometimes there would have been a cost connected with ignoring the new budget—a rebuke from an official or from certain congressmen, or a sacrifice in terms of conscience if the budget strongly suggested that certain policy changes were in the national interest (as perceived by the individual decision maker). Most of the time, however, the existence of the program budget would not have altered the trade-offs between parochial and national interests.

Possible Costs of Centralization. The shift of authority toward OSD made it possible, of course, for the program budget to have significant impacts. But such shifts, like most other moves, are unlikely to be costless. Note that program budgeting does not *cause* such shifts of power, but in considering program budgets it may be necessary to trade acceptance of further centralization for ability to make effective use of the budgetary apparatus. Walking this tightrope, too, can be considered another of the remaining difficulties in program budgeting.

If additional power is given to a central authority, it becomes less costly than before for that authority to ignore dissent—to ignore opposing views of the future, other beliefs about technological change, other appraisals of costs and gains, conflicting pictures of contingencies and uncertainties. If one service must bargain with the others, of if OSD must bargain with the services, it costs that agency something to ignore dissent about these matters. If less bargaining is necessary, neglecting criticism costs less. With increased centralization, therefore, programs are more nearly tailored to one view of the future and one utility function.

This may in turn make it less rewarding than before for lower-level officials to worry about their views of the future, their beliefs about technological change, their appraisals of costs and gains, their pictures of contingencies and uncertainties. In other words, the greater the extent to which higher levels make the choices, the less profitable it is for lower levels to devote their resources to thinking about those choices. Their time and energy can better be spent on matters that remain under their jurisdiction.

Another effect of further centralization is that of increasing the burdens on the shoulders of the central authority. As a consequence, the central management will find it more costly to do things that require time and energy, more rewarding than before to find ways to save time.

More specific impacts that could result from these forces include the following. Exploring alternatives in general could become more expensive, and there might be fewer alternatives explored. For example, rivalry under a rather decentralized system more than good analysis was probably responsible for the early development of Polaris and the subsequent Air Force interest in reducing vulnerability. The comprehensive examination of costs and gains might, with more pressure to reach decisions and less pressure to hear dissenting views, become more costly, and simplifying procedures and using rules of thumb might become more rewarding. (Indeed, with different OSD personnel, there might be a reversion to analyses in terms of the interceptor that flies the fastest, the tank that is the biggest, and so on.) Fewer hedges against contingencies and uncertainties might result. One decision maker would be more likely to regard fewer bets as being worth covering than would a diversity of decision makers; and lower levels, forced to live with their proposals, might find it less costly to themselves to propose relatively safe "conservative" actions.

One aspect of the exploration of alternatives becoming more expensive is that changing the recorded program might become more difficult. Higher officials would ultimately find that flexibility, that is, frequent change, was costly to them and that it would invite lower levels to use the "foot-in-the-door" tactic. Higher levels might then tend to reject PCP's, and lower levels might find it relatively unrewarding to propose many changes. Embedding choices in a five-year program and requiring lower levels to live with their cost estimates would almost certainly reduce flexibility. (This is a disadvantage that would have to be weighted against the advantages of the arrangement.) Along this same line, monitors of program elements, in order to carry out their tasks, are likely to be more concerned about visibility and control than about substitution possibilities and adaptability.

An especially important point is that, in a centralized situation, the cost-reward structures up and down the line depend more heavily than in a service-rivalry oriented system on the attitudes, values, beliefs, and decisions of one man—the Secretary of Defense. If Curtis LeMay were Secretary, the impacts on incentives and on outcomes would differ from those that would result if a purely political appointment were made. With some Secretaries, centralization could even mean decentralization: If an appointee refused to exercise authority, then there would, of course, be no effective centralization, and the above arguments would not apply.

CONCLUSIONS

There are still many difficulties with our budgeting system. As is almost always the case, each step that promises gain also entails some cost. To decide the type and quantity of budgetary data desired, hard-to-discern costs must be weighed against hard-to-assess gains. In this connection there should be exaggeration of neither the value of the fragments of information that can be presented nor the incentives of personnel to provide appropriate data or to use the information that is generated. Even though organizational reform might increase the likelihood of basing choices on this information, allowance should still be made for numerous imperfections. In fact, to reduce the costs entailed by centralization, decreased effectiveness of program budgets might deliberately be accepted.

We should recognize these difficulties and limitations not only in choosing how to apply program budgeting but also in deciding how to "sell" this analytical technique. A "hard sell" may lay the basis for misuse or for disillusionment and disuse of such tools. Some quarters seem to suggest that program budgeting could work miracles in all corners of government. Yet within the Defense Department it has appeared to be helpful in some programs but not especially useful in other packages—for example, General-purpose Forces and especially General Support and Research and Development. Accordingly, perhaps it should not be expected that program budgets will dramatically increase efficiency in everything from the judicial system to Medicare!

BIBLIOGRAPHY

1. Enthoven, Alain C. and Henry Rowen, "Defense Planning and Organization," *Public Finances: Needs, Sources, and Utilization.* Princeton, N. J.: National Bureau of Economic Research, Princeton University Press, 1961, pp. 365–417.

2. Hitch, Charles J., *Decision-Making for Defense.* Berkeley and Los Angeles: University of California Press, 1965.

3. ——— and Roland N. McKean, *The Economics of Defense in the Nuclear Age*. Cambridge: Harvard University Press, 1960.

4. Lindblom, Charles E., *Bargaining: The Hidden Hand in Government*, RM-1434-RC. The RAND Corporation, 1955.

5. McKean, Roland N., "The Unseen Hand in Government," *American Economic Review* (June, 1965), pp. 496–506.

6. Novick, David, ed., *Program Budgeting: Program Analysis and the Federal Budget*. Cambridge: Harvard University Press, 1965.

7. Quade, E. S., ed., *Analysis for Military Decisions*. Chicago: Rand McNally & Co., 1964.

8. Schlesinger, James R., "Quantitative Analysis and National Security," *World Politics* (January, 1963), pp. 295–315.

9. Smithies, Arthur, *The Budgetary Process in the United States*. New York: McGraw-Hill Book Company, 1955.

ARMEN A. ALCHIAN

University of California at Los Angeles

Armen A. Alchian is Professor of Economics at the University of California, Los Angeles. He was the first economist regularly engaged in research at The RAND Corporation, beginning his work in 1947. Between 1947 and 1964, he pioneered several important lines of inquiry there. The author has specialized in the methodology of systems analysis, their true costs, and in research and development management. He has been at UCLA since 1946, where his academic research and writings have dealt with inflation, costs, property, and behavior. He is the coauthor (with Professor William R. Allen) of a leading principles textbook. Professor Alchian received his Ph.D. in Economics from Stanford University. During World War II, he served for four years in the Air Force.

5

Cost Effectiveness of Cost Effectiveness

Why has a cost-effectiveness system only recently been applied to defense and government actions? Why had cost-effectiveness evaluation systems not previously been in use, as has long been the case in the private business sector? The answer is not that politicians and military people are slower, less discerning, and less rational—rather that the rewards and punishments imposed on businessmen who ignore this particular kind of cost-effectiveness calculus are more severe. As a matter of fact, cost-effectiveness analyses of one type or another have always been used in government and defense activities. But since the resulting decisions seemed to reflect too little concern for some factors and too much for others, 'inappropriate' (that is, different) weights were given to the various components of costs and benefits. The pertinent question, then, is what were the presumably correctible weights of the old system that the new was supposed to have corrected? And does the new system have new dangers or defects of its own that, hopefully, are less grievous than its added benefits?

I. COST-EFFECTIVENESS CONCEPT

There should first be agreement on what is meant by the new cost-effectiveness principles. Cost-effectiveness studies, as they are now commonly called in government, refer to a means of comparison, choice, and implementation of decisions among available, considered options with the assumption that the appropriate criteria are being used. An "assumption that the appropriate criteria are being used" is crucial; for without it, the description would be practically empty, because all selections of actions are based on something, ranging from a random choice generator or one's personal whims to a dictum from higher authority. A crucial feature of cost-effectiveness studies as currently recommended is that the appropriate criteria of cost and of effectiveness be used and that *all* costs and predictable effects of the *relevant decision* be given their appropriate weight in the choice.

That the emphasis upon explicit or appropriate cost-effectiveness studies comes from Economics does not mean that only narrow material effects, distinguished from some allegedly noneconomic effects, are the appropriate criteria. Beauty, truth, dignity, religious and personal freedoms, security of life, democratic processes, tolerance for disparate views, and so forth, are sometimes thought to be noneconomic factors or objectives that must be given separate weight. Thus sometimes it is contended that considering only economic values without remembering social, cultural, political values confines the decision maker to an incomplete, and probably biased, cost-effectiveness criterion. However, there is no exclusivity or conflict among economic values, political values, social and cultural values. Economic (that is, trade-off) values merely reflect and measure the trade-offs between the other values and goals. Any good capable of providing more desired political, social, cultural, esthetic, religious, nutritional objectives has economic value. Every good that helps achieve any goal is an economic good with (economic) value, for *the rate at which some amount of good can be substituted or traded for some of another good in achieving those various goals is precisely what is meant by its (economic) value or price*. To repeat, economic value is simply a measure of trade-offs or rates of substitutability between means (goods or resources) for achieving these various goals.

But a mythical difference between economic and other values must not be allowed to obscure a significant distinction among (a) effects for which it is possible to measure trade-off rates or values directly *via* market prices (market exchange rates via production or sale), (b) effects that can be quantified in some physical sense but cannot be valued in any generally accepted or valid way (as when the effect is not purchasable in the market), and (c) effects that cannot even be quantified in a way that would be valid for everyone (the impact on the probability of war, on morale, on morality, and so on).

Although already explained by Charles J. Hitch and Roland N. McKean,[1] this interaction of effects is worth repetition and emphasis, because there are still allegations that cost-effectiveness principles reduce everything to the dollar sign and ignore technological, social values. Vivid examples of the misunderstanding of the functions and implications of cost effectiveness are the charges that if we had used cost effectiveness in the nineteenth century we would still be using sailing ships, or that cost effectiveness will mean losing the war without going bankrupt.

II. DEFECTS OF OLD SYSTEM

What were believed to be some of the correctible faults of the prior system?

(1) *Span of Costs*. The wrong span of costs of a weapon system was used. The full cost of a system considered for procurement was not viewed as comprising the stream of payments now and in the future; usually only the present expenditures were given serious weight. This way of thinking resembles buying a car as if the initial down payment were the cost. Piecemeal expenditures were treated as total costs. Often, as a result, future expenditures were obligated and in time often become excessively large. A better allowance for the subsequent expenditures would have encouraged different and more efficient procurement decisions. To reduce this error, recent cost-effectiveness systems have promulgated a forecast spanning several years, with all expenditures in that interval counted in costs.

(2) *Component Costs*. The old system was even worse than buying a new car by contemplating only the initial down payment. It made decisions independently about interdependent or component parts of a system—as if a family

---

[1] Charles J. Hitch and Roland N. McKean, *The Economics of Defense in the Nuclear Age* (New York: Atheneum Publishers, 1965).

car were to be bought by four different members of the family, each being responsible for buying a different part of the car. Each would consider the cost to be only the payment on their particular part. In defense programming, decisions about bombers were made by one command, about fighter defense escorts of the bombers by another, about personnel by still another, and about air bases by another. Defense performance tasks were not costed as a task. Only the components were costed as end-items. Moreover, the Air Force, the Army, and the Navy sometimes acted as though the others did not exist. This is not to say that the agencies did not discuss, dispute, and argue with one another and in Congress for the right to be responsible for certain tasks. It says instead that the defense of the continental United States or the strategic striking power were not costed or evaluated by combining all strike forces into one performance or program package. Therefore, the costs of these general functions were not costed in ways that enabled a rational calculation of the approximate worths of such performance capability. And thus the next inadequacy is suggested.

(3) *Disregard of Incremental Gains and Costs.* The size of any program or even of a purchase (for example, a new bomber type) was not systematically treated as a variable. "Requirements and priorities" were bruited about as though they had to be met regardless of the costs (that is, sacrifices of other "requirements and needs"). As a result, the gain in one avenue of defense expenditure obtainable by spending less in some other avenue was not systematically considered. Because budgets and plans were specified in terms of inflexible requirements and needs, evaluations of trade-offs or of substitution among amounts of weapons and levels of goals were not elicited. The opposite error to thinking in terms of "requirements" and "priorities" was the specification of a total "essential" *budget* that presumably met our "needs"—with the implication that one dollar more would not contribute to greater defense, and that one dollar less would mean loss of all defense capability. The "requirements or priorities" extreme is tantamount to a "damn the cost" extreme; whereas the budget limit implies "damn the effectiveness." This approach was not at all conducive to systematic exploration and evaluation of the cost effectiveness of various programs.

(4) *Incentive Systems.* Even if the above faults are recognized, there remain difficulties arising from the *context* in which cost-effectiveness studies are used. For many institutions, a change of context often changes or frustrates effectiveness. In the present instance, the absence of (1) a market and of (2) private-property rights in the resources being allocated means that the effectiveness of a cost-effectiveness analysis in a private-property system cannot totally be transferred to government or socialist systems. The extent to which various costs and effects are discerned, measured, and *heeded* depends on the institutional system of incentive-punishment for the deciders. One system of rewards-punishment may increase the extent to which some objectives are heeded, whereas another may make other goals more influential. Thus *procedures* for making or controlling decisions in one rewards-incentive system are not necessarily the

"best" for some other system. In other words, the application of cost-effectiveness studies and principles (as used in a private-property, competitive-market context) to socialistic or governmental arenas involves some serious, undesirable side effects.

Of course the danger of serious, undesirable side effects does not mean that the achieved and desired effects may not be worth the costs; it should also be remembered that ancillary steps can reduce the undesirable side effects. In fact, this paper is intended to direct attention to such ancillary precautions—not to undermine cost effectiveness. Gratuitous meaning should not be read into these remarks. It is not here being contended that government or socialistic action is less desirable than a private-property, capitalistic context. The proposition is that various criteria differ in effectiveness.

In the competitive, private, open-market economy, the wealth-survival prospects are not as strong for firms (or their employees) who do not heed the market's test of cost effectiveness as for those firms who do. In the private, market-oriented sector of our economy, such behavior would mean a loss of wealth to other business firms. As a result, the market's criterion is more likely to be heeded and anticipated by business people. They have personal wealth incentives to make more thorough cost-effectiveness calculations about the products they could produce and offer for sale. In the government sector, two things are less effective. (1) The full cost and value consequences of decisions do not have as direct and severe a feedback impact on government employees as on people in the private sector. The *costs* of actions under their consideration are incomplete simply because the consequences of ignoring parts of the full span of costs are less likely to be imposed on them. Their decisions are conditioned by a different span of the resulting costs. The costs *they* bear more fully are the costs to which they give greater (though not necessarily, of course, exclusive) weight. (2) The effectiveness, in the sense of benefits, of their decisions has a different reward-incentive or feedback system: for example, a general who could save the economy one billion dollars, with unreduced defense capability over a ten-year span, has *less* incentive than in a market economy to heed that savings, particularly if it will impose a severe cost on him. Whatever his motivations and understanding of the "national interest," it is fallacious to assume that government officials are superhumans, who act solely with national interest in mind and are never influenced by the consequences to their own personal position.

Even if everyone could be imbued with a selfless spirit and attitude, what criterion or test of their wisdom, superiority, or efficiency would be ultimately decisive? Small-scale *tests* of wars or deterrence as a means of testing efficiency of decisions are not readily available. In the private civilian sector, open-market competition among competing buyers and sellers provides a continuing, effective test and a criterion of production and allocation decisions. None is so readily available for the military nor for a very wide class of government action. Again, a precautionary disclaimer. This is neither criticism of government nor praise for the private-sector decisions; it is not an innuendo that government should do less. The fact is that some tasks are delegated to governments or nonmarket group action because of a dissatisfaction with the appropriateness of the private-property, market process for allocating some resources.

In sum, the old system of decisions characterized by (a) incomplete, biased concepts of cost, (b) failure to properly categorize the item, service, or program to be costed, (c) failure to consider trade-offs among programs, their components, and the goals being sought led to what was believed to be inefficient military-defense programming and procurement. But the reward-punishment incentive system characterizing government activities must not be forgotten. It is worth examining just how the new cost-effectiveness system proposes to avoid or modify disabling characteristics.

III. OBSTACLES TO EFFECTIVENESS OF COST-EFFECTIVENESS

It is clear now in which ways the new cost-effectiveness system calculus and its *implementation* is intended to be an improvement. (1) The new system analyzes the costs of a whole program or function—not merely components or parts of a program. For example, the strategic strike force, the continental defense, the supply or logistics mission may be a basis for assemblage and comparisons of costs. This concept of costs has been characterized as program packaging. (2) Most programs are costed for at least five years into the future in order to give greater assurance that the full time-span of costs will be reflected in the present estimates of total costs. Initial outlays can no longer be officially interpreted as the relevant costs. Inherent in a combination of these two changes is the greater ease of comparing trade-offs among programs. (3) Program changes, which inevitably will occur as the future unfolds and greater information is discerned about capabilities and events, are to be implemented by "program-change proposals." Any proposal to change (substantially) a program can be initiated by any agency but must be approved by higher authority, usually the Office of the Secretary of Defense. This provision for program-change proposals is designed to ensure that costing continues to be done on a program basis and that coherence among components of a program is maintained.

In effect, the Defense Department now operates (on paper, at least) along the command and decision lines of a business firm. New products or production programs must be costed on an end-product (not simply on an input) basis. Competition among various possible products that a firm could produce is resolved by top management in the light of estimated realizable marketability and product costs. And so decision and control over procurement for various types of functions for arming the military is resolved at the high level of the Office of the Secretary of Defense. Operating details, as in a business, are delegated to lower-level management. The parallel is excellent—up to a point. Unfortunately, some ingredients in the business firm's environment are missing in government. Two of these merit some examination and notice.

(1) *Program definition.* The program being costed is not one that can be readily identified as the pertinent, complete package. Is the appropriate program defined as that of Defense, or the Air Force, or Air Defense, or Strategic Offense, or Minutemen system, or a single launch complex, or a single missile? The more narrowly it is construed, the more will there be interdependencies with other associated complementary programs that are likely to be ignored. Simply to consider a larger or more broadly defined program than before does not in itself ensure a more appropriate basis for costing and decisions. The larger the scope of the program, the greater will be the span of trade-offs and adjustments that are presumed to have been considered within the analysis. But the larger the scope, the larger is the uncertainty about the costs. At the extreme one could call the whole government a program, and we would end up with something like the federal budget proposal. A smaller program enables more explicit comparisons of alternative programs. But then the smaller the program, the less are the interdependencies explicitly and analytically taken into account. These considerations are not criticisms of a cost-effectiveness calculus; instead they are warnings against the belief that cost-effectiveness calculations for some program automatically lend that particular program the aura of the "appropriate" size program for decision making. However sophisticated may be our cost-effectiveness analyses of particular program packages, we still must recognize the unresolved problem of the appropriate scope of the defined program.

(2) *Reward-Incentive System and Centralization of Control.* The government decision context lacks competitive markets and private-property rights as incentive and control mechanisms for the decision makers. That these are missing is, of course, news neither to the Defense Department planners nor to those who are expanding the role of the new cost-effectiveness systems with centralized control. But the question still stands about the extent to which the new system can effectively overcome the absence of these two features and yield a better system.

Unfortunately, centralization of decisions in a single office over the three military sectors is not analogous to the centralization of business decisions in the head of the firm. In the private economy other competing firms can duplicate or take different points of view about the nature of desirable products. But there are not two departments of defense to provide the competitive survival and selection of preferred products. The existence of a market in which the results of competing independent producers or decision makers can be exposed to evaluation is crucial to business efficiency. Without competitors a monopoly situation develops, and centralization within a monopoly does not ensure that alternatives will be tested and explored with the efficiency of competing firms. In a government agency, the incentives of the managers to maximize the capitalized wealth of the agency are weaker than if there were identifiable owners of the agency who could reap the capital gains. Their incentives to maximize the wealth or economic efficiency of their decisions is reduced, since their own wealth and welfare is less tied to the resulting effects. This is, of course, precisely why the five-year programs are being advocated over a one-year program plan. But the incentive for decision is still not the same.

A quiet, uncomplicated life without so much bickering and fighting about wealth values of alternative products is more viable. Centralization under government contexts implies less exposure and testing of differences of opinion, easier suppression of alternatives, less effective response to costs, and less flexible adjustments of programs despite more exhortations to the contrary.

The new cost-effectiveness system offers no discernible protection against the tendency it has to facilitate or encourage greater *centralization* of the decision processes. The risks inherent in centralized control are well known: belief by the superior in his own superior judgment (otherwise, why would he be there?); reduced incentive to consider alternatives; less motivation for subordinates to risk testing alternatives not acceptable to the superior. In sum, centralization of decision making—a valid achievement within a privately owned business firm competing with others in an open market—has its dangers in government. A danger of centralization of government authority in conjunction with cost-effectiveness studies is the belief that *properly formulated studies* of cost effectiveness will provide a proper test that can dispense with the checks and balances of the decentralized political process. But, as has been stressed, government cost-effectiveness studies are not policed and tested in the political sector with the same enforcement system that pervades the private sector's market-exposure tests. There is a vast difference between properly formulated studies and realized results that correspond (a) to actions inherent in behavior responsive to those studies *and* (b) to the incentives and punishments policed by an open-market, private-property competition. Men can be less expected to heed a broad cost-effectiveness concept if punishment for failure to do so is weaker. To provide this "heed," a centralized system of estimation and conceptualization of costs and effects is used to police and select among alternatives, but the former system of effective political checks and balances is thereby weakened.

(3) *Costs of Current Decisions vs. Costs of Programs.* Program packaging for estimation of costs of procurement, production, and operation necessarily involves long time spans of estimates. The five-year or eight-year span of projection is popular and certainly better than the one-year, expenditure-cost identification. Yet beware. The danger here is the belief that if a decision is taken now, it will necessarily incur the costs forcasted. Attention is drawn not simply to errors of estimate, but instead to the fact that the cost estimated is the pertinent cost *if and only if* the program is carried out in its entirety over the projected future. A program that is expensive over five years may involve only a small cost if initiated *and then terminated* at the end of one year. The well-known mistake of paying regard to sunk or past costs (which the cost-effectiveness system is intended to avoid) may be matched by the opposite error of regarding full-time costs as the *incurred* and inescapable costs of a present decision to procure equipment. What the full-time cost estimate tells us is the costs that will be incurred *if and only if* the program is carried out. Neither that cost nor the past expended

costs are valid for present decisions; present decisions are not *now binding* upon the completion of the entire projected program. The costs incurred in the *selection* of some plan are not the costs incurred if that plan is carried through to fruition.

Of course, cost estimates of contemplated full programs are not irrelevant. They are useful for a comparison of the costs that will be expended for the selected plan if it is ultimately implemented over the projected interval. After a *plan* has been selected on the basis of that full time-span cost estimate, there is a temptation to stay with the plan thereafter; for after all, was it not the best one? Yes, but only if there is no uncertainty about the future. Where there is uncertainty, it may be wiser (more economical) to adopt a more expensive (full-time costs basis) action with a sufficiently lower *first*-year incurred cost than a less expensive one (full time-span costs) with a higher first-year incurred cost. For example, it may be better to lease for the first year and then buy in the next year if the postponement means a sufficiently good chance for a better procurement decision. Decisions are not made once and for all. With new developments and possibilities springing up each year, attention should be given to the costs of providing for revisions of plans. In other words, the five-year plan period with costs for the full period is a *forecast period*, not a commitment or budget-decision period. Therefore, in addition to full program costs, one should also compute and heed the costs that will be *incurred* by the current decision.

As an experienced colleague, Roland McKean, points out, the costs incurred by the act of marrying Miss A or Miss B (who has an exquisite taste for luxury) are relevant [even] to one's present choices about which girl to date. But, it would be absurd to fall into the trap of regarding the full cost of marriage as being incurred by one date. As in Research and Development, it is possible and desirable to date several girls to acquire more information about each before making a permanent procurement.

(4) *Research and Development vs. Procurement.* The distinctions developed in the preceding paragraphs become especially important if, as is suspected to be the case, the five-year cost-forecast interval tends to become a *decision interval*. If the five-year foresight becomes a five-year commitment, as if one were committed to that plan, flexibility and adaptability are unnecessarily restricted. Especially important are the dangers arising from inclusion of research and development activity in a procurement program. There has long existed in the military an unfortunate confounding of research and development decisions with the procurement or production decision. Research and development activity decisions are typically geared to some "optimally" designed end-item that is supposed to result from the planned research and development. Furthermore, that contemplated end-item is treated as a requirement or need. If there were not foreseeable need for that projected end-item, the research and development activity would not be supported. A justification of this basis for decisions about research and development makes the untenable assumption that the results of research and development are foreseeable with sufficient accuracy to determine

the nature and function of the end-item. It is difficult to imagine a more plausible, yet fallacious, assumption.

It is one thing to know desirable directions of changes in performance capabilities; it is quite another to know in which ways that greater capability can be performed—let alone, discovered. To desire faster planes is sensible. To ask for research to obtain faster planes is sensible. But to specify the kind of plane and the other joint attributes that it should yield is simply muddleheaded. To do so presumes knowledge about how and *when* the greater speed will be achieved, and about what trade-off between speed and other characteristics will be worthwhile. Such information is simply not available. Yet the research and development activity decision is tied to the criterion of full time-span costs for an item yet to be produced, a procured and operated end-item—as if all the costs were irrevocably incurred at the initial research and development stage. This kind of tie is not always desirable. Any decision system should avoid an implicit tie.

The official dogma of the Department of Defense is that Research and Development is *not* included in decisions about operational mission programs, at least until the project has passed the program definition stage and until the weapon system to be procured has reached a highly developed stage of engineering. But the history of the TFX decisions is sufficient, without going back to our rocket development program, to foster doubts about the meaningfulness of such doctrines of proscriptive behavior intended to separate decisions about production of operational end-items from Research and Development decisions.

Program packaging in terms of missions of military tasks is sensible, but the acquisition of knowledge, if always included in a mission or program package, amounts to a defective program definition. Acquisition of knowledge is itself a function or mission, and there is no obvious reason for distributing its cost among all the missions or programs, like some kind of overhead cost. To divide it and immerse its costs and activities in other program packages is exactly what the general principle of cost-effectiveness of coherent, alternative programs is intended to avoid.

(5) *What Type of Effectiveness?* Cost-effectiveness analysis found its hardest going in obtaining acceptance of the cost concept as a valid criterion. Less difficult was acceptance of the effectiveness criterion. More recently, however, the objective or criterion of effectiveness has been more and more difficult to identify. Number of targets destroyed, probability of being able to launch a counter strike given that the opponent has launched the initial attack are examples of two relatively simple criteria. But these are no longer, if they ever were, the only pertinent criteria. They are instead, component variables of the utility or criterion vector. Unfortunately, the difficulty, or impossibility, of discovering or formulating an acceptable effectiveness criterion has led many observers to use an "approximate" criterion so that an explicit answer could be obtained. In other words, the criterion has been formulated so as to facilitate the analytic method. And, of course, that is precisely why the "big" issues seem

always to be settled without formal cost-effectiveness analyses; there simply does not exist a formalized cost-effectiveness analysis capable of giving answers to those problems. It has not been possible to formulate the criteria in explicit, generally acceptable terms. The criterion vector itself is still open to debate. There is a tendency to be impatient with decisions not based on a formal analysis of an explicitly characterized problem because of the belief that such analysis is better than an informal, nonstructured "judgment" about the relevant problem. Uncertainty about objectives, let alone the means of best achieving them, attenuates (though it does *not* eliminate) the relevance of cost-effectiveness studies without objectively measureable objectives.

National military strategies are still open. Is our military capability to be a method of preserving a set of friendly governments, or one of the "containing" communism on the assumption that communist countries can be friendly and compatible with continuing coexistence? And so, the discussion could lead on and on into a host of unresolved issues, which certainly should be part of a full cost-effectiveness study.

(6) *Nondefense Activities.* An increasing portion of nondefense government activities will surely be submitted to cost-effectiveness evaluations by higher authorities in the government. The people in the Bureau of the Budget are insisting on more thorough analyses of programs by departments prior to inclusion in the budget request to Congress. Centralization via Presidential authority has always existed. What will be the effect of this enlarged scope of formal cost-effectiveness application? Most of the features mentioned earlier and regarded as potential dangers seem to apply here, even though a major advantage of this cost-effectiveness emphasis is that it will expose proposed activities to cost-effectiveness concepts broader than those viewed by the proposing agency. The interest of each director of an agency is to enlarge his realm of activity. The natural bias toward overestimating benefits and underestimating costs is not easy to avoid. A more clear-cut exposition of the cost-effectiveness or benefit study conducted by the lower-level agency will enable the higher authority to compare various proposals with less parochial interest in the competing proposals. Therefore, it is possible to conjecture that the cost-effectiveness estimates should be less biased toward the interests of the operating agency.

But there is the *danger* that duplication of services by various agencies will be avoided. We have in mind the duplication among regulatory agencies. Currently, many regulatory agencies control our banks. In each state a state agency and national agencies exist. Banks can be authorized by either. This competition among the regulators provides a protection from unacceptably capricious regulatory actions. Take another example; presently one regulatory agency regulates surface transportation and another regulates air transport. Had all been subjected to control by the same regulatory agency, it is safe to conjecture that the airlines would have been less free in attracting traffic away from rail and bus. The cartelizing propensity of regulatory agencies with respect to the industry being controlled (that is, protected from competition) is too well known to warrant being neglected. Clearly, the advantage of cost-effectiveness studies being cleared and policed by higher authorities is not without its dangers.

Now we clearly do not know how much centralization of review of cost-effectiveness studies will lead to these faults. Although experience and adequate measure of the effect is lacking, the danger is in no way eliminated, nor is the net advantage of cost-effectiveness studies at high levels of centralized authority automatically denied. Even driving a car has its dangers—but actions have been taken to reduce such dangers, at the expense of the other desired performance qualities. And it would seem similarly appropriate to devote some effort to reducing the prospects of those disadvantages in cost-effectiveness applications.

If all our foreign-aid or all our agricultural-aid programs, to name but two, are evaluated in terms of cost-effectiveness analysis at a higher level, the analysis of these programs as a package or as an integrated whole pushes toward centralization of decision about such activity in one agency—a not unmixed blessing. Exposure to alternatives actually undertaken enables better choices. Mere recognition of this danger is not sufficient. Some institutional system to protect competitive choices and behavior, in order to induce exposure of alternatives to some kind of realistic, public testing and evaluation, is desirable. Unfortunately desirability does not mean feasibility, and it is not clear how such a context might be provided. Like much else in this essay of evaluation, it is easier to detect dangers and undesirable forces than it is to suggest ways of eliminating or attenuating them. It can only be hoped that some awareness of these dangers will stimulate some caution or action intended to reduce those disadvantages.

IV. EFFECTIVENESS OF COST EFFECTIVENESS

Yet no one doubts that the new system has, in fact, achieved greater responsiveness to cost. What is the explanation?

The conjecture is offered that the proponents of the new cost-effectiveness analyses have a zeal for what we would all regard as desirable or good cost-effectiveness studies. The current proponents and executors understand the relevant concepts of costs and the obstacles to better decisions about programs and procurement decisions. And they have succeeded in achieving a level of authority from which to apply their desirable criteria.

But what will happen when new people inherit this new centralized cost-effectiveness machinery along with its system of control? Is there anything that suggests that it will be inherited by men equally able to enhance a career by *using* these more economically general cost-effectiveness studies? And even for the present incumbents, is there anything to assure that those now in command will be prepared seriously to modify approved plans if their prior plans look "bad"? Will not they, too, begin to observe the general laws that characterize viable political behavior?

RELATED READINGS

1. Dulles, Eleanor L. and Robert D. Crane, eds., *Detente: Cold War Strategies in Transition*. New York: Frederick A. Praeger, Inc., 1965.

2. Herzog, Arthur, *The War-Peace Establishment*. New York: Harper & Row, Publishers, 1965.

3. Hitch, Charles J. and Roland N. McKean. *The Economics of Defense in the Nuclear Age*. Cambridge: Harvard University Press, 1960.

4. Kahn, Herman, *Thinking About the Unthinkable*. New York: Avon Books, 1962.

5. Levine, Robert A., *The Arms Debate*. Cambridge: Harvard University Press, 1963.

6. Martin, Thomas L., Jr. and Donald C. Latham, *Strategy for Survival*. Tucson: University of Arizona Press, 1963.

7. Peck, Merton J. and Frederic M. Scherer, *The Weapons Acquisition Process: An Economic Analysis*. Boston: Harvard University Graduate School of Business Administration, 1962.

2

COST EFFECTIVENESS APPLICATIONS

JAMES R. SCHLESINGER
The RAND Corporation, Santa Monica, Calif.

James R. Schlesinger is a Senior Staff member with The RAND Corporation. Since joining RAND three years ago, he has specialized in strategic analysis with particular reference to nuclear weaponry. At present, he is Project Leader of the RAND study on Nuclear Proliferation. He also serves as consultant to the Bureau of the Budget on certain aspects of the national security program. Prior to moving to RAND, he taught economics at the University of Virginia, served as consultant to RAND and to the Board of Governors of the Federal Reserve System, and was a member of the Board of Associates of the Foreign Policy Research Institute, University of Pennsylvania. In 1957, he served as Academic Consultant in Economics at the United States Naval War College. His publications include *The Political Economy of National Security* (Praeger, 1960). He received all his academic training and Ph.D. at Harvard University.

6

The Changing Environment
for Systems Analysis

Any discussion of the changing environment and its implications for decision making must begin with that commonplace English word "uncertainty." Yet it is doubtful whether its introduction will serve to illuminate the knotty problems of choice implied by constant change. No word is used more eagerly or more glibly. All too frequently, however, "uncertainty" is employed as an incantation to exorcise from the analysis the troublesome questions that it cannot resolve:[1] the result being a genuflection toward what remains unknown before decisions are made on the basis of the limited picture of the unfolding environment, as it is perceived at a point in time.

For this reason I might be inclined, following Kierkegaard, to begin with a panegyric on uncertainty, but this would be misleading, in a sense, for the most interesting considerations in dealing with national policy is not so much uncertainty as certainty. In both analysis and planning we are too prone to ignore the certainty that things change over time: that a number of years hence national objectives and strategies will be different from what they are today. In planning for the future the appearance of uncertainty at a given time is perhaps less interesting than *the certainty that changes in objectives and strategies will take place over time.*

What is true for ourselves is true for others. The hopes and drives of one's opponents also change over time. A review of earlier analytical efforts reveals a failure to appreciate the eroding effect that time inevitably has both on the attitude and behavior of rivals and on our own perception of the threat they represent. Part of this failure undoubtedly has reflected the inability fully to anticipate the consequences of success. In conditions of conflict even partial success implies that one's foe will be forced to divert his energies to actions designed to exert pressures on those vulnerable points now made relatively more lucrative by one's previous successes. For the game theorist such a development is perfectly predictable, but in the real world the tendency of governments to concentrate attention on immediate and pressing concerns makes it difficult to give adequate weight to this insight. More allowance can be made in future work for the alteration over time of opponents' objectives and strategies (partially in response to our own moves) and for our own adaptation to these anticipable, if not predictable, changes in behavior.

There are other important, although more technical, reasons for the past failure to appreciate the erosive impact of time. First, systems-analytic work has been overly tied to the rather unique conditions in which it developed. It has been too much dominated by those relatively simple strategies appropriate for the early nuclear period—which permit the quantitatively precise evaluation of mutual destructiveness in a showdown clash, actual or hypothetical, between

Any views expressed in this paper are those of the author. They should not be interpreted as reflecting the views of The RAND Corporation or the official opinion or policy of any of its governmental or private research sponsors.

[1] Or to provide a form of personal insurance so that, if events go awry, the analyst need not be held accountable.

the two superpowers.[2] Second, and perhaps more fundamental, an illusion developed that systems analysis as a technique was not itself subject to change and that the basic methods were more or less impervious to time.

This identification of the evanescent with the permanent has introduced certain rigidities into analysis. These are in the process of disappearing, not only because of the changes in the environment *per se*, but also because the environment has changed in a particular direction: decision making in the sixties is increasing in its complexity and this carries with it implications, not only for the decision maker, but also for the analyst as well. A clear moral is implied for future systems-analytic work: there is a growing requirement for care in the design of studies or analyses and for ingenuity and flexibility in the design of systems. In developing this theme I shall attempt to do three things: (1) to indicate those trends that have intensified demands on the analyst, (2) to illustrate the general issues raised by reference to two specific analytical and choice problems confronting defense analysts, and (3) to draw a few inferences regarding future analytical work.

I. MAJOR ENVIRONMENTAL CHANGES

Since the developmental years of systems analysis, changes have occurred in the strategic, political, and technical environment which raise the level of sophistication required of the art. Four specific factors may be cited, which, operating together, have accentuated demands on the analyst. As we examine them individually, we will see that none of them is wholly new. Yet, growing weight must be assigned to each, and jointly they considerably augment the challenge to the imagination and insight of the analyst.

A. The Increase in (Perceived) Political Fluidity

In the past, the assumption of Soviet malevolence, accompanied by estimates of future Soviet capabilities based on production possibilities, led to the designation of specified threats in particular time periods. The challenge to the analyst was to design a broad system to deal with the assumed threat. This approach was employed in 1950 shortly after the first Soviet atomic test.[3] The year 1954 was specified as one of "maximum peril" on the hypothesis that by then the Soviets would have produced atomic weapons in sufficient number to neutralize the U.S. atomic deterrent. By that year, it was argued, conventional

[2] This bias is reflected in the continuing tendency for high DoD officials to present their rationale on the acquisition or continuation of the strategic systems in Packages I and II (and even to evaluate such systems) largely in terms of the destructiveness of a nuclear war in which the Soviets strike in an unconstrained manner.

[3] See Paul Hammond's study, "NSC-68: Prologue to Rearmament" in Schilling, Hammond, and Snyder, *Strategy, Politics, and Defense Budgets* (New York: Columbia University Press), 1962.

forces would be required to prevent an outthrust of Soviet power. Whatever the merits of the contemplated posture, the argument for it was temporarily eclipsed by the "new look" decisions of 1953–1954.

Again, in the "missile gap" controversies following the Soviet development of the ICBM in 1957, projections were developed indicating 1961–1962 as the period of maximum danger for a Soviet strike without warning. The degree of risk was properly regarded as dependent on the U.S. posture. The main objective of the analyst was to devise means for countering a clearly specified threat—one which implied the "worst possible" consequences. In such an environment, the "minimax rule" compelled attention for guiding analysis. Once again, the existence of an acknowledged and specific threat simplified the task of the analyst.

A procedure of specifying and responding to a single dominant threat is not always wrong. As a simplifying assumption in periods of revolutionary changes in military technology, it has its uses. Indeed, if once again the nation were confronted with another such revolutionary change, we might well return to using this analytical device.

But consider how different our situation is today. Instead of having to deal with a dominant threat in a specific time period, we deal with *a spectrum of vaguely perceived and more modest threats which may develop at some indefinite time in the future.* No longer do we feel that the Soviets can negate our second-strike capability without signs of buildup—and the absence of a dominant threat cancels out the "minimax rule" as a guide to action. We are less inclined to view the Soviets as either implacable foes or rational game-opponents or to attempt to anticipate their actions on such a basis. No longer do we seem to place much confidence in our ability to predict what the Soviets will do. As a result, we can no longer concentrate our resources on countering a single maximum threat. Instead, we must allocate resources so that we can deal with many (preferably all) of the broad array of vaguely perceived threats—threats that can be posed by the Chinese and others as well as by the Soviets.

B. Greater Sophistication Regarding the Character of Nuclear War

A second factor is the growing sophistication on both sides regarding the character of nuclear war. We will consider this subject in more detail in Section II; here we might simply note major changes. First, we now recognize both a number of conflicting objectives and a major uncertainty as to which of these objectives would be dominant in nuclear war. As a consequence, even greater attention must now be devoted to the criterion problem. In the fifties, analyses of possible nuclear exchanges did not get much beyond two-sided spasm wars.[4] In both the first-strike and second-strike variants, the objective was

---

[4] To assure that, if a Soviet attack came, the war would be at least two-sided, was the dominant concern—and in view of the character of the existing forces, it was then the appropriate concern.

clear-cut: destruction of the maximum number of enemy targets, either cities or highly vulnerable strategic air forces. The targets were known, immobile, and soft. Destruction was to be achieved without concern for collateral damage (which was, at that time, a "bonus" effect). Damage limitation for the United States emerged principally through the reduction of Soviet offensive capabilities either by pre-emption or quick retaliation subsequent to the Soviet first strike.

In reviewing these early-vintage studies of broad strategic systems, we are probably struck by the relative simplicity of the problem, as it then was seen. Only a single type of weapon system was involved. Penetration was a manageable problem. The focus of attention was on survivability, but it was the short-lived survivability necessary to hit back in a spasm-war strike. Thus, in the early fifties, the relative advantages of ZI basing versus overseas-basing in the two main contingencies would correctly become a major issue.

By current standards, the defects of this outlook are numerous—even if we confine ourselves to analysis of central war with the Soviets as the main foe and disregard complexities introduced into strategic planning by the rise of China. Forces and analysis have advanced. Conceptions regarding both objectives and strategy, if not wrong then, are now obsolete. Manipulation of a single offensive weapon system as the main variable for both deterrence and warfighting is now wholly inappropriate. The image of how nuclear war might come about—in massive initial strikes with little or no warning—must now be modified. As a consequence, a sharp line can no longer be drawn between strategic forces and general purpose forces. Today we are concerned with damage limitation and with combinations of offensive and defensive systems to attain that end. A variety of strategic offensive systems exists which potentially may contribute to our strike capabilities, but the optimal choice will depend upon the circumstances.

Partly because of the inherent difficulties if the Soviets take sensible counter-measures, partly because of the absence of really hard thinking on the part of the Services, partly because of high-level policy decisions, it is now generally accepted that the option of a highly successful disarming strike is not open to either side. A principal consequence of this view is the reinforced emphasis on minimizing damage to the civilian fabric of Soviet society as a consequence of counterforce strikes. If the Soviet offensive forces capable of inflicting drastic damage on the United States cannot be eliminated, the counsel of wisdom suggests that we provide every incentive to the Soviets to exercise restraint in the use of their surviving forces. This implies keeping the Soviets aware of how much remains at risk, if they behave rashly. This concern about collateral damage means that we must now give careful attention to balancing objectives to which we gave no thought in earlier systems studies—for example, knocking out a hardened target with a weapon of the smallest possible yield. Five years ago, as far as collateral effects were concerned, we were indifferent to the size of weapons to be dropped on point targets.

Two major consequences of this growing awareness of the complexities surrounding nuclear war should be underscored.

The first stems from the fact, mentioned earlier, that emphasis has shifted from the operating characteristics of individual weapon systems to the combination of numerous systems into an integrated package. The stress has shifted to the complementarities among weapon systems, and *a major goal in trade-off analysis is to improve compatibility between systems,* even if some otherwise desirable characteristics must be sacrificed. This trend is epitomized by major DoD studies in recent years, and perhaps most revealingly in the decision to combine Package I and Package II for analytical purposes.

This new emphasis on complementarities requires a major adjustment in studies for the Air Force. Historically such studies have relied on the weapon-system concept pioneered at RAND. But now the Air Force will have to grapple with the same intractable problems in integrating weapon systems that the other Services have always faced—at least implicitly. For the Army, the meaning of the weapon-system concept has always been rather fuzzy. Center-stage has been something like the infantry division, which ties together a large number of separate capabilities. What meaning could there be, for example, in a "howitzer weapon system" or an "armored car weapon system"? In the strategic field, at least, the Air Force has been fortunate in the past in having relatively clean-cut analytical devices at hand. But this increases the difficulty of adjusting to a package-oriented environment, and there is small comfort in having to pay the penalty for past success.

The second consequence that we must now recognize involves a related set of complicating factors, which stem from our changed image of how nuclear war may come about. Given the prospective strategic balance, with the potential for devastation embodied in the forces that would survive a disarming attack, it becomes very hard to envisage nuclear war being initiated suddenly with all-out strikes. If it were to come, it is most likely to come in a sequence of escalating steps from a lower-level confrontation. This implies the need for careful study of how best to mesh general purpose forces and strategic forces. Strategic forces will either serve to control or fail to control the process of escalation—"keep the lid on," in the current parlance. The less advantageous the strategic balance is to the United States, the bolder the enemy may be in any specific crisis. On the other hand, limited war forces, including selected nuclear forces, may through their existence or through their employment serve to control conditions that could escalate to central war. Thus, limited war forces—with or without fire-breaks—are part of the mechanism of deterrence of central war, and the complementarities and trade-offs between the two types of forces must be carefully analyzed. If crises and potential crises are the seedbed of central war, and if effective crisis management constitutes a principal means for reducing the risk of central war and for obtaining settlements on terms favorable to us, then some of the confidence generated in the past by systems studies must perforce disappear. Crises involve so many unpredictable elements—boldness, resolve, and determination in the pursuit of one's objectives; rapid and unforeseen adaptation or improvisation of military capabilities—that neatness and precision, if obtained in systems studies, will not be consistent with the messiness of real-life conditions.

Both the increased stress on packages, complementarities, and mission trade-offs (under conditions in which we hope that central war, if it comes, will be characterized by restraint), and the increased tie between strategic and limited war capabilities (stressing the recognition that a central war, if it comes, will result from escalation) diminish our ability to get a quantitative handle on strategic problems. The role of assumptions in providing a royal road to quantitative conclusions has increased by something like an order of magnitude. While varying degrees of confidence will be placed in such assumptions, the problem of analysis is markedly different from what it was in the fifties, when contingencies could be mapped out in advance. Whatever the confidence placed in assumptions, the probability that they will be wrong is very high.

C. Increased Emphasis on Highly Specialized Weapon Systems

The demands on the analyst, particularly in force-structure determination in an environment in which mission trade-offs have become critical, is heightened by the highly specialized nature of many modern weapon systems. In part, specialized systems may be required because of our altered objectives in nuclear war. Given a desire to avoid collateral damage, the option of going to higher levels of violence to achieve target destruction disappears. One must attain higher performance levels in target destruction. The end of reliance on big yields may imply a variety of highly specialized delivery vehicles.

Perhaps more importantly, specialized weapon systems are also needed to counter enemy advances or to exploit enemy vulnerabilities. But because of their inflexibility, such weapon systems will be required in the force structure only if the enemy adopts certain courses of action rather than others. A highly specialized system, by definition, invests major resources in a specific kind of capability. On a cost-effectiveness basis, however, the allocation of resources for a highly specialized purpose is warranted only if the enemy chooses to procure and deploy just those capabilities for which the highly specialized system is a countermeasure.

Let me illustrate this problem by reference to the growing variety of delivery vehicles and concepts. A decade ago there was only one delivery vehicle: the bomber. Before the order-of-magnitude improvement in air defense capabilities, the principal problem was to get the aircraft over the target. A system analysis concentrated on trade-offs among range, weight, payload, and speed and paid some additional attention to basing concept, alert status, vulnerability and the like. However, with the arrival of surface-to-air missiles, the picture began to change. Against extensive air defenses, even with defense suppression, high-altitude attack looked less promising. To circumvent Soviet SAMs, low-altitude penetration became the accepted concept. In principle, bombers optimized for low-altitude operations became attractive. At the same time, long-range missiles, free of any initial problems of penetration, were being deployed, and they had major cost advantages over bombers for most tasks involving known immobile targets.

Yet the possibility of effective ABM defenses has lurked in the background. Given the improvement in low-altitude air defense, major difficulties in penetration could develop with existing U.S. delivery vehicles. A case may exist for developing, as a hedge, advanced systems like SLAM, designed to circumvent such defenses through low-altitude penetration at Mach 3. But that case does not extend to procurement and deployment—until Soviet action makes so specialized and costly a system an attractive buy. If Soviet defenses do not improve to such a degree, other less costly measures will suffice—improved penetration aids, for example. The point is that much of U.S. R&D activity should be devoted to developing specialized capabilities designed to counter Soviet developments which would exploit vulnerabilities in existing U.S. systems. Yet the Soviets cannot acquire capabilities to exploit all our vulnerabilities; they will have to choose. Thus, many of our own specialized systems need never be procured. On cost-effectiveness grounds, appropriate actions for us depend upon those routes the Soviets actually choose to follow. And since force-structure decisions, more so than R&D decisions, are critically dependent upon intelligence, the broader the menu of capabilities from which we must choose, the more vital good intelligence becomes in analysis.

One additional consideration must be added. Development of specialized systems implies, almost by definition, that there are fewer hedges against the failures of *close substitutes*. In the fifties, the F-101, the F-104, and the F-102/106 programs were in some sense substitutes. The opportunities for transfer of subsystems from one program to another were sizable. But in recent years the increased specialization of systems and subsystems reduces this kind of hedge. Increased specialization means less opportunity for partial overlaps among programs. This imposes greater demands on the R&D program, a fact that leads us to our last point, which concerns the growing financial strains in R&D.

D. Rising Costs of R&D

Costs of developing military systems since the early fifties have been rising rapidly, seemingly exponentially. Opinions vary regarding causes and possible cures, but the fact itself is beyond dispute. Given relatively stable budgets, either the number and variety of systems both developed and procured will fall, or else a number of systems successfully designed will not be carried through the full and costly development cycle as it is now known.

At the same time that the supply of new weapons is under downward pressure, the demand is rising for varied weapon development to hedge against uncertainty. As mentioned earlier, we live in a period in which the strategic balance is likely to change slowly and in no clear predictable manner with respect to new weapons. Yet, though the direction of advance is not clearly charted, instability and change do lurk in the background. We must use our R&D resources to counter a number of potential Soviet threats.

Happily, the possibility does exist for directing the R&D more toward hedging against a large number of possible surprises and less toward developing a smaller number of operational systems. There are two contrasting approaches that can be taken to hedging against uncertainty. The first is to have in development a number of complete systems—one of which, as a threat crystallizes and a need is perceived, has qualities that make it adaptable to a new mission. This is the now traditional approach to aircraft development. It characterized bomber and fighter development during the fifties. It was comforting to discover, for example, that the B-52 did possess a low-altitude capability or that the F-104 could be adapted to the role of an attack aircraft.

The second approach is quite different. The stress is on a well-stocked R&D menu, with numerous specialized projects which can rapidly be moved into the procurement-deployment stage, if the need arises. The focus of the program is shifted away from *full systems* development to exploratory and advanced development *stages*. The goal is to create, in effect, a shelf of advanced weapon hedges. The key concepts here are technical building-blocks, preliminary compatibility studies, and system design. This may be called an option-creating and option-preserving strategy for R&D. It contrasts with a strategy in which the major effort on the scientific-technical base represented mainly feedback from the objective of full systems development. It involves recognition that successful development does not necessarily involve procurement, and that procurement and deployment will probably not follow from successful development in the majority of cases. A major problem with this strategy, of course, is that the willingness to cut off a successful program goes against the grain for both the technologists and the organizations responsible for its development.

If we are prudent in allocating our energies, there seems to be little reason to wonder which is the appropriate kind of hedge strategy to pursue in the foreseeable future. Given the rising cost of systems, the falling supply of new weapon systems, the growth of specialized potential threats which existing systems are unlikely to prove sufficiently flexible to counter, and the need for more specialized capabilities to counter specific threats, it appears that the appropriate means for hedging against surprises is through an enhanced R&D program, in which individual projects are austerely conducted—a program designed to create and preserve a multitude of options. As the Soviet Union gives indications of pursuing particular lines of attack, we could move with moderate speed to counter those actions. We must be aware that such a strategy involves the quick response of the American economy, when production and deployment prove necessary. But in light of the proved flexibility of U.S. industry and technology and the historical sluggishness of the Soviet economy, we can have a measure of confidence that, in the final race for completely operational forces, we would come out ahead.

Yet we should be aware of the greater challenge this strategy represents for system design and system analysis. The designer must deal more than he would like with preliminary work on incomplete systems. The analyst, as he looks to the future, must deal with more or less hypothetical forces on which it is extremely difficult to get even a rough quantitative handle.

II. TWO CONTEMPORARY ANALYTICAL PROBLEMS

Up to this point, the discussion has been largely in generalities—generalities which help to explain how the character of analytical studies has been altered since the mid-fifties. To provide additional substance, let us examine two recent analytical and decision problems: (1) the optimal resource allocation for damage limitation, and (2) the choice of a specific offensive force-mix and the limits this choice may impose on strategic options in subsequent time periods. The first is intended to illustrate the points made earlier regarding our growing sophistication about nuclear war and our changed perception of the threat. The second is intended to illustrate what has been said regarding the problem of covering a broad spectrum of threats in light of the increasing cost and decreasing flexibility of new weapon systems.

A. Criteria for Resource Allocation for Damage Limitation

The first problem is, of course, the subject of the on-going DoD studies on optimizing Packages I and II. Certain methodological aspects of the existing studies could be criticized—in particular, the deficiencies of parametric analysis for long-range force-structure planning in light of the absence of time-phasing and the impossibility of identifying or analyzing critical decision points. But it is perhaps better to concentrate attention on a single issue: that the quantitative results rest upon inherently subjective estimates. In the final analysis *the optimal allocation will depend upon assumptions regarding a subjective parameter: specifically, the probability and duration of a period of mutual restraint and city avoidance in nuclear war.* This is a case in which what previously was called "the royal road to quantitative conclusions" must be based upon some rather questionable initial assumptions. Either explicitly or implicitly, some estimate of the probability of city avoidance will enter into the analysis and determine the results. But since this highly subjective element will influence both resource allocation and strategic choice, it should be considered explicitly— rather than be ignored in the quest for deceptively firm quantitative conclusions.

Broadly speaking, current studies attempt to reveal, for various budget levels, the optimal point on constant-damage trade-off curves for allocating funds between strategic offensive forces, on the one hand, and optimized civil defense and terminal bomber defense, on the other (see Figure 6–1). But the optimal point is dependent on the degree of mutual restraint assumed—in that for a war which is primarily counterforce, it will be advisable to invest relatively greater resources in expanding, diversifying, and protecting our offensive capabilities.

Let us consider two extreme and hypothetical cases and explore their implications for resource allocations. In the first case, Mr. Brezhnev and his successor,

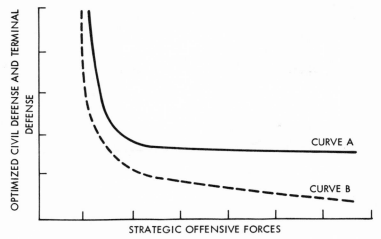

Figure 6–1   *Trade-Off Curve for Damage Limiting*

if any, as well as the American President, repeatedly emphasize in their public statements that nuclear war is a terrible thing: that it would be disastrous were it to come; that if it does come, the loss of life must be held down; and that "our" side would never initiate a strike at enemy cities, but reserve its "invulnerable" forces for retaliation should the foe strike cities first. Such declarations, if made repeatedly, would certainly influence our view as to the nature of nuclear war and the preparations we should make for it.

In the second case, we feel quite sure that the bulk of the Soviet missile force is pointed at our cities, and that the decision to launch will follow immediately upon any substantial U.S. strike—either because the missiles are, in effect, wired for an automatic response or because the authority to fire descends automatically to lower command levels when U.S. warheads impact on Soviet soil.

Clearly, under these two sets of hypothetical conditions, we would assign very different subjective probabilities to the existence and extent of a period of mutual city avoidance. But it should also be clear that, given these alternative probabilities, we are dealing with *two different trade-off functions* between strategic offensive and strategic defensive capabilities. Thus, in Figure 6–2, Curve A represents a trade-off function in the case of spasm or near-spasm war. For damage limitation in such a war, our strategic offensive forces, designed to deal with time-urgent targets, would consist largely of missiles. The force would tend to be limited, since very large additional expenditures on offensive capabilities would not buy much in the way of damage limitation. This is indicated by the elbow in Curve A. On the other hand, the payoff to additional defensive forces would be moderately high, so that relatively modest outlays for defensive capabilities would be the equivalent of very large expenditures on offensive capa-

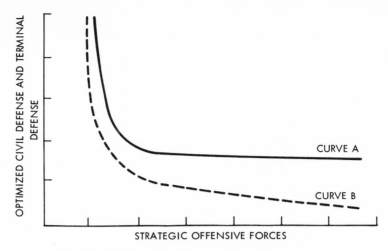

Figure 6–2   *Trade-Off Curves for Damage Limiting*

bilities. By contrast, Curve B indicates the trade-off function on the assumption that there will be an indefinite period of city avoidance. The entire curve is shifted downward and to the left, indicating that limiting damage to a *given* level can be obtained with lower outlays on Packages I and II. Under these conditions, the returns for additional outlays on strategic offensive forces may be moderately high. By contrast, beyond a limited initial investment in defensive capabilities, very large additional outlays on such capabilities may buy comparatively little—and relatively modest outlays on offense will be the equivalent of very large outlays on defense.

This sharp divergency exists because defensive capabilities (aside from fallout shelters) perform a somewhat different and more limited function than do offensive capabilities. This difference in function is obscured in many existing studies, which examine optimization in terms of alternative war outcomes based upon potential damage at a single point in time rather than provide a time-sequential analysis of the war that recognized the possibility of a period of mutual restraint. To illustrate this difference in the nature of the two force-sets, let us turn to Figure 6–3. As the arrows at the left of the figure suggest, both the offensive and defensive capabilities of the United States serve to reduce the Soviet *potential* for damage. But there is a difference which could prove to be very important. While both sets of forces from the very beginning do limit potential damage, *the United States could employ its strategic offensive forces immediately on the outbreak of war in order to alter the character of the Soviet threat.* The longer the period of restraint, the more extended is the *intra-war* opportunity to alter that threat. Moreover, the longer the period, the more options may be open to us to make such an attempt. By contrast, the defensive capabilities are, in a sense, "withheld." They perform their "active" role only in the relatively

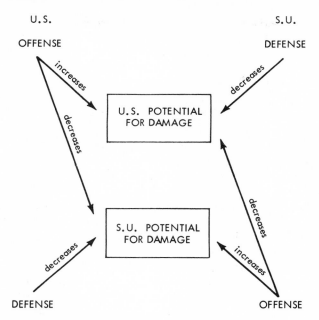

Figure 6–3   *Measuring War Outcomes*

brief period required for a Soviet strike against cities. *A period of restraint does not result, therefore, in an expansion of the list of interesting defensive options.*

Thus, if restraint is preserved for a period, the actual employment of defensive capabilities to blunt the Soviet attack would occur only after what may be a considerable lag—during which the strategic offensive forces could be employed to perform their function of reducing the possible weight of the attack that the Soviets must ultimately decide whether or not to launch.[5]

There is a need, therefore, to consider carefully how long such a lag might last, and to include the best probability estimates among the parameters used to optimize force allocation. But this important factor is neglected in many studies, which more or less implicitly assume near-spasm war. The reason for this is that only in the context of a near-spasm war can the strategic offensive and strategic defensive forces be compared simply and without qualification. Once the possibility of restraint is introduced and the contrasting functions of the two categories of forces are underscored, the complexity of the calculations is increased many times. And this complexity occurs not only in the calculations of systems effectiveness. Searching questions must be raised regarding what portion of the population is to be risked (for a limited but indeterminate time period) in order to provide greater capabilities for reducing long-run Soviet

---

[5] There is the added possibility, depending on the hardware characteristics and the command and control arrangements of the Soviet forces, that they could also be used to degrade Soviet targeting capabilities.

damage potential. There is no objective answer. Yet, avoiding such questions may result in a force structure optimized for dealing with what may be the least likely type of central war.

To illustrate the way such calculations may influence the optimal force structure, let us consider three hypothetical systems—distinguished in accordance with the speed of effective reaction. System A (say, missiles) can react immediately to destroy Soviet damage-inflicting capabilities. System B (say, reconnaissance-strike capabilities) reacts more slowly, its maximum effectiveness occurring from twelve hours to two weeks after the outbreak of war. System C (say, ASW capabilities) requires several weeks or even months to accomplish its mission. To limit damage in a near-spasm war, one would want to rely primarily on System A. But procurement would be relatively limited, with the balance of funds going into defensive capabilities because the *marginal cost* of killing additional Soviet offensive capabilities would rise rapidly for this system. However, if there is a lengthy period of restraint, Systems B and C may become attractive for reducing Soviet damage potential. If the period of restraint lasts for a week, for example, the marginal cost of destroying surviving Soviet land-based missiles through reconnaissance-strike capabilities may be relatively moderate—and this option *could* become interesting. If the war goes on for months, ASW capabilities designed to seek out and destroy Soviet missile-launching submarines might be very interesting. In a brief period, the marginal cost of destroying Soviet SLBMs could be infinite. But over an extended period, it might be moderate enough to be highly attractive, especially when it is remembered that knocking out a submarine represents a bargain in terms of missiles destroyed. In an extended counterforce war, all of the enemy's capabilities can be made vulnerable.

The moral of this story is that when enough time is available, a slow-reacting system may be relatively cheap in terms of the *marginal cost* of destroying additional enemy capabilities. The high marginal cost of damage limitation through strategic offensive forces applicable in a near-spasm war may cease to be relevant if an extended period of restraint occurs.

As a simple example of these points, let us examine several situations, defined by the data in Table 6–1, in which the Soviet forces consist entirely of missiles. There are 800 missiles, of which 200 are elusive targets that can be discovered only after some time has passed. If the war is essentially over after an

TABLE 6–1   Effects of Different Allocations of Strategic Forces

Type of Missile Attacked	Initial Force Size	Size after Initial Strike	Size after One Week	Size after Several Months
Targetable	600	150	40	25
Not initially targetable	200	200	200	30
Total	800	350	240	55

initial exchange, the use of strategic offensive forces to reduce enemy damage potential becomes too costly. The marginal cost of taking out enemy capabilities may be very high in relation to saving the lives of, say, a million people. Enough enemy missiles (350) survive, in any event, so that one should invest heavily in defensive capabilities. If, however, the war goes on for several months, one may be able, through the use of time-consuming offensive systems, to reduce enemy forces to the point that the surviving missiles (55) represent a much more modest threat to civil society. From the standpoint of damage limitation, the optimal mix in this case is skimpier defensive preparations and far heavier investment in strategic offensive forces—a solution that means little more than that the allocation of resources depends on the ratio in the final showdown between enemy vehicles and one's own lucrative civil targets. If one cannot reduce this ratio substantially through extended counterforce operations, then the payoff of heavy outlays on defensive measures will be much greater than if one can.

To demonstrate that for optimal resource allocation we are interested in the ratio, in the final showdown, between enemy vehicles and one's own civil targets, let us turn to Figure 6–4. The figure indicates (1) that the measure in which we are ultimately interested in studies of damage limitation is the Soviet potential for damage, and (2) that both offensive and defensive capabilities affect this variable, the offense by directly reducing Soviet offensive capabilities, the defense

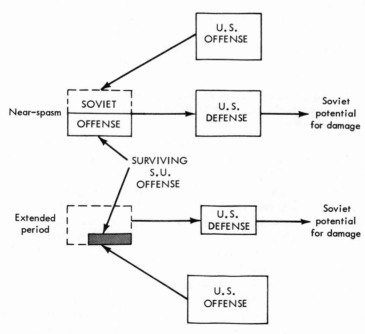

Figure 6–4   *Variation in Optimal Resource Allocation*
Depending on Assumed Character of
War

by blunting the effects of an attack, so that what is finally filtered through is Soviet potential for damage. The questions are: How much to U.S. offense, how much to defense? In the near-spasm context, the United States may be unable to make a very substantial dent in Soviet offense, and the optimal strategy would be to invest heavily in defense. Where, on the other hand, there is an extended period, U.S. offense, through a variety of measures, may reduce Soviet offense to a very low level—so low that much less should be allocated to defense to blunt the now much-reduced Soviet attack. The size of the boxes in the figure indicates that in the second case an entirely different allocation may be appropriate for the United States—one in which much more is invested in offense and far less in defense.

It should be acknowledged that the studies of damage limitation in the near-spasm context are unquestionably useful in providing an *initial* basis for analysis. From them one can speculate on the sequence of interactions as each side responds to the perceived outcomes by altering its intentions and capabilities. However, from the foregoing discussion, we can conclude that raising the issue of complementarities between missions enormously complicates analytical work and raises questions regarding the confidence that we can place in the results. To design an analysis which points to a single and unequivocal set of conclusions regarding strategic-forces resource allocation is well-nigh impossible. The point that should be remembered is that the ultimate decision regarding resource allocation must rest on nonquantifiable or subjectively quantifiable elements and that it cannot rest solely on presumably quantifiable technical data. Thus, an essentially unknowable parameter becomes critical in determining the ultimate results.

B. Constraining Future Strategic Options by an Early-on Force-Structure Decision

Let us turn now to our second illustration, which involves a problem in choice with which the DoD is continuously struggling, that is, determining the composition of U.S. missile forces. The purpose of this example is to underscore the desirability of maintaining flexibility in planning in order to cope with a gradually unfolding threat environment whose precise future character cannot be predicted. It was suggested earlier that the way to retain flexibility in such an environment is through an aggressive R&D program designed to develop multiple options and through avoidance of force-structure decisions until such decisions are forced upon us by the flow of events. The present example stresses the advisability of delaying major force-structure commitments until long lead-time elements force a decision. The case for such a decision-making pattern is quite strong *when one has moderate confidence that delay will permit the resolution of major uncertainties regarding the future strategic and technological environment.* This kind of flexibility may be contrasted with the premature foreclosing of strategic options implicit in commitments which are made at too early a date.

To indicate the advisability of such a decision-making pattern, let us examine the particular set of decisions, made early in 1961, which determined the character of our missile forces. Needless to say, the purpose in going back to these earlier decisions is not to indulge in some pointless second-guessing, but to learn what we can for the future.

The decisions made in March 1961 were advertised as part of a "quick and dirty look" at the force-structure program inherited from the Eisenhower administration. Major conclusions were to expand greatly the projected Minuteman (and Polaris) force and to reduce the size of, and the emphasis upon, the Titan II force. The effect of these decisions was to determine that the intermediate-run U.S. forces would be overwhelmingly composed of small payload missiles. Two background aspects of these decisions should be kept in mind. First, they were made before the new intelligence, then becoming available, had been fully absorbed. While fears of a major "missile gap" were being dissipated, we were still unaware of how great our strategic superiority was. Consequently, substantial emphasis remained on a quick buildup of a second-strike capability. Second, there existed certain political pressures for making changes (particularly in light of the preceding campaign) that would dramatize and highlight the shift away from the policies of the preceding administration. The atmosphere was one calling for decisiveness in a period of presumed crisis, as is perhaps suggested by the phrase "quick and dirty look." In any historically fair assessment of these decisions, these considerations must be kept in mind.

Nevertheless, we should ask ourselves a question: What can we as analysts learn in retrospect from these decisions? It now is clear that major difficulties existed in formulating the early-on cost-effectiveness studies which served as their basis. On the one hand, there were major uncertainties regarding the size and character of prospective Soviet forces and also regarding the strategic concept that we would adopt. In addition, major technical uncertainties regarding both Minuteman and Titan II remained unresolved. As a consequence of these deficiencies in information, it was inevitable that only the crudest observations could be made regarding the effectiveness component of the decision-making schema. Cost considerations, therefore, became dominant. Yet, even here, because of the unresolved technical problems, not much confidence could be placed in the cost calculations. As it turned out, these calculations were strongly biased against Titan II because of the drastic underestimation of missile operations and maintenance costs. This favored the missile with the lower initial capital cost, that is, Minuteman.

The upshot was that, as a result of calculations based mainly on cost, decisions were made, in effect, against large payload missiles and for small payload missiles. At the time, there was, to be sure, a developing emphasis on the desirability of avoiding collateral damage through the use of weapons of lower yield (which may have been associated with a stress on small payload vehicles), but it seems fair to say that cost was the main consideration pushing in the direction of a force composed of small payload missiles. Had it been necessary to make that decision at that time, of course, it would have been equally necessary to have based it on whatever information was then available. But we can say with reasonable confidence that there was then no compelling reason why it had to be made. It could have been delayed, and—in retrospect—we can see several still unresolved strategic and technical issues which suggest why it should have been delayed. Let us examine six of these issues.

1. Counterforce Strategy and the Prospective Hardening of Soviet Missiles. Perhaps the most important issue has been the elaboration of the counterforce strategy in its controlled response variant, with its emphasis on initial targeting of military targets exclusively and the attempt to avoid major damage to the fabric of Soviet civil society. In addition, although Soviet ICBMs were then soft, there was the prospect, later emphasized by Secretary McNamara in Congressional testimony, that in the future their ICBMs would be hardened. The extent of hardening and, *a fortiori*, the degree of hardness could not be anticipated with any precision. Particularly as the Soviets hardened their missiles, the United States might require higher-yield weapons to destroy Soviet capabilities. The degree to which our own CEPs could be lowered was unknown, and consequently, higher-yield weapons might be needed to substitute for targeting inaccuracies. Moreover, if the Soviets failed to press the development and procurement of missile-armed submarines, the pressure upon us to avoid the use of high-yield weapons out of concern for collateral damage would be much reduced, because we still might be able to achieve a major disarming blow. In light of the still unknown parameters, the prospective Soviet moves toward hardening should have led us to emphasize the large-payload hedge rather than commit ourselves too early to a force composed largely of small-payload missiles.

2. Possible Soviet ABM Deployment. Since we were aware of the possibility that the Soviets might deploy an ABM system, the implications of such an eventuality for a U.S. missile force composed primarily of small-payload missiles might well have been considered. Re-entry vehicles with small-yield weapons appear to be particularly vulnerable to ABM systems. Large-payload vehicles represented a hedge against Soviet ABM deployment in that the re-entry body could be toughened up, much higher-yield weapons could be employed, and a wide assortment of penetration aids could be packed into the vehicle. In short, the commitment to a force composed primarily of small-payload missiles should be regarded as an inadequate hedge against the possibility of the Soviet ABM system.

3. Test Moratorium and Test Ban. In early 1961, it could not be assumed with any confidence that the Soviets would break the test moratorium during the summer of 1961, thereby permitting our own test series and possible improvements in yield-to-weight ratios. In subsequent reviews, the possibility of the test ban treaty, which materialized in the summer of 1963, should have been kept in mind. The treaty now inhibits our ability to reduce the size and weight of warheads in Minuteman or to increase the yield with a warhead of given size. With given weight and size constraints in the re-entry vehicle, a reduced ability to vary the physical size of the weapon implies a lessened possibility of doing such things as toughening up the re-entry vehicle or packing in additional penetration aids.

4. Limitation on Numbers. Limiting the number of missiles available to both sides has been discussed at Geneva. Moreover, even in the absence of a formal agreement, some implicit bargaining has taken place between the two camps with the intention of holding numbers down. If numbers are held down, for whatever reason, much larger capabilities are provided by a force composed of large-payload as opposed to small-payload missiles. The large-payload vehicle represents a hedge to offset the effects of the likely inclination to hold numbers down.

5. Multiple Warhead Options. For quite obvious reasons, the possibility of a missile carrying multiple warheads, each individually delivered, very much increases the utility of a large-payload vehicle.

6. Questionable Systems Reliability. The fact that the technical characteristics of missile systems and subsystems were still unknown in 1961 points to one final possible advantage of the large-payload vehicle. In such a vehicle, if reliability problems were encountered, subsystems such as guidance packages could have been placed in parallel, thereby reducing the risk of unreliability—and possibly economizing on operation and maintenance costs.

The ultimate influence of any one of these considerations could have been such as to make it advisable to press forward with large-payload vehicles; yet decisions made earlier, largely on the basis of cost considerations which were crude in themselves, had already inclined the United States in the direction of small-payload missiles. The entire episode illustrates the need for flexibility, for hedging, and yet for *timely* decisions respecting force structure. It also demonstrates what should be obvious, how cost-effectiveness studies conducted at one point in time may become irrelevant as strategic objectives and circumstances change. The point here, however, is that the decision did not have to be made so soon. When the external environment permits delay, and when one has moderate confidence that major uncertainties will be largely resolved, delaying the decision is likely to be the wisest course of action.

These conclusions seem inescapable, but they still leave room for the observation that, for strategic purposes,[6] the Minuteman decision has not worked out

---

[6] With respect to the cost-effectiveness of the investment, on the other hand, the decision may turn out far less favorably than anticipated. In a hardened and dispersed missile system with sophisticated command and control, the ground environment rather than the missiles themselves represent the main cost. In moving toward more advanced missiles, we most certainly would desire to take advantage of such costs and have the existing silos service several generations of missiles. But the existing silos were designed for the relatively small Minuteman. This implies that, if the United States moves toward larger payload missiles, we shall be facing the tough—and expensive—compatibility problems involved in squeezing larger vehicles into the existing space-limited configuration. Substantial retrofitting costs over time make the original decision more questionable—though, admittedly, this is easier to see in hindsight.

too badly. This is due particularly to the slow buildup, hardening, and dispersal of Soviet forces and to the slow advance on ABM systems. The favorable resolution of technical problems and the brief resumption of testing by the United States have been helpful. But the point is, if we have been right, we have been right because of developments that could not have been predicted with high confidence. Whatever analysts may say, it is undoubtedly better to have been right for invalid reasons than wrong for the right reasons. Yet, since we cannot count on such good fortune in all cases, we are well advised to see what we can learn from earlier experiences. One lesson this example demonstrates is the desirability of maintaining options and of putting off critical force-structure decisions until forced to make them by long lead-time items. Another is that the dominant role of uncertainties in this example (like the role of assumptions regarding highly subjective parameters in the previous examples) indicates that undue expectations regarding precision in systems studies is likely to be self-defeating.

III. SOME FINAL INFERENCES

The purpose of this concluding section is to draw some inferences from the discussion that may prove helpful in future analytical work. We can group these inferences under six headings.

1. Uncertainties: State of the World, Objectives, and Strategies

Inevitably the first issue to be raised is that which normally falls under the heading "uncertainty." Three points in particular should be emphasized. First, in a number of important ways the environment has indeed become more fluid, more uncertain. This reflects the perceived reduction in the probability of all-out nuclear war and the depolarization of international politics. Second, we are now more aware of "uncertainties" that have always existed in the environment, but which earlier perceptions of the state of the world precluded our recognizing. Third, we should now be more willing to acknowledge the certainty of change—with its corollary that only the absence of surprises would be surprising. Heightened awareness of continuous change and the uncertainties it entails is reflected in our perceptions of the nature of opponents, the character of nuclear war and how it may be initiated, and the future array of military capabilities and the degree of coherence attainable within the array. But these uncertainties regarding the environment, objectives, and strategy vastly complicate the decision-making schema. One view of the decision process, taken from formal decision theory, has attracted some attention among systems analysts. The procedure is to assign subjective probabilities to possible states of the world, array them accordingly along one axis, examine strategies or alternative lines of action along another axis, and then make a choice among them by means of some decision rule.

This is a neat and intellectually elegant way to structure the problem, but, if improperly understood, may create more problems than it solves. Although a useful first approximation, such a model is inadequate in at least two respects. First, the assignment of probabilities to perceived possible states of the world will inevitably be misleading, because the chances are very great that the state of the world that does materialize will be one which was not perceived in advance. Second, both the optimal strategy and the strategy finally chosen are likely to be different from those which were arrayed in the payoff matrix. In assessing decision theory, it is important that we keep in mind the distinction that exists between *risk* and *uncertainty*. For risk, anticipation is possible and appropriate calculations, even if subjective, can be made. By contrast, how uncertainty will be resolved is impossible to foresee, and its existence will partially destroy the relevance of all advance calculations.

2. Disparate Approaches to Analysis

This matter of uncertainty raises the question of how to approach analysis. In the past, both within and without RAND, there have been two disparate points of view. A first group, whom we might call the contingency *planners*,[7] has felt some confidence in our ability to chart in advance successful policies for the unknown future. Their method has been to designate the probable states of the world and to design a system which can deal adequately with each of them. A second group, whom we might describe as *contingency* planners,[8] has tended to emphasize the uncertainties and our limited ability to predict the future. Those who hold this view have consequently stressed the need for sequential decision making, for improvisation, for hedging, and for adaptability. Heightened awareness of inevitable change should tend to make us more sympathetic to the latter approach.

3. Developing and Selecting U.S. Military Capabilities

We face a wide spectrum of threats, but we cannot tell which, if any, will actually materialize. Given the cost and specialization of our own weapon systems, we cannot afford to procure all the systems necessary to deal with such a multitude of threats. We may actually buy fewer systems, each of which is designed to deal with a relatively limited threat. For central war purposes the

---

[7] That is, those who believe that the array and character of future contingencies can be specified in advance, and that *detailed advance* planning can be done to deal with whichever one does occur.

[8] That is, those who believe that future developments will have a large element of the unforeseen, that contingencies cannot be specified precisely in advance, and that *whatever planning one does must be done so that it may be adapted to the contingent and the unforeseen.*

effectiveness of any given U.S. system depends on what is in the Soviet force structure. Many major force-structure decisions will have to be delayed until we have clear evidence of the direction in which the Soviets will proceed. On the other hand, although specialized weapon systems deal with narrow threats, we must protect ourselves against a broad range of threats. The chief way to do this is through a wide-ranging, austerely conducted R&D program, in which it is fully recognized that many successful developments will not lead to procurement.

Although the chief way of building flexibility into the future force structure should be an R&D program which provides a rich menu, we ought not to neglect the possibility of building flexibility into individual systems. In a continuously changing strategic environment, it must be kept in mind that the choice of a weapon system does not simply optimize—it also constrains the choice of future strategy. The adaptation of strategy should not be unduly limited by the selection of weapon systems through the choice of criteria that inherently reflect a single set of strategic conditions.

4. The Problem of Cherished Beliefs

A determination to stress adaptability and the avoidance of premature commitments in the future implies that we must be on our guard against the cherished beliefs that are carried forward from previous conditions and previous battles. Obviously, this admonition represents a counsel of perfection, one that sounds naive when directed toward frail human nature as it must perform in a bureaucratic environment. Yet such counsels of perfection are necessary to provide warning flags against the kind of error into which we fall through seduction rather than through bungling.

Consider once again a basic tenet of decision theory. In principle, our choice of force structure and strategy should be dependent upon, and subsequent to, our estimates of the probabilities pertaining to various states of the world. In practice, however, this is rarely the case. Partly, this may be ascribed to the long lead-time associated with the purchase and deployment of weapon systems— which implies that our strategic choices must be made well in advance of any hard intelligence about the state of the world. Much more important, however, in imposing obstacles to logical choices are bureaucratic pressures and the proclivity of most human beings to make decisions based on more or less pure intuition, and then adjust one's assessment of the state of the world accordingly. Rather than the state of the world determining one's strategy, as in the model, the assessment of the state of nature is not even arrived at independently, but all too frequently is merely a reflection of strategic choice. Thus analysis is made to reflect preconceptions. If we are to achieve true adaptability and to suppress cherished but obsolete beliefs, we must all try both individually and organizationally, to control such tendencies.

5. Complementarities and Mission Trade-Offs

Recognition of complementarities among major missions means that the problems of overall system design have become increasingly intricate and that more attention must be paid to them. More emphasis must be placed on force integration; less attention can be concentrated on the individual weapon system. As a result, the opportunity for traditional systems analysis—in the sense of analysis to assist a simple choice between several given systems for accomplishing a single objective—has diminished. This shift implies that in analytical work, choice becomes more dependent upon parameters which are only implicitly or subjectively quantifiable—and which may even be unknowable. Under these circumstances, it is probably preferable to have an acknowledged imprecision in systems studies rather than a spurious precision.

6. Quantitative Precision

Finally, we might observe that imprecision in analytical results, at least in the quantitative sense, stems from the lessened distinction between capabilities for central war and limited confrontations, from the absence of dominant threats, and from the general growth of uncertainty. This may imply that in military systems analysis we are undergoing a great transition. Previously, there may have been an overemphasis on intuition, but now that the battle for the recognition of quantitative studies has been won, the current problem may be an overemphasis on those objects of analysis that can be readily quantified. Now that the importance of the quantitative element has been recognized and stressed, we should be increasingly aware that it does not represent the whole story. We should be more inclined, perhaps, to recognize the element of art in systems analysis—and to stress what the best practitioners have always known: that judgment and educated intuition (in handling quantitative considerations, to be sure) remain the critical inputs.

BIBLIOGRAPHY

Chernoff, Hermann and Lincoln E. Moses, *Elementary Decision Theory*. New York: John Wiley & Sons, 1959.

Cohen, John, *Chance, Skill, and Luck*. Baltimore: Penguin Books, Inc., 1960.

Hoffman, Fred et al., *Counterforce and Damage-Limiting Capability in Central War*, **1970** (U), Secret-Restricted Data, R-420-PR. The RAND Corporation, August, 1963.

Kaufman, William W., *The McNamara Strategy.* New York: Harper & Row, Publishers, 1964.

Klein, Burton H., "The Decision-Making Problem in Development," in *The Rate and Direction of Incentive Activity.* Princeton, N.J.: Princeton University Press, 1962, p. 477ff.

Luce, R. Duncan and Howard Raiffa, *Games and Decisions.* New York: John Wiley & Sons, 1957.

Nelson, R. R., "Uncertainty, Learning, and the Economics of Parallel Research and Development Efforts," *Review of Economics and Statistics,* November 1961.

Quade, E. S. ed., *Analysis for Military Decisions.* Chicago: Rand McNally & Co., 1964.

Schelling, Thomas C., "Controlled Response and Strategic Warfare," Adelphi Papers #19, *Institute for Strategic Studies,* June 1965.

Schlesinger, J. R., "Quantitative Analysis and National Security," *World Politics,* January 1963, p. 295ff.

R. H. McMAHAN, JR.
TEMPO, General Electric

R. H. McMahan, Jr. is a member of the professional staff at TEMPO, General Electric's Center for Advanced Studies at Santa Barbara, California. His degree is in Electrical Engineering from Worcester Polytechnic Institute. He held a variety of positions with GE from 1950 to 1958, joining TEMPO in 1959. The author has managed a series of government-sponsored studies of such subjects as the arms control implications of urban ballistic missile defense (BMD) and hardsite defense, the interactions of arms control and BMD policies, and the influence of BMD on the stability of arms control environments. McMahan is a member of the Institute of General Semantics and the International Society for General Semantics. He is the author or coauthor of a number of classified reports and papers; recent unclassified publications include *Public Opinion and Ballistic Missile Defense— Report of an Exploratory Survey*, TEMPO report RM64TMP-50, and "Rationales for BMD Policy," in the *Bulletin of the Atomic Scientists* (March, 1965), TEMPO SP-286.

D. H. TAYLOR
TEMPO, General Electric

D. H. Taylor is a member of the professional staff at TEMPO, General Electric's Center for Advanced Studies at Santa Barbara, California. He holds B.S. and M.S. degrees in Electrical Engineering from the University of Idaho and has completed the General Electric Company's three-year Advanced Engineering Program.

For the past eight years, he has participated in and managed various studies relating to the effectiveness and cost of strategic and tactical weapon systems. These studies have ranged from the delivery efficiency of ballistic missiles and bombers to the allocation of defense budgets between forces for maintaining deterrence and forces for limiting damage, as well as possible enemy reactions to the deployment of such forces. The participation in these studies has required a close working relationship with the defense establishment.

His publications include many classified reports and papers. His unclassified TEMPO publications include *Optimum Defense Deployment—An Analysis of ABM's and Civil Defense* (SP-305, November, 1964) and *Force Structure Research Methodology* (RM64TMP-18, February, 1964).

His professional society affiliations include the Institute of Electrical and Electronic Engineers and Operations Research Society of America.

7

Central War Alternatives

CONTEXT FOR STRATEGIC ANALYSES

With the development of thermonuclear weapons, the explosive power deliverable in a single package increased more than a million times. The ability to deliver such weapons swiftly over intercontinental distances has fundamentally changed the role played by the instruments and the institution of warfare in the policies of major nations. No longer is the concept of strategic warfare restricted to a long-term process of erosion of a nation's capacity or will to fight a "conventional" war on its own or someone else's soil. It is now possible to destroy the economic and institutional essentials of a nation (for example, all its major cities) in an interval measured not in years or months, but in days or hours. Although such a strategic capability is complex and costly, the requisite economic and technological resources will be within reach of more and more nations as time goes by.

The topic of central-war or general-war alternatives is concerned with (but not limited to) choices among strategic military forces. In terms of current (mid-1965) DoD (Department of Defense) programming terminology, these are the forces involved in two major programs: the Strategic Offensive Forces and the Continental Air and Missile Defense Forces (including Civil Defense).

As currently expressed, the basic missions of US strategic or general nuclear-war forces are: first, to deter a deliberate nuclear attack on the United States or its allies and second, to limit damage to the United States should such a nuclear attack occur.[1]

Deterrence implies the maintenance of a convincing capability for inflicting unacceptable damage on any aggressor, even if he were to strike first at our retaliatory forces. The concept of deterrence rests upon the assumption that a major modern industrial nation would not rationally pursue a policy that would precipitate thermonuclear attack upon itself. No possible gains would be worth the price even of "victory" in an all-out nuclear war. In other words, nations who are presumed to be deterred from initiating thermonuclear war must indeed have something to lose in such a war and must share some common concept of rational behavior.

The exact nature or extent of "unacceptable damage" need not be specified,

[1] One might prefer other priorities, such as first guaranteeing protection for the US, and only then buying the means to inflict damage on others. But the deterrence-first ranking of these missions is largely determined by the technological and economic realities of strategic weaponry. Defense systems conceivable today can significantly reduce damage from any given threat; but even very expensive defenses can only "raise the price" of achieving any given level of damage. It may be possible to deny penetration to small numbers of relatively unsophisticated ballistic missiles (the "Nth country" threat, with today N equaling China). But an advanced country with sufficient resources (most notably, of course, the US and the Soviet Union) could maintain a substantial assured destruction potential against defensive measures taken by any other nation.

as long as a potential aggressor can perceive that the deterring nation has both the capability and the resolve to retaliate. Thus a nation must "advertise" its deterrent capability to some degree, but not too much. (If an opponent knows nothing about your strength, he has nothing to fear and may be reckless; if he knows too much, he may be able to counteract your capability.)

Another dimension of the concept of deterrence involves the kinds of actions (and by whom) that a given capability can credibly deter. The specific threat of a nuclear attack on Russia, in retaliation for a deliberate Soviet attack on US cities, is clearly credible. On the other hand, the US would not expect others to believe an American threat to initiate thermonuclear war in reprisal for, say, an isolated incident between Russian and American troops in Berlin, or for the burning of a USIS library in a non-nuclear nation.[2] Between such unambiguous extremes lies the question of how specifically the hostile acts that will bring nuclear retaliation should be prescribed. (If a nation convincingly draws a very fine line, it may be pushed dangerously close to it. If policy is too vague, it may be impossible safely to take a stand at the proper time.)

Although the *prevention* of general war (deterrence) is the dominant *raison d'être* of our strategic forces, damage-limiting is an important secondary goal.

Many rationales for damage-limiting may be found in the strategic literature. Among the most compelling today is recognition of the fact that deterrence could "fail" by degrees and perhaps be restored before "all is lost," or that nuclear attacks might occur that would not be "failures of deterrence" at all. Many examples of such contingincies have been cited: accidental launches of enemy weapons or detonations of one's own weapons, unauthorized firings (the "psychotic commander" scenario), inadvertent but limited attacks resulting from error or miscalculation by otherwise responsible leaders, attacks by smaller powers (the "Nth-country threat"), and so forth. In all such cases, great damage could occur, but some strategic weapons would remain that threaten even more damage. There would be incentives on all sides to "keep deterrence from failing" —that is, to find alternatives to conscious escalation to an all-out nuclear exchange. And any measures that could have been taken to mitigate the damage from such events would clearly be desirable.

These and many other issues have been discussed at length in the literature of deterrence, and they will never be finally resolved. They are mentioned here primarily to illustrate that deterrence involves a complex interaction of psychology, economics, politics, and technologically based military capability. In this chapter, however, the focus will be strategic-weapon capability, particularly those aspects that can, at least to a degree, be quantitatively analyzed.

---

[2] Indeed, we take considerable pains to make it clear that our strategic posture does *not* require spasmodic responses to trivial or ambiguous events—that we want to, and can, withhold nuclear retaliation until we are sure that the extremely provocative event that our deterrent is intended to discourage has actually occurred.

DESIGN OF STRATEGIC ANALYTIC MODELS

With the foregoing concepts established, the following question can be addressed: How can analytic models and the speed and precision of modern computers be best used to aid in selecting among strategic offense and defense force-structure alternatives?

Strategic forces are procured to assure the capability to punish an attacker, and to limit damage in the event of nuclear attack on the US. These objectives must be met within a variety of constraints, including budget, existing systems, technological state-of-the-art capabilities, and anticipated improvement as a result of research and development programs. Criteria for preference among alternatives are difficult to determine, particularly since many facets of the future threat are not known even to the potential opponent. Yet these very difficulties make it all the more necessary to quantify those aspects of the problem that can be rigorously tested, in order to reduce the range of uncertainties and identify important issues.

At the start, requirements for several sets of models, useful in the analysis of central-war alternatives, can be identified. These include damage models, weapon-system models, and various allocation models. The latter include models for buying and assigning strategic-offense systems, as well as models for selecting among defense alternatives.

Damage Models

An inherent part of the problem for all parties involved is the relative effectiveness of nuclear-weapon delivery systems. Offensive weapon systems are generally valued in terms of their delivery efficiency and damage capabilities when delivered. Defensive systems are valued in terms of their ability to prevent delivery or reduce damage from delivered weapons.

The selection of an adequate measure of damage is itself a complex matter. The capability of a deterrent force is usually calculated in terms of the damage it can inflict on strategically valuable things—that is, those resources and institutions essential to the viability of a modern nation. Various entities may be considered as measures of strategic value: population (overall, urban only, or specific segments); centers of government or other institutions; industrial capacity; selected resources, and so forth; or combinations of these with various relative weights assigned.

The measure of damage most commonly used is population fatalities. Some reasons for this are the following: (1) Population is unquestionably one of the most important strategic values; (2) reliable census data are more readily available on population than on other measures of value (particularly for countries other than the US); (3) the distribution of urban population is fairly closely correlated with that of some other values (such as industrial floor space); (4) data are available to determine fatalities or casualties from both prompt and delayed weapon effects, for various degrees of exposure or shelter conditions.

Model complexity varies from simple expected-value relationships to complicated Monte Carlo and simulation processes. In general, the most detailed model available is desirable; however, computer availability and cost, and time available for structuring analyses and interpreting results, frequently prohibit the extensive use of detailed models except for very special problems. The attainment of a preferred compromise among strategic-force alternatives requires a judicious selection of complicated models for selected, detailed analysis and of simpler models—with inputs based on detailed studies—for national deployment studies and studies of the interactions between the different countries involved. In any case, damage models are required to determine the effectiveness of various offensive and defensive alternatives. In this chapter, the discussion will concentrate on simple models that must be used repetitively when complicated interactions are involved.

Weapon System Models

There is a second class of models that will be referred to as weapon-system models. These are required to characterize both existing systems and alternative future systems. Consider, for example, a ballistic-missile system. Characteristics of importance include:

a. Availability: the probability that the missile will be available for launch when required.

b. Survivability: the probability that the missile will survive, given that it was fired upon by the enemy.

c. Reliability: the probability that the payload will attain the proper ballistic trajectory.

d. Penetration Probability: the probability that the warhead will penetrate the defenses, given that it arrives at the target and that the target was defended.

e. Kill Probability: the probability that the warhead will kill the target, given that it penetrates. This in turn is a function of (1) other weapon characteristics such as yield and accuracy; (2) target characteristics such as hardness, accuracy of attacker's knowledge of its location, and so on; and (3) the kill criterion established by the offense.

f. Cost: the research and development, investment, operating, and basic support costs of each system as a function of the number purchased.

Weapon-system models include procedures and techniques for defining and combining the characteristics identified above to determine the number and cost of weapons required under varying conditions.

Allocation Models

Allocation models describe the procedure followed by the offense in assigning weapons to a particular target when the defense will react to the contemplated assignment. In this case, a max-min solution is generally sought where the offense targets successive weapons for maximum value destroyed, and defense resources are allocated for minimum value destroyed. This problem affects the deployment of defenses within a target area, such as a defended city, as well as the targeting and defending of an entire complex of targets, such as all major cities in a nation. That is, defending one target to a very high level would merely permit an attacker to retarget his missiles to other undefended targets within the complex. This leads naturally to the national offense-targeting and defense-allocation problem. Allocation models to be discussed will include models for each single target as well as those dealing with the national allocation problem for both the offense and the defense.

In order to clarify these concepts, the nature of the models discussed above will be illustrated by a relatively simple example of methods that may be used to quantify some of the aspects of the problem of selecting forces for deterrence and damage limiting.

AN EXAMPLE

Consider a situation where the United States must, over a period of time, allocate a succession of constrained budgets to: (1) maintain the capability to achieve a specified level of damage; and (2) minimize damage to the United States should nuclear attack occur.

There is no absolute way to know just which physical quantities can best represent the operation of "deterrence," although, as discussed earlier, an estimate of population fatalities associated with blast damage to urban targets is widely used. Other targets, such as critical communications and air-defense sites, may be included on a basic "assured-destruction" target list. Even given such a qualitative criterion, a quantitative measure of deterrence—the levels of damage or probability of kill that must be assured on those targets—is a matter of judgment. Thus both of these parameters (target lists and damage level) must be varied, regardless of the criterion selected, in order to test for sensitivity.

With these objectives in mind, various models can be selected for quantifying deterrence levels and damage limits. A damage model has been developed that determines (1) the probability of kill[3] on a point target with a specified radius of uncertainty or (2) the expected overlap between a circular target and the lethal area of a given weapon, where the hit point has a known and specified distribution[4] about the aim point. This model expresses damage level or probability of kill as a function of various weapon-system parameters such as availability and reliability (expressed as probabilities), weapon yield, circular probable error, and target hardness and radius. With such a model, one can determine

---

[3] That is, the probability that the target will be within the contour of a specified weapon effect considered to be "lethal" for that target.

[4] The model used here assumes a circular normal distribution.

TABLE 7–1   Hypothetical Target Complex for Assured Destruction

Target Type*	Target Radius n. mi.**	Target Hardness psi	Damage Level (fraction)	Number of Targets Time Period			
				1	2	3	4
1. Large cities	2.9	6.4	0.75	50	50	50	50
2. Small cities	2.3	4.8	0.75	100	100	100	100
3. Second country cities	3.3	4.5	0.75	0	0	50	100
4. Air defense sites	1.0	12	0.90	257	132	59	10
5. Hardened control centers	1.0	1000	0.90	2	4	5	6
6. Missile launch sites	0.5	100	0.90	430	570	570	570

* The results in this chapter assume a nominal amount of defense in the last time period for target types 1 and 5.

* * Includes uncertainty of location (geodetic error).

the number of offensive weapons required to achieve various levels of expected damage to a target.

The first step in analyzing the assurred-destruction requirement is to describe the target system in the country or countries against which an assured-destruction threat is to be maintained. Table 7–1 displays a hypothetical, but typical, target complex, in which the US has a primary and a secondary opponent. Four time periods, each consisting of three years, are shown (the time-period structure can be an input to the process). The first target type represents the most populous cities in the primary country; the number to be threatened is constant over time as shown in the last column. The same assumption is indicated for target-type 2, except that there are more of these smaller cities. Target-type 3 shows a gradual increase in the number of threatened cities, paralleling an assumed build-up of a nuclear capability by the secondary opponent, with consequently increased deterrent requirements. Air-defense sites (Target-type 4) are assumed to decrease in number, whereas control centers (Target-type 5) increase as a function of time. Target-type 6 could represent missile launch sites in the primary and secondary countries.

Although obviously simplified, this target system illustrates the flexibility necessary to reflect changing requirements over time. The requirements for damage model are also partially specified, since the damage model must relate weapon parameters to these damage objectives.

The basic hypothesis involved in this example is that our primary mission—deterrence—requires maintaining an offense force capable of achieving the levels of damage indicated in the table on all the targets listed. Presumably, we would like to accomplish this objective with a minimum expenditure of resources. By using various weapon-system models, critical weapon-system parameters such as availability and survivability, may be determined for each existing and

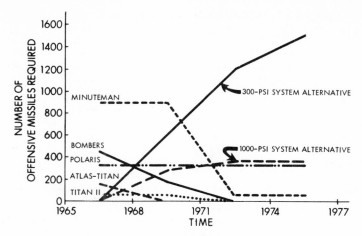

Figure 7–1   *Hypothetical US Strategic Offense Force Structure Required to Maintain Assured Destruction Threat on Target System of Table 7–1*

potential future weapon-system. Given these inputs, the damage model and weapon-system model can be used to determine the number of weapons required for each system in each time period and against each target. This is a measure of the effectiveness of the weapon systems for each potential assignment. If, in addition, the investment and operating cost of each system is known, the total cost of alternate weapon-target assignments can be computed. This computation would not be carried through for infeasible assignments; that is, the procedure would account for such constraints as the existing weapon inventory, production rate limitations, procurement lead times, delivery system range, and so forth.

In past studies, linear programming has been used to determine optimum allocations. An objective function is written representing the total cost, over a twelve-year time period, of alternate weapon-target assignments, and the constraints are written in a linear-programming format.[5] The computer then essentially compares all possible alternate weapon-target combinations and selects the combination that achieves the stipulated damage at a minimum total cost.

Figure 7–1 provides an example of the resulting time phasing of strategic weapon systems to threaten the damage levels on the total target complex indi-

---

[5] In this example, budget rates are not constant. Rather, the budgets required in each time period are summed to find the total budget. Thus these results are nonoptimum in that the beneficial effects of deferring expenditures to a later time period (which may inhere in some alternatives) are not considered, and they could influence the results. The introduction of such discount rates into the existing models would be conceptually straightforward but would complicate the discussion.

cated in Table 7–1. In this case, missile systems such as Minuteman, Atlas-Titan, Titan II, and Polaris[6] are compared to manned bombers and two future missile systems. The two future systems have payloads optimized to provide a minimum system cost over a five-year period against 1000- and 300-psi[7] point targets. Any assignment of weapons to targets other than the one corresponding to the weapons system procurement of Figure 7–1 will cost more than this optimum allocation. Research and development costs were not directly accounted for in the allocations of Figure 7–1, since such an accounting would make the problem nonlinear and thus preclude the use of linear programming. Similarly, the effect of learning as systems are procured and deployed is not included. More complicated techniques such as nonlinear programming and dynamic programming exist, which can be used to accommodate such factors.

With the linear-programming model used here, costs such as research and development can be included by making two runs—one with the new system in the mix and one without the new system. This will provide the total cost savings over twelve years if the new system is purchased. An assessment can then be made as to whether the research and development costs will exceed the expected savings. If not, the system is preferred, and the research and development can be added to the cost determined in the linear-programming solution.

This procedure provides the first result in the consideration of central-war alternatives on a quantitative basis—the most efficient allocation of strategic offensive weapon systems to accomplish deterrence.

The next step is to allocate the remaining resources so that damage to the US is minimized in the event that deterrence fails. Damage-limiting alternatives are listed below, grouped according to whether they function after an enemy weapon has been launched at its target (post-launch defenses), or whether they rely on preempting an attack by destroying the enemy weapon before it has been launched (pre-launch defenses).

Post-Launch Defenses

Civil Defense (CD) (also referred to here as passive defense). Civil defense measures include identifying and marking space in existing buildings that can be used as shelters against radioactive fallout; building blast shelters; dispersing stockpiles of such commodities as food, raw materials, and tools for postwar recovery; developing city evacuation plans; and so forth.

Ballistic Missile Defense (BMD), also referred to here as active defense, or anti-ballistic missile (ABM) systems. BMD options include both area and point defenses, or combinations of the two. Area defenses are so called because their interceptor missiles have a range of several hundred miles and can thus defend regions in which a number of targets may be located. Intercepting at those ranges means that the attacking reentry vehicles (RV's) are still in the mid-course part of their trajectory and have not yet begun to reenter the earth's atmosphere. It is easy for the attacker to create a very large "threat cloud" in space, composed of booster tank fragments, decoys (even balloons), chaff, and so forth, making it impossible for defense

---

[6] In Figure 7–1, the level of Polaris missiles was held constant. In the study for which this example was determined, the tactic of holding Polaris level constant resulted in a negligible difference in total system cost over twelve years.

[7] Nominal target hardness in pounds per square inch (psi) peak overpressure.

radars to discriminate threatening from harmless objects. Thus area defenses must rely on "volume kill"—that is, the use of defensive warheads that have a high probability of killing an attacking RV anywhere in this large threat cloud.

As this threat cloud reenters the atmosphere, lighter objects are burned up or slowed down more rapidly than the warhead-carrying RV's, and defensive discrimination is easier. Terminal defense systems rely on this atmospheric sorting and launch high-acceleration interceptors at individual threatening bodies, with intercepts occurring relatively close to the target. These are sometimes referred to as "point defense" systems, since the size of the defended region is small compared with an area defense.

Bomber Defense. This category comprises defense against manned bombers, both area and point. These include early-warning systems, command and control facilities, and interceptor missiles and aircraft.

Pre-Launch Defenses

Antisubmarine Warfare (ASW) Defense. These systems are used for nullifying the threat of submarine-launched missiles by countering the launch platform (the submarine) itself.[8]

Strategic Offensive Forces (SOF). Both manned bombers and missiles may be employed in a counterforce mode to destroy enemy airfields, missile sites, or other military targets. Whether to include such military targets on the assured destruction target list (Table 7–1) or deal with them as part of the damage-limiting mission must be resolved for each particular analysis.

Each of these alternatives can limit damage to the United States resulting from attacks by particular enemy weapons. Each has a cost and relative effectiveness under specified conditions. The problem is to find the allocation of funds remaining, after guaranteeing deterrence as a time function, that will minimize damage to the US. This allocation procedure should consider as a basic input the weapon systems in being for guaranteeing deterrence. That is, part of the forces acquired for the purpose of maintaining deterrence may be included in the initial inventory for the damage-limiting process. This allows for the possible use of some of the strategic forces in a manner different from their initial purpose, should deterrence "fail" and damage limitation become the principal United States objective.

A method has been developed within the defense establishment to allocate remaining resources among the damage-limiting alternatives, in order to maximize the protected population per damage-limiting dollar invested.

Consider first the post-launch defense problem. We will limit the scope of this example to these alternatives:

Active defense:	Terminal ("point") BMD
Passive defense:	Fallout shelters
	Blast shelters

This omits some important alternatives but still leaves many interesting and complicated interactions to be illustrated.

---

[8] System concepts involving intercept of submarine-launched missiles in the early phases of their flight are also sometimes classified as ASW systems.

In these terms, the post-launch defense problem reduces to one of allocating between terminal active defense and passive defense for the defended area. The offense has the option of selecting among a large number of penetration aids, each requiring payload weight that could otherwise be used for higher-yield warheads. The best defense deployment is a function of the offense option selected, and the best offense allocation is a function of the defense deployment. If a common measure of effectiveness for the offense and defense can be identified, the problem of offensive and defensive allocation can be at least partially resolved. The measure of effectiveness, in this example, is the exposed population or the population killed.

For this example, consider the use of heavy decoys for the offense and the allocation between active and passive defense for the defense. Heavy decoys are of enough weight (expressed as a per cent of the RV weight) to be indiscriminable from RV's to below the interception altitude of the active defense.

The offense will design a payload configuration for each defended target having an optimum allocation to heavy decoys under the assumption that the defense will optimally allocate between active and passive defense. The general problem is depicted by the matrix of Figure 7-2. Here various offensive and

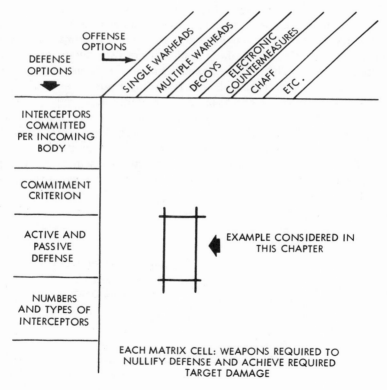

Figure 7-2 *Offense-Defense End-Game Options*

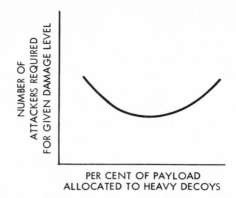

Figure 7–3   *Preferred Offense Option*

defensive options are identified. Entries in the matrix are the number of offensive weapons required for the offense to nullify the defense and accomplish the desired damage to that target. This eliminates the sometimes controversial problem of defining a penetration probability: that is, penetration probability and kill probability are determined jointly. A fundamental assumption for the process is that the offense will select the option minimizing the required number of weapons and that the defense will select the option maximizing this number.

In general, the offense can hide the identity of the selected option (payload composition), whereas the defense has two kinds of options, only one of which can be concealed. The defense's choices regarding resource allocation to active defense, as well as numbers and type of interceptors deployed, types of shelter programs, and so forth, will probably be known in advance to the offense, who can design accordingly. The defense can presumably keep secret such things as ABM system discrimination procedures, interceptor commitment philosophies, and so forth. In the first case, a search of the matrix will yield the optimum solution, whereas in the second case (concealed options) a game-theory solution is required.

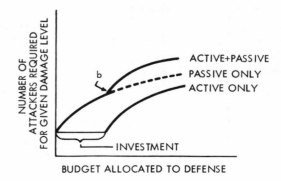

Figure 7–4   *Preferred Defense Option*

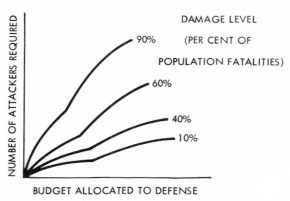

NUMBER OF ATTACKERS REQUIRED

DAMAGE LEVEL

(PER CENT OF

POPULATION FATALITIES)

90%

60%

40%

10%

BUDGET ALLOCATED TO DEFENSE

Figure 7–5   *Max-Min Solution*

Within the restrictions identified above, the offense option is shown in Figure 7–3 and the defense option in Figure 4. In Figure 7–4, "b" indicates the point below which passive defense alone is preferred and above which a combination of active and passive defense is preferred. A computer program has been used to find the offensive and defensive options satisfying the stated criteria. Results similar to Figure 7–5 can be determined for each defended area when varying damage levels are considered. Each point in the figure has associated with it an optimum allocation to heavy decoys for the offense and an optimum defense allocation between BMD and fallout and blast shelters.

Armed with these data, and having selected a national deployment doctrine, optimum allocation can be determined between terminal active defense and passive defense. A rationale for national deployment must first be developed. Such deployment procedure can then be applied to active defense or to suggestions for civil defense deployments, including blast shelters and recuperation facilities.

National deployment involves the interplay between the offense and the defense. A 'max-min' solution, in which the offense targets for maximum exposed population under the assumption that the defense will allocate for minimum destruction, is sought. Consider the case in which the offense consists of only one missile type in varying numbers for use against a group of cities. The best that the offense can do is to target each succeeding missile in an attack so that the "return" from that missile (in terms of expected damage achieved) is greatest. This procedure will result in a function of value destroyed (population fatalities) versus attack size shown by the "no defense" curve in Figure 7–6. The numbered dots along this curve indicate the points at which successively less lucrative targets are first attacked.

The defense now has the option of defending a number of cities to some particular "defense level," k, considering the budget and the number of enemy weapons that may be used. The defense level represents a limit on the vulnerability of the defended cities, expressed in terms of marginal expected fatalities

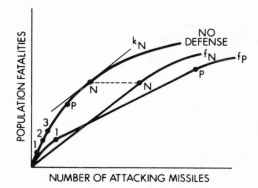

Figure 7–6   *National Damage Function for Various Defense Conditions*

per attacking weapon to which the defense wants to limit the offense in attacks on those cities. It is represented by the slope of the damage curve in Figure 7–6. The defense could select some city (for example, the Nth city on the target list in this example) and deploy defenses at cities $1, 2 \ldots (N - 1)$ so as to reduce their vulnerability to that of N. This would produce the defended damage function f_N. The linear portion of this curve has the same slope (k_N) as the no-defense curve at point N. This function has associated with it an optimum budget. Alternatively, for the same budget, fewer cities (for example, P cities) could be defended to a better defense level—that is, less value lost per attacking weapon (lower slope, k) at the defended cities. But the offense would then target some more-lucrative undefended cities first, then the defended cities 1 through P, then the remaining undefended cities, resulting in damage curve f_P. For small threats f_N is preferred, whereas f_P would be preferred against large threats.

Optimum defense deployments for small threats (those with functions like f_N in Figure 7–6) may be determined by the following process:

1. Construct a no-defense exposed-population curve assuming optimum enemy targeting, and assume a national deployment rationale, such as that of specifying a limit (k) on the "attractiveness" of defended cities as strategic targets.

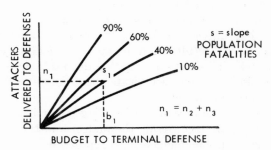

Figure 7–7   *The Max-Min Solution*

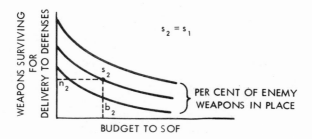

Figure 7–8   *SOF for Damage Limiting*

2. Given this model of undefended vulnerability and deployment rationale, select a defense level, k (damage from one enemy weapon) and the corresponding number of defended cities.

3. Then, using k, compute the price in weapons that the defense must charge at each defended city, as well as the offensive allocation to penetration aids and the allocation between active and passive defense.

4. Repeat for different values of k and numbers of cities defended to determine optimum defense deployments as the defense budget varies.

This process will yield data similar to Figure 7–7 for the United States population. This represents an optimum allocation between terminal active defense, fallout shelters, blast shelters, and recuperation facilities as a function of delivered enemy weapons.

For specified enemy threats, curves similar to Figures 7–8 and 7–9 can be determined for the pre-launch damage-limiting alternatives, SOF and ASW[9].

The final question is how best to allocate resources among these damage-limiting alternatives. The allocation procedure is indicated by the relationships between Figures 7–7 through 7–10. In past studies, the functions of delivered weapons in relation to terminal defense budget (Figure 7–7) have been nearly

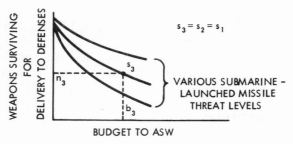

Figure 7–9   *ASW Forces for Damage Limiting*

[9] For the purpose of this example, submarine-launched weapons will be assumed to have the same accuracy and yield as land-launched missiles. Accounting for the differences is conceptually straightforward, although it does make the analysis more burdensome.

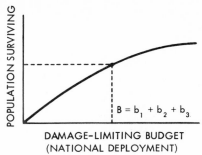

Figure 7–10   *Composite Damage Function*

linear. So for a given damage level, say 40 per cent, in Figure 7–7 there is an associated value of weapons per dollar, slope s_1. By finding similar slopes on curves of Figures 7–8 and 7–9 (points s_2 and s_3) and adding the associated allocations to SOF and ASW (b_2 and b_3), it is possible to find preferred allocations to these two alternatives. Note that these allocations have associated with them deliverable weapons n_2 and n_3. Then Figure 7–7 is entered at a value of delivered weapons, n_1, equal to the sum of n_2 and n_3, to find a budget for terminal defense. The sum of budgets b_1, b_2, and b_3 is the total damage-limiting budget. This corresponds to point B of Figure 7–10. Population surviving as a function of damage-limiting dollars invested is maximized when B is allocated between terminal defense, SOF, and ASW in these quantities. Then, by repeating this procedure for different values of population surviving, it is possible to complete Figure 7–10. This is the desired result.

The damage-limiting budget and assured-damage budget (for example, minimum budget for accomplishing the desired damage levels of Table 7–1) must add to the total available budget. In this example, the following steps were pursued: (1) a total budget level was assumed, (2) deterrence objectives over time (Table 7–1) were specified, (3) a minimum offensive budget was determined, and (4) the resulting damage-limiting budget was determined for entry in Figure 7–10.

Although no interaction between the resulting US deployment and enemy choices has been shown, the final selection of weapon systems must reflect possible reactions of others to US deployments. The same models can be applied to the enemy if the required parameters and criteria can be specified.

CAVEATS AND CONCLUSIONS

Analytic models can be used wisely or foolishly. The results they produce can be helpful or misleading, depending on the skill and judgment with which analyses are designed, conducted, and reported. Hopefully the simplified examples in this chapter will serve to illustrate not only the potential of analytical techniques for dealing with the quantifiable aspects of complex strategic choices but also some of their limitations.

An important contribution made by such analytical techniques in the process of making complex decisions is in forcing interested parties to define rigorously a problem, or a portion of a problem. The analyst, in adapting or devising mathematical models to represent real-world quantities and relationships, requires that the problem be expressed in a set of quantifiable parameters with precisely defined relationships.

But this very quantification can itself be the source of difficulties. It is impossible to present here an exhaustive list of these difficulties or complete guidelines for avoiding or overcoming them. Rather, the example presented earlier in the chapter will be used to illustrate the kinds of questions that must be kept in mind in reporting and using the results of quantitative analysis as aids in strategic decision making.

The process of defining a problem in terms amenable to quantitative analyses, for example, raises many questions such as these:

(1) Is it reasonable to calculate "deterrence" on the basis of levels of damage to strategically important targets in different countries?

(2) Given that the answer to (1) is at least conditionally "yes," is population a reasonable measure of strategic value?

(3) Does threatening a given level of strategic damage first, followed by limiting damage with remaining funds, constitute a reasonable policy?

(4) Is budget an adequate measure of resource limitations for the United States?

Answers to the first three questions cannot be precise. They depend on many intuitive processes and judgments and can only be estimated. The fact that certain answers to these questions have proven acceptable and useful for a period of time should not obscure the fact that the answers (or even the questions) may change under altered circumstances. As a minimum, force deployments based on such estimates should be tested for sensitivity to the principal parameters.

The examples of this chapter used population fatalities as a measure for both US assured damage and US damage-limiting. As mentioned above, other measures of strategic value could have been used. The relative weights assigned to various measures of strategic value can significantly affect force deployments. And although the examples used here assumed identical US and Soviet value measures, asymmetries in the value systems of different nations could have further effect on force requirements.[9]

[9] For example, each nation must ask such questions as: Should a nation give highest defense priority to that which it values most, to that which it thinks an enemy thinks it values most, or to that which it thinks an enemy might most want to destroy?

Consider also that the discussion in this chapter deals with absolute levels of damage (for example, the criteria in Table 7–1). Alternatively attention could be given to the ratio of, or difference between, US and Soviet damage potential (out of concern, perhaps, for relative postwar strength). Although such "score-of-the-war" calculations can be pushed to meaningless extremes, some estimates of relative capability are at least implicit in any discussion of "strategic stability."

Regarding question (4) above, budgets can only be considered as an approximation of all the relevant resource constraints; yet they are clearly the easiest to measure and a useful common denominator. When budget is selected as a single measure, resulting deployments must be checked to see if some other relevant resource, such as available personnel, has not become a controlling constraint. If so, appropriate adjustments in force deployments will be necessary.

Once a problem has been defined in quantitative terms, other difficulties arise concerning the analytic methods to be used. For example:

(1) How valid are expected-value models?

(2) What is the appropriate role of complicated, detailed models compared to simple, general models?

(3) Does a linear-programming model (such as the one used in determining force mixes in this chapter's example) hide many desirable solutions that are nearly optimum?

Expected-value models can lead to significant distortions when used to predict the outcome of a small number of trials. On the other hand, when many trials are involved, little error is introduced by their use. In the evaluation of central war alternatives, where hundreds of missiles and hundreds of targets are involved, expected-value models can be valid. Especially when used in judicious combination with more detailed models (such as Monte-Carlo models of damage to selected cities used to validate expected-value results for national deployments), expected-value models can provide useful inputs otherwise unattainable to the defense-management process.

The analyses on which this chapter's example is based have been discussed in some detail with a fairly wide cross section of defense analysts during the past several years. One criticism raised is that too many decisions are turned over to the machine, since linear programming as used may hide many solutions which were near optimum (and which may be very desirable when factors outside the scope of the analysis are considered) by not printing them out. The only reasonable rejoinder is that computerized techniques allow the comparison of far more alternatives than would be possible by other methods. If in the process some alternatives are overlooked because of the optimization criteria used in a given analysis, it is still true that a larger number of relevant solutions can be brought forth if analytic models are used than otherwise.

The kinds of procedures and models illustrated in this chapter have made and can continue to make vital contributions to defense-management decisions relevant to central-war alternatives. They do not provide ultimate answers. They can be misleading if carelessly used. But if such techniques are used conscientiously, better decisions should result.

RELATED READINGS

1. Dulles, Eleanor L. and Robert D. Crane, eds., *Detente: Cold War Strategies in Transition.* New York: Frederick A. Praeger, Inc., 1965.

2. Herzog, Arthur, *The War-Peace Establishment.* New York: Harper & Row, Publishers, 1965.

3. Hitch, Charles J. and Roland N. McKean, *The Economics of Defense in the Nuclear Age.* Cambridge: Harvard University Press, 1960.

4. Kahn, Herman, *Thinking About the Unthinkable.* New York: Avon Books, 1962.

5. Levine, Robert A., *The Arms Debate.* Cambridge: Harvard University Press, 1963.

6. Martin, Thomas L., Jr. and Donald C. Latham, *Strategy for Survival.* Tucson: University of Arizona Press, 1963.

7. Peck, Merton J. and Frederic M. Scherer, *The Weapons Acquisition Process: An Economic Analysis.* Boston: Harvard University Graduate School of Business Administration, 1962.

HERMAN KAHN
Hudson Institute

Herman Kahn is Director of Hudson Institute and was its principal founder in 1961. Among his major interests at Hudson Institute have been studies on Latin American and other development problems, inquiries into alternative world futures and long-run (10 to 35 years) political, economic, technological and cultural changes, and research into strategic warfare, civil defense, and basic national security policies. Earlier, he was associated for twelve years with The RAND Corporation, where he worked on problems in applied physics and mathematics, operations research and systems analysis, weapon design, particle and radiation diffusion, gamma ray absorption, Monte Carlo methods, war gaming, game theory, civil defense, defense and foreign policies, and strategic warfare. He is the author of *On Thermonuclear War*, *Thinking About the Unthinkable*, and *On Escalation: Metaphors and Scenarios*, as well as many articles for professional journals, periodicals, and books. He has lectured at war colleges, universities, and defense study centers throughout the world and has served as a consultant to numerous governmental commissions and industrial and scientific concerns. Mr. Kahn holds a B.S. degree in physics and mathematics from U.C.L.A. and an M.S. degree in physics from California Institute of Technology.

ANTHONY J. WIENER
Hudson Institute

Anthony J. Wiener is Chairman of the Research Management Council and Assistant to the Director of Hudson Institute, which he joined at its founding in 1961, and where he specializes in political and behavioral science aspects of public policy problems. Previously he was a consultant on political and economic aspects of science and technology with Arthur D. Little, Inc., and taught political science at MIT, where he was a staff member of the Center for International Studies. Earlier positions include Research Fellow of the Society for the Investigation of Human Ecology, Research Associate of the U.S. Joint Commission on Mental Illness and Health, and consultant to various public policy agencies and research projects. His recent researches and publications have dealt with international crises, arms controls, civil defense, NATO, behavioral sciences and international relations, race relations, and poverty. His earlier reports dealt with topics such as social and forensic psychiatry, law and behavioral science, public opinion research, politics and sociology of science in the U.S. and U.S.S.R., and economic development. He is a graduate of Harvard College and Harvard Law School.

8

New Perspective on Civil Defense

INTRODUCTION

Since the inception of the Federal Civil Defense Agency in 1950, Congress has regularly slashed two-thirds to nine-tenths from Administration requests for civil defense. Yet these requests seemed wholly inadequate compared to the potential destructiveness of the all-out, surprise attacks against cities that were until very recently the only threat envisioned. Indeed, the requests were cut as much because of, as in spite of, this perception of inadequacy.

The FCDA itself and a series of authoritative study groups and commissions periodically reached the conclusion that much more extensive programs ($20 to $40 billion dollars) were urgently needed. Yet these "full-scale" proposals did not strengthen Administration bargaining positions for much more modest requests; on the contrary, they added to the prevailing impression that the government programs were hopelessly small compared to the threat. At the same time, the "full-scale" proposals strengthened the fears of those who considered the modest programs a wedge for a new, exorbitantly expensive, and politically powerful federal agency. The "full-scale" proposals seemed to some competitive with the costs of maintaining an adequate deterrent and to others likely to increase international tensions and to create domestic political problems (Ref. 16).

During the past few years however, new possibilities for more effective protection relative to expenditures at various budgetary levels have been studied. Some of these are now being emphasized because of important changes in the international and technological environments. (These changes are discussed at greater length in Ref. 6.) One implication of these studies is to make "low-casualty" programs appear surprisingly feasible for a wide range of contingencies and at much lower cost than previously estimated. This chapter summarizes some of the more important developments (especially those currently being studied at Hudson Institute)[1]. They serve to create novel perspectives on the appropriate criteria, of effectiveness and of economic and political costs, for the evaluation of civil defense programs. These new perspectives lead to new orientations and organizational criteria for future civil defense programs.

Effectiveness for What Contingencies?

The current strategic environment is characterized by (1) a reduction of tension between the United States and the Soviet Union, especially concerning strategic warfare; (2) a widespread belief that nuclear weapons will not be used,

[1] We wish to acknowledge the contributions, in the form of prior work done on this and related subjects, that were made to this paper by our Hudson Institute colleagues, especially Paul C. Berry, William M. Brown, Raymond D. Gastil, Frederick C. Rockett and Max Singer. (See References.) The views expressed, however, are not necessarily those of our colleagues, nor can they be attributed to the Hudson Institute or any of its contract sponsors; they are the responsibility of the authors alone.

at least for the next decade or so; and (3) an increasing strategic invulnerability on both sides, combined with U.S. preponderance. At the same time, the history of Soviet military behavior suggests a high degree of conservatism and defensive emphasis. These factors suggest that the threat of a deliberate, planned, large-scale Soviet attack is very small compared to other possibilities for the outbreak of nuclear war. In both the current and the expected situation, no one seems likely to jump into thermonuclear war—but backing in remains a possibility.

Analysis of the kinds of escalations and crises (Refs. 11, 17) that could least implausibly result in the detonation of nuclear weapons on the United States suggests that the "design cases" for civil defense planning should be some variations of the following scenario: (1) a very intense crisis; (2) some kind of "strategic warning" of hours, days, or weeks; (3) some likelihood of limited counterforce attacks on U.S. allies, and/or explicit threats and very small counterforce; (4) possibly followed by small or "ragged" countervalue attacks on the United States; (5) before a large city attack—if any—would be carried out.[2]

The major conclusion for civil defense planning is that small or intrawar attacks, arising out of deep crises, are (1) apparently the least unlikely, (2) the easiest and cheapest to prepare against, (3) and yet, as of this writing, among the most neglected of civil defense contingencies. Although the possibility of unforeshadowed, massive attack should not be ignored, the relative overemphasis on it has hampered realistic planning efforts.

New Program Elements

A more realistic allocation of emphases leads to increased interest in civil defense and emergency planning programs containing some or all of the following elements: (1) a tension mobilization base; (2) a crisis mobilization base; (3) a postattack recuperation base; (4) low-casualty fallout programs that utilize movement of population outside of likely blast areas and to fallout shelters of a protection factor proportionate to likely fallout intensity; (5) programs that increase blast protection in proportion to population density, in order to increase the efficiency of money spent on blast shelters by reducing to some constant the number of casualties that can be caused anywhere by a single warhead of a given size; and (6) possible agreements on arms control and increased defense, including some cooperation between the U.S., the Soviet Union, and others, on civil defense measures.

In the following sections, we discuss some of the strategic and political aspects of such program elements and indicate how they suggest new perspectives on costs and on effectiveness of civil defense programs. New understandings of the

---

[2] Although it is necessary to use some such term as "strategic warning" or "crisis warning," it is important to be conscious of how complex such a concept is; whether a signal or event is "warning" depends on many difficult-to-predict factors, especially the perceived costs and value of the response being considered (see Refs. 13 and 8).

strategic and political situation now provide an opportunity to create a civil defense and emergency planning program, both more appropriate to the threat and more realistic in cost. This might be a federalized, professionalized program oriented toward creating a comparatively inexpensive base from which rapid and important increases in protection could be achieved if tensions increased or an emergency arose.

A well-designed program based on these concepts should attract more serious consideration by Congress and the public than civil defense programs have had before: Because mobilization bases cost relatively little (unless and until they are activated), the cost of such insurance might for the first time seem proportionate to its probable usefulness. Because a relatively limited nuclear attack arising relatively slowly from an escalating crisis would allow the time for planned expansion and for improvised measures, the program might both appear and actually be adequate for a wide range of important contingencies. Of course, such a program should also provide a meaningful capability against "worst cases," though relatively unlikely "worst cases" should not be "design cases."

New Orientations

Reorienting the civil defense program toward these new requirements might warrant increased professionalization of personnel and strengthened federal control over local organization and operations. This would decrease the dependence on untrained or poorly trained local personnel and volunteers and would almost eliminate the interactions of civil defense and local politics and the direct involvement of the public in civil defense decisions. Primarily, such reorganization would enable better civil defense; in addition, there would be important political advantages in shifting such decisions to the realm of professional expertise and ordinary defense procedures, subject to the usual public scrutiny; but not embroiled in local political decision processes.

Improvements in organization, doctrine, and capability introduced since 1961 have strengthened civil defense considerably. At the same time, the 1961–62 controversy probably left a long-lasting potential for public controversy over civil defense. Nevertheless, a reoriented program could incorporate civil defense into U.S. national security policies and perhaps remove it from political imbroglio to new effectiveness and acceptability. However, the effect of civil defense and emergency planning on local interests and on other federal agencies will probably preclude as much freedom from controversy as, for example, air defense. Programs within the traditional scope of military expertise tend not to be closely questioned by Congress or the public, but civil defense, which seems less technical, may be disputed and cut back in spite of its possibly superior cost-effectiveness. Furthermore, new civil defense programs involve elements such as construction budgets on which, unlike many military items, members of Congress may feel well-qualified to dispute.

One important by-product of a more expert, centralized, and professionalized civil defense program is that the present uncertainty concerning the performance of the program could be significantly reduced. In fact, it should be possible to design expert professional programs whose performance, under many contingencies, can be relatively accurately estimated, thus gaining greater advantages from cost-effectiveness studies.

A program that has become independent of direct local support, has been strengthened in its professional and expert character, and has been integrated with current strategic thinking through reorientation to mobilization bases might receive increased support from Congress, the public, the military, and the Administration. Once the changes have been made, the program might have good prospects for being continued routinely, without the need for continual Presidential intervention to save it.

THE PLACE OF CIVIL DEFENSE IN OVER-ALL NATIONAL POLICY

Civil Defense and Strategy

The present strategic and political situation should reduce concern about the effect of civil defense programs on the "balance of terror." Unless some unexpected vulnerability is discovered, present and prospective weapons balances are such that surprise attack would make little or no sense for either side, regardless of civil defense measures. In the absence of any but the most elaborate and improbable active defense, both sides seem likely to retain an ability to retaliate after a counterforce first strike and to destroy, at a minimum, an enormous amount of property in empty cities, even if the population were entirely protected.

Under these conditions, civil defense functions primarily as insurance, as one aspect of the government's acceptance of its civic and moral responsibility to try to defend people against disasters, whatever their cause. However, it can still serve as a strategic element: in severe crises a civil defense capability may aid the resolve of decision makers countering the pressure of aggressive, reckless or foolish opponents. The capability may help stabilize a situation strategically by increasing extended deterrence,[3] and in psychological ways by minimizing the likelihood of irrational behavior a leader who can determine the risk and perceive its limits may be less likely to panic, lose control, or bluff unreasonably. He may be better able to make calculations without fear of a catastrophic loss of will or morale. His situation contrasts favorably with that of the leader who feels nuclear war will inevitably mean the end of his society, and yet feels he must risk it or threaten it credibly in order to deter aggression.

[3] That is, deterrence not only of direct attacks, but of extreme provocations. At a minimum, extended deterrence requires perception by the opponent of national willingness to execute war-risking policies or even to make deliberate and credible threats in some extremely grave crisis.

Arms Control and the Détente

Arms limitations and disarmament may be quite consistent with civil defense, since they both attempt to reduce the level of destruction of wars. Thus, while both sides may gain through symmetrical or parallel offensive weapon reduction, both would lose protection through symmetrical or parallel CD limitations. Soviet CD will not threaten us in the next decade (unless combined with surprisingly effective ABM capabilities and unexpectedly large increases in offensive capabilities).

There seems to be a sound basis for U.S.-S.U. cooperation in civil defense—it would reduce both domestic and international political costs of deploying defensive systems. Furthermore, if the United States had more effective civil defense capabilities, inspection requirements for future arms control agreements would be reduced and comprehensive arms control would be more feasible and therefore more likely (since a well-defended country is not so vulnerable if an agreement is violated). It is possible that civil defense can be most useful when combined with arms control, and perhaps even vice versa (see Refs. 1 and 9).

Under the current conditions of détente and mutual invulnerability, it seems highly unlikely that adding moderate capabilities for active and passive defense would accelerate an offense-defense arms race. Furthermore, adding such capabilities would buy—on the margin—much more damage-limiting potential than would comparable spending for offensive weapons.

SOME NEW PROGRAM ELEMENTS

A Tension Mobilization Base

Lessened emphasis on the problems of central war, which has resulted from diminished tension between the great powers, is, of course, desirable, but can lead to official neglect of issues that require continuous thought and discussion. As history has often illustrated, international tensions can build up quite rapidly. Renewed tensions might create a sudden demand for a civil defense capability that normally would take several years to develop. The OCD should develop an operational plan to reduce sharply the time ordinarily required for obtaining an improved posture. Indeed, plans are needed for a range of options that could be activated as alternatives or simultaneously. A complete urban blast shelter posture would normally require a lead time of five to ten years, but combined with other programs it may be possible to develop a "stockpile" of plans, experimental shelters, supplies, siting analyses, and contractor experience that would enable very rapid construction. (For example, if proper plans, preparations, and motivation existed, it might be possible to spend effectively

$20 to $40 billion on a shelter program in well under one year.[4]) Suggestions for "mass-producing" blast shelters should be solicited and studied seriously.

The Soviets have suffered a considerable economic strain by their reaction to our defense budget increases since 1950 and should wish to avoid being drawn into any new "race." Thus the speed with which we could deploy a significant active or passive defense capability could be important for deterrence as well as damage-limiting if the present détente deteriorates seriously.

A CRISIS MOBILIZATION BASE

Even if tensions remain low, it is still possible for an intense crisis to escalate relatively rapidly (see Ref. 17). If budgets remain low, OCD could probably devote much of its current effort to developing and maintaining a capability to utilize the few days, weeks, or months the country may have to increase protection if a severe crisis develops. Preparations before a crisis begins could include some mixture of paper plans for evacuation, training of necessary personnel (for example, those concerned with emergency control of food and transportation), the development or improvement of fallout shelters, especially outside of major urban areas, and work on mobilization bases for significant blast shelter programs.

If well directed and supplied, most of the required new shelters might be constructed, in most weather conditions, by the evacuees themselves. (Frozen ground in northern winters would require special supplies or alternatives, of course.) The fact that public fallout shelters are an accepted, if not fully budgeted, part of national policy would facilitate the development of a powerful core of rural shelters and shelter managers that could be extremely useful in a crisis.[5]

It is necessary for the development in peacetime of crisis programs involving evacuation that the appropriate officials understand the following points:

(1) Currently discussed evacuation concepts are not based on the idea of "outrunning the missile," but rather on the important possibility that the development of crises and wars would give sufficient "strategic warning," perhaps days or weeks.

(2) Prevention of evacuee "panic" is probably manageable, as indicated by a great deal of

---

[4] The U.S. construction industry currently has a capacity of more than $100 billion a year. Unlike most military or industrial suppliers, it is readily deployable if advanced plans have been made. Of course, time-consuming operations, such as land acquisition, must be achieved in advance, or bypassed in the crisis. For example, land could be acquired on a contingent basis, or at least selected.

[5] Three years ago a Hudson Institute study estimated that with appropriate plans, proper motivation, and good leadership, American resources are sufficient that in two days' time it should be possible "to develop more civil defense capability during this time than has been obtained during the . . . years following World War II." (See Ref. 5.) That estimate does not seem to need revision because of the civil defense capability that has been added in the last three years.

indirect evidence, analysis of analogies, and some recent experiences with hurricanes and other disasters with comparable warning times.

(3) For many reasons the Soviets (or Nth countries) are unlikely to have, or be able to use, or have sufficient reason to use enough weapons so effectively to blanket great rural areas with blast, fire, or sufficient fallout, as to nullify all or most of the increased protection afforded by improvised shelters.

(4) Current studies of the Soviet threat, the American economy, and comparable historical situations indicate that for most of the central war possibilities that can be termed *likely* in the next decade, the country would have the physical capability to recover from the damage in a relatively rapid fashion (5 to 15 years in much the same way that Japan and West Germany did).

(5) In the event that a very intense crisis should occur with no other preparations having been made, analogous experience indicates that public cooperation with emergency evacuation measures would probably take place reasonably smoothly, and mainly on the basis of self-protecting, humane, prudent, and altruistic motives, rather than the often-feared panic and bellicosity.

One crisis evacuation measure which might save as many as 20 to 30 million Americans has been described as "medium-city evacuation" (see Ref. 15). Aside from the twelve largest metropolitan areas and those areas without an adequate nearby reception area, about one hundred cities may be evacuated in less than ten hours to a close "ring" area containing reception fallout shelters (including, in the cheaper programs, crisis-prepared shelters). These rings might include communities 15 to 50 miles from the urban center. These distances would enable many persons to commute to city jobs during part of the intra-war or crisis period. Aside from being a useful concept for saving citizens, medium-city evacuation would work well in a program that initially provides blast protection for only the largest cities, whether or not such a program was undertaken in fact.

A Postattack Recuperation Base[6]

Although the public fallout shelter program has been generally accepted, the creation of new strategic systems arouses widespread (and in some cases valid) fears of the arms race and growing international tension. Those who share these fears might object strongly to any large civil defense efforts beyond fallout protection. Even these opponents of defense might agree, however, that the current arms control and détente atmosphere could be preserved while a related and alternative capability is developed through a program of national supply management.

It is widely recognized that in the initial postattack environment there would be much more gross production capacity than production because of

---

[6] Under P.L. 920 and Executive Order 10,952, postattack recovery is not included among the tasks of the Office of Civil Defense, Department of the Army, but remains the responsibility of the Office of Emergency Planning, Executive Office of the President. Civil defense, however, obviously can and should be designed to alleviate the recovery task, and civil defense programs should be evaluated on the basis of their potential contributions to long-term recovery, as well as by other criteria.

organizational problems and bottlenecks in critical parts and materials. The men and machines needed to fabricate these parts and materials might, for example, be destroyed together with the warehoused stocks. It is important to determine what postattack supplies may be in widest demand and shortest supply either regionally or nationally. The most important items could then be stockpiled in dispersed locations. (Medical organizations, for example, have successfully advanced a program for widely dispersed hospital and medical supplies.) Such stockpiling would not reduce the number of direct casualties the Soviets could inflict, but might increase greatly the ability of the immediate survivors to recover. It would give the country a better "theory of survival," and help fulfill current Federal responsibilities to these potential survivors.

Stockpiling is usually an expensive option, and is frequently beset by problems of deterioration, maintenance, and obsolescence. These drawbacks can largely be overcome by judicious employment of crisis preparations and post-tension mobilization. During relatively peaceful times, plans and preparations might consist mostly of thinking through and organizing a system for necessary action if international relations deteriorated seriously. Thus, were we to enter a threatening new situation, we might not only wish to budget perhaps $20 billion on shelters, but a similar or greater amount on recovery stockpiles and methods of protecting property. In a rapidly intensifying crisis, emergency measures for improving recuperation prospects are possible, though they would require the cooperation of most of the population. These would, of course, be phased in with emergency survival measures.

"Balanced" Fallout Protection

Using fallout shelters located in expected non-target areas is a practical, inexpensive design for civil defense which could save almost the entire population in many of the plausible attacks. Such a design requires sufficient planning and adequate strategic warning for movement of civilians from urban areas. In most places in the United States, radiation intensities could be controlled in all but large wars, since outside the target areas there seems to be sufficient shelter potential to provide the minimum survival protection (Ref. 14). Furthermore, movement of almost all the population from metropolitan areas in a matter of hours or days, during crises, appears feasible (Ref. 5).

There are two approaches to the goal of providing at least minimum radiation protection for everybody: (1) levels of fallout protection can be graded ("balanced") to meet predicted threats of radiation at some specified level of confidence, or (2) protection can be so ample that variations in predicted threats can be ignored. The "balanced" protection concepts could lead to comparatively inexpensive programs of high effectiveness, since they avoid the inherent risks of programs in which an arbitrary minimum protection factor qualifies a structure as a fallout shelter anywhere in the nation.

Studies of past civil defense programs (and the recently proposed full fallout shelter program) have estimated large numbers of casualties from city attacks, partly because they assumed urban shelters, vulnerable to blast. In moderate to large countercity attacks, nearly complete destruction of the urban population must indeed be predicted, unless blast shelters are used or evacuation is carried out.

Relocation of the urban population, if completed in time, can produce almost complete protection from the primary effects of weapons delivered against cities and military targets, and capabilities for doing this can be found at a relatively modest peacetime cost. In contrast, urban blast shelters offer less complete protection, are relatively expensive, and for political, economic, and technical reasons may not be available in time for use. Moreover, they might not be fully used in crises, because a significant number of people might prefer to leave the cities, rather than trust the shelters. Thus, if a highquality blast shelter system is not developed in peacetime, civil defense programs based on timely movement from target areas may be the best alternative. (In the next section, however, we suggest some perspectives on comparatively inexpensive and high-quality blast protection.)

There have been several studies on the feasibility of evacuation based on "strategic warning." As yet, no single negating factor has been found, although there are obviously uncertainties and difficulties about deciding when the situation justifies the government ordering an evacuation, estimating how much time can be allowed, and deciding how long, and to what degree, to try to keep people from returning to the cities. Historical evidence indicates that millions have successfully moved away from war's dangers under a variety of circumstances. Evacuation is an important aspect of civil defense programs in Sweden, Britain, the U.S.S.R., and other countries. Moreover, evacuation may not only be feasible in the United States, but in many crisis situations at least partial evacuation would occur, officially sponsored or not (Ref. 13).

For attacks delivering less than about 3,000 megatons, people could survive with modest shelter (with protection factors of about 20) in most non-target areas, because the intensity of fallout radiation generally declines rapidly with distance from targets. With some advance preparations, available shelters could be developed in most plausible emergency situations to meet local minimum requirements for radiation protection. (In the years ahead, however, much larger attacks might become important possibilities, and readily available shelter such as basements and low PF rural buildings would then be even less adequate even for minimum protection.)

Except for planning errors, substandard preparations, and the possibility of relatively ineffective attacks against evacuees, the number of casualties should be low if a balanced fallout shelter program is implemented and used successfully. Analysis of the kinds of strategic situations, threats, and attempts to bargain that are most likely to precede an attack indicates that sufficiently recognizable and timely warning will probably be present. The benefits of conducting studies and preparing plans that keep available the option to evacuate to prepared and improvised balanced fallout protection seem very large, relative to the peacetime costs.

Blast Shelters of Varying Hardness

Although deploying any substantial blast shelter protection may be undesirable in the present détente, there are several reasons not to drop interest in research, planning, and possibly in acquiring a significant mobilization base:

First, it would appear that although the lack of a good Soviet counterforce capability makes *any* attack very unlikely, a small attack aimed at cities should be taken as seriously as any other possibility.

Second, system designs have been developed recently that rationalize and improve the effectiveness of blast shelter programs by using shelters of varying hardness to limit the damage that any one enemy bomb can cause. In one such system design, each standard enemy weapon is limited by the shelter system to a specified maximum number of blast fatalities, no matter what its point of impact.[7] For example, each one-megaton weapon might be limited to 10,000 blast fatalities by varying the psi (pounds per square inch of blast overpressure) ratings of urban area shelters from 10 to 300, in proportion to population density. Central New York City and a few other extraordinarily densely populated areas would be treated as special cases, and for these a partial local dispersion of people to blast shelters outside downtown areas is a possible solution. In this case, the program must have a few hours of effective "tactical" warning to achieve maximum protection. With this posture, during a prolonged crisis the essential activities of even these few cities would not depend on workers commuting from outlying shelters (Ref. 2).

Third, studies have indicated great savings from reducing shelter space per occupant below current assumptions about minimum standards. The feasibility of this reduction is based upon: (1) analysis and comparison with other "bearable" crowded situations; (2) reorganization of shelter space; (3) improved management of environmental factors other than area; (4) increased willingness to accept some risks of casualties from overcrowding; and (5) the need for providing interim protection during the early phases of a more extensive program.

Fourth, recent intense discussion of projected active defense systems has led to cost-effectiveness comparisons of blast shelters and active defense, as well as to consideration of the possible optimum mixture of these two systems. It now seems quite clear that with substantial programs (in excess of $15–20 billion) and no opportunity for evacuation to distant fallout shelters, a preferred defense would combine fallout shelters in rural areas and both blast shelters and active defenses in urban areas. With smaller programs (less than $15 billion), it becomes difficult to justify much expenditure on ballistic-missile defense, unless one assigns either a surprisingly high performance to BMD or an unusually high utility to property compared to people. However, a few billion dollars

---

[7] Of course, there are other targeting criteria, such as the value of buildings, and these could be introduced into the model to reduce further the relative attractiveness of any particular target to the attacker.

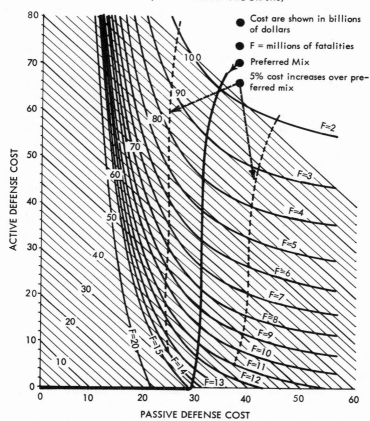

Figure 8–1   *Example of Cost Effectiveness of Varying Active-Passive Defense Mixes (with Specified Programs)*

(beyond programmed R&D) even out of a $15 billion total might be a good investment in active defense against the possibility of unsophisticated attacks and to provide a capability for rapid future expansion of the active defense. This seems to be justifiable even though some recent cost-effectiveness calculations, based primarily upon the criterion of civilian fatalities, indicate that all funds available for defense should be allocated for civil defense, up to a critical amount, beyond which most funds should be spent for active defense. The critical amount is related to a number of choices in deployment, system costs, and the nature of the attacks the system is optimized against. One "typical" result is shown in Figure 8–1, which assumes a 5,000-MT urban threat, much larger than the "design case" we suggested before. The figure is not intended as an argument for a particular program but as an illustration of the kinds of results that are reached if one uses the kinds of assumptions about the cost effectiveness of the defense components and the nature of the attack which we have argued are reasonable. (For more details, see Ref. 3 and the discussion of alternative specified programs. This illustration is drawn from Figure 9 of Ref. 3, which shows one of a family of possible mixes.)

Despite the superficially complicated appearance, this diagram is quite straightforward. The "preferred mix" curve simply connects the points that represent the lowest total costs at each level of fatalities. The dotted lines show the sensitivity of the preferred mix to an increase of 5 per cent over the minimum-cost program for each level of fatalities. Because of the improved design of the civil defense component, our calculations allocate relatively more to civil defense than do most other studies; if comparable improvements could be made in active defense, the preferred mix would, of course, be shifted to the left.

Blast and fallout shelter programs can be designed that would enable very high percentages to survive the short-term effects of an attack, but would still leave possibly critical questions of recovery and recuperation from moderate or large attacks. Improved protective designs present a reasonably feasible solution to the technical problems of insuring the survival of most of the population from the immediate effects of even large and irrationally malevolent attacks, up to about 10,000 MT, and the costs involved would not prevent future reduction of the per cent of GNP devoted to defense; but potential recovery and long-term recuperation from moderate or large malevolent attacks involve great uncertainties. One of the best potentials for alleviating postattack problems is probably the addition of active defense systems, which can aid recovery by protecting property as well as people, by reducing the total of megatonnage delivered, and by reducing the proportion of weapons that are groundburst and create large amounts of "local" fallout. However, using the standard assumptions, much more spending on passive defense would be worthwhile before active defense begins to offer cost-effectiveness advantages.

Arms Control and Civil Defense

It is sometimes argued that under certain circumstances defensive systems could reduce the costs of nuclear war enough to make war more likely. However, the goals of civil defense are basically very similar to the goals of arms control, that is, to reduce the probability and/or the destructiveness of war. Thus, it is useful to consider possibilities that combine the advantages of both approaches to damage reduction.

Arms Control and Defense. One interesting possibility is a policy we have described as "Arms Control and Defense" (see Ref. 7, 12, and 18). This policy attempts to improve actual defense of the country in a nuclear war, without increasing the danger of an arms race in peacetime, by freezing or substantially reducing the nuclear weapons inventories of the great powers, while procuring extensive active and passive defenses. The two objectives support one another, for the limits on offensive weapons may make the defense procurements politically and economically acceptable in a détente world, while the improved defenses reduce inspection requirements for arms control agreements by reducing the marginal advantages of cheating.

In a world in which combined arms control and defense agreements had been made, nations would not only be deterred by the threat of nuclear war, but also by the knowledge that their opponents are more difficult to intimidate through "nuclear blackmail." Furthermore, smaller nations that otherwise could compete with the superpowers in the capacity to destroy largely undefended cities, would find it much more difficult, psychologically as well as economically and technologically, to threaten (or deter) the superpowers (except possibly for comparatively small and esoteric attacks, such as "suitcase bombs"). Thus two of the major incentives for nuclear proliferation would be reduced: policing by the superpowers of crises involving Nth countries would be easier, and potential Nth countries would probably realize that they have been "priced out of the market" for competitive strategic systems.

Cooperative Civil Defense. Another of the mutually reinforcing possibilities for civil defense and arms control is cooperative civil defense.[8] In a détente in which the primary strategic problems of the superpowers may become, at least in public, the prevention of dangers of nuclear use through accident or by Nth countries, cooperative civil defense arrangements (implicit or explicit) embracing the United States, its closer allies, and the Soviet Union might be acceptable. By this means, the civil defense efforts of all nations concerned would more likely be considered prudential and humane, rather than strategic, war-supporting goals. (The advantages of extended deterrence in crises would remain for the superpowers against Nth countries, though not so much against each other.)

Agreements to cooperate in deploying civil defense would be in the national interest for at least the following reasons:

(1) Such an agreement would provide experience in working together for U.S. and Soviet officials—experience that should be transferable to other areas.

(2) Fears that defense deployment might be "provocative" would be allayed if it were done by agreement.

(3) There would be less vocal internal opposition to a more comprehensive program, including elements of blast and CBR protection.

(4) It is worth repeating that, according to publicly projected force balances for the next decade, no matter how good either side's ABM-CD programs might become within realistic limits, then barring the unlikely possibility of certain bizarre crises, choosing nuclear war would be likely to result in unacceptable destruction, i.e., it would not be a preferred alternative even to a relatively irrational decision maker.

(5) Protecting citizens of either side makes possible a less destructive counterforce option for the other side's forces in the event of initially unintended escalation to nuclear war. (This may be an advantage for either or both sides.)

---

[8] The proposal is discussed in more detail in Ref. 1, especially Chapter VII.

Although there have been some favorable reactions, it would be politically unrealistic to expect much enthusiasm in the near future for cooperative civil defense in the U.S. government, or the Soviet, of course. However, an agreement to cooperate in civil defense development would still be a valuable arms control measure, since it would symbolize most dramatically the common interest in protecting citizens. This may be politically much clearer under many conceivable circumstances, e.g., extreme nuclear proliferation or (an admittedly impossible degree of) Chinese nuclear bellicosity.

SOME POLITICAL COSTS OF CIVIL DEFENSE

Analysis of the domestic political controversy begun by the civil defense program of 1961 indicated that civil defense programs mainly do not (and need not) have socio-political effects unfavorable to arms control (see Ref. 16). Opposition came from a very small (but influential) segment of the population, according to public opinion data, and was expressed primarily in terms of arguments that were also intrinsically arguments against deterrence. (Indeed, it was also argued frequently that civil defense *was* necessarily part of deterrence and could not properly be considered insurance. Once this point was made, the anti-deterrence arguments could be invoked.) If it is argued that civil defense can enable the President to deter hostile actions by increasing his willingness to risk, threaten, or engage in a use of nuclear weapons that risks retaliation, opposition to extended deterrence will probably continue, although many opinion leaders will probably understand and favor an increased capacity to deter crises.

However, the arms control and defense and cooperative civil defense programs suggested here as alternatives would be much more difficult to depict or perceive as anything but prudential. The mobilization bases would not require anxiety-provoking actions and decisions from individuals and local communities. The equal-casualty or equal-risk (rather than equal-protection-factor or equal-expenditure) principle of the blast shelter program should not be too difficult to clarify for those who ultimately shape public opinion.

Something is lost, of course, if civil defense programs are advocated solely as insurance, and not as "part of the deterrent." In 1961 CD was opposed by some who did not consider "mere insurance" worth the premium, preferring to rely entirely on deterrence provided by strategic weapons. The most vocal opposition, however, came from those to whom deterrence (especially extended deterrence) seemed provocative and arms-race tending, or who feared that U.S. civil defense would impair the present stability of deterrence—that is, those who feared U.S. civil defense would weaken the Soviet capacity to deter the U.S. from striking first.

Current objections on the basis of these political costs should be greatly diminished compared to 1961. The programs discussed in this chapter consist primarily of mobilization bases and cooperative measures in a context of mutual strategic invulnerability and détente. Although such programs could have some strategic value for a very intense crisis, they are not likely to disturb current stability. Opposition to CD as "not worth the money" should also be reduced, for from a cost-effectiveness point of view, both mobilization bases and programs designed for other than "worst cases" are much better investments than either large programs designed against massive attacks or small programs that cannot handle massive attacks.

But, as has often been pointed out, civil defense needs steady support from the Executive Office to achieve even modest population protection. A substantially larger civil defense program than the current one could provide a considerable degree of protection for the country. But it would have to be effectively supported by the President, the Secretary of Defense, and the Department of the Army and be presented not as a response to new dangers, but as insurance and as a further rationalization of our strategic defense posture toward a more balanced and stable international situation.

CONCLUSION

Reorganization for New Roles

So long as civil defense was not an integrated part of national security doctrine and the normal military establishment, its effectiveness seemed at best conjectural, the costs of a "reasonable" program seemed excessive, if not absurd, and funds and political support remained inadequate. Inevitably, organizational arrangements were also unsatisfactory. Responsibility for a large range of functions, including long-range planning, coordination with the military and with other agencies, peacetime disaster relief, shelter marking and management, training, warning, construction, evacuation, rescue, and postattack resource management and recovery was divided among many agencies, all undergoing frequent reorganization. Important functions were delegated to other agencies, where they were understandably neglected in favor of more immediate tasks. Action programs and immediate survival were organizationally separated from long-range planning and post-attack recovery, and the latter, important but less urgent concerns, were comparatively neglected. Finally, troublesome gaps in immediate programs were left unfilled because of dependence on state, local and volunteer contributions.

Alternatives for organizing the wide range of civil defense functions and for locating them in the governmental system have been studied frequently. Many different arrangements have been suggested and quite a few have actually been tried—yet none has seemed satisfactory for long.

However, if a program were to be adopted emphasizing a federalized, professionalized cadre, commissioned to prepare a mobilization base, the incentive to try another administrative structure would be greatly diminished. The current organization—or any reasonable alternative—would probably work fairly well with such a program, given adequate financing. Yet a new orientation for the program would itself provide new criteria for improving the organization. For example, the present division between OEP/NSC and OCD/DOA/DOD and the current distribution of Federal and state and local responsibilities may be ripe for reappraisal.

Such a reappraisal would be pointless if it merely weighed once again the considerations involved in each of the many reorganizations of the last fifteen years. The recent progress of the civil defense program would merely vindicate current arrangements. But if the progress is to continue, more of the planning, line, and "delegated" functions may need to be consolidated in one organization that contains no elements of facade. The new strategic and political situation, combined with new possibilities for program elements of very high cost-effectiveness, lend hope that such a reoriented and reorganized civil defense program could attain new effectiveness.

Criteria for Evaluating Effectiveness

There are never absolute guarantees of security. One cannot properly judge a program by asking, "Is it *guaranteed* to work?" A more useful criterion is the standard implied in such questions as: "Under what likely circumstances are the program's results useful enough to justify its various costs and disutilities?"

On this basis, we believe that programs including some or all the elements we have discussed—especially the mobilization bases—should now be considered seriously. We believe that such programs would very likely have significant effectiveness, in the unlikely but not-impossible event of war, against a large range of plausible Soviet, Chinese, and other weapons systems and tactics. Such programs could have some peacetime value in deterring crises and supporting foreign policy and would not tend to stimulate offense-defense arms races. The costs would be low compared to previous and future reductions in the strategic defense budget and very low compared to projected expenditures for nuclear weapons and delivery systems. Neither the domestic nor the international political difficulties seem excessive in comparison with the benefits that may be obtained. In sum, these new developments, in the new situation, can lead to much more effective and, in the broadest sense, much less costly programs for protecting populations than have heretofore been thought possible.

REFERENCES*

1. Brennan, Donald G., ed., *Arms Control and Civil Defense*, HI-216-RR. Harmon-on-Hudson, New York: Hudson Institute, December 2, 1963.

   * Since this chapter focuses on new perspectives on civil defense being developed at Hudson Institute, we have not supplied references beyond our own supporting studies.

2. Brown, William M., *The Design and Performance of "Optimum" Blast Shelter Programs*, HI-361-RR/2. Harmon-on-Hudson, New York: Hudson Institute, June 11, 1964.

3. ———., *Potential of Damage-Limiting Systems*, HI-651-RR, Harmon-on-Hudson, New York: Hudson Institute, February 14, 1966.

4. ———., *A New Look at the Design of Low-Budget Civil Defense Systems*, HI-478-RR. Harmon-on-Hudson, New York: Hudson Institute, August 2, 1965.

5. ———., *Strategic and Tactical Aspects of Civil Defense with Special Emphasis on Crisis Programs*, HI-160-RR. Harmon-on-Hudson, New York: Hudson Institute, January 7, 1964, Chapter IV, p. 7.

6. Brown, William M., Raymond D. Gastil, Herman Kahn, and Anthony J. Wiener, *Changing Prospects, Missions and Roles for Civil Defense: 1965–1975*, HI-447-RR. Harmon-on-Hudson, New York: Hudson Institute, February 22, 1965.

7. Gastil, Raymond D., "Comments on Strategic Alternatives and Arms Control and Defense," in *Some Approaches to Damage-Limiting Studies*, Part II, HI-459-RR/11. Harmon-on-Hudson, New York: Hudson Institute, November 20, 1964.

8. ———., *Problems in the Usability of Strategic Warning for Increased Readiness*, HI-488-D. Harmon-on-Hudson, New York: Hudson Institute, February 15, 1965.

9. ———., "A Prudential Nuclear Policy," Chapter 10. (Draft volume.)

10. ———., *The Relation of Increased Readiness Programs to Peacetime Strategic Choices and Arms Control*, HI-489-D. Harmon-on-Hudson, New York: Hudson Institute, February 17, 1965.

11. Kahn, Herman, *On Escalation: Metaphors and Scenarios*. New York: Frederick A. Praeger, Inc., 1965.

12. ———., *A Paradigm for the 1965–1975 Strategic Debate*, HI-202-FR. Harmon-on-Hudson, New York: Hudson Institute, November 22, 1963.

13. Rockett, Frederick C., *A Discussion of a Policy of Increased Readiness for Civil Defense*, HI-477-RR (Rev.). Harmon-on-Hudson, New York: Hudson Institute, May 20, 1965.

14. Rockett, Frederick C. and William M. Brown, *An Analysis of Local Protection Factor Requirements and Resources*, HI-486-RR. Harmon-on-Hudson, New York: Hudson Institute, June 11, 1965.

15. Singer, Max, *Phasing of Crisis Civil Defense Programs*, HI-330-D. Harmon-on-Hudson, New York: Hudson Institute, February 14, 1964.

16. Wiener, Anthony J., *Arms Control and Civil Defense: The Domestic Political Interactions*, HI-216-RR/IV. Harmon-on-Hudson: New York, Hudson Institute: August 20, 1963.

17. Wiener, Anthony J. and Herman Kahn, *Crises and Arms Control*, HI-180-RR. Harmon-on-Hudson, New York: Hudson Institute, October 9, 1962.

18. Williamson, Paul, *On a New Arms Control Strategy*, HI-390-RR. Harmon-on-Hudson, New York: Hudson Institute, February 24, 1965.

RICHARD B. RAINEY, JR.

The RAND Corporation

Richard B. Rainey, Jr. has been a staff member of The RAND Corporation since 1956. He was, until recently, leader of a group in the Logistics Department which has done many studies of military airlift, sealift, and prepositioning as well as many comparisons of the relative ability of Western powers and the Chinese and Soviet Blocs to project and support military power in remote areas. Recently he began the direction of a major new interdisciplinary project which is examining the structure and function of United States general purpose and airlift-sealift forces as instruments of foreign policy. The study will also relate these policy instruments to others, such as military assistance and economic aid.

9

Mobility-

Airlift, Sealift, and Prepositioning

United States national security policy extends our interests to all parts of the world. Thus, defense planners must consider how best to deploy our military forces outside the United States. Because the containment of communism is a principal foreign policy objective, the military objective of the United States and its allies is to *maintain* or *project* some measure of military power along the periphery of the Soviet Bloc and China. Either the peacetime maintenance of power close to the periphery, or the ability to project it to the area very rapidly is required by such a national objective. Therefore, power must be projected from the continental United States, where the industrial base of this power is located.

This chapter is concerned with defense planning issues that are important in the deployment of military forces to a theater of operations and the support of their combat operations in nonnuclear conflict. The problem facing the planner is the choice of a combination of transport systems and the peacetime basing of combat units, their equipment, and their support. In particular, the planner must concentrate on rapid ways of utilizing force at remote locations.

VALUE OF RAPID RESPONSE

Why is rapid response a desirable or even necessary attribute of a military force? First, it is believed that wars or other undesirable political events may be deterred if substantial forces can be summoned quickly. When the United States intervened in the Dominican Revolution the response was both rapid and massive. Once the decision had been made to intervene, our forces were ashore within a few hours. In the next few days over 20,000 U.S. troops were in the country. This kind of response seemed to reflect the belief of the President and his advisors that only intervention on such a scale would be sufficient.

Second, rapid response might affect the actual fighting of a war. Rapid movement of forces into an area might enable defense of that area with smaller total forces than if the response were slower. Further, since less territory might have to be yielded, the eventual counter-offensive to regain objectives might be smaller.

The key question is: for a given budget how should resources be allocated to implement our national security policy; or, alternatively, given a set of requirements what allocation will be lowest in cost? Any answer must consider all resources necessary to attain a particular level of capability. A transportation system must be designed that will not only enable rapid introduction of forces into an area, but also will provide the support necessary to maintain the forces in combat.

PROJECTION OF POWER

In projecting power to overseas locations, several options are open to the United States. 1) Forces may be located overseas wherever they are thought to be required. 2) All forces may be retained in the continental United States to be deployed wherever required. 3) A combination of these postures may be used, with some forces and support overseas plus a strategic reserve in the United States with a capability to deploy it to overseas locations. Apart from cost, location of forces overseas is accompanied by both advantages and disadvantages. One advantage is that forces located in an area provide a visible indication of U.S. intent. They also represent an obvious commitment on the part of the United States, out of proportion often to their military capability. Further, forces located in an area represent ready power if they are required there.

Among the disadvantages, the most important probably is that such forces tend to be tied to their peacetime location. It is more difficult politically to remove forces from one overseas location to another than to deploy similar forces from the strategic reserve in the United States. In some areas such as Korea, the nature of the assignment is such that tours of duty are quite short; the result is frequent rotation of personnel, with a consequent loss in capability.

The dual or combined posture can also include storing excess materiel overseas—usually stocks of equipment and war consumables. If it becomes necessary to introduce more forces into the theater, the extra supplies and equipment can be used by personnel deployed from the United States. Such an arrangement requires fewer airlift resources, for example, than if all equipment and supplies must be moved when personnel are moved.

Another way to preposition capability, aside from the combat forces themselves, is a support structure that enables rapid introduction of combat forces into an area. This can take the form of peacetime theater infrastructure—air bases, communications, depot facilities. This support structure can have an expansion capability enabling it to support large forces much more quickly than if the support must be moved along with combat forces.

TRANSPORT SYSTEM PRODUCTIVITY

Any of these postures must include a transportation system that allows men and materiel to be moved either from the United States to the required overseas location, to move forces from one part of a theater to another, or to move from one theater to another. Almost any system will include some elements of both airlift and sealift. Planning for overseas operations must estimate the productivity of transportation systems which include varying quantities of air and sealift. Within any mix—particularly in the case of airlift—there may be a wide choice of designs to provide the capability. The choice involves quantities of air, sea, and ground capability as well as appropriate mixes within each type of transportation.

AIRLIFT

Much attention has been given in recent years to techniques for estimating the productivity of transport aircraft—particularly the problems of transportation of ground forces. The most important problem in the Army transportation job is its enormous bulk of requirements. Also, vehicles are a large part of any Army unit, and they represent a peculiar problem in air transportation.

Some of the earliest work on the airlift characteristics of the Army deployment mission was done by William F. Sharpe[1] at The RAND Corporation. Most of the Army cargo is vehicular; while peacetime cargo principally consists of small units which can be arranged more flexibly. He concluded that: 1) while aircraft cargo-compartment cubage may be an acceptable measure for space requirements in determining peacetime airlift capability, requirements of Army deployment cargo demand a more accurate measure; 2) The best single measure of the space requirement for the Army equipment was cargo-compartment floor area rather than cubage. In most jet aircraft entering the fleet, the constraint on aircraft capacity for the Army deployment mission would be floor space rather than payload. If aircraft were designed with payloads greater than 51 lbs. per sq. ft. of cargo compartment area, the constraint would be floor space. If the design was for payloads less than this, the aircraft would typically be weight limited.

In later work Sharpe[2] combined a method for simulating the loading of aircraft with Army equipment with a network flow routine. A computer program was designed to simulate the deployment of Army units in transport aircraft from peacetime locations to an area of actual or potential combat. This technique enabled much more extensive studies of deployments, providing an inexpensive tool for varying the kinds of payload to be moved, the location of units in peacetime, and the war zones involved.

Sharpe has since used the Army Deployment Simulator to develop a technique for evaluating the productivity of various large transport aircraft in Army deployments. This study[3] used results obtained from previous deployment simu-

[1] "Aircraft compartment design criteria for the army deployment mission," RM-2566, The RAND Corporation, May 1, 1960.

[2] "The Army Deployment Simulator," RM-4219-ISA (Abridged), The RAND Corporation, March, 1965.

[3] "Estimating the Productivity of Large Transport Aircraft in Army Deployments: A Simplified Method," RM-4312-PR, The RAND Corporation, November, 1964.

lations to estimate aircraft productivity for a number of cases without additional simulations. For any specified type of deployment, he found that results from a limited number of cases could be used to derive tables which, together with an aircraft's payload range curve, determined the minimum fleet size required for a specific task or what size task a specific fleet could perform.

He used the results to aid in evaluating alternative designs for a proposed heavy logistics aircraft, enabling a comparison of this new aircraft with the C-141. This method provides a useful tool for comparing productivities of aircraft within a proposed airlift fleet. When combined with the system costs of alternative aircraft, it can help determine a preferred *airlift* fleet which can be part of a larger study to determine preferred combinations of airlift, sealift, and prepositioning.

SEALIFT

Estimating the productivity of sealift is similar to, although more straightforward than, estimating airlift productivity. The delivery capability of sealift depends on the carrying capacity of the ships, the time required to load and discharge them, and the steaming time between the materiel and the place of delivery. In Army deployments, the fact that the cargo consists of vehicles is important for sealift as well as airlift.

The capacity of a ship to carry vehicles is measured by the floor area of the storage space. In conventional shipping, vehicles cannot be stacked without constructing false decks, and because of the lengthy construction process, such ships are an unlikely way to provide rapid response. An alternative to conventional merchant vessels is the development of the so-called roll-on/roll-off ship. They attempt to provide a fast deployment logistics ship with higher speed and more rapid loading and unloading capability than conventional ships.

PROBLEMS IN MEASURING EFFECTIVENESS

Although point-to-point estimates of the productivity of air or sealift systems are sometimes complicated—particularly when most of the cargo is vehicular—development of these techniques in the last few years has greatly eased the analysis of this part of the problem. Possibly the most troublesome difficulty remaining is the choice of an appropriate measure of the "war fighting" productivity of transportation systems. A purely economic comparison of sealift and airlift, *initial* responsiveness, and capability in subsequent redeployments, indicates that sealift is a much cheaper way of transporting the kinds of materiel required for support of ground forces.

Until now, most studies have used the time pattern of delivery of men and materiel to an assumed objective area or areas. Different airlift fleets or mixes of airlift, sealift, and prepositioning at the same budget level can give widely different delivery profiles over time. For example, a system emphasizing sealift would show a much higher eventual delivery capability than an equal cost system emphasizing airlift. The latter system, however, would undoubtedly deliver *some* units earlier. Which system is preferred would depend upon the relative worth of some early capability, obtained at the cost of a smaller eventual capability.

The answer, unfortunately, nearly always depends upon the specific situation. It is influenced by the geography, the specific characteristics of the threat, the political environment (which might affect overflight or staging rights), and so on. Attempting to estimate the influence of these situational variables is going to be difficult, imprecise, and above all, time consuming.

One of the most important situational influences is the need for quick response at particular points, not just generally in a combat theater. The point of need is, moreover, likely to be near the fighting rather than at a port or airfield in the rear. Much emphasis is now being placed on developing a capability for operating from short, low-strength airfields in the proposed new C-5A heavy transport aircraft. Planners have become convinced that unless troops and equipment can be routinely delivered well forward in the theater, many of the advantages of airlift would be lost.

A study of quick response to particular points of need, however, requires studying the entire transportation process from origin to final destination. In addition to estimating intercontinental delivery capability, air and surface movement capability in the theater must also be analyzed. Consider, for example, a quite plausible situation occurring in connection with a commitment to Thailand arising from obligations under the Southeast Asia Treaty Organization. To make the example simpler, assume that only United States and local Thai forces are involved in defending Thailand against an invasion of North Vietnamese and Chinese troops coming through Laos. U.S. ground and air units must be moved into the area quickly enough to stop the invasion before it has penetrated very far into Thai territory.

If the forces are to halt aggression before it is well under way, they must be introduced somewhere close to the Thai-Laos border. This means that equipment, supplies, and people must be moved several hundred miles from the nearest port. To devise the preferred system, one must consider combinations of the varied transportation methods available along with prepositioning materiel somewhere in the theater. One possibility is the prepositioning of materiel on ships in the theater, using airlift to bring personnel from both the United States and the theater. When the equipment has been unloaded from the ships, it must be moved overland by rail and road to the objective areas.

The performance of such a system compared with an equal cost system which used airlift to move equipment and supplies from land prepositioning sites in the theater would depend to some extent upon the time available. The system emphasizing sealift might start landing equipment at Bangkok in three or four days and use another week to move it by highway and rail to the combat zone. Thus, in about ten days forces would be arriving in the combat area. The system relying more heavily on airlift and land-based prepositioning might be able to get *some* forces into place in two or three days, but might show lower total deliveries after two weeks. The issue is the value of having smaller forces arrive very early as opposed to larger forces arriving somewhat later. A study, described briefly later in this chapter, attempted to answer this question. Although reasonably clear answers are possible for any particular case, such answers are usually so peculiar to the particular situation that studies must allow meaningful choices among competing combinations of airlift, sealift, and prepositioning.

MAJOR UNRESOLVED ISSUES

The importance of the points discussed thus far is generally recognized. Although there is considerable controversy over details of the analyses—particularly about interservice questions—there is agreement about the relevance of the key issues and the general approach to their study. Forward prepositioning of equipment and supplies and the size of the economic credit which should be given to the peacetime use of the airlift fleet have been debated for years. These issues will be discussed in more detail, both for their intrinsic interest, and because they illustrate the analytic process used to develop preferred postures for force deployment.

PREPOSITIONING

Although the details are not available in the open literature, systematic studies were done at The RAND Corporation as early as 1958 on the use of land-based prepositioning as a complement to airlift in the rapid deployment of forces. One such study examined the desirability of stocking overseas some of the materiel required to support the theater operations of tactical air units which were located in the United States in peacetime.

Briefly, this study considered two contrasting policies—one requiring comparatively modest amounts of materiel in the hands of using units at their peacetime locations that are accompanied by a large transport fleet, and the other requiring greater amounts of materiel but fewer transports. The second policy involved overseas stockage or prepositioning. In addition to those items required for the peacetime training functions of the units, an equal amount of each materiel necessary for combat operations was assumed to be stocked in two war theaters. The study assumed that this material would be at central locations in two theaters. The aircraft and personnel of the unit would move from their peacetime locations to wartime employment bases; the materiel stocked at the overseas location would then be airlifted to these employment bases.

The study estimated the costs incurred by each policy in meeting a wartime requirement stated in terms of a minimum number of days for delivery of support personnel and materiel to any location along the Sino-Soviet periphery. The cost of the support system was computed for each policy and for varying deployment requirements. A second study made at about the same time compared the total system costs of tactical air units based in the United States with the costs of such units based in overseas theaters. Instead of comparing the costs and capabilities of locating only prepositioned materiel in the theaters, it compared the costs and capabilities of forces in the theaters. The forces from each posture were required to deploy a tactical air wing to any of several areas of potential limited war within a specified number of days. The costs to procure and operate the combat aircraft, air transports, and aerial tankers necessary to meet this requirement were then compared.

More recent analyses have included additional complexities: considering systems including both land and seabased prepositioning in systems, different types of ships and a wider variety of aircraft types; more diversity in types of units to be deployed; a greater range of possible combat situations. One such study compared the ability of equal-cost postures to deploy Army divisions to a number of different locations. They varied from one in which all equipment and personnel are moved from the United States to various assumed war locations to one in which all Army vehicles are prepositioned overseas and only personnel and non-vehicular equipment are airlifted to the theater of operations. One posture assumed that the entire budget was spent on the airlift fleet. The others spent less for airlift and used the remaining money to preposition selected equipment at several overseas locations. They were then compared in their ability to move the Army forces to different war theaters.

Most studies, including those discussed, consider the problem a choice among alternative combinations of prepositioning and airlift, rather than complete reliance on either. In all realistic alternatives, there is some prepositioning overseas and in the continental U.S. and some airlift capability for the deployment of troops and materiel to points where they may be needed. The question then concerns the locations and quantities of items and how much airlift and sealift capability should be provided.

The principal cost tradeoffs concern the acquisition and storage costs of additional materiel under an extensive prepositioning concept as opposed to the cost of acquiring and operating military air transport forces in a limited operation while maintaining comparable responsiveness and flexibility.

The speed with which combat forces can be delivered to wartime theaters is determined by the distance involved, and the speed, capacity, and number of vehicles available to do the moving. A simple explanation is that given speed, capacity, and availability of delivery vehicles, the closer the forces (or any part of them, such as some of their equipment) to the destination, the faster the response. The same is true for each factor considered separately. In each case, however, a change that improves speed of response can be made only at a cost— either in resources or in increased risk. The relevant problem is to estimate how changes in the parameters affect both performance and cost.

The costs of prepositioning to be considered are those incurred by forward prepositioning as opposed to costs incurred without it. They are very dependent on whether or not prepositioning involves larger total stocks.

If the total stock of a particular item is to be the same with or without overseas prepositioning, the alternative postures simply involve alternative geographical distributions of the same total stock. In that case the cost of prepositioning is the difference between the cost of holding the item overseas and holding it in the United States. Prepositioning costs, wherever incurred, must include the costs of storage, periodic replacement of deteriorated or obsolete items, maintenance of items in serviceable condition, and protection against pilferage and sabotage. If, as may well be the case for most items in most locations, it costs more to store an item overseas, then the cost for the item will be positive, but only to the extent of the cost difference. If, on the other hand, prepositioning involves acquiring additional stocks for overseas storage, the cost must include the full cost of acquiring the additional items, cost of movement to the overseas location, overseas storage, maintenance, and protection. The cost of the prepositioning in this case will be greater than the cost attributable to prepositioning with a fixed total stock.

In comparing the cost of prepositioning with the cost of providing the extra wartime airlift to deploy the items from the United States, the prepositioning costs must be based on appropriate assumptions about which of the two cases pertains. This will depend on the particular item considered; for some items the total stock is the same with or without prepositioning; for others every unit prepositioned may represent an addition to the total stock; in other cases, prepositioning involves greater total stocks than without prepositioning but does not account for the total difference.

Prepositioning is a change of the distance which forces or equipment must be moved which, other things being equal, will increase rapid response capability. If equal cost cases are being considered, one of the three determinants of deployment time must be changed to compensate for the increase in prepositioning cost. Either cheaper delivery vehicles must be purchased or the total number of vehicles must be smaller. If the loss in intercontinental transport capability is more than offset by the improvement in capability obtained by prepositioning, the posture including more prepositioning will be preferred.

In the last few years the Defense Department has moved toward a posture which emphasizes overseas prepositioning much more than in the past. A number of merchant ships have been converted to "forward floating depots" containing

Army equipment and supplies. Located in the Pacific, these ships can be moved fairly quickly to ports in Southeast Asia if required. Personnel could be moved— probably by air—from either the United States or the Pacific.

Perhaps the only study which has considered not only the appropriate mix of airlift, sealift, and prepositioning, but also the "value" of rapid response was done in 1964 by the Special Studies Group of the Joint Chiefs of Staff. It estimated transport and prepositioning requirements for three strategies: (1) a forward strategy which provided the ability to introduce fairly large forces within a few days; (2) an intermediate strategy which moved forces in somewhat later; and, (3) a defensive strategy which introduced forces much later and anticipated a slow buildup and eventual counter-attack. It compared the peacetime costs of these strategies—including not only the different transportation system costs, but the total ground and tactical air force requirements for each one, along with the cost of fighting under each strategy in terms of casualties, material losses, and other war-fighting costs. Thus, perhaps for the first time, a value could be placed on rapid response; in this case, it can be regarded as the difference between the total system costs—both for maintaining the force in peacetime and using it to fight a war—for the various postures.

ECONOMIC CREDIT FOR PEACETIME USE

The economic credit accorded the use of military cargo airlift in peacetime is another highly significant and still unresolved issue. The credit given this peacetime use can affect both the quantity of airlift in a transportation mix at a given budget and whether or not to procure new transport aircraft.

Useful airlift performed on military transport aircraft in peacetime includes that performed in relative peace and in an almost continual succession of small-scale emergencies as well as a sustained conflict such as the Vietnam war. Military airlift at a minimum can save the cost of shipping by sea, including the associated extra handling costs, and sometimes can reduce total stocks of certain items in the inventory. At the most it saves the cost of alternatively shipping by commercial air, when air shipment is justified as more economical than sealift or is required for rapid response to unanticipated urgent needs. The credit for useful peacetime lift may thus range from a few cents per ton mile if commercial sealift is the alternative up to ten or twenty cents per ton mile depending on the kinds of items airlifted.

The proper credit cannot be established by simply projecting some demand for airlift over the future and costing it at the commercial airlift rates. The key question is what the credit should be, that is, how much of the peacetime airlift should be credited at the air tariff rate and how much at sea rates. Determining the proper credit to be applied is difficult. Data on past shipments by air or sea usually can only be suggestive. Although air shipment was used in a certain case, possibly a better method could have been used. Data on shipments usually only suggest that certain categories of shipment may be worth closer scrutiny because they appear particularly questionable—for example, large-scale shipments of cheap bulky items which are demanded on a fairly continuous basis.

The question of what to ship by air and what by sea is of current interest for two quite different reasons. The current tight airlift situation has created pressures to utilize available airlift only for necessary air shipments, not for items suitable for sea shipments. Also, appropriate credit for useful peacetime airlift must be determined to estimate the next cost of the military airlift force (total peacetime expenditures for investment and operating minus peacetime credits) and the best combination of airlift, sealift, and prepositioning.

In comparing smaller versus larger airlift forces, what is of interest is the *incremental* credit for additional useful peacetime airlift capability. A choice could be, for example, between acquiring an extra squadron of aircraft or spending the money for more ships or more prepositioning. The net cost of the additional squadron depends partly on the credit for additional peacetime airlift provided by the squadron. If, without that squadron, there is insufficient peacetime military airlift for all items which should go by air, the commercial air tariff would be the appropriate credit for some or all the peacetime airlift provided by the extra squadron. However, if without the extra squadron enough peacetime military airlift exists and some items are airlifted which otherwise would have gone by sea, the appropriate credit for the extra squadron would be only the sea tariff, plus other costs associated with sea shipment and the cost of additional materiel if this is relevant.

The proper credit for useful peacetime airlift must be determined by study of military support requirements overseas and how best to meet them. Whether the incremental credit is two to four cents or ten to twenty cents per ton mile is extremely important, as is whether the military airlift force is credited with two or four hours of useful airlift per day per aircraft. At one extreme the peacetime credit would be an almost negligible fraction of total peacetime expenditures on the airlift force. However, the peacetime credit might offset most or all expenditures and thus make the military airlift force virtually free. The choice of the best combination of airlift, sealift, and prepositioning is thus highly sensitive to the peacetime credit. A choice based on the wrong assumption could be disastrous in the choice of the appropriate transportation mix.

COSTS OF PEACETIME USE

Related to the issue of the appropriate economic credit to give peacetime use of the airlift fleet is the cost associated with such use, in terms of both operational capability and peacetime operating cost. The transport fleet must be operated in peacetime at a level high enough to enable response to peak demands early in an emergency. The exact level required is undecided, but it concerns how much exercise of parts of the system is necessary to enable the system to expand its output rapidly.

The peacetime operating cost implications of various flying rates can be estimated reasonably well. The effects on wartime capability, however, are much more difficult to investigate. Peacetime flying can be categorized into two broad classes: one consists of training missions for aircrew proficiency purposes, exercises, and special assignments such as refugee evacuation; the other includes so-called channel traffic over the overseas route structure. Some channel traffic may contribute to wartime proficiency, but the amount is difficult to determine.

Channel traffic missions other than those required to maintain the wartime proficiency of the airlift system affect the wartime capability of the fleet even though they may be "productive" by providing support to peacetime overseas forces. With a given manning level there is clearly some level of peacetime flying, suitably allocated, which provides maximum wartime airlift capability. At lower levels of peacetime flying, increasing the rate will probably decrease it. In general, more flying will provide more practice, but it will contribute to greater crew fatigue, increase the number of aircraft out of commission, and result in more dispersal of the fleet. All these things can degrade emergency airlift capability.

Another aspect of the cost of peacetime airlift is important. If airlift has been employed to reduce stocks of spare parts and to allow the closing of overseas depots during peacetime then this kind of support must clearly be continued in wartime. Some airlift must be diverted from wartime tasks to continue this support or such support must be shifted to civil carriers. The first alternative imposes a cost in terms of the airlift which is not available for the wartime requirements. The cost of the second is that incurred to assure, with high confidence, the wartime availability of commercial airlift on very short notice—even during peak tourist seasons.

INTRATHEATER TRANSPORT

Support of combat operations after the initial deployment is in many ways more difficult to analyze than questions concerning intertheater movement or prepositioning. The intratheater transport system must be designed to support the highly variable needs of ground and air units engaged in combat. Particularly in fluid combat situations, the quantity of resupply can change drastically and quickly; the composition of demands and the locations where supplies are needed change frequently.

Resupply of conventional ordnance and fuel compose the bulk of the support requirements for both ground forces and tactical air units. Determining the interaction between demand for such commodities and combat action is extremely difficult. Ground force resupply requirements are generally based on data from previous wars, modified to reflect changes in equipping and manning. There is considerable question about whether planning factors based on historical experience reflect the demand for supplies or the amount which the logistic system was able to supply. History seldom provides details about a particular situation sufficient for precise analysis.

In principle, intratheater transport requirements should be determined from an analysis of the entire package of combat forces and their transportation support. For a fixed budget, the combination of airlift, surface lift, and combat forces which provide the greatest combat capability is preferred. Such an analysis is extremely difficult as there is virtually no agreement about how to measure combat capability—particularly for ground forces. Slight knowledge of the interaction between supply support and combat capability makes examining the effects of exchanging weapons for support almost impossible.

The determination of the best combination of combat forces and their support depends on the particular situation. Detailed examination of road and rail capacity and the availability of airfields for a wide variety of potential combat areas is necessary. A range of threats and possible strategies must be considered. Blending all these variables into a comprehensive analysis is enormously difficult, given the current state of knowledge of most of them.

The intratheater transportation system, of course, affects and is affected by the intertheater system. For example, if the analysis is done part by part (as is almost necessary), the preferred intertheater system might contain a large number of ships and little airlift. This, in turn, would mean an intratheater system which must provide support from ports to combat operations occurring inland. It would be very different from one designed for use in an intertheater system containing aircraft able to operate into primitive airfields near or in the combat zone.

The problem still remains of designing a total system of combat forces and inter and intratheater transportation which can be quickly adapted to operations under a wide variety of circumstances. A combination which is dominant for all likely kinds of wars in varied geographic locations is unlikely. Much research must be done on practically all aspects of the problem.

Previous discussion has concerned determining preferred combinations of various kinds of resources for a given budget; or, for a postulated set of requirements, the least cost combination of such resources. The problem remains of determining total force size for the general purpose as well as the airlift-sealift forces. Knowledge of the relationship between national security policy and the various instruments necessary to implement it is extremely sparse. The best approach is to provide decision makers with various budget levels, at which the best possible combination of resources given the current state of knowledge.

In summary, the key issues in the choice of airlift and sealift are the value of being able to project military power rapidly to remote locations and the appropriate costing of the systems which provide that capability. While these issues remain difficult to resolve, defense planners have been able to employ much more sophisticated techniques of analysis than a few years ago.

BIBLIOGRAPHY

1. Borchers, C. R. and M. J. O'Brien, *Effect of Dimensional Variations in Transport Aircraft Cargo Compartments on Sortie Requirements and Space Utilization in Deployment of Army Units.* Maryland: The Johns Hopkins University Press, January, 1961.

2. Brown, Neville, *Strategic Mobility,* Studies in International Security: 7. London: Chatto & Windus, 1963.

3. Fitzpatrick, G. R. and M. J. O'Brien, *A Method of Estimating Aircraft Fleet Requirements in Strategic Deployments.* Maryland: Operations Research Office, The Johns Hopkins University Press, July, 1960.

4. Sharpe, W. F., *Aircraft Compartment Design Criteria for the Army Deployment Mission,* RM-2566, The RAND Corporation, May 1, 1960.

5. ———, *The Army Deployment Simulator,* RM-4219-ISA (Abridged). The RAND Corporation, March, 1965.

6. ———, *Estimating the Productivity of Large Transport Aircraft in Army Deployments: A Simplified Method,* RM-4312-PR. The RAND Corporation, November, 1964.

JOHN J. McCALL

The RAND Corporation

Dr. John J. McCall is Associate Professor of Management
Science at The University of Chicago. He is a consultant to The
RAND Corporation. He served as a Research Economist at The
RAND Corporation from 1959 to 1966 and was a National
Science Foundation Postdoctoral Fellow at the Netherlands
School of Economics (1963–64). His publications in economics
and management science have appeared in *the Journal of Political
Economy, Operations Research, The Journal of Business*, and
Management Science. A monograph, *Optimal Maintenance of
Stochastically Failing Equipment* (with D. W. Jorgenson and R.
Radner) will be published in 1966. He received his Ph.D. from
The University of Chicago (1959).

10

Maintenance

I. INTRODUCTION

This Chapter* reviews recent developments in the theory and application of maintenance policies. A maintenance policy is a rule that assigns a specific action, like repairing, inspecting, or doing nothing, to each moment in the life of an equipment or 'weapon system'. The need for maintenance policies has been long recognized both in the military and in defense and nondefense industries. Indeed, "rule of thumb" policies have been followed for many years. The use of very expensive and complex equipment like jet airliners, ballistic missiles, and electronic computers has necessitated a reassessment of "rule of thumb" policies. Fortunately, the concurrent development of mathematical decision theory provided the tools required for a successful reevaluation.

At the outset it is important to note that maintenance is usually only one of several substitute activities that improve equipment performance. The optimal allocation of a fixed budget among these activities must logically precede the design of optimal maintenance policies. For example, if the per-unit cost of equipment is small relative to the cost of maintenance, the production process should use more pieces of equipment and less maintenance. Similarly, if maintenance is less expensive than alternative stockage policies, the production process should concentrate more upon maintenance than upon inventory. In this paper the importance of these more global allocation problems is recognized, but the discussion focuses on allocations among various maintenance activities.

The theory of maintenance falls under two rather divergent disciplines: capital theory (a topic in economics) and reliability theory (a topic in applied probability). The presence of both economic and stochastic factors in maintenance models accounts for this dual membership. The maintenance of equipment is first of all a special problem in the theory of capital. The equipment produces a flow of output over its useful life. The rate of flow, the length of life, and the salvage value are all affected by the level of maintenance activity. The general problem is to ascertain the "best" relation among these variables when the exogenous factor, technical change, is also considered. This general problem has been divided into two parts. The first is determining when old equipment should be replaced by new equipment, where the rate of output declines with equipment age. This has been called the deterioration problem. A complete deterministic solution was first presented by A. A. Alchian [1]*. A solution using a more convenient computational procedure was developed by R. Bellman and S. Dreyfus [5]. This procedure possessed the added advantage that it was easily extended to equipment that deteriorates stochastically. The problem of technological change was also easily treated within this framework.

---

* Any views expressed in this paper are those of the author. They should not be interpreted as reflecting the views of The RAND Corporation or the official opinion or policy of any of its government or private research sponsors.

* Numbers appearing in brackets, refer to references listed at the end of the chapter.

The second subproblem focuses on the maintenance actions taken during the life of the equipment. Most of the research on these problems has considered equipment that fails stochastically, that is, equipment whose time to failure is a random variable with a given probability distribution. Study of these micro-scheduling problems has been quite extensive[1]. Many interesting theoretical models have been developed, most with significant practical applications. These maintenance models are almost all probabilistic in character and represent important applications of probability theory. More specifically, the theory of maintenance developed for these stochastic problems belongs to the second discipline mentioned above—reliability theory.

There are two basic categories of stochastic models. The first is the class of preparedness models in which the equipment fails stochastically and, at least for some of its parts, its actual state—good or failed—is not known with certainty. Preventive maintenance models comprise the second class of maintenance models. In these models the equipment is subject to stochastic failure and the state of the equipment is always known with certainty. If the equipment exhibits an increasing failure rate, and furthermore a failure in operation is more costly than replacement before failure, then it may be advantageous to replace the equipment before failure. The problem is to determine a suitable replacement schedule.

The techniques used to analyze stochastic maintenance problems belong to the methodology associated with decision making under uncertainty. The general structure of these problems possesses those features that are characteristic of decision-theoretic models. While in operation the equipment under consideration is assumed to occupy one of several states, the two extreme states being "new" and "failed." These two boundary states enclose a set of intermediate states that denote different degrees of deterioration. The movement from state to state is governed by a probability mechanism whose law may be completely known, partially known, or unknown by the decision maker. Unattended equipment moves stochastically from state to state in a natural manner until it reaches the absorbing state of failure. The behavior of the equipment can, however, be regulated by choosing a particular action at each decision point. These actions include: doing nothing, inspection (if the equipment is not continuously observed), several types of repair, and replacement or complete overhaul, both of which "renew" the equipment. When the equipment is composed of several parts, a specific action must be assigned to each part; the action chosen for one part may depend on the state of one or more of the remaining parts. The sequence of actions chosen by the decision maker reflects a maintenance policy, and the difference between the regulated and natural behavior of the equipment is a measure of the policy's influence. A policy's performance can be measured in cost by assigning an occupancy cost to each state and an intervention cost to each action. These costs are calculated to measure the money and downtime costs of each maintenance action as well as the downtime cost

---

[1] A survey of this literature is presented in [19].

associated with each operational state. The objective of the decision maker is to choose maintenance actions so that the expected cost per unit time of operating the equipment is minimized. Any rule that assigns a specific action to any possible realization in the equipment's life is called a maintenance policy.

An optimal policy is a rule that is best in the sense of minimizing expected cost per unit time. A policy that required a detailed description of each possible realization, such as the state of the equipment, its age and the number, types, and times of previous actions, would be analytically difficult and costly to implement. Similarly, any policy with a complicated form has both theoretical and practical disadvantages. Therefore, research in stochastic maintenance scheduling has for the most part confined its attention to policies that have modest informational requirements and simple forms. It is perhaps remarkable that optimal policies of *practical importance* have been obtained that satisfy both of the simplicity criteria. Nevertheless, the title of optimality has so far been conferred on only a small number of maintenance policies, and many practical maintenance problems await optimal solutions.

In the absence of optimal policies a sensible strategy is to assume that the optimal policy possesses a simple form and then to choose the best policy within this class. As an illustration, a simple maintenance policy is the age-replacement policy that replaces the equipment at failure or at age, N, whichever occurs first. This policy is optimal for a single piece of equipment under certain circumstances. In general, the existence of interdependence among replacement costs makes it difficult to obtain optimal policies for several pieces of equipment. In view of this difficulty, the best alternative may be to assume that the simple age-replacement policy is optimal and calculate the best replacement interval for each piece of equipment. The restriction to simple policies has been justified on the grounds of administrative feasibility, analytical simplicity, and, sometimes, demonstrated optimality in a different, but related, environment.

Adherence to any simple maintenance policy generates a stochastic process whose steady-state behavior is usually amenable to analysis. Probably the most important operating characteristic of the policy's steady-state behavior is the long-run expected cost per unit time. Its importance derives from the fact that the decision parameters of a particular policy are usually calculated to minimize the long-run expected cost per unit time. It is usually a simple matter to devise a computational routine for obtaining the "optimal" values of the decision parameters.

Having disposed of optimality in one way or another, either by beginning with an optimal policy or calculating the "optimal" decision parameters of a simple but nonoptimal policy, the calculation of additional operating characteristics is frequently useful. Two operating characteristics that sometimes aid in predicting future maintenance and supply requirements are the expected rate of failure and the expected rate of replacement. The evaluation of equally attractive nonoptimal policies is also facilitated by a comparison of their corresponding operating characteristics.

The methodology and development of stochastic maintenance theory bear a striking resemblance to those of stochastic inventory theory.[2] Both have their roots in simple deterministic models. The stochastic models of inventory theory usually assume that, for a particular item, the demand per unit time is a random variable; some also assume that the time until delivery is a random variable. The corresponding stochastic element in maintenance is the equipment's time-to-failure. Dynamic programming [5] has been the primary method for achieving optimal inventory policies. Proofs of optimality in maintenance theory have also relied primarily on this technique. Even the structure of some optimal maintenance policies is similar to optimal inventory policies. Finally, analogous renewal theoretical arguments are employed to obtain operating characteristics for both inventory and maintenance models.

The design and improvement of complex equipment constitute another set of maintenance problems. The maintainability or ease of equipment repair is a critical performance characteristic. A second performance characteristic of equal criticality is the frequency of equipment failure. In the development and improvement of military equipment, special importance has been attached to these maintenance characteristics. An important problem is determining the "best" allocation of a fixed budget between these two performance characteristics.

The criteria used to evaluate alternative maintenance policies vary from one application to another. Equipment-replacement problems usually select the replacement interval to maximize the present value of the net stream of services produced. An alternative criterion is to minimize the present value of the stream of expenses for a specified level of service. This criterion is especially appropriate in military application, where it is difficult to place a monetary value on the stream of services. The criterion defining optimality for stochastic maintenance policies is usually to minimize the expected cost per-expected-unit of equipment operation. In most applications it is assumed that a maintenance action restores the equipment to a condition "good as new." Thus, neglecting discounting, optimizing over a single cycle of operation, from one renewal to the next, is equivalent to optimizing over an infinite time span. Indeed, it has been shown that policies optimal over a single cycle of operations with no discounting are a limiting case of policies that minimize discounted costs as the discount rate goes to zero [22]. Incorporation of a non-zero discount rate is a straightforward extension of the models discussed here. An alternative criterion that is sometimes used to assess stochastic maintenance policies is to maximize the probability that a fixed number of equipments will be operational at any randomly chosen time. Policies guided by this probabilistic criterion have not been examined in the same detail as those adhering to an expected-value criterion. The allocation of resources among various performance characteristics like maintainability and reliability use similar criteria.

The remainder of the chapter is divided into four sections. Section 2 presents

---

[2] See Chapter 8 in this book by H. S. Campbell for a description of inventory policies.

results for deterministic maintenance policies. In particular, the economic replacement problem is examined; all stochastic properties are suppressed, and the analysis is purely economic. Section 3 is a brief survey of stochastic maintenance models. Both preventive maintenance models and preparedness maintenance models are described; simple examples of each are presented. The steady-state behavior of these policies is also discussed, and the usefulness of operating characteristics is illustrated. Finally, an adaptive policy is discussed in which the distribution of time-to-failure is not known with certainty. The substitution relationship between the performance characteristics, reliability, and maintainability is explored in Section 4. The concluding remarks together with some suggestions for future research are contained in Section 5. The Appendix contains a more technical discussion of the reliability-maintainability trade-off.

II. DETERMINISTIC MAINTENANCE POLICIES [3]

The replacement of deteriorating equipment is the first problem considered in the theory of maintenance. Aging has a twofold impact on equipment performance. First, the costs of operation are an increasing function of age; second, the rate of output decreases with equipment age. Consequently, the equipment's net benefits are a decreasing function of equipment age. Abstracting from the regular maintenance actions that occur over the equipment's life, the decision maker is assumed to control only one action—the time of equipment replacement. The consequence of this action is to restore the equipment to its original state: that is, it is replaced by an identical piece of equipment, except that its age is zero. This renewal assumption simplifies the analysis and is tantamount to assuming zero technical change.[4] For an optimal replacement policy the sequence of replacement actions beginning at one renewal point is the same as at any other renewal point. This implies that the optimal policy over an infinite horizon is purely periodic: that is, there is a fixed period of time between replacement actions.

Let $b(t)$ denote the instantaneous rate of net operating benefits per-unit-time for equipment of age t. The net benefit is simply the gross value of equipment output less operating expenses. The cost of replacement includes both a monetary cost and a downtime cost. The monetary cost of replacement equals the acquisition and installation costs less the salvage value of the used equipment. The downtime cost is simply the net operating benefits that would have been produced over the replacement time. Let $C(t)$ represent the net cost of replacing equipment of age t; finally, let K denote the time required for replacement. If N represents

---

[3] This Section is based on Chapter 1 of [14].

[4] The inclusion of technical change, that is, replacement with equipment superior to the original, complicates the analysis and for expository reasons will not be discussed here. The interested reader should consult [5] and [14].

the replacement age, then the length of a complete cycle from the beginning of one replacement action to the next is $(N + K)$.

For a policy of replacing equipment at age N, let $B(N)$ denote total discounted net benefits. The decision maker simply chooses the value of N that maximizes $B(N)$[5].

III. STOCHASTIC MAINTENANCE POLICIES

As previously noted, stochastic maintenance models can be divided into two groups, the preventive models and the preparedness models. All of the preventive maintenance models discussed in the literature are designed for randomly failing equipment whose state is assumed to be known with certainty. Changes of state are immediately detected, thereby signalling the initiation of the appropriate maintenance action. Preventive maintenance models are therefore affected by a single source of uncertainty, the inability to predict the exact time of state changes. And it is precisely this uncertainty that creates opportunities for replacing or repairing equipment before it fails. If it is more costly

[5] The total discounted net benefit over the first cycle is:

$$(1) \qquad \int_0^N e^{-\alpha t} b(t) \, dt - e^{-\alpha N} C(N),$$

where the discount rate is denoted by α. Since every subsequent cycle is a repetition of the first, the sum of the discounted net benefits over all cycles is:

$$(2) \qquad B(N) = \sum_{n=1}^{\infty} e^{-(n-1)(N+K)\alpha} \left[\int_0^N e^{-\alpha t} b(t) \, dt - e^{-\alpha N} C(N) \right]$$

Since this is a convergent geometric series it can be evaluated directly to give:

$$(3) \qquad B(N) = \frac{\int_0^N e^{-\alpha t} b(t) \, dt - e^{-\alpha N} C(N)}{1 - e^{-\alpha(N+K)}}$$

Differentiating $B(N)$ and setting the derivative equal to zero produces:

$$(4) \qquad b(\hat{N}) - C'(\hat{N}) = \alpha e^{-\alpha K} B(\hat{N}) - \alpha C(\hat{N})$$

where $\hat{N}$ denotes the optimal replacement interval. Taking the limit of the right side of (4) as $\alpha \to 0$ yields the interesting result:

$$(5) \qquad b(\hat{N}) - C'(\hat{N}) = \frac{\int b(t) \, dt - C(\hat{N})}{N + K}.$$

That is, the optimal replacement interval is chosen so that the marginal net benefit per-unit-time (left-hand side of [5]) equals the average net benefit per cycle (right-hand side of [5]). For a discussion of the assumptions ensuring the existence of a finite and non-zero optimal replacement age, see Chapter 1 of [14].

to replace a part after failure than before, then in the absence of uncertainty the equipment will be replaced just before it fails. When the equipment fails randomly, it is impossible to replace just before failure; and in these circumstances it may be advantageous to replace the equipment well in advance of an actual failure. In the presence of uncertainty it sometimes pays to "waste" equipment life in order to avoid the high cost of failure; however, this is true only if uncertainty assumes a particular form. The conditional probability that the equipment will fail in the interval $(t, t + \Delta t)$, given that it has survived to time t is denoted by $\rho(t)\,\Delta t$, where $\rho(t)$ is the equipment's failure rate.[6] Replacement before failure is advantageous only if the failure rate is strictly increasing. For example, consider equipment with a constant failure rate. By definition, replacement before failure does not affect the probability that the equipment will fail in the next instant given that it is good now. Thus if replacement costs are positive, it will never be advisable to replace before failure. The same argument applies *a fortiori* if the failure rate decreases with time.

On the other hand, preparedness models were developed for equipment whose state is ascertained only when the maintenance action is performed. Thus, preparedness models are affected by three different uncertainties. First, it is impossible to predict the exact time of equipment failure. Second, the time at which the equipment will be required to perform is not susceptible to exact prediction. Finally, the state of the equipment is known only at the time of particular maintenance actions.

The simplest and best known of the preventive policies is the strictly periodic policy [3, 16]. This policy is designed for equipment that is continuously inspected and possesses an increasing failure rate. The equipment is repaired whenever a failure is detected. The motivation for preventive maintenance stems from the fact that the in-service failure of an equipment is frequently costly relative to the alternative of replacing before failure.[7]

---

[6] Letting $F(t)$ denote the probability that the equipment fails by age t, the failure rate can be expressed as

$$\rho(t) = \frac{d}{dt}\{\log[1 - F(t)]\} = \frac{f(t)}{1 - F(t)}.$$

[7] Let C and C^* be, respectively, costs of replacing before and after failure. Then $\bar{C}$, the asymptotic cost per-unit-time of operating the equipment when the equipment is replaced at failure or at age N, whichever occurs first is

$$(7) \qquad \bar{C}(N) = \lim_{t \to \infty}\left\{\frac{C^*m(N, t)}{t} + \frac{Cs(N, t)}{t}\right\} = \frac{C[1 - F(N)] + C^*F(N)}{\displaystyle\int_0^N [1 - F(t)]\,dt}$$

where $m(N, t)$ and $s(N, t)$ are, respectively, the expected number of preventive maintenance actions and the expected number of in-service failures in the interval $(0, t)$ when the replacement interval is N. This assumes a zero rate of discount. Positive discount rates require the usual modifications. For an excellent discussion of policy criteria and the role of discount rates see [22].

R. Barlow and F. Proschan [3] have shown that for infinite time spans this strictly periodic replacement policy is the best of the class of random periodic policies, that is, that class for which the replacement interval is a random variable.[8]

As an example of a periodic preventive maintenance policy, consider the replacement policy for a commercially used electron tube.[9] The tube fails according to a normal distribution (truncated at zero) with a mean operating life of 9080 hours and a standard deviation of 3027. If $C^* = \$1100$ and $C = \$100$, then solving Eq. (8) gives an optimal replacement interval of 4540 hours. The average cost per hour of operating this tube under the optimal policy is $\$.05$. The cost per hour of replacing the tube only at failure is $\$.12$.

Preventive maintenance models have been developed for equipment with several parts:[10] for example, consider equipment composed of two parts labeled (1) and (2). Part (1) has the same structure as the equipment in the periodic preventive maintenance model; it is the victim of an increasing failure rate and C_1, the cost of replacing before failure is less than C_1^*, the cost of replacing after failure. On the other hand, part (2) fails exponentially (constant failure rate). The parts fail independently, and the failure of either causes an equipment failure that is immediately detected. Letting C_2 and C_{12} denote, respectively, the cost of replacing part (2) separately and the cost of replacing both parts together, the inequality

$$(9) \qquad\qquad C_{12} < C_1 + C_2$$

signifies the presence of economics of scale in maintenance.

R. Radner [23] has shown that the optimal policy for this equipment is characterized by two decision parameters, n and N, such that

    (i) if $x < n$, replace part (1) only if it fails;

---

[8] The optimal replacement interval is obtained by setting the derivative of $\bar{C}(N)$ equal to zero. This gives the expression

$$(8) \qquad\qquad \rho(N) \int_0^N [1 - F(n)]\, dt - F(N) = \frac{C}{C^* - C}.$$

Since $\bar{C}''(N)$ is greater than zero, the solution to Eq. (8) is the optimal preventive maintenance interval in that it minimizes $\bar{C}(N)$. The solution to Eq. (8) is unique if $\rho(t)$ is strictly increasing; the failure rate is increasing if and only if the second derivative of $\log [1 - F(t)]$ is nonpositive, that is, if and only if $\log [1 - F(t)]$ is concave. Some important probability distribution possessing an increasing failure rate are the normal, the gamma, and the Weibull, for some values of its parameters. (The criterion of minimizing costs per-unit-time is easily converted to the criterion of minimizing costs per expected piece of equipment good per period of time. This conversion is effected by replacing C and C^* by, respectively, $K + C/A$ and $K^* + C^*/A$ where the C's denote the money costs of maintenance actions, the K's denote downtime costs, and A is the rate of amortization. Minimizing this revised criterion is equivalent to minimizing the cost of producing a given level of performance, provided the unit cost of the equipment is a constant.)

[9] This example was obtained from [3]. p. 90.

[10] An application of the two-part preventive maintenance model is contained in [17].

(ii) if $n \leq x < N$, replace part (1) if either part fails;

(iii) if $N \leq x$, replace part (1) at once, where x is the age of the equipment.[11] The calculation of these decision parameters can be accomplished directly by expressing the criterion, expected cost per-unit-time per expected proportion of equipment good, as a function of the parameters and then minimizing this function with respect to n and N. The generalization of this model to a system composed of part (1) and M exponentially failing parts is straightforward.

The implementation of a particular policy generates a stochastic process that with the aid of several renewal theoretic results is easily analyzed. The analysis is useful in predicting the behavior of the stochastic process and also in assessing the performance of a particular policy. The choice among nonoptimal maintenance policies is greatly facilitated by an analysis of this kind. Furthermore, with a particular policy having been chosen, operating characteristics can then be used to predict supply and maintenance requirements.[12]

The simplest preparedness policy is the replacement of a single piece of equipment. The time-to-failure is a random variable with an arbitrary probability distribution. The equipment cannot be inspected before replacement, and the only decision is to determine the replacement interval. Since replacement yields an equipment as good as new, there is a natural renewal cycle from one replacement to the next, and neglecting discounting it is appropriate to minimize costs over a single cycle. Letting N and K denote, respectively, the replacement interval and the time-to-replace, L, the cycle length is simply $N + K$. The expected good time over a cycle is

$$(15) \qquad T = \int_0^N [1 - F(t)]\, dt.$$

---

[11] Notice the analogy between the (n, N) structure of this optimal maintenance policy and that of the (s, S) inventory model. For a description of the inventory model, see [2].

[12] Three of the most important operating characteristics for the periodic preventive maintenance model are: the expected rate of replacement, $r_.$, the expected rate of failure, r_0, and the expected rate of preventive replacement, r_1. The steady state values of these operating characteristics are:

$$(10) \qquad r_. = [E(Y)]^{-1}$$

$$(11) \qquad r_0 = p[E(Y)]^{-1}$$

$$(12) \qquad r_1 = (1 - p)\,[(E(Y))]^{-1}$$

where

$$(13) \qquad E(Y) = \int_0^N (1 - F(t))\, dt$$

$$(14) \qquad p = F(N)$$

and F is the cumulative failure distribution (Calculations of operating characteristics for other maintenance models are contained in [3], [14] and [18].)

Thus the proportion of time good over the cycle is

(16) $$G(N) = \frac{T}{L}.$$

The criterion to be minimized is $\bar{C}(N)$, the cost per proportion of good time per-unit-time,

(17) $$\bar{C}(N) = \frac{A + (C/(N + K))}{G(N)}$$

where C is the dollar cost of a replacement and A is the cost per period amortization. Assuming a constant unit cost of producing equipments, minimizing $\bar{C}(N)$ is equivalent to minimizing the cost of maintaining a fixed expected number of good equipments. The unique optimal replacement interval is obtained by setting the derivative of (17) equal to zero and solving for N. For example, if $R(t)$ is exponential with failure rate, λ, a quadratic approximation to $e^{\lambda N}$ yields the following optimal replacement interval:

(18) $$N \approx \left[\frac{2(K + C/A)}{\lambda} \right]^{1/2}.$$

If the distribution of times to failure is exponential, equipment inspection has the same renewal property as replacement; regardless of age, an unfailed equipment is as good as new. The calculation of an optimal inspection interval is essentially the same as for replacement.[13] M. Kamins [15] and J. Coleman and I. Jack Abrams [6] have generalized the inspection model to include the possibility that inspection may be imperfect. Two imperfections are recognized. First, the detection procedure may not detect an existing failure and, second, inspection may register a failure when the equipment is good. The presence of either of these imperfections does not alter the policy's periodicity but does

---

[13] The expected cost per proportion of good time per-unit-time is now

(19) $$\bar{C}(N) = \frac{AL + B + (1 - \sigma e^{\lambda N})C}{\displaystyle\int_0^N R(t)\, dt}$$

where L the expected cycle length is:

(20) $$L = N + H + [1 - \sigma e^{-\lambda N}]K,$$

and B, H, and σ are, respectively, the dollar cost of inspection, the time to inspect, and the probability that the equipment survives inspection. Setting the derivative of Eq. (19) equal to zero, a quadratic approximation to the unique solution, the optimal inspection interval is:

(21) $$N \cong \left[\frac{2[H + B/A + (1 - \sigma)\,(K + C/A)]}{\lambda} \right]^{1/2}$$

impair the validity of Eq. (19). The necessary modifications are presented in Refs. 6 and 15.[14]

It is important to note the significance of the exponential distribution in the development of maintenance policies. It is the only probability distribution that has no memory: that is, if exponentially failing equipment has survived to age t, the probability that it will fail in the interval $(t, t + dt)$ is independent of t. This property facilitates mathematical analysis. In addition, many complex equipments have been observed to fail exponentially. This combination of mathematical charm and empirical validity accounts for the distribution's popularity. For further discussion of the exponential distribution see D. R. Cox and W. L. Smith [7], and D. J. Davis [8].

Both the military and industry have shown a great interest in the periodic preventive and preparedness models. The number and variety of military and industrial applications testifies to their practical value. Many of the major airlines of the world calculate their engine overhaul schedules according to the preventive maintenance model. These same airlines use both periodic models to determine inspection and replacement intervals for many other equipments. Many defense industries have also implemented these models, and the increasing cost of procuring and maintaining industrial equipment provides a natural stimulus for further applications. Military interest in periodic policies has paralleled that of industry. The implementation of these policies has been most conspicious in the case of expensive equipment like submarines, missiles, and aircraft, with more and more equipments entering the expensive class. An application of the preparedness maintenance model to a ballistic missile with several subsystems is contained in Ref. [13]. Military applications of the periodic preventive maintenance model have frequently led to the discovery that the replacement interval in effect was too short. The reason for this is not that the cost of an in-service failure is almost equal to the cost of a preventive removal— the cost of failure, especially within a military milieu, is often very high. Rather, the reason for replacing equipments too frequently is simply that many equipments fail exponentially; and when equipments fail exponentially the best policy is to replace *only* at failure. A conservative policy of frequent replacement guarantees nothing but higher operating costs for exponentially failing equipment.

In many applications the probability distribution of the time-to-failure is not known with certainty. Adaptive maintenance policies have been devised to cope with this uncertainty. These policies have a Bayes structure.[15] The form of the equipment's failure distribution is known, but one or more parameters are unknown. Initially, the decision maker's limited information is summarized by

---

[14] Preparedness models have also been developed for equipment possessing more than one part. See [22]. Operating characteristics can also be calculated for these preparedness models. The interested reader should consult Refs. [3], [18], and [22].

[15] For a discussion of the Bayes methodology, see [24].

a subjective probability distribution defined on all possible values of the unknown parameters. The initial maintenance policy is chosen to minimize the
expected value of the expected cost per-unit-time, where the second expectation
is with respect to the subjective probability distribution. Acquisition of new
information about the unknown parameters is accompanied by a revision of the
initial or prior distribution. The revision is conducted in Bayesian fashion, and
the ensuing posterior distribution is used to recompute the maintenance policy.[16]
A summary of these methods was presented in [12], and an application is
contained in [13].

IV. THE RELATIONSHIP BETWEEN MAINTAINABILITY
AND RELIABILITY

In the design and improvement of equipment it is desirable to achieve
the most favorable balance between maintainability and reliability. Maintainability refers to the ease with which repairs can be performed, whereas reliability
measures the frequency of failure. At the design or improvement stage, the decision maker must determine the relative investment in maintainability and
reliability. The decision maker might invest most of his funds in achieving high
reliability, in which case the equipment fails infrequently, but repairs are costly
and lengthy. Alternatively, the major investment might be in maintainability,
in which case the equipment fails frequently, but is repaired easily and quickly.
Assuming a constant rate of output from an operational equipment, either in

---

[16] As an illustration an adaptive policy will be calculated for the periodic preventive replacement policy. The equipment is assumed to fail exponentially with an unknown failure
rate, λ. The prior distribution of λ, $h(\lambda)$ is assumed to be Gamma with parameters a and b,

$$(22) \qquad h(\lambda) = \begin{cases} b^a \lambda^{a-1} e^{-b\lambda} d\lambda, & \lambda \geq 0 \\ 0 & \text{elsewhere.} \end{cases}$$

The equipment is observed to fail at times $(t_1, t_2, \ldots, t_n)$. The posterior density, g, given this
information is also Gamma with parameters d and f, where $d = n + a$ and $f = b + \Sigma\, t_i$. The
adaptive replacement policy is obtained by minimizing the expected value of the expected cost
per-unit-time with respect to the posterior distribution. More precisely, the replacement interval
is chosen to

$$(23) \qquad \text{Min}_N \int_0^\infty \bar{C}(N, \lambda) g(\lambda \mid t_1, \ldots, t_n)\, d\lambda.$$

Differentiating with respect to N and integrating over λ yield:

$$(24) \qquad \frac{N + f^d}{f^{d-1}} - Nd - \left(K + \frac{C}{A}\right)(d - 1) = 0.$$

The solution of this equation—the adaptive replacement interval—is obtainable by standard
numerical techniques.

the form of a physical product or, as in the case for many 'weapon systems', in the form of readiness, the optimal allocation of funds between maintainability and reliability maximizes the in-commission rate. The in-commission rate is the fraction of time the equipment is operational. Using standard economic theory, the optimal allocation is achieved when the incremental increase in the in-commission rate, the marginal product, per dollar spent on reliability equals the corresponding incremental increase per dollar spent on maintainability. Symbolically, this optimal allocation occurs when

$$(25) \qquad \frac{mp_r}{p_r} = \frac{mp_m}{p_m}$$

where mp_r and mp_m are, respectively, the marginal products of reliability and maintainability, and p_r and p_m are the per unit prices, assumed constant, of reliability and maintainability. Although this excursion into price theory yields some insight, the proposed solution is too general to be operationally useful.[17] The Appendix contains a more specific formulation of the problem, which, although exceedingly simple, captures the distinctive elements of this allocation problem. The problem is to improve the performance of a particular 'weapon system' by allocating a fixed budget between reliability improvement and maintainability improvement. Such problems of product improvement frequently occur in the military and defense industry. Furthermore, the improvements are frequently achieved by altering reliability and maintainability parameters. Nevertheless, it is sometimes more important to improve another performance characteristic rather than invest in either reliability or maintainability. Determining the best combination of reliability, maintainability, and other performance parameters necessitates an analysis somewhat different from that presented here. The criterion to be maximized then would be mission value instead of the in-commission rate. The alternative investments would be measured by their cost and the amount by which each enhances mission value.

V. CONCLUSIONS

The topics discussed in this chapter represent only a small part of the research that has been recently accomplished in the analysis of maintenance policies. Many maintenance models have been studied in which queuing plays a prominent role. The research on queuing is, however, so vast that any discussion of these models would either be inadequate or require a separate chapter.[18] It

---

[17] More importantly, some of the assumptions underlying the price-theory model are invalid. In particular, it is unlikely that the production function, the relationship between the in-commission rate and the factors, maintainability and reliability, exhibits constant returns to scale.

[18] The reader interested in queuing applications should consult [3] and [19].

should be noted, however, that virtually all the maintenance models that include queuing are those in which the equipment is replaced at failure. Queuing techniques are then employed to calculate the optimal number of equipments and repair teams. To the best of the author's knowledge, nontrivial maintenance policies have never been embedded in a queuing milieu. Analysis of these problems is an important area for further research.

Applications of simulation models to maintenance problems comprise another significant segment of maintenance research. These results were excluded from the presentation for essentially the same reasons as those for queuing.[19]

The relation between maintenance and system operation has been explored in much more detail than our discussion suggests. The interested reader is referred to the work of C. F. Bell [4] and R. A. Levine and R. B. Rainey, [11] and the other references listed in each.

At several points in the chapter the relation between inventory and maintenance models has been observed. The interaction between the two processes has, however, never been analyzed. For example, how is the optimality of an inventory model affected when demands are stochastically generated by equipment that is preventively maintained; or conversely, how is an optimal preventive maintenance policy derived when it is connected with a particular inventory policy? Questions like these merit additional research.[20]

APPENDIX [21]

At any point of time the weapon system is assumed to be in one of two states—either operating or undergoing repair. Sufficient resources are devoted to repair so that queues never develop; that is, a failed 'weapon system' is always assured of immediate service. The 'weapon system' fails according to a geometric probability distribution with parameter p_2, where p_2 is the probability of not failing during a specific time interval. The distribution of times to repair is also geometric with parameter p_1, where p_1 is the probability of completing a repair during a specified time interval. The description implies that the

---

[19] The reader interested in simulation applications should consult [10], [25], [26], and [27].

[20] Medical application of maintenance scheduling theory is another important area that has received virtually no attention. These applications could contribute significantly to that discipline probably best described as the economics of health. Large sums of money are spent every year on preventive medicine in both the military and civilian sectors. The effectiveness of these expenditures has not been measured very precisely. The mathematical techniques that were derived for equipment maintenance problems should be useful in assessing the value of these expenditures and in suggesting alternative preventive medicine programs. For example, these techniques could be used to determine the optimal time between medical and dental examinations and also to measure the rewards from improving detection techniques.

[21] A substantial portion of this Appendix is based on [4].

transitions from the operational state s_1 to the repair state s_2 and vice versa are governed by a Markov chain with transition matrix,

$$
(26) \qquad T = \begin{array}{c} \\ s_1 \\ \\ s_2 \end{array} \begin{array}{cc} s_1 & s_2 \\ \left| \begin{array}{cc} p_2 & 1 - p_2 \\ \\ p_1 & 1 - p_1 \end{array} \right| \end{array}.
$$

Since T has no zero entries, the Markov chain is regular. Regularity implies the existence of a unique fixed vector W such that

$$
(27) \qquad WT = W.
$$

The ith element of W, W_i, is the probability of being in state s_i in the long run. W_1 and W_2 can be obtained by solving the state equations:

$$
(28) \qquad W_1 p_2 + W_2 p_1 = W_1;
$$

$$
(29) \qquad W_1 (1 - p_2) + W_2 (1 - p_1) = W_2.
$$

The nontrivial, normalized ($\Sigma W_i = 1$) solution is:

$$
(30) \qquad W_1 = \frac{p_1}{(1 - p_2) + p_1};
$$

$$
(31) \qquad W_2 = 1 - W_1 = \frac{1 - p_2}{(1 - p_2) + p_1}.
$$

In the long run the system will be in operation W_1 per cent of the time and in repair W_2 per cent of the time.

Assume that when funds for product improvement become available, the system has given repair and reliability characteristics, p_1^0 and p_2^0, respectively. Then, in the absence of product improvement the long run in-commission rate is denoted by

$$
(32) \qquad W_1 = \frac{p_1^0}{1 - p_2^0 + p_1^0}.
$$

The product-improvement funds may be spent on either improving the repair facility (increasing p_1^0 by x_1) and/or improving the reliability (increasing p_2^0 by x_2). After the funds are spent and the system adjusts, the in-commission rate is then denoted by

$$
(33) \qquad W_1 = \frac{p_1^0 + x_1}{1 - (p_2^0 + x_2) + (p_1^0 + x_1)}
$$

where

$$
0 \le x_1 \le 1 - p_1^0, \qquad 0 < p_1^0 \le 1;
$$

$$
0 \le x_2 \le 1 - p_2^0, \qquad 0 < p_2^0 \le 1.
$$

The relative sizes of x_1 and x_2 will depend on $C(x_1, x_2)$, the cost of these improvements. The cost of x_1 is independent of the amount of x_2 purchased, that is,

(34) $$C(x_1, x_2) = C_1(x_1) + C_2(x_2).$$

Furthermore, these functions are assumed convex in the relevant regions, with their first and second derivative satisfying the following inequalities,

$$C_1'(x_1) > 0, \qquad C_2'(x_2) > 0;$$
$$C_1''(x_1) \geq 0, \qquad C_2''(x_2) \geq 0,$$
$$0 \leq x_1 \leq 1 - p_1^0,$$
$$0 \leq x_2 \leq 1 - p_2^0.$$

The object of product improvement is to purchase the largest possible in-commission rate with the funds available. Or, letting C denote the size of the product-improvement budget, the object of product improvement is to

(35) $$\text{Max} \frac{p_1^0 + x_1}{1 - (p_2^0 + x_2) + (p_1^0 + x_1)}$$

subject to

$$C_1(x_1) + C_2(x_2) - C = 0,$$
$$0 \leq x_1 \leq 1 - p_1^0,$$
$$0 \leq x_2 \leq 1 - p_2^0.$$

The solution to this problem, (x_1^*, x_2^*), specifies the optimal division of the product-improvement budget between the two technical alternatives. The size of the product-improvement budget determines the output eventually achieved.

There are several methods available for solving problems of this kind (external problems with constraints). The simplest method is the so-called method of direct elimination. The constraining equation (budget constraint) is solved for one variable in terms of the other. The function to be maximized is then reexpressed in terms of the independent variable alone, and the solution obtained in the usual way. This procedure will be illustrated for linear cost functions.

PRODUCT IMPROVEMENT WHEN COSTS ARE LINEAR

Assume the costs of the incremental improvements, x_1 and x_2, are cost of repair improvement,

(36) $$C_1(x_1) = \alpha x_1, \qquad \alpha > 0,$$

and cost of reliability improvement,

$$(37) \qquad C_2(x_2) = \beta x_2, \qquad \beta > 0;$$

and that all available money is spent,

$$(38) \qquad C_1(x_1) + C_2(x_2) = C.$$

Under these conditions the object is to

$$(39) \qquad \text{Max} \frac{p_1^0 + x_1}{1 - (p_2^0 + x_2) + (p_1^0 + x_1)}$$

subject to

$$0 \leq x_1 \leq 1 - p_1^0,$$

$$0 \leq x_2 \leq 1 - p_2^0,$$

$$\alpha x_1 + \beta x_2 = C.$$

Note that the in-commission rate W_1 can be written

$$(40) \qquad W_1 = \frac{p_1^0 + x_1}{1 - (p_2^0 + x_2) + (p_1^0 + x_1)} = \frac{1}{\dfrac{1 - p_2^0 - x_2}{p_1^0 + x_1} + 1}$$

Consequently, maximizing W_1 is equivalent to minimizing

$$(41) \qquad H = \frac{1 - p_2^0 - x_2}{p_1^0 + x_1}.$$

Solving the budget constraint for x_2 gives

$$(42) \qquad x_2 = \frac{C - \alpha x_1}{\beta}.$$

Rewriting (41) in terms of x_1 yields

$$(43) \qquad \text{Min} \frac{\beta(1 - p_2^0) - C + \alpha x_1}{\beta p_1^0 + \beta x_1} = H,$$

subject to

$$0 \leq x_1 \leq 1 - p_1^0,$$

$$0 \leq x_2 = \frac{C - \alpha x_1}{\beta} \leq 1 - p_2^0.$$

Differentiating H with respect to x_1 yields

$$(44) \qquad \frac{dH}{dx_1} = \frac{\alpha \beta p_1^0 - \beta^2(1 - p_2^0) + \beta C}{(\beta p_1^0 + \beta x_1)^2}.$$

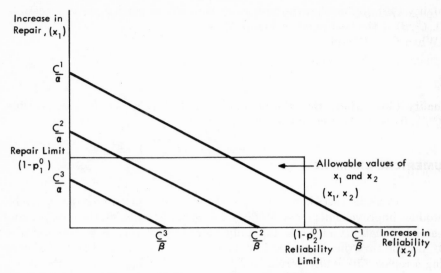

Figure 10–1   *Allocation Policy as a Function of Expenditure Level*

Therefore, H is a decreasing function of x_1 when the numerator is negative or when

$$(45) \qquad\qquad 1 - p_2^0 > \frac{\alpha}{\beta} p_1^0 + \frac{C}{\beta};$$

and an increasing function of x_1 when the numerator is positive, or when

$$(46) \qquad\qquad 1 - p_2^0 < \frac{\alpha}{\beta} p_1^0 + \frac{C}{\beta}.$$

If H is a decreasing function of x_1, as much x_1 as possible is purchased, whereas if H is an increasing function of x_1, as much x_2 as possible is purchased. This policy is illustrated in Figure 10–1 for three different total expenditure levels, C^1, C^2 and C^3.

Since α and β are positive and p_1 is non-negative, $C = C^1$ and

$$\frac{C^1}{\beta} > 1 - p_2^0$$

implies (see inequality 46) that the best policy is to buy as much x_2 as possible. Therefore, the desired point in Figure 10–1 is (x_1, x_2).

When $C = C^2$ and

$$\frac{C^2}{\beta} > (1 - p_2) - \frac{\alpha}{\beta p_1},$$

inequality (46) implies that the best policy is to buy as much x_1, x_2 as is possible, so $(0, C^2/\beta)$ is the best point in Figure 10–1.

When $C = C^3$ and

$$\frac{C^3}{\beta} < (1 - p_2) - \frac{\alpha}{p_1},$$

inequality (45) implies that the best policy is to buy as much x_1 as possible, so $(C^3/\alpha, 0)$ is the best combination.

A NUMERICAL EXAMPLE

Consider cases in which one of the following three budgets is available for product improvement: $C^1 = \$1000$; $C^2 = \$750$; $C^3 = \$250$; the cost-per-unit increases in reliability and maintainability are, respectively, $\beta = 100$ and $\alpha = 1000$. Assume that the original reliability is $p_2^0 = \frac{1}{8}$ and the probability of completing a repair during any period is $p_1^0 = \frac{1}{4}$. For a budget of size C_1 then,

$$1 - p_2^0 = \frac{7}{8}, \qquad \frac{\alpha}{\beta} p_1^0 + \frac{C^1}{\beta} = \frac{5}{4},$$

and the original availability, W_1^0, is 22 per cent.

Since

$$1 - p_2^0 < \frac{\alpha}{\beta} p_1^0 + \frac{C^1}{\beta}$$

then from inequality (46) we should buy as much reliability as possible. So $x_2 = \frac{7}{8}$ and $x_1 = \frac{1}{8}$. The new reliability is $p_2^0 + x_2 = 1$, and the repair parameter is $p_1^0 + x_1 = \frac{3}{8}$. The in-commission rate W_1 is

$$W_1 = \frac{p_1^0 + x_1}{1 - (p_2^0 + x_2) + (p_1^0 + x_1)} = 100 \text{ per cent.}$$

If the budget is of size C^2,

$$1 - p_2^0 = \frac{7}{8}, \qquad \frac{\alpha}{\beta} p_1^0 + \frac{C^2}{\beta} = 1,$$

and the initial in-commission rate is 22 per cent. Since

$$1 - p_2^0 < \frac{\alpha}{\beta} p_1^0 + \frac{C^2}{\beta},$$

as much x_2 as possible is purchased so $x_2 = \frac{3}{4}$. At this point, the funds are depleted so $x_1 = 0$. The new system parameters are reliability, $p_2^0 + x_2 = \frac{7}{8}$; repair

$p_1^0 = \frac{1}{4}$; and in-commission rate, $W_1 = 67$ per cent. Finally, if the budget is of size C^3,

$$1 - p_2^0 = \frac{7}{8}, \qquad \frac{\alpha}{\beta} p_1^0 + \frac{C^3}{\beta} = \frac{1}{2},$$

and the initial availability is again 22 per cent, since

$$1 = p_2^0 > \frac{\alpha}{\beta} p_1^0 + \frac{C^3}{\beta},$$

in this case as much maintainability as possible is purchased, all of the budget is spent on x_1. The new system parameters are $p_2^0 = \frac{1}{8}$, $p_1^0 + x_1 = \frac{1}{2}$ and $W_1 = 36$ per cent. If, alternatively, all the money is expended on x_2, the system parameters are $p_2^0 + x_2 = \frac{3}{8}$, $p_1^0 = \frac{1}{4}$, and $W_1 = 28.5$ per cent.

REFERENCES

1. Alchian, A. A., *Economic Replacement Policy*. R-225 The RAND Corporation, April, 1952.

2. Arrow, K. J., S. Karlin, and H. Scarf, *Studies in the Mathematical Theory of Inventory and Production*. Stanford: Stanford University Press, 1958.

3. Barlow, R. and F. Proschan, *Mathematical Theory of Reliability*, New York: John Wiley & Sons, Inc., 1965.

4. Bell, C. F., *Influence of Resource and Policy Changes on Aircraft Capabilities*. R-382 The RAND Corporation, August, 1961.

5. Bellman, R. and S. Dreyfus, *Applied Dynamic Programming*. Princeton, N. J.: Princeton University Press, 1962.

6. Coleman, John J. and I. Jack Abrams, "Mathematical Model for Operations Readiness." *Operations Research*, Vol. 10, No. 1, (January–February, 1962), pp. 126–38.

7. Cox, D. R. and W. L. Smith, "On the Superposition of Renewal Processes." *Biometrica*, Vol. 41 (1954), pp. 91–99.

8. Davis, D. J., "An Analysis of Some Failure Data." *Journal of the American Statistical Association*, Vol. 47, No. 258 (June, 1952).

9. Deavers, K. L. and J. J. McCall, *An Analysis of Procurement and Product Improvement Decisions*, RM-3859-PR. The RAND Corporation, December, 1963.

10. Ginsberg, A. S. and B. A. King, *Base Operations-Maintenance Simulator*. RM-4072-PR, The RAND Corporation (September, 1964).

11. Levine, R. A. and R. B. Rainey, *The Base Operations-Maintenance Model Used in RAND Logistics Research*, RM-2374. The RAND Corporation, May, 1959.

12. Jorgenson, D. W. and J. J. McCall, "Optimal Scheduling of Replacement and Inspection." *Operations Research* (October, 1963), pp. 732–46.

13. ———, "Optimal Replacement Policies for a Ballistic Missile." *Management Science* (April, 1963), pp. 358–79.

14. ——— and R. Radner, *Optimal Maintenance of Stochastically Failing Equipment*, R-437-PR, The RAND Corporation, April, 1966.

15. Kamins, M., *Determining Checkout Intervals for Systems Subject to Random Failures*, RM-2578. The RAND Corporation, June, 1960.

16. ——— and J. J. McCall, *Planned Replacement of Aircraft and Missile Parts*, RM-2810-PR. The RAND Corporation, November, 1961.

17. McCall, J. J., *Solution of a Simple Overhaul Model*, RM-2989-PR. The RAND Corporation, February, 1962.

18. ———, "Operating Characteristics of Opportunistic Replacement and Inspection Policies." *Management Science*, Vol. 10, No. 1 (October, 1963), pp. 85–97.

19. ———, "Maintenance Policies For Stochastically Failing Equipment: A Survey." *Management Science*, Vol. 11, No. 5 (March, 1965).

20. Morse, P. M., "Maintenance of Equipment," *Queues, Inventories, and Maintenance.* New York: John Wiley and Sons, 1958, Chapter 11, pp. 157–79.

21. Radner, R. and D. W. Jorgenson, "Optimal Replacement and Inspection of Stochastically Failing Equipment," *Studies in Applied Probability and Management Science*, K. J. Arrow, S. Karlin and H. Scarf (eds.), Stanford University Press, Stanford, California, 1962, pp. 184–206.

22. ——— ———, "Opportunistic Replacement of a Single Part in the Presence of Several Monitored Parts." *Management Science*, Vol. 10, No. 1 (October, 1963), pp. 70–84.

23. ———, "Maintenance Policies for Systems with Several Parts." Technical Report No. 8, Berkeley: Center for Research in Management Science, University of California (November, 1962).

24. Raiffa, Howard and Robert Schlaifer, *Applied Statistical Decision Theory.* Cambridge: Division of Research, Harvard Business School, 1961.

25. Smith, T. C., *SAMSON: Support-Availability Multi-System Operations Model.* RM-4077-PR, The RAND Corporation (June, 1964).

26. Steorts, R. C., *A Simulation Model of an Inertial Guidance System Repair Shop: A Planning Tool.* RM-3599-PR, The RAND Corporation (March, 1964).

27. Voosen, B. J. and D. Goldman, *PLANET: Planned Logistics Analysis and Evaluation Technique—Availability and Base Cadre Model*, RM-4659-PR. The RAND Corporation, September, 1966.

HARRISON S. CAMPBELL

The RAND Corporation

Harrison Campbell is a member of the Staff of The RAND Corporation's Logistics Department. He received his B.S. degree from Massachusetts Institute of Technology in 1950 and holds an M.A. and a Ph.D. in Economics from Columbia University. Formerly with the Department of Commerce and General Dynamics, Fort Worth, he joined RAND in 1957, where his work has included extensive experience with military inventory management problems.

11

Procurement and

Management of Spares

INTRODUCTION *

It is important to remember that, although the military materiel system is large and diverse, it provides but one of the inputs to the creation of military capability. The fundamental objective of spares management, therefore, is to furnish the desired level of one input to a productive process that also uses maintenance personnel, equipment, and supplies (other than spares). Implicitly or otherwise, some judgment must be formed as to the desired level of the spare-parts input; and it becomes the task of spares management to accomplish this as efficiently as possible.[1]

This management job is rightfully a major preoccupation of the military departments and the Department of Defense. The Air Force alone stocks about 1,200,000 spare items, with an acquisition value of more than 5 billion dollars (active inventory, not including spare engines). Additions to spares stocks amount to nearly three-quarters of a billion dollars annually. This inventory creates a managerial task of tremendous scale.

Spares management has many facets—such as organization, transportation, storage and handling of materiel, repair of parts, and cataloguing—but the most fundamental area concerns policies for stock control and spares requirements determination. This aspect of spares management will be the main concern of this chapter, with attention focused primarily upon the application of the tools of inventory-control theory to the analysis of spares procurement and management.

In other words, the discussion will concern the rules for deciding which inventory levels are optimal or preferred at the various stockage points in a system. The focus is dictated by the key role played by stockage decisions in a materiel system. Stockage policy has a pervasive, if implicit, control over the systems operating costs: It determines the level of investment and the frequency of shortages, of requisitions, of new procurements, and of repair actions.

An introductory survey of the subject, such as this, cannot cover the entire field of inventory theory or its applications. Instead, the chapter will be broken down into three parts: (1) a discussion of the main choices in modeling logistics inventory systems and the interpretation of inventory models and their results; (2) a review of some inventory models representing basic analytic approaches that should have had—or can be expected to have—the largest role in application

---

* Numbers appearing in brackets refer to references listed at the end of the chapter.

[1] The view taken here is that spares, maintenance personnel and equipment, and the major equipment items themselves (for example, B-52 aircraft) are inputs to a productive process and substitutable for each other within limits. Spares management is then, technically, a problem in suboptimization of the system providing the spares input for any specified level of that input. References [6], [7], and [18] develop these ideas more completely. Various approaches have been suggested or tried for fixing the level of the spares input. These will be discussed in this chapter.

to logistics systems; and (3) a presentation of several special topics of importance to the study of spares management.

Inventory Analysis—Generalities

It is important to realize that inventory models are, as a class, severe abstractions of the real world. As with other decision-oriented models, their value lies in a systematic relating of the main elements of a problem, so that a large volume of recurring decisions of the same type can be made consistently in accordance with agreed-upon criteria. But before an outline of the structure of inventory analyses is presented, some discussion of present-day inventory management may be in order.

Spares management presents a considerable problem of choice to the would-be analyst. He can be concerned with the determination of future requirements or with the distribution of present stocks. He may deal with the entire system of stockage points, including depots or primary supply points, intermediate storage sites, repair points, and final users, or with some subgrouping of points; or he may be able to treat points independently of one another for analytic purposes. In some problems it may be appropriate to deal with spares according to a property-class grouping (Aircraft Wheel and Brake Systems), and for other purposes identification of the specific weapon (C-130 Aircraft) may be important.

The existing framework for data collection and management control, which must limit an investigation to some extent, will be more or less elaborate, depending on the category of cost and repairability to which a particular set of spares belongs. In the Air Force, for example, although high-cost, recoverable spares represent only some 3 per cent of the number of items, they account for nearly 70 per cent of total spares investment. Clearly, more elaborate management methods are justifiable for these articles than for low-cost material. This management framework may be taken as given for many purposes, though ultimately some judgment must be reached as to the appropriate cost of data collection, accounting, and other forms of management input.

As a commodity, spare parts possess several attributes with particular implications for management. Procurement lead-times may be quite long, on the order of a year or more for high-cost spares. Future spares usage is very difficult to predict, partly because of its characteristic randomness, partly because of the need to forecast the operational program of the end-use weapon, and partly because of obsolescence due to design change. Initial estimates are particularly error-prone [19], a fact that is important in studies of the provisioning area.

How much of the total spares-management system must be embraced in a single analytic formulation? It is certainly neither practical nor necessary to deal with everything at once. Simplifications of the problem are obviously desirable from the standpoint of facilitating computation of policies and managerial understanding; however, a valid analysis does require that all interacting features of the problem be included in a meaningful way.

For many purposes, for example, it is important to consider related sets of spares, such as those associated with a particular weapon, rather than to deal with individual items. This broader view is necessary because different spares are, within limits, substitutes for each other as inputs to weapon maintenance. Maintenance efficiency and weapon up-time are sensitive to aggregate supply effectiveness, and single-item models are not well suited to analysis or display of aggregate costs and outcomes. It is frequently not enough to know that a policy in force possesses optimal properties for each item; it may also be important to determine the relation between *total* cost and effectiveness for decision-making purposes.

Interaction also exists among echelons. The stock levels held at depot in part determine the depot-base resupply time, which affects the stock levels needed at the base. Further, the frequency of ordering from the base affects the cost of depot operation, through the number of orders the depot must process and the effect on the variance of depot issues. These considerations argue for comprehensive multiechelon, multibase analyses, but such approaches have met with limited success.

The Structure of Inventory Analyses

The conventional approach is to cast the problem in the form of an economic model, for which either (1) costs are the only relevant consideration and are minimized by the choice of stockage policy or (2) policy is chosen to minimize costs for some given level of effectiveness.[2] These models must embody assumptions or rules about a number of different components of the real-world counterpart system: a policy structure or format, a particular model of the demand process, a model of the replenishment process, and a statement about the dependence of the relevant costs upon these factors.

The Ordering Policy. The ordering discipline is frequently dictated by the problem or, more rarely, is one of the things to be determined by analysis. By far the commonest is the (s, S), or two-bin, policy, for which a large body of theory also exists. When the stock, x, falls below the predetermined level, s, an order is placed for $S - x$ units, S and s being chosen so as to minimize costs. A related discipline is the (s, Q) policy, in which the order placed when the stock falls to or below s is of a fixed size, Q. These ordering policies may be coupled with a system of continuous review, in which it is known when the reorder point is passed. This implies current knowledge of balances, which may be a trivial requirement if a single location is involved, but may involve elaborate reporting of transactions in larger systems.

An alternative to continuous review is periodic review. This corresponds to the wholesale-requirements methods in a number of areas where stocks on hand are compared, quarterly perhaps, to desired stocks and the difference placed on procurement each time. Or, a periodic review system may be combined with an (s, S) or (s, Q) policy, in which stock is reordered up to S (or ordered in batches of size Q) if below s at the time of review (otherwise no order is placed).

---

[2] Alternatively, effectiveness may be maximized for some given budget.

An important special case of the (s, S) policy is the $(S - 1, S)$ policy, in which "one-to-one" ordering is practiced (the reorder point being one less than the maximum stock). When this policy form can be assumed to be optimal (typically, where higher-cost spares are involved), it is only necessary to compute values for a single policy variable, S, and certain other analytic simplifications obtain. This makes possible more comprehensive analysis for this case.

Models of Demand. The representation of the way in which demands for inventory arise is an important part of the analysis of inventory problems. It is usual to treat spares demand as a random process described by an appropriate probability distribution function (inventory studies have also dealt with known, or deterministic, demand, but these are not relevant to the spares problem). The modeling task then becomes one of selecting the best function by considering empirical fit, analytic convenience, and the physical process embodied by the probability model.

The physical assumptions corresponding to the Poisson distribution are suggestive of the conditions under which spares demand occurs. A Poisson distribution arises where (1) the number of demands occurring in any interval of time is statistically independent of the number occurring in any other non-overlapping interval (that is, the fact that a demand occurred today gives no information about the number of demands tomorrow), (2) the process is stable over time, and (3) if time is divided into small enough intervals, the probability of two or more demands in the same interval is negligible ([12], pp. 143–54).

The advantages of the Poisson model are compelling: Its assumptions seem to be satisfied in practice; its shape (skewed to the left) corresponds well to empirical frequency distributions of demand; it is analytically tractable; and it is a one-parameter distribution, requiring only the mean rate of demand (or average issue rate) for estimation purposes.

But often the Poisson does not give a good fit to spares-demand data, and some other model of the underlying demand process is chosen [13], [9]. This inadequacy can be attributed to circumstances interfering with the simple Poisson assumptions: There may be "contagion" effects in maintenance if discovery of a defective part on one piece of equipment leads to inspection of other units (and possibly preventive replacement); some parts are liable to damage during installation, and activity of different aircraft is usually correlated so that the exposures to the possibility of failure are bunched in time.

The effect of these, or possibly other, unknown circumstances is to raise the apparent variance of demand to values inconsistent with the Poisson hypothesis. A two-parameter distribution is then needed that will, in effect, allow a more exaggerated skewness. Compound Poisson distribution functions are a natural choice: They are two-parameter distributions (allowing a fit to any empirically determined mean and variance); they retain some correspondence to the assumptions suggested by the physical process; and they possess some of the analytical advantages of the simple Poisson.[3] The commoner forms are the

---

[3] Reference [12], pp. 268–72, contains a description of the compound Poisson family.

geometric, or stuttering, Poisson and the negative binomial. Without discussing the particulars of either distribution, the physical process they describe is that demands arise in bursts, or clusters. The number in any burst is governed by the geometric or logarithm distributions, respectively, and the occurrence of the bursts themselves constitutes a simple Poisson process.

Whatever probability model is used, an implicit problem of estimation exists in the application of the inventory policy. The model may assume that the distribution and its parameter values are known, but in practice these must be estimated from past data. Estimation errors are one of the most serious causes of poor performance by inventory proposals. It may be advantageous to reflect any uncertainty about the estimate of the mean rate of demand by means of a Bayesian model (for an example, see [10]).[4] Inventory policies incorporating Bayesian procedures involve considerably increased computation but possess significant advantages. There is no restriction expressing uncertainty about future demand in a single set of probabilities that may not correspond very well to reasonable assumptions about the demand process; rather, it is possible to view the mean (or other parameters) of the underlying demand distribution as itself subject to uncertainty, expressed in a prior distribution. Demand is then viewed as a two-stage process of a random choice of the parameter(s) of some type of distribution from the prior distribution and a subsequent random draw of the size of demand from the particular distribution selected. The probabilities of any demand level for this two-stage process can be computed, and, when a sample of actual demand data is observed, the prior distribution can be modified by the application of Bayes theorem and the demand probabilities re-calculated. This *ex posteriori* distribution will exhibit a smaller variance, thus reflecting "learning" or reduced uncertainty about the parameter(s) of the basic or underlying demand distribution. Indeed, the major advantage of the Bayesian approach in inventory models, is that it provides a systematic way of reflecting increased knowledge into the estimate of the future. Exploitation of this learning in most cases presupposes a multiperiod inventory analysis.

So far demand has been discussed as though it were a stationary process, that is, identically distributed in every time period. Obviously, this assumption does not hold for some of the most important spares-decision situations, because spares usage is related to weapon activity, which changes continuously as weapons phase in and out. It is still possible to assume that the distribution is stationary with respect to some "program element," such as aircraft flying hours, but models reflecting a varying program are necessarily computationally more complex than "steady-state" models.

The case where demand is not stationary, whether due to varying operational programs (per unit time) or other causes, has been treated as a problem in adaptive forecasting through the use of exponential smoothing [2].

The Replenishment Process. The process by which resupply is accomplished must be described by the inventory model. This may involve resupply from a

---

[4] See [23] for a general treatment of the subject of Bayesian statistics.

higher echelon, procurement from outside the materiel system, or repair of spares turned in at the time of demand—depending on the echelon of stockage and the category of spare parts.

A considerable simplification in the analysis is possible if the replenishment time can be treated as fixed or known. When it cannot be a known constant, it is represented as a randomly determined delay, in which the response times are independent of each other and of the stock-level position. This delay may be drawn from an empirical distribution, or an analytic function may be fitted to the data. The significance of these alternatives will become clearer in connection with the specific inventory analyses in the next section.

The Relevant Costs. The relevant costs are, of course, those that vary when the inventory policy changes. Since the cost structure permitted by inventory models is rather simple, the estimation of cost parameters requires careful interpretation and judgment. The costs can be classified under several headings: cost of procurement, cost of ordering and shipping inventories to the point of use, cost of "holding," or keeping inventories in stock, and cost of shortages.

Procurement Costs: This is usually taken to be the unit purchase price plus first-destination transportation cost. In some problems price "breaks," as a function of order size, must be considered. In steady-state models, procurement costs or unit costs do not enter directly, though holding cost is usually estimated as a function of procurement cost.

Holding Costs: These are all costs associated with holding stocks in the logistics system: warehousing costs, inventory-taking costs, cost of modification or maintenance performed on stocks in storage, and so forth. These are related to the time the stocks are held and are typically estimated as a fraction of the value invested in spares. It is also common to include an "obsolescence risk" factor and an interest charge. The interest charge is, in principle, the foregone earnings on the invested sum if it could be devoted to some other, profitable use. Presumably the government's alternative use of funds is debt-retirement, and studies of military inventory systems have generally used the average cost of the public debt as the interest charge. Where it is desirable to reflect a ceiling or constraint on funds, however, the interest charge may be varied to ration the available funds among competing items.

Ordering Costs: These are the costs associated with preparing a purchase order or contract, in the case of procurement of spares, or with preparing a requisition on a wholesale supply point for internal transfers. They are incurred once per purchase or order. Average cost of shipping materiel from depot to base is sometimes treated as part of base ordering cost.

The Shortage Cost: A distinction is made here between the shortage cost and the shortage penalty. Later in this section the penalty will be seen to be equivalent to a policy variable or control; however, there are also objectively measurable costs associated with unfilled demands. These are the extra costs of rapid or premium ordering, transportation, or repair actions that are taken in response to a shortage.

A few words on cost estimation. The overall costs of the inventory activity depend on such things as the volume and value of the stock warehoused and the frequency of orders. If these costs are estimated by standard cost-accounting methods and used in single-item inventory formulas, the overall level of activity is in turn determined, and the cost estimates may change. This circularity can lead to adjustment effects when inventory decision rules are installed.

This is one of the more persuasive arguments for dealing with systems or sets of items rather than with individual items. Management is enabled to focus on overall costs and outcomes for some large part of the supply activity, reaching the desired position directly rather than by trial and error. (For a discussion of this point, see [8], p. 76.)

Other types of costs may be important, especially if changes to the spares-management system itself are being studied. Chief among these are the costs of data processing accompanying more elaborate control systems (central accounting for assets, transactions reporting, or demand forecasting techniques). Also important may be the increase or decrease of costs accompanying changes in response times—requisition processing, transportation, or repair times.

Models and System Objectives. The point has already been made that spares supply is a technical input to a productive process and that the managerial problem has two aspects: to determine the desired level of that input and to provide that chosen level in the more efficient way. The study of logistics has been much more fruitful in the latter task than in the former: Determination of the preferred level of spares input is not well understood as an analytic process (although the problem can certainly be stated formally).

There are essentially two ways of linking the spares subsystem to the overall logistics system. One is to include in the cost function a depletion penalty or shortage penalty representing the cost of compensating for the shortage, over the long run, with increased amounts of other inputs (this procedure will be described more precisely below). Minimization of this cost function with respect to the policy variable will, under the assumptions of the model, provide a stockage policy that is consistent with the desired overall results.

The other method is to require the inventory policy to achieve some specified rate of depletions or shortage, by item or overall. This approach is less commonly used but has several advantages. The rate of shortage occurrences (or their duration, or some similar index of merit) can be compared directly to the occurrence rate in the live inventory system, which allows the performance of the policy and the system to be monitored and permits managerial experience to be applied, directly and naturally, to choosing an appropriate level of effectiveness.

Fundamentally, choosing the effectiveness level and estimating the shortage penalty involve very much the same considerations and information. Consider the following simplified two-part inventory system. The costs of each part, C_1 and C_2, and the number of shortages of each for some time period, N_1 and N_2, are both functions of the stocks, q_1 and q_2.

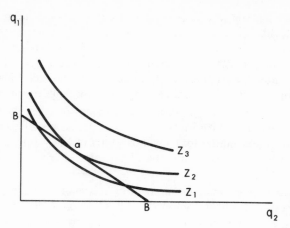

Figure 11-1   *Minimization of Spares Budget for*
                    Given Expected Shortage Rates

Since it is somewhat more convenient to work in terms of the expected number of demands satisfied than expected shortages, we define:

$$(1) \qquad\qquad Z = \bar{X} - N$$

where $\bar{X}$ is the total expected demand and N the total expected shortage. The minimization of the spares budget, B, can be displayed graphically as in Figure 11-1. The curves Z_1, Z_2, and Z_3 represent several of the many possible isoquants showing the combinations of q_1 and q_2 that produce the given value of Z. The line BB is the combinations of q_1 and q_2 that can be purchased with a given budget (costs are here assumed to be linear with the q's). The largest value of Z that can be obtained with a given budget, or the lowest budget that will achieve a particular level, is obviously at a point of tangency of a budget line with a Z isoquant. This occurs in Figure 11-1 at the point a, which is the lowest budget line that will permit the level Z_2 to be reached. At this point of tangency, the rate at which q_1 is being exchanged for q_2 along the constant-Z curve, Z_2, is equal to the rate of exchange of q_1 for q_2 along the constant budget line. Mathematically, this is equivalent to the following:

$$(2) \qquad\qquad \frac{\dfrac{\partial Z}{\partial q_2}}{\dfrac{\partial Z}{\partial q_1}} = \frac{\dfrac{\partial B}{\partial q_2}}{\dfrac{\partial B}{\partial q_1}}$$

$$(3) \qquad\qquad \frac{\dfrac{\partial B}{\partial q_1}}{\dfrac{\partial Z}{\partial q_1}} = \frac{\dfrac{\partial B}{\partial q_2}}{\dfrac{\partial Z}{\partial q_2}} = \lambda$$

Equation (3) simply states the familiar condition for minimum cost of a given product: marginal costs of inputs should be proportional to marginal physical products.

If λ is now used as a shortage penalty, it is possible to write a conventional cost function for either of the two spare parts.

(4) $$C(q) = B(q) + \lambda N(q)$$

The choice of q will minimize $C(q)$ by taking the derivative and setting it equal to zero.

(5) $$\frac{dC}{dq} = \frac{dB}{dq} + \lambda \frac{dN}{dq} = 0$$

Since $dN/dq = -dZ/dq$, Equation (5) is easily seen to be identical with (3). Thus it is possible to use λ as a shortage cost in the set of single-part equations (4) or assign a value of N to each part as in (3). Either procedure yields the same stockage policy, and both require the same considerations, information, and analysis.

Of course, the aggregate shortage objective, N (or Z), must be arrived at in some fashion. By an extension of the foregoing analysis, it is possible to show, conceptually, how it derives from the relationship of inventory inputs to other logistics inputs.

Now consider finding some overall output, F (which might be in-commission weapons, flying hours, or cargo ton-miles). For illustrative purposes, F will be determined by two input factors, the inventory-system input, Z, and one other, M, which represents perhaps balanced doses of maintenance manpower and equipment. Production isoquants and constant outlay curves will again be used. (See Figure 11–2.) By the same reasoning as before, the minimum-cost point is

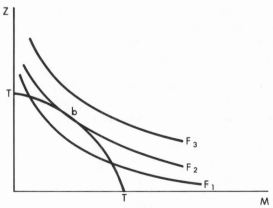

Figure 11–2   *Minimization of Over-All Logistics Budget for Given Levels of Output*

at b for output F_2 (or alternatively, F_2 is the maximum output for the budget represented by TT), and it is characterized by these relations, where T is the total cost.

$$(6) \qquad \frac{\dfrac{\partial F}{\partial Z}}{\dfrac{\partial F}{\partial M}} = \frac{\dfrac{\partial T}{\partial Z}}{\dfrac{\partial T}{\partial M}}$$

$$(7) \qquad \frac{\dfrac{\partial F}{\partial Z}}{\dfrac{\partial T}{\partial Z}} = \frac{\dfrac{\partial F}{\partial M}}{\dfrac{\partial T}{\partial M}}$$

Again, the interpretation of (7) is that all marginal physical products should be proportional to marginal costs, as a condition of efficient production. Since $\partial T/\partial Z$ represents the rate of increase of total cost as the expected number of demands met increases, this value is simply the imputed value of satisfying a demand under equilibrium conditions. Thus it is the negative of the shortage penalty, which has been designated λ. With the substitution, the result is:

$$(8) \qquad \frac{\dfrac{\partial F}{\partial Z}}{-\lambda} = \frac{\dfrac{\partial F}{\partial M}}{\dfrac{\partial T}{\partial M}}$$

$$(9) \qquad \lambda = -\frac{\partial F}{\partial Z}\frac{\dfrac{\partial T}{\partial M}}{\dfrac{\partial F}{\partial M}}$$

Equation (9) allows an interpretation of the shortage penalty, λ, in the context of overall resource allocation. It is the value of a small change in the overall product due to a change in Z (that is, $\partial F/\partial Z$), measured by the marginal cost per unit of product in terms of other resource inputs—in this case "maintenance and equipment." The ratio $(\partial T/\partial M)/(\partial F/\partial M)$ is the rate of increase in total cost per unit added of the M resource, divided by the rate of increase in the product, F, per unit of M. This is the marginal cost per unit of F. Thus the shortage "cost," λ, can be derived from the optimizing solution for the overall logistics system.

This illustration has been carried out in terms of two parts and two classes of input for illustrative purposes, but in principle it can be generalized to any number of parts and inputs.[5] Note that λ does not in theory involve the valuation

---

[5] It has been assumed that the production relation and the constraint are concave functions that are continuous and differentiable and that all inputs are used in positive amounts. A deeper analysis must allow for departures from these assumptions.

of military worth or the utility lost due to weapon down time; it is determined by the marginal relations between inputs characterizing the minimum-cost (or maximum-output) solution of the logistics resource allocation problem. One has the choice of using the determined value of N (or Z) or the ratio, λ. Examination of (9) shows what is involved in treating λ as a cost to be estimated by engineering and accounting means. One must be able to assume that the entire system has been approximately optimized, to pick one of the other resource inputs, and to evaluate the derivatives involved: the rate of increase of output per unit of the resource added, rate of increase in cost per unit of this resource added, and the rate of decrease of output per unit shortage increase. In general, it is not correct to use the average cost of some input per unit output, for example, the cost of a missile divided by its average alert hours, as a shortage penalty [although this may be a lower bound on the true value of $(\partial T/\partial M)/(\partial F/\partial M)$].

Bear in mind that, in practice, the general optimization of a logistics budget is rarely attempted. Efficient use of resources comes about by long-run adaptation, through trial and error. It should be the aim of a spares-management policy to provide "acceptable" service in the most efficient way and, if possible, to present data on the relevant range of efficient alternatives. This will frequently mean that some measure of physical results— back-order rates or number of shortages—is more meaningful than an estimate of the ratio, λ, itself.

INVENTORY MODELS

Inventory models can be roughly classified by two principles: They may be steady-state or dynamic, according to their assumptions about the future, and single-point or multipoint (including multiechelon). Another important distinction may be made between single-item and multi-item models. Most applications to logistics problems have been based on single-item, single-point, steady-state models.

As was emphasized in the previous section, the underlying problem in designing a spares-management system is to choose an appropriate activity or level for optimization and to bring into the solution a means of relating stockage policy to an effectiveness objective. We will now examine an important policy area and an inventory model for this area.

The (S-1, S) Inventory Policy in a Multi-item System

The ($S - 1$, S) inventory policy with continuous review lends itself to an accurate analytical formulation and the multi-item approach, and it represents an important policy in logistics applications. High-cost, repairable-type spares are stocked according to this policy, at least at base or final-user level, and represent, as we have observed, a dominating fraction of total spares investment. One-to-one ordering is the desirable policy when the part in question is so expensive that the economic lot size is one unit.

In the repairable-item problem, replenishment of inventories may be either by local repair in an average fraction of the cases, α, or by resupply from a higher echelon in the remaining fraction, $1 - \alpha$. Both repair and resupply times are characteristically random. Since order size is not a variable, the relevant costs (that is, the ones affected by the choice of S) are the shortage penalty and the cost of holding; the relevant policy outcomes are the number of shortages and the total investment.

A sensible policy would be one that provided less stock for items with short average-response times (perhaps because α was near one) than those with long times, less for very expensive items than cheaper ones, and less for low demand items than active ones.

The solution of this problem requires calculation of the probability distribution of the number of items in "resupply": that is, the number that have been placed in repair or on order. If this number goes above the spare stock, S, one or more shortages occur. In the most general form of such a problem, the probability distribution of the number of units in resupply must be estimated by Monte Carlo methods or approximated numerically, involving a large amount of computation; however, if the demand-probability function is restricted to the Poisson family (simple or compound), it has been shown that the distribution of the number of units in resupply is of the same Poisson type as the demand and depends only on the average resupply time [9]. Thus any arbitrary (random) resupply distribution can be analyzed quite simply for this class of demand distribution.

This permits a rather extensive treatment of the $(S - 1, S)$ policy for a multi-item system, under steady-state conditions and compound Poisson demand [9], [10], [11]. One can formulate quite simply a number of alternative performance measures for an item; one of these is the expected number of shortages[6] at any point in time, N, as a function of the stock, S.

$$(10) \qquad N(S) = \sum_{x=S+1}^{\infty} (x - S) P(x; R)$$

$P(x; t)$ is the compound Poisson probability of observing a demand of x in an interval of time t, and R is the average resupply time, defined above.

Now let us consider a related set of high-cost, repairable items, perhaps those applicable to a particular 'weapon system'. The expected cost is given by the following, where c is the unit cost, h the annual holding-cost rate, and d the shortage penalty.

$$(11) \qquad\qquad C = dN(S) + hcS$$

---

[6] The referenced studies consider three measures: "fills," the expected number of demands per time period that can be filled immediately; "units in service," the expected number of units in routine resupply at a random point in time; and "ready rate," the probability that the item, observed at a random point in time, has no back orders. "Expected shortages" is the complement of "units of service," which is used here because the earlier discussion of inventory performance has been in terms of shortages rather than fills or units in service.

Shortages are assumed to be back ordered (this chapter will omit "lost sales"). The minimum-cost value of S is found by taking the derivative of C with respect to S and equating it to zero (or more properly, the difference of C, since S is a discrete variable). This provides the following approximate formula for minimum cost which implicitly determines S.

$$(12) \qquad -d[N(S+1) - N(S)] = hc$$

This says that we should increase S until the value of the decrease in expected shortages just equals the increase in holding cost of adding one more unit to the stock. Since this equation never holds (because S is discrete), the exact procedure is to locate S and $S + 1$ by the following and evaluate C for both.

$$(13) \qquad [N(S-1) - N(S)] > \frac{hc}{d} \geq [N(S) - N(S+1)]$$

The inventory model involved here is certainly easy to understand and use, and it is worthwhile to stop and briefly summarize the assumptions involved. Besides the form of the policy and the particular demand-probability distribution, the model allows for no interactions between stock levels and repair time: The value of S given by (12) does not anticipate use of priorities in out-of-stock situations. Also, the possibility of parts queueing in repair is neglected—repair times are independent random draws. These are typically the kinds of assumptions accepted by inventory models in order to gain the advantages of a systematic, computable stockage-decision rule.

There are, however, more important objections to this single-item formulation, for it assumes that h and d are perfectly known and that minimizing these costs for each item satisfies the objectives for the whole set. As the discussion of cost estimating suggested, the "physical" holding-cost portion of h is apt to be affected by the overall storage requirements of the system, and the interest-charge portion depends on the availability of funds. The shortage penalty, d, is more usefully viewed as a device for regulating the number of shortages than as an objectively measured cost. Finally, even if sensible values of h and d are presumed, the solution of Equation (12) for any (or every) item reveals nothing directly about the aggregate outcomes for the set of items. Therefore, a further step is indicated.[7] Note that the stock level for any item depends on the ratio h/d, which is designated K. If K is treated as a policy-control ratio and applied to all items, there is provided an efficient stockage policy for any values of h and d that are consistent with the ratio. By varying K over an appropriate range it is possible to generate a family of efficient policies and to display the aggregate

---

[7] For the sake of brevity, there is no discussion at this point of an important aspect of the studies references in this section and inventory analysis generally: the problem that the parameters of the demand distribution are not known with certainty. The particular work summarized here included an extensive Bayesian treatment of the matter of demand uncertainty [10].

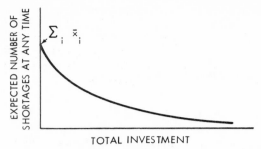

Figure 11–3   *Shortages vs. Investment for a Set of*
                       High Cost Parts

results in the fashion of Figure 11–3. This shows the expected number of shortages as a function of investment for the system of related items, where each point on the curve corresponds to the set of policies generated by a particular choice of K.[8] The expected shortages approach zero asymptotically. Each set of policies generated by a particular K is efficient, for the model chosen: Every item in the system is optimized for that value of the control ratio, and no reallocation of investment among the items can reduce the number of shortages.

A manager can select h and d and see, in Figure 11–1, the broad consequences of his selection. Alternatively, and more directly, he can simply select the point on the curve of relationship that represents either the available funds or the highest acceptable rate of shortage. He implements this policy with the implicit value of K, which becomes a parameter used purely for control purposes.

In application, a particular set of items must be chosen to which the computation is to apply. Since it is a single-point formulation, each base, ship, or other using activity must be treated separately (though we may wish to aggregate the results). It may be appropriate to deal with all the $(S - 1, S)$ type items at, for example, an air base, as one set; or it may be better management to deal with each major 'weapon system' or mission separately.

In this connection, it might be noted that one of the simplifications of the model as presented here is that all shortages have been treated as being of equal importance, so that their aggregate number has a definite meaning to management. This would not be true if different parts have different mission essentialities (although high-cost parts are typically important to the mission), in which case essentiality weights might be assigned to each part and the weighted shortage function minimized for each investment level. This is mathematically simple to reflect in models of this type, but deriving essentiality weights is a major undertaking.[9]

---

[8] The mathematical formulation and computer procedures for generating the relation can be found in [11]. This paper deals with effectiveness measures that approach 100 per cent with increasing total investment, but the two procedures are quite analogous.

[9] Similarly, we have assumed that additional shortages for the same part have the same importance. Very little has been done with nonlinear shortage penalties in inventory analyses.

It is probably best to treat major differences in importance associated with different missions, or weapon as opposed to nonweapon uses, by defining different systems or sets of items accordingly.

The Economic Order Size, Reorder Point Model

The steady-state, (s, Q) model of a single item at a single point is the most frequently applied inventory analysis in the logistical area, and elsewhere. The particular formulation shown here is based on [13], but very similar versions can be found in [26] and elsewhere.

In contrast to the $(S - 1, S)$ policy, (s, Q) policies are suitable for low-cost spares, in which reordering by batches is desirable, and where, by reason of the large number of items and their low unit cost, it is good management strategy to limit the amount of individual attention and exception actions.

Now, consider the cost relevant to policy determination where an amount Q is to be ordered whenever the stock level falls to (or below) s. Reorders cost r each and are received after a random delay p, subject to a probability distribution $h(p)$. N_s is the expected number of shortages associated with any reorder cycle if the reorder point is s. Other expectations are denoted with a bar over the variable, and the annual cost is written as a function of s and Q as follows ($\bar{x}$ is the average annual demand).

$$(13) \qquad C = r\frac{\bar{x}}{Q} + hc\bar{y}(s, Q) + dN_s\frac{\bar{x}}{Q}$$

$\bar{x}/Q$ is simply the number of orders per unit time. An approximation of $\bar{y}$ is $Q/2 + \frac{1}{2} + s - \bar{x}_p$, if $\bar{x}_p$ is the expected demand during a reorder time. This neglects the possibility of periods of zero stock in which the system is experiencing back orders. Whether or not $\bar{x}_p$ is subtracted depends on when costs begin to accrue—upon receipt or placement of the order. A more refined model might charge costs against stock in pipeline at a different rate than stock on hand. Equation (13) can be written more explicitly as follows:

$$(14) \qquad C = \frac{\bar{x}}{Q}(r + dN_s) + hc\left(\frac{Q + 1}{2} + s - \bar{x}_p\right)$$

Calculation of N_s requires the marginal distribution of demand during the randomly distributed reorder time. If $g(x)$ is this distribution and $P(x; t)$ is the probability distribution of demand in any time of length t, then the marginal distribution is the following:

$$(15) \qquad g(x) = \int_{p=0}^{\infty} P(x; p)h(p)dp$$

The distributions, $P(x;p)$ and $h(p)$ can be of any form, but the computation of probabilities is simplified if these are chosen so that $g(x)$ is analytically specified. For example, if $P(x;t)$ is Poisson, and $h(p)$ can be represented by the gamma distribution, $g(x)$ will be negative binomial in form. N_s is given by (16):

$$(16) \qquad\qquad N_s = \sum_{x=s+1}^{\infty} (x - s)g(x)$$

This formulation assumes that the spacing between orders is large enough so that orders always arrive in the same sequence in which they were placed or that crossing of orders is permissible.

The objective of policy is to minimize (14) by the choice of s and Q, which is done by finding the first differences of C with respect to s and Q and setting them equal to zero. These can be rearranged to yield the following formulas: s is implicitly determined by (18), and Q and s are solved iteratively, first finding Q on the assumption that dN_s is very small and then finding s using this Q, re-

$$(17) \qquad\qquad Q = \sqrt{\frac{2\bar{x}(r + dN_s)}{hc}}$$

$$(18) \qquad\qquad N_{s-1} - N_s > \frac{hc}{d\dfrac{\bar{x}}{Q}} \geq N_s - N_{s+1}$$

solving for Q with the new s, and so forth, until convergence is reached. Iteration is not necessary if dN_s is small enough relative to r, in which case the order quantity is determined independently of the reorder point.

These formulas are easily interpreted. Q, obviously, should be inversely related to holding cost, but directly related to the costs associated with reordering (since the larger Q is, the less frequently these costs will be incurred). The logic of the formula determining s is interpreted in the same way as the formula for S in the $(S - 1, S)$ case, except that the shortages are incurred only periodically (every $\bar{x}/Q$ years). If (18) is rewritten as $d(\bar{x}/Q)(N_s - N_{s+1}) = hc$, it can be seen that the object is to balance an annual decrease in cost of shortage against the annual holding cost of one unit.

This type of model is applied to the various stockage points of large systems, taking advantage of the relative independence of these points. Q and s should be large enough, however, to make shortages rare and keep the possibility small that a depot-level shortage will react on the lower level with a series of unusually long resupply times.

The model has a number of assumptions in common with the $(S - 1, S)$ model: It assumes that resupply times are random, that the probability distribution of demand is known, and that the present demand conditions prevail for the indefinite future (the steady-state assumption). These last two assumptions are always violated in practice to a greater or lesser extent: In particular, the steady-state assumption may be quite significant for the depot application because the order quantity may well cover a period of years. During this time bases may enter or leave the program as far as particular items are concerned, and the average demand level will vary accordingly. Base programs are usually level for a number of years, and the Q value will typically be much less than at the higher level ($\bar{x}$ and r are smaller). The life of the item will be longer at depot level, however, and applications of the model can utilize rules for adjusting the order quantity as the end of the program approaches.

The (r, Q) model can be more elaborately and precisely stated than in the foregoing version. A true (s, S) policy computation might be preferable: It is optimal for this problem and often will be the ordering format in use. The (r, Q) model ignores the "overshoot" of the reorder point when more than one demand occurs at the moment the reorder point is reached. In general, however, the system costs are not very sensitive to small errors in s and Q, and there is less at stake in the low-cost area than with the high-cost parts to which the $(S - 1, S)$ analysis applies. The limitations of lot-size reorder-point formulas have more to do with their scope than their accuracy as such.

The same objections or difficulties to an item-by-item approach, related in the discussion of the $(S - 1, S)$ analysis, apply to the economic order-quantity area as well. Minimizing each item's cost function may fail to minimize total-system costs because the cost parameters are not really constants when total activity varies, and the item-by-item approach tells management nothing about the important aggregate outcomes. In the low-cost area, there may be, in the short run, constraints on manpower or machine capacity for procurement actions or requisitions as well as constraints on funds.

One approach is to extend the control-parameters approach exploited in the $(S - 1, S)$ multi-item model. If dN_s is neglected as being probably small where economic order-quantity materiel is involved (this, at any rate, is a common simplification of the problem), (17) and (18) can be rewritten as (19) and (20) below:

$$(19) \qquad Q = K_1\sqrt{\frac{\bar{x}}{c}} \qquad \text{where } K_1 = \sqrt{\frac{2r}{h}}$$

$$(20) \qquad N_{s-1} - N_s > \frac{K_2 c}{\dfrac{\bar{x}}{Q}} \geq N_s - N_{s+1} \qquad \text{where } K_2 = \frac{h}{d}$$

K_1 and K_2 may be interpreted as cost ratios for understanding the general logic of the system but used as controls to determine the overall outcomes for the set of items. K_1 then fixes the ordering frequency and the average investment in order-quantity stocks, and K_2 fixes the expected shortages (given the ordering frequency) and the investment in lead-time plus safety-level stocks. The resulting stock levels are efficient in that they optimize stockage for this model and for the particular ratios of costs in the corresponding values of K_1 and K_2 (recall, however, that this simplified formulation is a further approximation of the model of (13); a more complete scheme would allow for the interaction between s and Q).

Management may simply rely on observing the effects of its choices of K_1 and K_2 from accounting reports of the supply activity and make adjustments of the ratios to achieve desired long-run results. Additional apparatus is required if management is to be provided with aggregate data for decision-making purposes. This might involve display of overall outcomes after the fashion of Figure 11–3, except that three variables are involved: number or rate of shortages, number of reorders, and investment. Again, management might use this knowledge of the system's behavior in two ways: to check the results of applying the "best estimates" of the cost factors or to relate item policy systematically to his overall constraints and objectives.[10] Such systems for providing management with overall information on the outcomes resulting from the choice of stockage policy have not been widely used because of the computational work load involved.

Dynamic Models

Steady-state models are useful for many situations in which the time horizon, or program end, is in the future and demand-rate changes are slow enough for the policy to adapt to them. The limitations of the steady-state approach may be overcome with dynamic programming models, although these are of a higher order of computational complexity. Such models are of great theoretical importance [1], although their application in logistics lies largely in the future.

The basic approach is to divide time into periods that are independent of one another with respect to demand. Demand need not have the same probability distribution in each period, and any desired program length and activity profile can be directly incorporated. The basic analysis involves defining costs in any one period as a function of demand, stock on hand, and amount ordered. The procedure is to solve the model for the final (n^{th}) period, obtaining expected cost as a function of the inherited stock (and the final order in the case of zero lag in delivery of orders). The cost and ordering rules of period $n - 1$ can then be determined, which include the (discounted) costs associated with any level of stock carried forward to period n. The computation continues recursively until the expected cost and ordering rule for the initial period are obtained.

The dynamic formulation is necessary to obtain exact (s, S) policies for the case of periodic review. It is also the basis for the proof that the (s, S) form is optimal under fairly broad conditions, namely that the expected cost of carrying

---

[10] An application and discussion of this general approach is found in [8]. See also [4].

inventory and back-order incidence in each period is a convex function of the starting stock. Unit cost must be constant (in any period), and a fixed cost of placing an order is permitted [24].

Dynamic programming models are very flexible, and can accommodate relatively elaborate systems. Increasing the complexity of the system considered makes it more difficult to generalize the solutions, however, and computation of specific solutions may become costly, even with large-frame computers.

An example of a large, dynamic model will be given in the following section on the multiechelon problem.

The Multiechelon Problem

In view of the circumstance that logistics-supply systems are multi-echelon systems,[11] it is perhaps sobering to note that very little has been accomplished with the analysis of such systems (although they are currently the object of study in several quarters). Interactions among echelons and between repair scheduling and stockage performance can certainly be uncovered, however, that attest to the practical importance of developing this area.

One type of interaction arises because the stock level needed at a lower echelon to provide a stated protection against shortage is a function of the response time (or resupply time) from the next higher echelon, and this response time is in turn a function of the stock level at the higher echelon. Repair scheduling at depot similarly interacts with stockage requirements. Another interaction arises from the determination of base-level order sizes independently of the higher echelon. The frequency of ordering directly affects higher-echelon operating costs, and the size of the order affects the apparent variance of depot issues and increases the stocks required accordingly.

One *n*-period dynamic, multiechelon model has been formulated, however, the optimality of its policy rules investigated, and some solutions computed [3], [17]. This analysis represents perhaps the most ambitious attempt to date to incorporate a substantial system of higher- and lower-level installations—depots and bases—in a single cost-minimizing computation. The model generally applies to items for which there is no ordering or setup cost for shipment within the system—that is, high-cost items for which one-for-one ordering is the accepted discipline. It does permit a fixed cost independent of order size at the highest echelon, however. Procurement and shipping costs, holding costs, and shortage costs are assumed to be linear. Demand originates at the lowest installation or level, and shortages at each echelon are back-ordered.

The policy computation provides the levels to which it pays to order for each point in the system, for each time period in the item's life. The conditions

---

[11] There are exceptions to this statement. From the standpoint of the Defense Supply Agency or any of the military Departments, they are single-echelon systems for DSA items. From the standpoint of the Department of Defense as a whole, of course, these organizations comprise a two-echelon system.

under which Bayesian estimation can be employed with this model have also been investigated [14].

The Clark multiechelon model demonstrates that optimal policies, or, at least, policies that are preferred within some reasonable class, can be computed for extremely complex systems of stockage points. Such techniques involve a considerable investment in data assembly and computer time; and one question involved in considering an application is whether the future can actually be specified in the great detail required with enough certainty to justify the effort.

It might also be noted that the technique just briefly summarized relates to a single item. Little consideration has been given to imposing multi-item constraints on such relatively elaborate one-item models. However, the static multi-item analysis for the $(S - 1, S)$ ordering policy under conditions of compound Poisson demand, described earlier in this section, has also been extended to the multibase, multiechelon problem [25]. In the larger context, the problem becomes one of allocating successive units of each spare item to one of the bases, or the the depot, so as to achieve the greatest marginal increase in performance. Performance is measured at the lowest echelon, or base level, by an aggregative criterion such as fill rate or the expected number of outstanding back orders. Back orders or non-fills at the depot echelon are not counted in the criterion, but the allocation of units of stock reflects the fact that a unit assigned to the depot does affect base-level performance by way of the average depot-to-base response time. Allocation of an investment budget among the spare items is then accomplished by marginal analysis, exactly as in the simpler, single-point model.

SPECIAL TOPICS

Deferred Procurement and Phased Provisioning

Perhaps the most vulnerable aspect of the application of decision models to inventory problems relates to the knowledge that must be assumed about demand. In practice, demand probabilities are not known quantities but must be estimated, and this becomes an important source of error in calculating inventory policies. Indeed, much careful optimizing of stockage decisions is simply wasted because of the poor precision with which the parameters and form of the demand distribution can be determined.

This is a particularly important problem in the case of initial stockage decisions for the new spares associated with a 'weapon-system' phase-in. These decisions, which frequently represent a large part of the total spares buy, must be based on technical or engineering estimates, made prior to any actual operational experience with the weapon. Such estimates are usually conservative—that is, they overstate the demand activity that may be expected—and are at best subject to considerable error [19]. The conservatism, or bias, is apparently a product of the difficulty inherent in making such estimates and of the realization that large underestimates on one or a few important parts could cause serious problems for a new 'weapon system'.

One line of attack on this problem is to attempt to refine the methods by which such estimates are formed or to devise ways of using the information that they do contain. A different approach is represented by the set of ideas or concepts called "deferred procurement" [21], "responsive production," or most recently, "phased provisioning." These systems differ in detail but have a common principle: the substitution of increased management inputs, information processing, and contractor responsiveness for some portion of the spares that would ordinarily have been bought. Under phased provisioning, the current system, the manufacturer advances the production date on units being assembled for eventual incorporation in the end item. This provides a production-line "float" while the weapon concerned is in production. The support manager then buys only a portion of his total computed requirement, drawing on the float when—and if—the need materializes.

Such arrangements do have a cost to the user and quite possibly would not represent the most efficient way of doing business if the demand rate were more certainly known. But under the conditions of relative uncertainty in a weapon's early life, they represent a way of buying some time to form better demand estimates before making a commitment on the entire spares buy. Thus, they may contribute materially to better system-stockage decisions.

Systems Analyses

So far the discussion has mainly concerned the methods and choices involved in analyzing the problem of stocking a given support system in as efficient a manner as possible; however, an immediate object of a study of spares management may be to determine the desired performance characteristics of the system itself. It is apparent that inventories are only one of the inputs and that the quantities needed depend importantly on the time lags—procurement lead times, transportation times, transaction-processing times, repair-cycle times—and on accounting accuracy and frequency of review.[12] A comprehensive analysis of spares management must consider all these inputs as substitutes for one another.

Inventory theory is also essential to this type of study, of course, because the comparison of alternative systems is not meaningful unless inventory levels are adapted to the characteristics of each. But studies oriented toward the design or modification of spares systems typically bring into focus a different type of problem and require different methods. Complete optimization of all the inputs

---

[12] These considerations are particularly important in view of the current rapid changes in computer technology and the increasing application of large-frame computers to inventory management.

or processes of such complex systems is not feasible, and the process of developing improved support structures is much more an engineering or design problem than a model-building task.

It is sometimes fruitful to specify or design a number of alternative systems with differing characteristics and simulate the performance of each under the same conditions of demand or stress [22]. This procedure allows a much more elaborate representation of costs, priority rules, and interactions between system elements than any purely analytic approach. It may, for example, be important to study the effect of repair-capacity constraints, in conjunction with rules governing which spares items to repair first, on the performance of a multi-item stockage system. Stockage rules can be based on a relatively simple model of the process and tested in the more elaborate computer simulation, and alternative repair policies or capacities can be compared on the basis of cost and effectiveness.

A related kind of system analysis concerns the location of parts repair within a multipoint stockage system. Accomplishing repair at the lowest echelon reduces the stock-level requirements at those points by shortening the replenishment time but requires specialized equipment and other inputs to create the repair capability. The cost of alternative repair postures can be compared, providing that stock levels are adjusted to hold the effectiveness of the combined repair and stockage system constant for all comparisons.

Computation of Kits and War-Reserve Levels

Another sort of stockage problem is represented by kits or reserve stocks for specific purposes: for example, the fly-away kit or mobility kit that is designed to provide spares support for some fixed period or number of missions, without resupply. Other related examples are the prestockage of war reserves at aircraft-dispersal sites and determination of shipboard-allowance kit quantities. In such problems the constraint generally is not cost, or at least not cost alone, but may instead be weight or cubage.

A particular problem connected with such kits is that, in most applications, the conditions under which spares-demand data are obtained can be expected to differ from those in which the kit will be used. One partial solution to this difficulty may be to collect demand data from realistic exercises, but it is generally difficult to obtain large enough samples in this way. It is frequently necessary to use consumption data from routine operations, making judgment adjustments to reflect the likely conditions under which the kit is to be used. In this way, allowance can be made for the effect on spares demand of differing maintenance capabilities and, to some extent, for the effect of specific types of missions.

The inventory problem here typically takes the form of minimizing the expected shortages (or, in some versions, maximizing the probability of no shortage) for the value of the constraint. If J_i is a criticality factor and W_i the weight for the ith part, the problem may take the form of minimizing the following for n candidates for the kit:[13]

(19)
$$\sum_{i=1}^{n} J_i \sum_{x=S}^{\infty} (x - S) p_i(x; t)$$

Subject to

(20)
$$\sum_{i=1}^{n} W_i S_i = W$$

This requires a computer solution analogous to that described for the allocation of investment in the multi-item $(S - 1, S)$ problem. Values of a constant, λ, are chosen and solutions found for the following i equations.

(21)
$$\frac{\lambda W_i}{J_i} = \sum_{S_1^*}^{\infty} p_i(x; t)$$

Then $\sum_{i=1} W_i S_i$ is checked to see if it is greater or less than the constraint W, λ is revised accordingly, and (21) is resolved. It is usually possible to reach a satisfactory solution in a few iterations. As in previous examples, the interpretation of (21) must recognize that S_i is an integer. Linear programming methods can be used to optimize a spares kit for more than one constraint: that is, a kit can be designed to minimize shortages for a target weight and volume or for weight, volume, and cost.

Determination of the essentiality or criticality weights is a large subject in itself. In some problems it is reasonable to assume that all candidates for a kit are equally essential, but in other applications differences in essentiality have been considered [5] [20]. Determining the weights involves the application of maintenance and operational expert judgment to derive a ranking of the candidate parts with regard to essentiality, considering the importance of each component to the mission, the degree to which it can be compensated for, if lost, by repair or redundant systems, and the urgency with which it must be replaced if defective. The parts are then grouped by major essentiality category and the weights, J_i, determined by judgment. The resulting kit can thus reflect, to some degree, the opinions of the users as to the relative importance of different spare parts to the mission for which the kit is designed.

CONCLUDING REMARKS

In this survey a great deal of attention has been given to theories of multi-item management, because such systems represent the most promising

[13] The "kit problem" has received a number of formulations; this one follows [16].

and useful tools currently being considered or applied. The major decisions of spares management—the determination of the total requirement and the procurement budget—pertain to the system as a whole, even though the budget must be implemented at the level of line-item detail. Management's concern is to find an allocation of its budget to spares purchases that will be reasonably efficient, that is, one under which no reallocation of the same budget could raise the overall effectiveness of the system. The ability to move between the domain of the individual spare part and that of an efficient system of many, related spare items is, perhaps, the main practical contribution that inventory studies can make at present.

But, each approach to inventory control has its characteristic shortcomings as well as its advantages. As we have seen, it is possible to develop rather elaborate dynamic models of single items, which explicitly allow for varying programs and finite time horizons and embrace multiple points and echelon relationships. Thus, these include elements of reality not present in the multi-item techniques already discussed, useful though these techniques are. The search for ways of combining these two approaches—the multi-item model for a single point under steady-state conditions and the complex dynamic model for a single item—is an important research task. Bear in mind that computational practicality is always a required condition of a proposed solution for an inventory problem.

We have touched on another sense in which inventory analyses are limited representations of reality, without, perhaps, fully evaluating the consequences. This is the general area of prediction of demand and the related problem of forecasting the incidence of obsolescence. Spares-demand rates are often too low for satisfactory statistical prediction, and it seems quite likely that the underlying conditions governing demand are unstable for any very long forecast period.

Much progress has been made in this area, particularly in the development of Bayesian methods and the better understanding of multi-item models with aggregative criteria, but the demand problem remains as the least tractable (and most treacherous) aspect of inventory analyses generally. This is particularly true of the initial provisioning of spares, based on engineering estimates. Not only are the estimates, as such, highly subject to error, but design changes with, consequent obsolescence, are most common at this time. This suggests that an important characteristic of any inventory policy and the wider support framework in which it is embedded is its vulnerability to demand-prediction errors (or, more generally, to an improper specification of the demand model). Uncertainty is a dominating characteristic of the spares-management problem.

Such investigations will often lead to design studies of the whole support system, of the type described in the preceding section. In this connection, better methods are needed for studying large spares-support systems to find the preferred mix between inventory investment, data processing and management, transportation, and repair inputs. Ideally, "trade-off" studies of particular parts of the system should give way to a more general optimizing approach.

As a final comment, the criterion or performance measure for a spares inventory system is an arguable question. Judgmental considerations will influence the choice of both the criterion function itself and of the desired value of the function to be specified as part of the policy. This is because of the limited state of our knowledge of how spares availability, other logistics inputs, and the resultant military capability are related to each other. Simple aggregative measures such as the average number of units backordered or the fill rate appear to be fruitful criteria for suboptimizing the spare parts input, but more elaborate measures may eventually prove to be useful.

REFERENCES

1. Arrow, K. J., S. Karlin and H. Scarf, *Studies in the Mathematical Theory of Inventory and Production*. Stanford: Stanford University Press, 1958.

2. Brown, R. G., *Smoothing, Forecasting and Prediction of Discrete Time Series*. Englewood Cliffs, N. J.: Prentice-Hall, Inc., 1962.

3. Clark, A. J. and H. Scarf, *Optimal Policies for a Multi-Echelon Inventory Problem*. PRC R-113. Los Angeles: Planning Research Corporation, 1959.

4. Davis, R. H., "Optimal Inventory Control Decision Rules for a Large Supply System," *Operations Research*, VII, No. 6, November–December 1959.

5. Denicoff, M., J. Fennell, S. E. Haber, W. H. Marlow, F. W. Segel and Henry Solomon' *The Polaris Military Essentiality System*, T-171. Washington: George Washington University (Logistics Research Project), 1964.

6. Enke, S., "An Economist Looks at Air Force Logistics," *The Review of Economics and Statistics*, XL, No. 3, August, 1958.

7. Enthoven, A. C., "The Simple Mathematics of Maximization," P-1833. The RAND Corporation, 1959.

8. Feeney, G. J., "A Basis for Strategic Decisions in Inventory Control Operations," *Management Science*, II, No. 1, October, 1955.

9. ——— and C. C. Sherbrooke, "The $(S-1, S)$ Inventory Policy Under Compound Poisson Demand: A Theory of Recoverable Item Stockage," RM-4176-1-PR. The RAND Corporation, 1966.

10. ———, "An Objective Bayes Approach For Inventory Decisions," RM-4362-PR. The RAND Corporation, 1965.

11. ———, "A System Approach to Base Stockage of Recoverable Items," RM-4720-PR. The RAND Corporation, 1965.

12. Feller, W., *An Introduction to Probability Theory and Its Applications* (2nd ed.), I New York: John Wiley & Sons, Inc., 1961.

13. Ferguson, A. R. and L. Fisher, "Stockage Policy for Medium and Low-Cost Parts," RM-1962. The RAND Corporation, 1958.

14. Fukuda, Y., *Bayes and Maximum Likelihood Policies for a Multi-Echelon Inventory Problem*, PRC R-161. Los Angeles: Planning Research Corporation, 1960.

15. Galliher, H. P., P. M. Morse and M. Simond, "Dynamics of Two Classes of Continuous-Review Inventory Systems," *Operations Research*, VII, No. 3, May–June, 1959.

16. Geisler, M. A. and H. W. Karr, "The Design of Military Supply Tables for Spare Parts," *Operations Research*, IV, No. 4, August, 1956.

17. Gradwohl, A. J., *Case Studies in the Multi-Echelon Inventory Problem*, PRC R-133. Los Angeles: Planning Research Corporation, 1959.

18. Hitch, C. J., "Suboptimization in Operations Problems," *Operations Research*, I, No. 4, August, 1953.

19. McGlothlin, W. H., "Development of Bayesian Parameters for Spare-Parts Demand Prediction," RM-3699-PR. The RAND Corporation, 1963.

20. Okun, B., "Design, Test, and Evaluation of an Experimental Flyaway Kit," *Naval Research Logistics Quarterly*, VII, No. 2, June, 1960.

21. Petersen, J. W., *Savings from Procurement Deferral with Interim Contractor Support: The Case of High Value Airframe Spares*, RM-2085. The RAND Corporation, 1958.

22. —— and H. W. Nelson, *Integrated Materiel Management*, RM-2870-PR. The RAND Corporation, 1961.

23. Raiffa, H. and R. Schlaifer, *Applied Statistical Decision Theory*. Cambridge: Division of Research, Harvard Business School, 1961.

24. Scarf, H., "The Optimality of (S, s) Policies in the Dynamic Inventory Problem," *Mathematical Methods in the Social Sciences, 1959*, ed. K. J. Arrow, S. Karlin and P. Suppes. Stanford: Stanford University Press, 1960.

25. Sherbrooke, C. C., *METRIC: A Multi-Echelon Technique for Recoverable Item Control*, RM-5078-PR. The RAND Corporation, 1966.

26. Whitin, T. M. and G. Hadley, *Analysis of Inventory Systems*. Englewood Cliffs, N. J.: Prentice-Hall, Inc., 1963.

FREDERICK T. MOORE

The RAND Corporation

Frederick T. Moore has been a member of the Senior Staff of The RAND Corporation since 1953. Before that he was on the faculties at the University of California at Berkeley and the University of Illinois. He has also been a consultant to the governments of Brazil and Venezuela as well as to several government and private agencies. He has written on a variety of economic problems and for several years was involved in developing a research program for The RAND Corporation on problems of procurement in the Department of Defense. His publications in this area include *Military Procurement and Contracting: An Economic Analysis*, The RAND Corporation, RM-2948-PR, June, 1962 and "Efficiency and Public Policy in Defense Procurement," *Law and Contemporary Problems*, Duke University Law School, Winter, 1964.

12

Incentive Contracts

INTRODUCTION

Since the beginning of World War II Department of Defense expenditures for the development and procurement of planes, missiles, and other military items have risen to levels many times higher than prewar levels. In recent years, total procurement by the Department of Defense has been $20–$25 billion annually. Moreover, large sectors of American industry are dependent in whole or in large part on government contracts. Both government and private resources devoted to defense procurement are large and interest in increasing the efficiency of the market is correspondingly high. Improved management of procurement could result in substantial total savings.

Among the instruments available to the Department of Defense, major attention has been given in recent years to improvements in contracting, including the selection of appropriate contract types and improved contract terms that procure the items economically.

Before World War II there were only two main types of contracts—the firm fixed price contract (FFP) and the cost plus a fixed fee contract (CPFF)—of which, the CPFF contract was much more widely used to procure new military hardware. The deficiencies of that contract type have been widely discussed: the lack of any requirement for complete performance for the cost specified and the apparent lack of incentive for the contractor to conserve resources and keep costs down.

The incentive contract, which avoids some of these deficiencies, has become important since its introduction, primarily as a substitute for the CPFF contract. During the late 1950's the CPFF contract accounted for almost 40 per cent of new contract dollars; by 1964 that figure was under 15 per cent, and the incentive contract accounted for virtually all the change. The Secretary of Defense has said that shifting from CPFF to fixed price and incentive contracts has saved ten cents in costs per dollar. At recent average levels of procurement, this implies total savings of between a quarter and a half billion dollars annually —a truly impressive increase in efficiency if we accept such estimates at face value.

The incentive contract has become an important instrument in the management of defense procurement. What features of the incentive contract are conducive to increased efficiency of procurement? Are there limitations on its effectiveness in the sense that the incentives offered may not operate in the way they are intended? Such questions occur in assessing the significance of an instrument that has had such a resounding acceptance.

The Form of Incentive Contracts

Incentive contracts fall midway between FFP and CPFF contracts, which are the two polar cases, and resemble both in some respects. The FFP contract, as the name implies, specifies a price at which an item is to be delivered. If the contractor is efficient and keeps costs low, he retains all of the extra profit—that is, the difference between his costs and the fixed price. The CPFF contract establishes a cost level to perform a particular task and then adds a fixed dollar fee that is determined as a percentage of the cost. Unlike the FFP contract, the contractor is not actually required to complete the task for the contract cost, though he must "use his best efforts" to do so. If the funds are exhausted before the work is completed, the contractor is absolved from any further performance. If performance is not complete initially, additional funds are often added to the contract so the work can be completed. Thus there is a tendency for costs to escalate in CPFF contracts and they are criticized because they offer few, if any, incentives for the contractor to act efficiently. There is also a fee limitation in CPFF contracts; the Armed Services Procurement Regulations stipulate a maximum fee of 7 per cent on procurement contracts, though in special circumstances, this can be raised to a statutory limit of 10 per cent.[1] In the FFP contract, price is unresponsive and profit directly responsive to changes in actual cost; the opposite is true for the CPFF contract. That is the simple but significant difference in the degree of incentive offered by these two contract types.

The incentive contracts involve negotiation of a target cost (a cost considered reasonable for performing the task) and a target profit which together make up the target price. In addition, a sharing formula is negotiated that prescribes the terms for sharing apparent cost savings between the government and the contractor. For example, a sharing formula of 80/20 means that 80 per cent of any savings go to the government and 20 per cent to the contractor; if actual costs exceed the target costs, the overages are shared in the same proportion so that the treatment of savings and overages is symmetrical. A numerical example may help illustrate the terms:

Target cost	$100,000	
Target profit	8,000	(8 per cent of target cost)
Target price	$108,000	
Price ceiling	$125,000	(125 per cent of target cost)
Sharing formula	80/20	

These are the negotiated elements in the contract. The formula for sharing cost overruns or underruns is the primary distinction between the incentive contract and the FFP or CPFF contracts. Let us suppose that the contractor successfully

[1] There are other contract types than the two mentioned, including redeterminable, fixed price with escalation of selected cost items, and labor and materials. These are of minor importance but for a description of them, see F. T. Moore, *Military Procurement Contracting: An Economic Analysis*, RM-2948-PR, The RAND Corporation (June, 1962).

performs the task at an actual cost of \$90,000. What is the price paid by the government and what profits does the contractor earn?

a) Profits: $\pi_A = \pi_T + b(C_T - C_A)$

$$= \$8,000 + .2(\$100,000 - \$90,000)$$

$$= \$10,000$$

b) Price paid by the government: $P = C_A + \pi_A$

$$= \$90,000 + \$10,000 = \$100,000$$

π_A stands for actual profits; π_T target profits; C_T and C_A the target and actual costs respectively; and b is the contractor's share of the savings.

The same calculations are performed in the case in which actual costs exceed target costs (a cost overrun). If the contractor incurs costs of \$110,000 to complete the task, his profits are \$6,000 (\$8,000 − .2(\$10,000)), and the price paid by the government is \$116,000. However, the government protects itself against extremely large cost overruns by imposing a price ceiling that is usually expressed as a per cent (for example, 125 per cent) of the target cost. If costs exceed the ceiling, the contractor must absorb the excess and often incurs a loss.

In one variant of the contract, the targets and the sharing formula are firmly fixed before any work begins. However, at times the target costs and profits are set provisionally when work commences and adjustments are made later after the contractor has acquired some experience. When a particular point in production is reached, the target costs and profits are revised in accordance with that experience. Less frequently the original sharing formula is also changed.

The incentive contracts just described are called "fixed price incentive fee" because the contractor is expected to complete his performance within the conditions imposed by the contract terms. Incentive fees are also attached to cost-type contracts. In a cost plus incentive fee contract, the total cost is estimated and a target fee is established. There is also a sharing formula specified; however, this type of incentive contract differs in two other respects. A maximum and minimum fee are specified so that the sharing formula only operates within the limits thus prescribed, and, as in CPFF contracts, there is no requirement that the task be completed within the limits of funds in the contract. Consequently, the cost plus incentive fee contract does not contain a price ceiling.

The major innovation in the incentive contract is the use of a formula for sharing cost underruns or overruns. In the incentive contract, the contractor's share is less than one but greater than zero. In the firm fixed price contract, the contractor claims the whole of an underrun and absorbs all the overrun, that is, the sharing formula is 0/100, and in the CPFF contract, he shares in neither.

Cost reductions are not the only mark of improved performance, particularly when the products being purchased are not as competitively comparable as commercial products, such as refrigerators or typewriters. The character of the military product is frequently somewhat uncertain; product quality and performance can fluctuate a good deal. In recognition of this fact, incentive contracts can be modified to reward improvements in the "timeliness of delivery, capability and serviceability of the product, ease and simplicity of operation, economy of maintenance, etc."[2] Cost incentives have been supplemented by adding options for the inclusion of incentive payments for superior performance on a wide variety of technical elements. The purpose is to give a better total measure of the performance of the contractor.

The extension of incentives to performance measures other than cost is limited only by the ability to formulate meaningful measurements on the product and to agree on them in the negotiation. The performance measures may be few and restricted to key elements in the program or they may cover dozens of specific items that span most significant aspects of the product. Technical performance targets can be most precisely defined for specific pieces of equipment as, for example, a rocket engine, gyroscope, or fire control system. The targets are expressed in engineering terms such as pounds of thrust delivered, number of successful firings, accuracy of control, and similar measures that can be determined by fairly direct measurement.

Performance targets for complete weapon systems tend to differ in character and mix technical elements with more general measures of performance. The first contract for a certain airplane illustrates the way the targets can be set. The contract was a cost plus incentive with incentives attached to cost, the delivery schedule, and technical performance of the aircraft. The target fee was set at 5.5 per cent with a minimum fee of 4 per cent and a maximum fee of 7 per cent. The possible fees that could be earned by the contractor are summarized below.

Performance Measure	*Weight (%)*	*Min.*	*($ Millions)* *Target*	*Max.*
1. Cost	$16\frac{2}{3}$	2.0	2.7	3.5
2. Delivery rate	$33\frac{1}{3}$	3.9	5.4	6.9
3. Technical	50	5.9	8.1	10.3
Total		11.8	16.2	20.7

The requirements on the delivery rate adjusted the fee depending on how well the contractor met a particular schedule. The technical performance measures covered the range and altitude capabilities of the aircraft and certain weight characteristics of major subsystems. It is particularly interesting to note the different weights attached to the three performance measures; technical performance of the aircraft was given the greatest weight in fee determination, and deviations of the actual delivery rate from the schedule were weighted twice as

[2] Armed Services Procurement Regulation 3-406, 2a.

heavily as variations in actual cost from target cost. Changing the weights in the formula for determining the fee can emphasize one performance measure at the (relative) expense of others so that the structure of incentives is altered and presumably would be reflected in the behavior of the contractor.

Actual profit earned can be represented in simple symbols:

$$\pi_A = \pi_T + b_1 c + b_2 d + b_3 r + \cdots$$

where c, d, and r are the differences between actual values and target values for costs, delivery rate, and technical performance respectively, and the b_i's are the weights attached to each, expressed either as specific amounts of fee or, in the case of costs, of percentage shares. In this formula, the actual profit is the sum of the individual items, and the total profit is a linear function of the individual variables; profit is increased if actual costs fall below the target, the delivery rate is increased, or technical performance exceeds the target. Other measures of performance may be added to the list if it is desirable.

Not all incentive contracts include provision for performance incentives, though the use of the option is increasing. The basic logic of the option seems inescapable: since costs may be kept low by sacrificing the quality of the product, rewards should be given as much for improving product performance as for reducing costs. The appropriate measures of total performance by the contractor have many dimensions. Criteria for performance apply strictly to the end-item itself; the method of achieving the result is not in question. Evaluation of performance waits on the completion of the item and on operational tests of it.

Recently the use of incentives has undergone a further expansion. They have been attached not only to the end-item itself but to the activities of the contractor in undertaking the work. This has been done through the extensive use of PERT charts (Program Evaluation and Review Techniques). A PERT chart diagrams in great detail the activities or processes required during development and procurement, estimates the time each process will take, shows whether these can be engaged in concurrently or consecutively, and identifies "events" (such as the completion of a process), and "milestones" (which mark completion of some major phase of the program). It is a detailed presentation of the physical flow of work and of the managerial decisions necessary to complete it on schedule. In some current contracts, "points" are given for successful achievement of events and milestones, and incentive payments and penalties are attached to each of them. These exist in addition to incentives attached to the performance of the end-item itself. In a contract for the Titan III missile, it is reported that the contractor "had more than 2,200 PERT event deadlines; 316 of these carried 'incentive' penalties ranging from \$2,000 to more than \$10,000. Twenty 'milestones' were staked out, each worth \$120,000."[3] In this contract, the incentives associated with the achievement of some event or milestone in the program

---

[3] "Move Up in Space—Win Points," *Business Week*. September 25, 1965, pp. 92 ff.

amount to about $4 million. These incentives are separate from those related to final cost or technical performance of the missile in its finished form. They are directly related to the management of the program.

In summary, the evolution of incentive contracts has had three distinct phases of increasing complexity in the specification of appropriate measures of performance. In its initial construction, the incentive was simply for cost reduction and was represented by the introduction of the sharing formula and the setting of a target cost. In the second phase the incentives were expanded to include special performance criteria for the end-item itself (including subsystems); this step made the calculation of performance a multidimensional one. The final elaboration extends the incentive provisions to the management of a program and further specifies the particular path that must be followed to meet the standards.

These developments of the incentive contract were undertaken in an attempt to inject performance tests in a market that was notable in the past primarily by the absence of such tests. But this development has created new problems that must be satisfactorily solved if the program is to be successful. The multiplication of performance criteria raises difficult problems of choice among alternative sets of incentives. A set of incentives may not complement, but rather offset, one another. Policing multiple incentives may change the institutional relationship between buyer and seller in ways that blur judgments about the efficiency achieved. Since the primary purpose of creating a system of incentives is to improve efficiency by lowering costs and raising the level of performance, it is necessary to inquire whether and to what extent the incentives now incorporated in these contracts have the desired effect.

COST INCENTIVES AND RISK AVERSION

The incentives that were first offered involved provisions for sharing apparent cost savings between the government and the contractor. To evaluate the effectiveness of these incentives requires an understanding of the interactions among three elements in the contract: the target cost, the target profit, and the sharing formula. A change in any one of the three will change both the over-all expectation of profit and the relative attractiveness of profit expectations determined by provisions made on the other two items.

One of the most difficult problems is setting a reasonable target cost. Contracts have often been criticized for poor estimation of target costs and particularly for setting the target artificially high. If target costs are systematically higher than actual costs, any extra profits will appear to result from the contractor's efficiency but will actually be due to poor cost estimating. A Congressional committee has expressed the opinion that the incentive contract "is a lazy man's contract for the government because mistakes in overpricing cost only 20 per cent when discovered. It is not necessary to add or subtract; merely learn to divide 80 − 20. . . ."[4] To hand a contractor a large windfall profit that results from an exaggerated target cost is the antithesis of an incentive and weakens the effectiveness of the sharing formula. If the contractor expects to maintain costs below the target, changes in the sharing formula will have small effect because extra profits will accrue to him in any case. There is a real incentive for him to negotiate as high a target cost as he reasonably can to protect himself against the uncertainties involved in producing new items for the military. Typically, the costs of military items cannot be estimated with the same accuracy as for commercial items. Since actual costs may increase sharply during the work, the appropriate strategy for the contractor, to avoid a serious cost overrun that would deplete his profit, is to negotiate a target cost that exceeds his expected costs. The government's position is to negotiate a target as close to expected costs as possible.

The final relationship between target costs and actual costs depends upon the degree of uncertainty in the outcome and the skill of the two parties in negotiating. The information available to each side may differ both in coverage and depth; in fact, asymmetry in information is frequently stressed in criticisms of incentive contracts. The advantage is for the contractor who knows the circumstances and limitations of his operation better than the government possibly can. Several steps have been taken to redress the balance including adding specialists to the team of government negotiators and requiring contractors to sign a certificate that their cost estimates are realistic. Yet there is no way of knowing whether bargaining power is equal or whether, if it is, the targets will closely approximate costs actually realized by the contractor. Equality of bargaining power does not guarantee that the effects of uncertainty will be overcome nor does it necessarily instill confidence in the accurate prediction of costs.

The real question is whether uncertainties and possible asymmetries in bargaining power create a systematic tendency for target costs to exceed actual costs, and, if so, how much of the difference might plausibly be attributed to poor cost estimating rather than to economies realized by the efficiency of the contractors. The evidence does not provide an unequivocal distinction between errors of estimation and the results of efficiency, for there is no way to separate the effects of the one from the other. However, the magnitude of the joint effects can be reasonably measured, and the effects of estimation errors may be roughly approximated.

The evidence on cost behavior in incentive contracts is provided by the statistics on completed contracts. Samples of such data are available and the

---

[4] U. S. Congress, House Committee on Armed Services, Special Subcommittee on Procurement Practices in the Department of Defense, House Report 1959 (Washington: GPO, June 23, 1960), p. 30.

results derived from one sample are shown in the table below with cost overruns distinguished from cost underruns.

Sample Cost Outcomes in Incentive Contracts

Cost Overrun or Underrun (%)	Number of Contracts	Per Cent
1. Underrun		
Over 20	10	4.4
10–19	43	18.9
5–9	64	28.1
0–4	51	22.4
Subtotal	168	73.4
2. Overrun		
0–4	31	13.6
5–9	12	5.3
10–19	8	3.5
Over 20	9	3.9
Subtotal	60	26.6

The table shows that there are more underruns than overruns. Almost three-fourths of the contracts show a cost underrun. Another investigation showed the same result, though only two-thirds of the contracts showed cost underruns.[5] The difference between these two samples results from the type of contracts covered and normal sample variability. In any case, the difference is rather small. In the sample, about 50 per cent of the contracts show underruns of less than 10 per cent; that is, in one out of two cases, the actual cost was less than 10 per cent below target cost. The extremes in overruns and underruns seem to occur more frequently in small contracts, not contracts for major weapons systems.

One further characteristic of the sample distribution of actual costs helps determine the likely maximum error in estimating target costs. The distributions of the sample data are markedly symmetrical around a central measure; there is little or no evidence of skewness in the distributions. Scherer has extended the analysis by applying a *chi*-square test to determine whether the distributions depart radically from the normal distribution. In all cases involving incentive contracts, he found that the samples were consistent with the hypothesis of theoretical normality of distribution.[6] The test for normality is obviously more

[5] F. M. Scherer, *The Weapons Acquisition Process: Economic Incentives* (Cambridge: Harvard University Press, 1964), Ch. 8; *Idem.*, "Contractual Incentives," *QJE*, p. 274.

[6] Scherer, *Economic Incentives*, pp. 194–95.

stringent than the test for simple symmetry in the distributions; however, only symmetry need be established to advance the analysis. A symmetrical (or normal) distribution of actual costs means that, given the mean of the distribution, the contractors are equally likely to be efficient or inefficient. A 5, 10, or any other per cent deviation from the mean is equally likely in either direction.

It may be argued that *if* target costs are estimated accurately (that is, are the "true" costs that a representative firm in the industry would incur), and *if* contractors are as likely to be efficient as inefficient, the theoretical distribution of the differences between actual and target costs would be symmetrical and have a zero mean. The distribution would have a zero mean because on the average actual costs, and target costs would coincide. The dispersion around that mean represents the varying efficiency of the contractors.

Incentive contracts are criticized because of the likelihood of profits increasing because of poor cost estimating. This shows up in the data as a distribution of differences between actual and target costs that has a nonzero mean. The sample data indicate that on the average (for several samples), actual costs are 3 to 8 per cent below target costs. To avoid underestimating the possible bias, it will be assumed that the average difference between actual and target costs is 8 per cent. This difference may, as a first approximation, be interpreted as the maximum likely error due to poor cost estimating. If there were no such errors, the average difference, $C_T - \bar{C}_A$, would be zero; since empirically the difference is 8 per cent, this is attributed to the errors of estimation. It is a *maximum* estimate of the error since some of it *may* be due to the contractors' efficiency. It is impossible to completely separate the part attributable to errors of estimation from the part attributable to efficiency.

These figures indicate that the contractor should expect a cost underrun, in the probabilistic sense, since two-thirds to three-quarters of the time an underrun has occurred; and the average underrun has been about 8 per cent. In these circumstances, however, why should the contractor choose an incentive contract when he typically shares only 20 per cent in the cost saving, when with a FFP contract he could retain all the savings? Why settle for a sharing formula less than 0/100?

There are several possible explanations. The incentive contract may be the choice of the government rather than that of the contractor, a choice dictated by the belief that the alternative is not a FFP but a CPFF contract for which costs may rise without penalizing the contractor. Alternatively the contractor may prefer the incentive contract to a FFP contract at the same target cost because he reacts differently to the probability of a cost overrun than an underrun. Even though the target cost may be loosely negotiated and create an expectation of a cost underrun, the contractor may be averse to accepting the risks of a FFP contract, because the (smaller) probability of a cost overrun times the loss in profit has a greater weight than the (larger) probability of a cost underrun times the gain in profit. In this sense the contractor is a "risk averter."

   Profit maximization by a firm implies an assessment of the risks associated with any bid price (that is, target cost) and, over the span of a number of bids (or contracts), maximization of the expectation of profit. Profit maximization then involves a willingness to risk possible poor results and adversely affected profit. Risk aversion means that the firm prefers a smaller but surer profit to a larger but less sure one, even though by being ingenious and enterprising the firm might obtain the larger reward. A counter example may help illustrate the point. In Case 1 below, the expected profit is 6 and the dispersion is 1; and similarly for Case 2. The firm may prefer Case 1 to Case 2 because it is safer. The incentives are not sufficient to overcome the desire to hedge against uncertainty, although the probabilities are favorable.

Case	$E(\pi)$	σ	Range $\pm 1\sigma$
1	6	1	5–7
2	9	6	3–15

   Case 1 might occur with a sharing formula of 95/5, whereas Case 2 would be consistent with a formula of 70/30. An expected profit maximizing firm would prefer the latter, but his more timid brother would respond favorably only if

$$C_T - E(C_A) > K$$

where K is some rather large number; that is, the firm must be virtually certain that it can "beat" the target before it responds to a larger sharing formula. This illustrates the close interdependence between setting target cost and the sharing formula in evaluating the incentive effects of the contract. This example shows favorable conditions for the contractor, but it is most unfavorable for the government since it implies that the price will be high.
   An experiment conducted on bidding strategy tends to confirm this evaluation of likely response to risk. The experiment specified several sharing rates ranging from 90/10 to 50/50, and in a simulated competitive atmosphere the participants bid for contracts, that is, they specified a bid price. The results showed that the prices bid increased as the sharing rate increased, for the participants interpreted a rising share rate as indicative of greater uncertainty in the actual costs that they would incur. Higher costs could only be offset by raising the bid price.[7] They acted as risk averters.
   Such behavior may be explained by saying that profit maximization is not the sole, nor necessarily the dominant, motive of the firm, and, if that is true, incentives in that direction are less effective. Preservation of the market share, increasing (or maximizing) sales, stabilization of earnings, and retention of a

   [7] G. J. Feeney, W. H. McGlothlin, and R. J. Wolfson, *Risk-Aversion in Incentive Contracting: An Experiment*, RM-4231-PR, The RAND Corporation (August, 1964).

skilled labor force may be of equal importance, for the firm has multiple objectives.[8] Incentives to reduce cost, to lower prices, and to use resources more efficiently compete with incentives to satisfy the other objectives. At present the typical relationship between the level of target profits and the sharing formula tends to lessen the incentive features of the latter.

The total profit of the firm in an incentive contract is the sum of the basic target profit and the additional profit earned via the sharing formula. The incentive feature lies solely in the latter item, since the target profit is fixed independently at the time of negotiation. Typically, the target profit is set at 8 per cent. In the sample of incentive contracts described previously, the average cost underrun is 7–8 per cent and the average sharing formula is 80/20, so that the additional profit earned in this way is 1.4–1.6 per cent, for a total profit of 9.4–9.6 per cent. The significant comparison is between the relative contribution of the target profit to that of the incentive profits in the total. Approximately 83–85 per cent of the total profit is accounted for by the basic target profit; the much smaller remainder is attributable to the sharing formula, yet it is the only part responsive to cost savings. The sharing formula does not alter the total profit very much in contrast to the cushion provided by the basic target profit. To increase the incentive to cut costs and to utilize resources more efficiently would require more emphasis on the sharing formula and less on the target profit, although the contractor would probably try to counter by raising the target cost. In actual practice there has not been much tendency to experiment with alternative combinations of target profits and sharing formulas. A sampling of incentive contracts shows that an 8 per cent target profit is most commonly agreed upon and two-thirds of the formulas were either 80/20 or 75/25. It is rare indeed to find a sharing formula below 70/30, that is, 60/40 or 50/50.

There is much more to be learned about the likely response of contractors to different combinations of the three elements of target cost, target profit, and sharing formula. Some combinations offer stronger incentives for cost reduction and generally increased efficiency than others and do not so obviously provide windfall profits to the contractor. No optimum combination of elements exists since the degree of uncertainty in the work directly affects the terms of the bargain. The wholesale displacement of CPFF contracts by incentive contracts may have resulted in inappropriate uses of the latter in that the contractor has only accepted the incentive form if the target cost was suitably high. A study of the likely price outcomes for a sample of contracts under alternative contractual arrangements must be done.

---

[8] Cf. W. L. Baldwin, "The Motives of Managers, Environmental Restraints, and the Theory of Managerial Enterprise," *Quarterly Journal of Economics* (May, 1964). See also W. J. Baumol, *Business Behavior, Value and Growth* (New York: The Macmillan Company, 1959).

SPECIFICATION OF MULTIPLE PERFORMANCE CRITERIA

Cost is not the sole measure of contractual performance; the quality of the product is of particular importance in the defense area and changes in quality do not automatically result in price changes. Since incentives can be attached to cost reduction, better over-all results may be achieved by rewarding separately superior performance in important technical areas. The argument is logical; the chief problems are to define the relative importance of the performance measures and to reward them appropriately so the contractor assigns them the same relative importance as the government does. If the incentive system is successful, any set of outcomes in performance that are equally acceptable to the buyer must provide equal rewards for the seller and require equal effort from him. Incentives might be so poorly constructed that a set of results equally acceptable to one party will contain one or more undesirable outcomes for the other party. If that occurs, the incentive system fails to achieve the desired results. The adjustments of rewards and standards necessary to satisfy this dual objective constitute the heart of the problem.

The difficulties of choosing an appropriate set of performance criteria and rewards can be illustrated by an example. Suppose a contract is being let for a new aircraft and that criteria are set for cost, technical performance (represented here by an index number that could be translated into some specific physical measure), and the delivery rate. The target figures are set respectively at: $C_T = \$100$; $R_T = 72$; and $D_T = 45$. The incentive rewards (penalties) for exceeding (falling short of) the targets are 70/30 on cost; $\$.50$ change in profit for each change in the performance index; and $\$.25$ for each item delivered above or below the target rate. The profit function for the firm is:

$$\pi_A = .3c + .5r + .25d$$

where c, r, and d are deviations from the target. We can omit, for simplification, specification of a target profit and assume that if the targets are exactly met, the profit is zero.

The set of incentive rewards completely defines the government's indifference surface for performance in the three specified dimensions, and alternatively defines the profit possibility surface for the contractor. The government, by accepting the set of incentive rewards, has defined the "value" of an improvement in performance. The government is presumed to be equally well satisfied by any of the sets of performance outcomes that give the same total profit to the contractor. For example, a total profit of $\$.5$ can be achieved by each of the three configurations shown here (given the targets and incentives listed previously) as well as by many other configurations. An increased total profit means

Outcome	C	R	D
1	95	70	45
2	100	72	47
3	103.3	67	61

that the government prefers that configuration of outcomes to any for which total profit is less. Since total profit is the same for all three cases, the government is presumably as ready to accept one outcome as either of the others. It has defined the value of trade-offs among the measures by the incentive rewards. In comparing Outcomes 2 and 3, an increase of 14 in the delivery rate is equivalent to a decrease of 5 points in performance and \$3.3 in extra cost.

In short the government's preferences on trade-offs are fully revealed, for any pair of measures, by the simple ratios, b_i/b_j, of the incentive rewards. Because these are fixed and not variable, the implied marginal utility of an improvement in performance is the same for an increase from 70 to 71 as from 80 to 81. Yet it seems obvious that in many cases the government's utility functions would be nonlinear. At some levels of performance, an increase would be worth more than at other levels. A variable incentive reward is necessary to reflect such preferences but it is seldom if ever recognized in typical incentive contracts.

Unlike the government, the contractor is not indifferent to alternative outcomes that yield the same total profit. The reason is found in the varying difficulty (expense) of exceeding the target figures in the three areas, and in the fact that the relative size of the incentive rewards does not necessarily coincide with the relative difficulty of performance. In terms of the previous example, the contractor might say to himself: "To raise the performance from 72 to 74 will be extremely difficult because it depends on things going just exactly right and even then, I'll be incurring a cost penalty because I'll have to sink a good deal into quality control; on the other hand, it should be relatively easy to raise the delivery rate and once the learning curve effects are felt, my unit costs should fall enough to offset any decline in performance." Hence, the contractor's choices are determined not only by the size of the incentive reward but also by the difficulty of increasing performance in one area in contrast to another. Consequently he will order the outcomes of equal total profit according to the probability of his achieving them, with the outcome that seems easiest (cheapest) heading the list. If the incentives seem to reward delivery relatively highly, he will sacrifice performance somewhat to achieve prompt delivery. In short the contractor also has an indifference surface showing combinations of qualities or outcomes that he considers equally difficult to achieve. These surfaces are defined by the contractor's evaluation of the probabilities of improving performance in a particular quality of the product. Since these probability functions are almost certainly nonlinear and since they may be either independent of each other or interdependent, the indifference surfaces may be of varying shapes depending on the assumption made. However, for any given profit level, the contractor will choose that combination of outcomes that he believes will require minimum effort. There is, of course, nothing necessarily inconsistent between the valuations of the government and the contractor. If the incentive rewards truly reflect the government's preferences, the contractor's preferences will lead to results that satisfy both parties; however, this is not necessarily true if the government's utility functions are nonlinear.

It is tempting to increase the number of criteria to be satisfied, but the trade-offs that must be considered increase roughly as the square of the number of criteria. Thus, doubling the number of performance criteria increases the trade-off calculations four times. There are of course practical limits to the ability of a contractor to choose among alternative outcomes. Although the addition of performance incentives to cost incentives offers many possibilities for improving the measurement of total performance, if this is to be successful the analysis of trade-offs must be rigorous and consistent. Even when such calculations are crudely done, the results may be preferable to the alternative of doing nothing, as in a CPFF contract, but still greatly short of what is feasible to do.

MANAGEMENT INCENTIVES AND THE RESPONSIBILITY FOR DECISIONS

Initially incentives were attached to performance of the end-item itself and to the specific costs that could be identified with the work. Recently, additional incentives have been attached to the management of the contract work through the utilization of PERT charts. This development raises several new problems for an evaluation of efficiency in procurement.

The PERT charts necessary to delineate the development and production of a major military end-item are formidable documents. Each phase and activity of the work must be carefully depicted, the scheduling of each operation in the sequence must be shown, plus the amount of time necessary for each, and the milestones indicating completion of significant stages must be identified and dated since the incentives apply to them. The negotiations of these problems occur during contract definition and before work actually begins, although this preliminary work accelerates the later work. In typical incentive contracts involving cost and performance incentives, contract definition normally takes a few weeks or months. But the institution of incentives on program management has lengthened the process to a year or more. It apparently is also a costly operation. Fragmentary evidence indicates that the costs of contract definition may at times amount to 5 per cent of the estimated total cost of the work. The reports that are prepared are also voluminous and measured in tens of linear feet or tons of paper. When the exact magnitude of the costs can be determined, the benefits from this concentration of effort on contract definition should be arranged against its costs to determine whether, on these grounds, the effort was well spent.

Because the programs that the PERT charts describe typically take two or three years to complete, a major forecasting job must be done. The many milestones to which incentive rewards are attached must be set for several years in the future. Moreover, there may well be more than one efficient path to get from one milestone to the next. The uncertainties that beset the fixing of a single target cost are magnified when dozens or more milestones must be set and appropriately sequenced. The possible range of error in the estimates is substantial. The contractor has the same incentive to delay the date of a milestone as to raise the target cost, and the multiplicity of events that must be covered might seem to favor a negotiating strategy aimed at delay. One may well be skeptical of basing incentive rewards on such a forecasting scheme.

The argument in favor of management incentives emphasizes the closer control that the firm must impose on its work force and its schedules. A tighter discipline and attention to deadlines means better results. This argument is a persuasive one, but it has an aspect that may be forgotten. To determine if the contractor is on schedule and meeting the PERT points requires the attention of a substantial team of government representatives. Project offices staffed by such representatives have always existed to check on various matters concerning compliance with the contract, but management incentives increase the number of problems that require decision. The necessity for continuous agreement on schedules, all the additional problems requiring approval of government representatives, and the closer control those representatives exercise over decisions increase the probability that what will really emerge from the work is a test of the *joint* abilities of the contractor *and* the government. To that extent, the incentive features of the contract are vitiated. Closer control of and involvement in the contractor's operations may mean a failure of the test of performance.

Finally, sharing responsibility may raise the costs of a program through increased claims by the contractor. When decision-making authority is shared, it becomes difficult to fix responsibility for decisions that ostensibly lead to nonperformance by the contractor, and that in turn creates disputes and differing interpretations of who is at fault. Though the sources of disagreement may occur at any time, the filing of claims for reimbursement are usually delayed so that with contracts involving management incentives several years may pass before the incidence of these costs can be assessed. As a result, these contracts might result in a bonanza for the lawyers. At this point, a discussion of the virtues and defects of management incentives is necessarily speculative, for there is no history of experience with them.

The Mix of Contract-types in the Firm

The business of a defense contractor combines work under different types of contracts and frequently includes both commercial and defense contracts. The incentive contracts comprise only a part of the total, and the dollar volume relative to total volume is likely to be small. A firm interested in profit maximization must consider this diversity in contracts and adjust to it.

Obviously cost reductions are most profitable to the firm if they are accomplished for the fixed price contracts, since every dollar of cost saved is a profit dollar earned. The incentive contracts offer a smaller reward for cost savings, and the CPFF contracts offer virtually no rewards. In allocating management effort the greatest attention will be given to cost reduction in fixed price contracts and somewhat less attention to incentive contracts. The practical consequences of this in any given situation are obviously difficult to judge, but the motivation does not obviously work in favor of the incentive contracts.

The allocation of overhead expenses may also be arranged to accomplish similar effects. Profit would be improved if overhead expenses can be transferred from fixed price contracts to CPFF contracts, and to a lesser extent to incentive contracts. This follows from the fact that the fee earned is not at all adversely affected or affected only partially if there are cost overruns on CPFF and incentive contracts, whereas they are reduced dollar for dollar on cost overruns in a fixed price contract. For example, a dollar of overhead cost transferred to an incentive contract may cost the contractor only twenty cents in profit but mean a full dollar of profit on a fixed price contract. Thus in a firm with mixed contractual business, the incentives in the incentive contract may become blunted. Allocation of overhead expenses is largely an arbitrary matter, but a consistent rule for allocation should be followed to insure that transfers of costs are not made only to enhance profits.

A combination of contract-types obviously provides circumstances in a firm's operations that may make incentives less than fully operative. The importance of these circumstances in practical situations and the impact on incentive systems require further study before firm conclusions can be drawn.

CONCLUSION

The incentive contract, as originally conceived, represented the first real innovation in procurement practices in the Department of Defense. It is a halfway house between the CPFF contract and the FFP contract, and has been extensively substituted for the former. That fact alone is evidence of the reliance on it to improve efficiency, and specifically to cut costs. The case for the incentive contract is *prima facie* a rather good one, and the empirical evidence on contractual outcomes seems at first glance to confirm expectations. However, no stronger statement than that can be made to support the incentive contract because of the difficulty of isolating cost "savings" that truly result from increased efficiency, and those that result from overestimating costs. The evidence available on contractual outcomes does not, of itself, support the statement that there is a saving of ten cents for every dollar of procurement transferred from a CPFF contract to fixed price and incentive contracts.

While a case can be made for cost incentives and for additional performance incentives, the argument in favor of management incentives is weaker. Although no one expects arm's-length bargains between government and contractor in defense business, it *is* the performance of the contractor that incentives are designed to test and to stimulate, and the intermingling of responsibility for decisions implied in management incentives (as here described) does not necessarily improve efficiency.

Doubts about the effectiveness of cost and performance incentives as an instrument for defense management revolve around several issues. What happens during negotiations particularly in the setting of target costs? What are the effects of uncertainty on the elements of the bargain? Could incentives be sharpened within the existing framework by, for example, altering sharing formulas in a more drastic way? And are the trade-offs among multiple criteria sufficiently well understood to give us confidence in the relative incentive rewards? These and similar questions merit further attention, for the field of research on preferred policies in procurement is still an open one.

Last, the contract form is only one among several instruments that the Department of Defense has developed to affect procurement practices. In this brief chapter, it has not been possible to consider either the weighted guidelines approach to fee determination or the program package concept of procurement, though both are intimately related to the choice and administration of contracts. The institutional fact of renegotiation also affects procurement policies. Thus the discussion of incentive contracts is only a partial approach to evaluating management of procurement in the Department of Defense.

BIBLIOGRAPHY

1. Bickner, R. E., *The Changing Relationship Between the Air Force and the Aerospace Industry*, RM-4101-PR. The RAND Corporation, July, 1964.

2. Deavers, K. L. and J. J. McCall, *An Analysis of Procurement and Product-Improvement Decisions*, RM-3859-PR. The RAND Corporation, December, 1963.

3. Feeney, G. J., W. H. McGlothlin, and R. J. Wolfson, *Risk-Aversion in Incentive Contracting: An Experiment*, RM-4231-PR. The RAND Corporation, August, 1964.

4. Fisher, I. N., *Cost Incentives and Contract Outcomes: An Empirical Analysis*, RM-5120-PR. The RAND Corporation, August, 1966.

5. Hall, G. R. and R. E. Johnson, *A Review of Air Force Procurement, 1962–1964*, RM-4500-PR. The RAND Corporation, May, 1965.

6. Handel, S. S., and R. M. Paulson, *A Study of Formally Advertised Procurement*, RM-4984-PR. The RAND Corporation, June, 1966.

7. Moore, F. T., *Military Procurement and Contracting: An Economic Analysis*, RM-2948-PR. The RAND Corporation, June, 1962.

8. ———, "Efficiency and Public Policy in Defense Procurement," *Law and Contemporary Problems*. Durham, N. C.: Duke University Law School, Winter, 1964.

9. Peck, M. J., and F. M. Scherer, *The Weapons Acquisition Process: An Economic Analysis*. Cambridge: Harvard University Press, 1962.

10. Scherer, F. M., *The Weapons Acquisition Process: Economic Incentives*. Cambridge: Harvard University Press, 1964.

11. ———, "The Theory of Contractual Incentives for Efficiency," *Quarterly Journal of Economics*, May, 1964.

12. Summers, R., *Cost Estimates as Predictors of Actual Weapon Costs: A Study of Major Hardware Articles*, RM-3061-PR (Abridged). The RAND Corporation, March, 1965.

13. Weiner, N. S., "Multiples Incentive Fee Maximization: An Economic Model," *Quarterly Journal of Economics*, November, 1963.

14. Williamson, O. E., *Defense Contracts: An Analysis of Adaptive Response*, RM-4363-PR. The RAND Corporation, June, 1965.

JORA R. MINASIAN

Institute for Defense Analyses and
State University of New York at Buffalo

Jora R. Minasian, Ph.D., The University of Chicago, is presently
Associate Professor of Economics at the State University of
New York at Buffalo and consultant to the Institute for Defense
Analyses. He has taught at The Universities of Chicago, California (Los Angeles and Santa Barbara campuses), and Rochester.
He has been on the research staffs of The RAND Corporation—an
organization conducting research primarily for the Air Force—
(1960–63) and the Institute for Defense Analyses, supplying
research studies mainly to the Department of Defense (1964).

He has received his B.S. (1953) and M.B.A. (1954) from De
Paul University and Ph.D. (1960) from The University of
Chicago, Department of Economics. He has been active in groups
of professional economic societies.

His articles have appeared in the *Journal of Political
Economy, National Bureau of Economic Research, Econometrica,
American Economic Review, Journal of Law and Economics*, and
other such journals.

13

Land Utilization for Defense

INTRODUCTION

Decisions in the United States concerning the use of land for defense purposes are made within complex organizational arrangements. The interested participants include the military services as demanders of land resource, Department of Defense (DoD), Bureau of the Budget, General Services Administration (GSA), Corps of Engineers, Department of the Interior, Department of Justice, Congress, and finally the executive branch. The extent of the participation by any one of the departments is determined by the nature of the problem requiring a decision; for example, a case involving land disposal will normally involve the GSA, but not the Department of the Interior.

TABLE 13—1   Federally Owned Land in the Continental United States, by Agency, Method of Acquisition, as of June 30, 1962

Agency	Public Domain Acres (1)	Acquired Acres (2)	Total Acres (3)
Department of Agriculture	160,363,775.6	26,213,296.7	186,577,072.3
Department of Commerce	300.6	9,211.3	9,511.9
Department of Health, Education, and Welfare	663.8	4,712.5	5,376.3
Department of the Interior	541,107,904.9	11,878,515.3	552,986,420.2
Department of Justice	3,667.3	22,661.3	26,328.6
Department of Labor	0	1.5	1.5
Post Office Department	0.7	1,668.6	1,669.3
Department of State	3,535.2	70,848.1	74,383.3
Treasury Department	59,117.2	12,108.6	71,225.8
General Services Administration	48.3	14,719.9	14,768.2
Housing and Home Finance Agency	0	286.1	286.1
Other Civil Agencies	1,543,621.9	1,456,345.2	2,999,967.1
Total Civil Agencies	703,085,942.5	39,707,828.7	742,793,771.2
Department of Defense	16,287,181.0	11,715,890.9	28,003,071.9
Total Federally Owned Land	719,373,123.5	51,423,719.6	770,796,843.1

Source: *Public Land Statistics*, United States Department of the Interior, The United States Government Printing Office, Washington, D. C., 1963, pp. 1–2 and 15–29.

A study of land utilization for defense entails an investigation of the nature of the decision-making processes governing resource allocation within the existing political institutional arrangement. This study of government (or organization) behavior will utilize economic methods of analysis. Such a study is only useful if it yields information about rewards and costs as defined by the impacts of the processes, rules, regulations, and laws under which the nature and operation of the organization is delineated. The present methodology, therefore, describes the institutional arrangement to find the impacts on cost-reward structures and to assess the effect of incentives on the decision maker(s).

Three points should be emphasized. First, the DoD is not a significant user of land compared with other governmental agencies. Table 13–1 provides land statistics which show the land holdings by agencies and their relative positions as of June 30, 1962. The DoD holds land (about 28 million acres) amounting to 3.7 per cent of the total amount of land held by Federal agencies (about 771 million acres, which is 34 per cent of total acreage of the U.S.). Second, the nature of the outcome of decision making should not be related to individuals in their capacity as decision makers. Indeed, just the opposite should be true, since methodology of economics is founded on the premise that the outcome is de- termined by the system of decision making in operation—the cost-reward struc- ture—not by the participants in that system. Therefore, if different results are desired, the system should be altered to generate appropriate incentives for the participants in the decision-making process. Finally, this analysis does not give even qualitative information about the relative efficiency of the DoD in compari- son with other government agencies. Such information may be obtained only by studying the incentive structures in other agencies.

DEPARTMENT OF DEFENSE LAND HOLDING

As of June 30, 1963, the Department of Defense (DoD) "controlled" 30.2 million acres of land which was distributed geographically as follows: 26.8 million acres (about 89 per cent) within the United States,[1] 0.2 million acres (about 1 per cent) in the United States possessions,[2] and 3.2 million acres (about 10 per cent) in foreign countries. "Control" means the possession of rights to direct the use of the property. Land rights may be acquired through: (1) donation, transfer, purchase with or without condemnation, (2) lease, (3) either temporary or permanent withdrawal of public domain lands, (4) tem- porary use permits (public land order or executive order), (5) easements, and (6) foreign rights.

---

[1] Excluded are 5,947,703 acres under the jurisdiction of the Civil Works Division, Office, Chief of Engineers, Department of the Army.

[2] Excluded are six acres under the jurisdiction of the Civil Works Division, Office, Chief of Engineers, Department of the Army.

**TABLE 13–2   Acreage of Land Under DoD Control by Geographic
Location and Type of Tenure as of June 30, 1963**

Type of Tenure	United States	Possessions	Foreign Countries	Total	Per Cent of Total DoD Land
Owned	6,780,917	97,067	0	6,877,984	22.8
Public Domain	16,768,156	0	0	16,768,156	55.6
Temporary Use	1,551,010	55,562	12	1,606,584	5.3
Leased	1,369,588	1,394	109,191	1,480,173	4.9
Easements & Public Lands	321,721	41,024	283	363,028	1.2
Foreign Rights	0	26,160	3,052,816	3,078,976	10.2
Total	26,791,392	221,207	3,162,302	30,174,901	100.0

Source: U. S. Congress, House Committee on Government Operations, *Federal Real and Personal Property Inventory Report (Civilian and Military) of the United States Government Covering Its Properties Located in The United States, in the Territories, and Overseas, as of June 30, 1963*, 88th Cong., 1st sess. Washington: U. S. Government Printing Office, 1964, p. 78.

The DoD total land holding by geographical distribution and the type of tenure are given in Table 13–2. Over 50 per cent of the land used comes from public domain and more than 20 per cent is obtained through purchase, transfer, or donations. There are, unfortunately, no accurate data on the value of these lands.

There are two reasons for paucity of such data: (1) the acquisition of land through purchase generates historical costs which do not represent the present value of the resource, and (2) there is no market transaction establishing values for donated and public domain lands withdrawn (see next section). Moreover, the data on rentals paid on leased property are not suitable for capitalization purposes, since the rentals reflect some in-kind services rendered by the DoD and incorporate property other than land.[3] Similarly, rental data received by the DoD from leased land cannot be capitalized, since they only reflect the arrangements under which grazing and mineral rights are granted to private citizens rather than the economic value of the lands.[4] Thus, we must judge the

[3] Annual rental paid for military property leased from outside sources as of June 30, 1963, was $19.2 million in the United States, $0.1 million in the United States possessions, and $17.6 million in foreign countries, a total of $36.9 million; see p. 75 of the source given for Table 13–2 above.

[4] Annual rental received for military property leased to outside sources as of June 30, 1963, was $10.9 million in the United States, $0.2 million in the United States possessions, and $0.2 million in foreign countries, a total of $11.2 million, *ibid.*

economic value of the resource essentially by the amount of acreage employed in providing defense.

LAWS, REGULATIONS, AND RULES[5]

The ultimate source of authority resides in the Congress, which annually authorizes acquisition of land as part of military construction. Any acquisition of land rights that entails expenditures of money must be provided by congressional appropriation. Congress also generates acts and public laws specifying the policy and methods of land acquisition and disposal. These acts and laws are given initial impetus by directives and instructions of Secretary of Defense to the Secretaries of the three military services. The services then establish regulations defining policy and procedural matters related to acquisition and disposal of real property.

There are four alternative ways of acquiring or disposing of land rights: (1) land may be purchased or sold directly in the market; (2) public domain lands may be withdrawn from (returned to) the Department of the Interior, the custodian of such lands, or the GSA; (3) land may be acquired (disposed) through transfer from (to) other military departments, government agencies, such as states or municipalities, civic organizations, and private citizens; and (4) land may be leased from (to) other governmental agencies or private citizens.

The laws, regulations, and rules pertaining to these four alternatives define different incentive systems. The costs and rewards of a given decision depend on the alternative chosen. This chapter provides only a brief description of the major laws concerning acquisition of and conditions of disposals of land rights in the United States.

Acquisition of Land Rights

Purchase. The Secretary of a military department is empowered by law to acquire land not exceeding $25,000 exclusive of administrative costs. For purchases of land exceeding $25,000, the Secretary must first obtain the approval of the Assistant Secretary of Defense (Properties and Installations[6]), and then

---

[5] Sources of information for this section may be found in (1) United States Code (USC), Titles 10, 42, and 43, in particular, which contains acts and public laws passed by the Congress; (2) the directives and instructions issued by the Secretary of Defense to Secretaries of the military services; (3) regulations and rules prescribed by each of the Secretaries to his subordinates (I have been unable to obtain such information for the Department of the Navy); (4) Federal Property and Administrative Services Act of 1949, as amended, and Regulations of the General Services Administration, Title 2, Real Property Management; and (5) regulations issued by the Secretary of the Interior in C.F.R.

[6] This designation has changed to Assistant Secretary of Defense (Installations and Logistics). Throughout this chapter the old designation will be used as it appears in most of the statutes and regulations mentioned here.

seek congressional authorization of such a purchase in an approved Military Construction Act. In addition, the Senate and House Armed Services Committees must be notified thirty days before the Secretary of a military department enters a transaction involving an acquisition of real property in excess of $50,000.[7]

The Corps of Engineers acts as real estate agent for the Army and Air Force, while the Bureau of Yards and Docks represents the Navy and Marine Corps in real estate transactions. The military services and their real estate agents have power of eminent domain and may bring condemnation procedures when a mutually agreeable exchange does not present itself.

Withdrawal of Public Domain Lands. "Public domain" or "public lands" are those which never left government ownership or which have reverted to Federal ownership through operation of the public land laws (laws or statutes passed by Congress concerning administration of public lands and the resources thereon). They include federal lands as well as the waters of the outer continental shelf.

A withdrawal of public land is effected by a public land order issued by the Secretary of the Interior, which limits the disposal of public lands and holds them for specific purposes. A withdrawal order makes government-owned land unavailable for private use. A withdrawal may exclude in whole or part the potential uses available to citizens. For example, land may be withdrawn either "from all forms of expropriation under the public land laws," or only "from application under the non-mineral public land laws," or "from disposition under the homestead act," and so forth.

A withdrawal may be temporary, if the land will be used currently, or permanent, if the land is designated for present and future use. A withdrawal is a reservation if it specifies the use and agency responsible for its management. Thus, a reservation is defined as lands "set aside" for specific use under the administration of a particular agency; for example, the first large-scale public land reservation, Yellowstone National Park, was created by an act dated March 1, 1872. The use of public lands may also be obtained by "use permits." The Department of the Interior may issue use permits to federal agencies, but such lands remain open to prospecting under the mining laws, as well as to other uses.

A military department requesting the withdrawal of public domain land of over 500 acres first obtains approval of the Assistant Secretary of Defense (Properties and Installations). Moreover, withdrawals, reservations, or restrictions of more than 5,000 acres of public domain lands of the United States for

---

[7] If the acquisition is part of a project, then the report to the Committee must also include an estimate of the total cost of the lands to be acquired or leases to be made. Moreover a Secretary of a military department must report to the Committee quarterly on transactions that involve an estimated value of more than $5,000 but not more than $50,000.

any one defense project or facility of the DoD must be approved by an act of Congress.[8]

Transfer. The law provides that a military department may obtain real property, *without reimbursement*, from other military departments, including the Coast Guard. If the property is valued in excess of $25,000, the receiving military department must obtain approval from the appropriate military department and the Assistant Secretary of Defense (Properties and Installations). If the property is valued in excess of $50,000, the Senate and House Armed Services Committees must be notified, and, after a thirty-day congressional period elapses, the appropriate real estate agent may obtain the transfer for the military department.

If desired Government-owned property has already been reported as excess land to the General Services Administration (GSA), these transfers are made in accordance with GSA Real Property Management Regulations (see following discussion of disposals). Normally such transfers will require reimbursement of 50 per cent of the appraised fair market value. Military land may also be exchanged for state, private, and national forest lands. In the latter case, the Secretary of Agriculture may effect such exchange without reimbursement.

Leases. No general statute specifically authorizes the Secretary of a military department to acquire real property by lease. The GSA is the sole leasing agency for general purpose space in urban centers and special purpose space in the District of Columbia and vicinity. Otherwise, a military department is authorized to lease property by the Department of Defense Appropriation Act for a *given year.* This annual congressional appropriation defines the acreage, space, or costs in the military department's Construction Program.

As in the case of acquisition of land by purchase, the Secretary of a military department must obtain the approval of the Assistant Secretary of Defense (Properties and Installations) for lease of land when the annual rental exceeds $25,000. He must also receive congressional clearance (allowing 30 days to pass) for leases which involve rentals in excess of $50,000.[9]

Disposal of Land Rights

Land controlled by a military department may be sold if it is first declared "excess" to the DoD and then found to be "surplus" or of no value to other government departments. The conditions and procedures that lead to the declaration that certain land is excess and surplus are somewhat complex and require some explanation.

[8] In 1964, a Public Land Law Review Commission was established to study existing laws and procedures relating to the administration of public lands of the United States. As an interim measure, the Secretary of the Interior is required to report to the President of the Senate and the Speaker of the House of Representatives and allow sixty days to pass before effecting withdrawal, reservation, restriction, or change in the use and classification involving more than 2,560 acres of public land.

[9] See note 7.

If a unit or a command of a military department sees neither present nor foreseeable "requirements" for a given land, it declares the land excess and transmits this information to headquarters. Headquarters then decides if the proposed excess property is required by another unit in the department, in which case the Secretary of the department can reassign it. Otherwise, headquarters "screens" and circulates a notice of availability of the property to other military departments. If other military departments do not require the land, disposal action is recommended to the Assistant Secretary of Defense (Properties and Installations).

A disposal directive is issued to the real estate agent (1) when the Assistant Secretary of Defense approves the disposal action, and (2) if the estimated value of the land exceeds $50,000 and the Armed Services Committees of the Congress has not objected to the disposal action in the thirty-day period. The real estate agent will then arrange with GSA and/or the Department of the Interior to complete the disposal. If the land were originally withdrawn from public domain, and if the "character" of the land were not "substantially" changed by subsequent improvements, the Department of the Interior will accept the land and become solely responsible for its management. Otherwise, GSA will accept the land if it concurs with findings of the Department of the Interior. If by screening other government nonmilitary departments and agencies, no new requirements arise, the land becomes surplus and may be disposed of by sale or other arrangements defined in the Federal Properties and Administration Services Act of 1949, as amended. GSA may delegate the administration of the disposal to the agency in possession of the land, but will prescribe the terms and the conditions of the disposal.[10] However, all proceeds from sale of the excess land will be deposited in the Treasury as miscellaneous receipts, without direct benefit to the department excessing the land.

The procedures described concerned cases where a military department gave up all rights to the land. However, transactions concerning particular rights to land may also be carried out. In the case of nonexcess land—land for which no current need exists but is retained for future use—a military department may grant temporary use if it does not prevent future use. The temporary use may be granted either for exclusive or joint use to (1) another military department, (2) other federal agencies, (3) state or local governmental agencies, and (4) private organizations or individuals.

Granting temporary permits to other military departments is similar to transfer arrangements discussed under acquisition procedures. The Secretaries of the Department of the Interior and of Agriculture and others, with the approval of Secretary of a military department, may grant to the above mentioned parties rights to explore for minerals, rights to graze or to sell the agricultural products derived from such land.

[10] The Secretary of Defense may transfer (through GSA) without reimbursement military land to educational activities of special interest to the Armed Services, for example, military preparatory school.

State and local governmental agencies have priority over private organizations and individuals to lease available land. However, with the consent of the Department of the Interior and/or GSA, a military department may bypass other federal agencies.

The approval of the Assistant Secretary of Defense (Properties and Installations) is required for outlease of land when the estimated annual rental is more than $25,000. Except for leases for agriculture or grazing purposes, the congressional committees on Armed Services must be notified and clearance obtained if the estimated rental is more than $50,000. As noted previously, the *Treasury* receives the rentals from outleasing of lands, but the leasing military department receives *no* direct benefits.

THE PROPERTY RIGHTS OF LAND AND THE IMPLIED RESOURCE ALLOCATION

Acquisition of Land Rights

An acquisition of land rights creates money expenditures in the case of a purchase or a lease, but not when withdrawal, donation, or transfer is involved. The cost of a military project employing land as a resource depends upon the method used in acquiring the additional land. It requires a smaller additional appropriation of funds when the real estate transaction does not involve money expenditures.

The supplier of funds will tend to prefer a smaller budget to a larger one. In this context, it does not matter whether the Executive, the Congress, and the Secretaries of the military departments are guided by patriotism, politics, or economic considerations. Everything else being equal, a larger rather than smaller appropriation (1) imposes a higher cost on the decision makers in charge of the funds (ultimately the members of the Congress) or (2) reduces the probability of success for those requesting the funds. It must be remembered that each of the Secretaries of military departments competes for funds from the Secretary of Defense, the latter competes with other federal agencies for expenditure categories from the President, who faces the Congress and finally the voters.

It should be emphasized here that the proposition just made does not mean that a proposal to use "free land" is both a necessary and a sufficient condition for a commander to suceed in attaining approval of a new activity. It is not the absolute but the relative probabilities that are relevant. That is, regardless of the merit of the new activity (in the absolute sense), its chances are increased when the new activity involves "free land" use.

First, consider the relationship between a commander of a unit and his superior, the Secretary of the military department. There are more alternatives and thus possibilities for trade-offs between activities at the Secretarial than at the base or post level. But the Secretary will not be indifferent whether the activity is projected to cost one million or one and one-tenth of one million dollars; he will tend to prefer the former. This preference results from the competition that the Secretaries of the three military departments face, which in particular is reinforced by the use of "cost effectiveness" criterion. Competition for approval, and thus funds, induces each Secretary to show more "effectiveness" per "cost" (which means favoring "free" mode of land acquisition).

This discussion can readily be extended to the Secretary of Defense vis-à-vis other governmental agencies. Considering a budget constraint that is brought to bear ultimately by the voters' attitudes, the least costly mode of obtaining land will be preferred. We would, therefore, expect a demander of additional resources to use the method of acquisition that enables him to obtain land "free of charge," and thus increase the chances of getting his "requirements" granted.

We have discussed in general the conditions underlying the demand for additional lands without explicitly considering the supply of the land that is donated, transferred, or subject to withdrawal. The supply of donated lands is limited, constitutes a small portion of land held by the DoD, and is not a reliable source. The source of land acquisition through transfer is also limited for the reasons discussed in the next subsection. The main source of the land under discussion is public domain lands. The Secretaries of the three military and/or the defense departments compete, implicitly if not explicitly, with other governmental agencies, of which the Department of the Interior is in effect the most important one (due to its reluctance to issue orders for the withdrawals).

Although competition at this level may potentially cause the incentives of the Secretaries to differ from that of the decision makers at a lower level, it has little practical effect. First, meticulous congressional scrutiny of construction projects indicates the costs incurred by the demander of funds in terms of congressional testimony, justification, and negotiation in general. Second, the Department of the Interior has not greatly hindered withdrawal of lands; its basic reluctance seems to have been in giving up the surface rights such as mineral, mining, and so forth, rights that are safeguarded by the wording of withdrawal orders issued to the military departments. Hence one expects that public domain lands generally will represent a more favorable supply of the resource, as the constraints are looser outside than inside the Congress.

The Exercise of Existing Rights

The Nature of Rights of Land. What are the potential alternative uses of a certain amount of land? A commander of a base or post might search for ways to economize the use of land under his jurisdiction. If he could exchange part of all of the land for return of some other land, for resources, or for money, rights would be a set of *transferable* rights.

But recall the laws and regulations defining the conditions surrounding the sal of land. As a result of a commander's attempt to "maximize the value e output" generated by the employment of the land, the rights of land may be transferred elsewhere. It may be transferred to other activities in the same or other military departments, to nonmilitary governmental departments, to state agencies, or to private citizens. None of these exchanges yields a direct benefit to the commander. On the contrary, he loses a part or all the rights of land he possessed before the exchange. This is true whether or not the recipients of the rights were required by law to part with money or other resources, since the commander normally has no claim over such returns. The Treasury receives the money arising from a sale of the property. Under these circumstances the rights of land have value to the commander only when used by the commander. Its value to him in alternative uses and/or by the users is essentially zero. Therefore, the rights of land possessed by a commander of a base or of a post *are not transferable* under existing institutional arrangements.

Can a commander of a base or a post deny the use of the land to others? He enjoys protection against trespassing. But he may lose part or all "his" rights to the land in question as a result of reassignment within his military department, a change in his mission, or a lack of appropriation. In other words, the commander cannot deny other uses and/or users. Thus, his property rights in land *are not exclusive.*

Whether this threat of loss may compel a commander to consider alternative uses for the land in his decisions depends upon the nature of and the extent to which incentives at various decision levels differ. If the survival or success of a commander were partly determined by the efficiency with which he managed the land, then from his viewpoint the value in alternative uses would not be zero. And this would be reflected in his decisions.

There are few grounds to suppose that this appropriate relationship exists. One rarely hears of a commander being cited for winning a contest for "excessing" land or independently initiating joint use with other units. On the contrary, in practice the importance of a command tends to be judged by the size of the resources, including land, under its jurisdiction.

Divergence of Incentives. As determined by alternative available uses, a certain amount of land has different values to the Secretary of a military department than to the commander of a unit in the same department. The basis for such a divergence is the extent of economic trade-offs available at each level. Alternatives uses of land available to the Secretary of a military department include reassignment to different units in his department, transfer for return of other resources (including land) from other military, nonmilitary federal and state departments, and private citizens.

These exchanges occur through barter transactions that are ever more costly and cumbersome than barter deals ordinarily are. This is because several gover ment agencies are involved. To gain some perspective, consider two relati recent cases involving the Navy: one case involved the State of Oregon other involved Kern County, in California.

In the first case, the State of Oregon wished to exchange some lands f federal lands constituting Boardman Bombing Range of the Navy. With th sent of the Secretaries of the Navy and the Department of the Interior, Congress, in the Military Construction Act of 1960, authorized the full exchange of the lands. Subsequently, it was found that a full exchange was not feasible, and an act was sought to allow the Navy to exchange only a portion of the lands in question. In October, 1961, Congress authorized the revised exchange. The State of Oregon embarked on a program for acquiring lands necessary for the exchange. The State purchased privately held lands, withdrew land from public domain, and appealed to the Corps of Engineers and the Federal Power Commission to restore to public domain some land involved in a power site withdrawal. Moreover, it advised the Bureau of Land Management of its intention to exchange state lands for the lands restored by the Corps of Engineers and requested the Federal Aviation Administration for grant of airspace easements. Finally, in October, 1963, after mutual agreements were reached on terms, the exchange of lands was consummated.[11]

In the second case, the Navy agreed, and GSA approved, to "excess" some lands to Kern County for the specific purpose of providing recreation and park services. The plan for the transfer of the land was initiated in late 1959 and was not effected as of February, 1965. The difficulty arose because the law, but not the Navy,[12] specified a payment of 50 per cent of the market value of land for the transfer in question. This was not acceptable to Kern County. Although every participant (including the White House) in the plan was sympathetic, there was no way for Kern County to receive the lands without reimbursement.

These examples show how the present institutional arrangements, by imposing high transactions costs, tend to limit the extent of exchanges that are open. The potential gains must be high enough to compensate for the costs of transaction and yield a net return. Or putting it in another way, the value yielded by the land when used within the particular Service need not be as high as it must otherwise be to justify its retention.

Reinforcing this tendency is the limited scope of beneficial exchanges available to the service. This weakens the incentives to reallocate land resources to uses outside the military service. The effect is to make rights to land at the Secretarial level by and large not transferable. However, as in the commander's situation, the Secretary's rights to land are not exclusive. For, as a result of approval of projects in general and appropriation of funds in particular, the Office of the Secretary of Defense (OSD) may both directly and indirectly affect the land holdings of a military department.

The Role of the Department of Defense. The fate of a base or an installation will depend upon whether the "project" or mission assigned to it is approved by DoD and funded by Congress through an appropriation act. Failure to

a pe
his 1
[11] Incidentally, as part of the exchange, the State of Oregon paid a sum of money, which
ot available to the Navy to meet the conversion expenditures entailed by the exchange,
ich a specific appropriation had to be authorized subsequently by Congress.
dispo The Navy was in position to receive a payment-in-kind, the attendant services for the
of th el at the adjoining base.

obtain approval will result in the loss of rights to resources at a base or an installation, unless a substitute project is approved for the unit or the retention of the facilities can be justified on grounds of future use. Joint use or outleasing arrangements may result in the latter case.

Changes in landholding or use are brought about by Property Management, particularly the Base Utilization Division (Properties and Installations) of the DoD, which was established in 1961. The division is responsible for developing concepts and procedures with the intermediate and long-range objectives of improving the utilization of all military installations throughout the world. As of June 30, 1963, these numbered over 4,073. But the division's staff numbers less than ten and includes military personnel of civil engineering background, three of whom are on loan and represent the three Services. This division initiates surveys of the installations in response to information supplied "internally" or on direct order from higher echelon, for example, the Secretary of Defense. Typically the survey group will have a chairman, not on loan from a Service, and will include the three military representatives.

Naturally, incentives at the level of Property Management will reflect those present at the OSD. OSD will have a relatively strong incentive to allocate the land within a military service rather than in a nonmilitary department. There are alternative civilian uses for military land, but incentives to release land to outside uses depends on the gains resulting compared to costs of future acquisition of additional lands, and the costs of retention of land by the DoD.

The prevailing institutional arrangement limits the extent of gain, since the direct benefits derived from exchanges, if not payment-in-kind—DoD land for other lands—are uncertain. The costs of retention may vary and will depend partly upon the political mood existing in Congress and the Executive at a given time. These kinds of pressures caused passage of the 1958 Act and creation of the Public Land Law Review Commission in 1964, which together restrict, or impose additional costs on the military of withdrawing public domain lands over 5,000 acres. (See preceding section.)

It should be pointed out that even if the members of the Base Utilization Division were given appropriate incentives, the results of their efforts would still be unsatisfactory. It is not the meager size of the staff, the large number of the installations, and the substantial number of continuously changing tasks and missions that must be studied. The basic defect is a lack of any economic criterion. There is no way to assess the relative value of land used in Base A rather than B, in activities in other military or nonmilitary departments, or in the private sector.

A SUMMARY AND THE PROBLEM

The preceding discussion of existing laws and regulations revealed a set of rights to land that in essence are neither transferable nor exclusive. Transferability and exclusiveness are the two foundation stones of the economic theory of property rights. One economic implication of nontransferable rights is that, from the viewpoint of the holder of such rights, the economic cost of the resource is zero since the highest value generated by the resource in a foregone alternative is zero. Consequently, there is no incentive to economize the use of such rights, since the economic cost of the resource is zero whether a part or all is used. Moreover, there is no appropriate mechanism by which such resources find their way to their highest valued uses.

Resource allocation is also affected by the nonexclusivity of such property rights. For example, decisions of the Secretaries of the Services and/or the Department of Defense are external to the use holder, but they do affect resource use. An attempt was made to ascertain the potency of such forces operating from higher echelons and the resultant changes in the utilization of land rights. The analysis in the preceding section concluded that changes effected by these forces did not materially affect the transferability of such rights or its effect thereby on resource allocation. A change in use or holding of land will tend to reflect changes in missions and task assignments, as a result of policy decisions at the OSD level rather than from a mechanism that guides the resource into its most valued alternative from the vantage point of society.

These unfortunate results should *not* be attributed to the character or ability of the various decision makers. Instead, the outcome is the direct result of laws and regulations that exclude the true economic choice. In this respect land is not unique. Annually, Congress appropriates in detail for specific military construction projects that are "funded" separately from procurement of weapons and personnel. This process and the usual detailed specifications prevent decisions on trade-offs that exist between different factors of production used in construction and also trade-offs between construction and other categories of expenditures.

The basic obstacle to efficient use of land, in the sense that land tends to be used in its highest valued alternative, is lack of any alternatives through exchange. Nontransferability of the rights is the essential problem. As a result, there is no economic criterion to evaluate alternatives and no appropriate mechanism to effect trade-offs.

This conclusion should not imply that the deficiency is inevitable. It could be remedied by introducing suitable changes in the system. But it is outside the scope of this chapter to develop in detail an institutional arrangement that provides appropriate incentives for decision makers.[13]

Generally, changes that will constitute an improvement over the current system may be classed broadly into two types: (1) the DoD may, independently of other governmental agencies and the Congress, innovate arrangements whereby the economic cost of a resource is felt by the users; or (2) the Congress may embark on a major change which would involve re-enacting laws and regulations giving incentives to decision makers to incorporate the value of a resource in alternative uses when deciding on its employment.

---

[13] A forthcoming report by the author discusses an alternative institutional arrangement.

HARRY J. GILMAN

University of Rochester

The author is currently Associate Professor of Business Administration at the University of Rochester. But the ideas presented in this chapter were developed while he was a member of the research staff of the Center for Naval Analyses and while he served as Director of Military Compensation and Retention Studies in the Office of the Assistant Secretary of Defense (Manpower). He wishes to acknowledge his debt to Dr. Stuart Altman and Lt. Colonel Herman T. Boland, Jr. for their helpful comments on an earlier draft of this chapter. His special thanks go to Dr. Arnold Moore for his numerous criticisms and suggestions during the period of writing. The views expressed herein are entirely the author's and do not reflect the official position of any employer past or present.

14

Military Manpower Utilization

Chronic problems in the recruiting and retention of military personnel suggest that there are important differences between the management of labor in the military and civilian (nongovernment) sectors of the economy.[1] Some of these differences may result from the unique services performed by the military establishment. Others, however, are the result of the special nature of the institutional and budgetary constraints facing the military services. This paper examines several of these special factors and evaluates their impact on military manpower utilization.

In order to ensure that the best use is made of military manpower, efficiency is needed in (1) the allocation of funds between capital and labor, (2) the allocation of labor among the services and among outputs within a service, and (3) the allocation of funds among the different kinds of labor within each of the services. Sections I, II, and III examine allocation decisions (1), (2), and (3), respectively. Section IV is a summary of findings.

I. ALLOCATION OF FUNDS BETWEEN CAPITAL AND LABOR

The civilian firm and the military services must continually decide how to allocate their funds between capital and labor. Their problems are similar. As with goods and services produced in the civilian economy, a specific level of defense output, such as a state of readiness or level of combat capability, can be produced by combining capital and labor in a number of different proportions. For example, a given level of combat effectiveness can be maintained with a reduced labor input, provided expenditures on capital are increased sufficiently to offset the reduction in output caused by the reduction in labor. Such substitutions are possible throughout the defense establishment: automatic equipment can be substituted for men watching temperature gauges or oiling machinery in the engine rooms of naval vessels, for signalmen, or for ordnance and supply handlers; gas turbine engines can be substituted for conventional steam engines at significant savings in manpower, and so forth.

What conditions determine the specific proportion of capital to labor in both the military and private sectors of the economy? A private firm operating in a competitive economy will tend to combine these two broad groups of factors in the proportions that minimize costs. This will occur when the last dollar spent on labor adds to output the same amount that it would have added had that dollar been spent on additional capital. Were it otherwise, it would obviously be in the interest of the businessman to shift expenditures from the less productive to the more productive factor, thereby reducing his costs per unit of output and increasing his profit.

---

[1] Federal employment of civilians is not discussed here, but parts of this paper apply with equal force to the utilization of nonmilitary personnel.

In the private sector of the economy, the tendency toward minimum cost production exists because the firm (a) desires to increase its profits and (b) is able to shift its funds from one input to another in response to changes in the prices or productivity of inputs. Moreover, with some exceptions, minimum cost production is socially desirable because it assures relatively less use of scarce (costly) resources and greater use of more abundant (less costly) resources.

Should resource allocation in the defense establishment be subject to constraints that will assure minimum costs of production? The answer to this question is yes, provided that it is the social, not the Department of Defense, cost that is being minimized. In the case of labor, for example, the cost that is relevant for the defense production decision is the cost that is necessary to attract a completely voluntary force. This is the social cost of labor, which, under the conditions of an operable draft, as at present, exceeds the Department of Defense cost of labor.[2]

The importance of the voluntary cost for military manpower-utilization decisions is best illustrated with the case where the level of military compensation is below that for comparable labor (of like age, education, occupation, and so forth) working under similar conditions in the civilian sector. In such a case, a shift of an individual from the civilian to the military sector will reduce civilian income and output by an amount equal to his civilian earnings. If his utilization in the military services were determined by his level of military compensation, his output in the military would be smaller than that in the civilian sector. Use of the voluntary price would, therefore, ensure that the resultant gain of product in the military sector would be no smaller than the product lost in the civilian sector.[3]

Recognizing the social desirability of minimum cost production, it is appropriate to ask whether the military services have the incentives to be, and are *able* to be, efficient in their use of resources? The lack of a quantitative measure of military effectiveness (output) prevents an accurate assessment of the degree of efficiency in defense activity. But there are at least two factors that work unequivocally toward making the allocation of funds between capital and labor in the services less than optimal. The first of these relates to the deficiencies in

---

[2] It is not the purpose of this paper to estimate the increase in military pay that would be required for a completely voluntary force. This amount would obviously be a function (1) of the size of the force desired relative to the size of the relevant manpower pool and (2) of the non-monetary conditions of military service and the level of economic activity in the civilian sector of the economy. Neither does this paper address itself to the question of whether society's tax for defense should fall disproportionately on its young males (the draft) or whether it should be more evenly distributed among all income earners (the case of higher pay for a voluntary force). The principal concern of this part of the paper is the estimation of the impact of the draft on military manpower utilization.

[3] Similar considerations apply to the case in which the draft price equals the level of civilian earnings but in which military service is performed under more onerous conditions than those in the civilian sector. In this case, the voluntary price would have to exceed the earnings of comparable civilian labor by an amount that would compensate military personnel for the differences in conditions of service.

the current budgeting system that interfere with the proper allocation of funds between these two inputs. The second relates to the existence of the draft and the concomitant underestimation of the social cost of labor.

A. The Military Budgeting System

The incentive to allocate funds between capital and labor in a way that will minimize cost is, in the case of the private firm, provided by the desire to maximize profits. This incentive operates in the presence or absence of changes in the prices or productivity of either of these two inputs. There is little value in reemphasizing the fact that there is no similar incentive in military, or in most other government activities. What is worth emphasizing, however, is that the military budget is so compartmentalized as to make efficient allocation unlikely and difficult even if an incentive could be created. For example, once funds have been allocated to a specific input, such as military personnel at the beginning of the year, they can rarely be shifted to any other input during the year. Indeed, this compartmentalization often discourages efficiency, for the existence of unused funds (savings) in one year may result in a reduced allocation of such funds in the next budget year with no offsetting increase elsewhere.

Moreover, throughout the development of the budget, the allocation decisions center around very specific line items, such as aircraft procurement (Navy), military personnel (Army), and so forth. This process is not likely to highlight the possible trade-offs between capital and labor. For example, the capability of an aircraft carrier is a function of the number and type of aircraft, the design of the carrier, and the number and type of personnel. Each of these inputs can be substituted for the other, to some extent. Rarely, however, are such trade-offs considered; the three inputs are funded separately and are generally reviewed and approved by different persons.

Nevertheless, a considerable amount of substitution of new capital for older capital and thereby of capital for labor actually does take place on an intermittent basis. These substitutions generally occur in conjunction with the development of new equipment such as the light machine gun, recoilless rifles, and missiles, each of which requires smaller crews for equal firepower. But factor substitutions seldom occur at a given level of technology, and the technological changes do not seem to be produced in response to the relative prices or productivity of inputs. There is little evidence to suggest that the development of ships or aircraft, for instance, is significantly affected by the relative prices of either capital or labor.

In the author's opinion, these deficiencies in the allocation of funds between capital and labor in Defense are partly the result of the compartmentalized nature of the budgeting and review process. A process that centers around the levels of specific inputs rather than output is not designed to bring into sharp focus the possibilities of substitution of one input for another; neither does this process provide the maximum incentives for substitution when the possibilities become apparent.

B. The Impact of the Draft

The preceding section suggested that the current defense budgeting system does not provide the incentives necessary to encourage economic efficiency. This conclusion does not depend on the services' ability to acquire either men or equipment at below market prices and does not specify whether the military services underutilize men, overinvest in equipment, or both.

The draft, however, enables the services to acquire manpower at an average price lower than that necessary to attract a completely voluntary force.[4] Equipment, on the other hand, continues to be purchased at market prices. To the extent, then, that the services have the opportunity and incentive to increase effectiveness at a given budget, they are likely to want to buy more labor out of that budget with the draft than without the draft. Since the labor cost to the military understates, in the presence of the draft, the real cost of its labor to the society, such an increase in the force will raise military effectiveness by a smaller amount than the concomitant loss in output in the civilian sector.

Although the lower labor costs to the military (under the draft) are not the sole determinants of the utilization of labor in defense activity,[5] it is evident that the draft has a significant impact on both the size and quality of the military force. This is apparent from the fact that the draft is applicable, at most, to those individuals who have not fulfilled their initial service obligation. Those beyond their initial term of service are in the military on a voluntary basis. Consequently, the draft lowers the cost of less-experienced (first-term) relative to that of more-experienced (career) personnel.

The lower cost of first-term personnel may be, however, more apparent than real. First, the existence of the draft contributes to a lowering of the level of experience of the military force, thereby increasing the number of men required for a given level of effectiveness.[6] Second, the higher rate of turnover of personnel

---

[4] The draft does not, of course, prevent some individuals, particularly those in the lower-skilled military specialties, from being overpaid. Indeed, the services have a surplus of careerists in low-skilled specialties.

[5] There is some evidence that the size of the force is also subject to nonmarket constraints. And both the Administration and Congress are subject to continuous pressures to develop capital intensive weapon systems.

[6] Partial support for this proposition is found in the composition of the military force by years of service. For example, about 50 per cent of the force on active duty at the end of FY 1964 had less than three years of service. That this is at least partly the result of the draft is evidenced by the differences in retention rates for first-term regulars and inductees. For example, in recent years, the reenlistment rates for first-term regulars have varied between about 22.0 and 29.0 per cent, whereas those for inductees have been around 10.0 per cent. In FY 1964, the respective rates were 25.2 and 3.6 per cent. It may be assumed that the retention rates for first-term regulars understate the retention rates for true volunteers. This is because some of the regulars have joined in preference to being drafted. Source: Directorate for Statistical Services, Office of the Secretary of Defense.

resulting from the draft contributes to the need to maintain a large network of military training centers to train the new and inexperienced entrants in order to qualify them for assignment to a military specialty. Much of this training is done by military instructors and supported by military personnel. Consequently, reduced turnover would enable the services to operate with fewer men.[7]

Finally, by lowering the apparent cost of first-term personnel to the military, the draft encourages the underutilization of such personnel, thereby increasing further the size of the force required and the social costs for any level of effectiveness. This effect of the draft is particularly noticeable when one views the size of the force as the resultant of (a) the number of men in uniform and (b) their average level of skill. Since the draft enables the military to acquire both high-skilled and low-skilled labor at the same money prices, the services are encouraged to raise the qualitative requirements for recruits. But there is little evidence to suggest that the improved quality of initial entrants is paralleled by either a proportionate decrease in the number of men in uniform or by a proportionate increase in effectiveness. Instead, there is some evidence to suggest that the lower relative cost of higher quality labor results in the relative underutilization of such labor. For example, both low- and high-quality inductees are generally assigned to activities requiring relatively little technical training. Moreover, because of the draft, the services are able to set mental, educational, and physical requirements for voluntary enlistees and officer personnel that are clearly in excess of those necessary for the satisfactory performance of many duties assigned to first-term personnel.

It has been argued that the high-quality initial entrants, although underutilized during the first term of service, are necessary to assure a high-quality base from which to draw the career force. Individuals in the latter group are generally assigned to the more demanding activities. But the vast majority of those with higher levels of education, for example, do not remain in the military beyond the initial service obligation. Recent data reveal that the first-term reenlistment rate is about twice as high for non-grade-school graduates than for high-school graduates. Consequently, the individuals in the career force have a lower average level of education than those who are in the military for relatively short periods of time. The latter are, therefore, rarely assigned to activities requiring high levels of education. The difference in the selectivity criteria between first-term and career personnel can be explained by the services' ability to acquire higher-quality first-term, but not career, personnel at low costs.

The effect of the draft on the average quality of initial entrants can be illustrated by the high rejection rates, for both medical and mental reasons, for

---

[7] The total training costs for military personnel in FY 1964 have been estimated at about $4 billion. Since these costs are exclusive of the rent of land and much of the capital used for training, the 4 billion figure is a significant underestimate of the annual training bill.

TABLE 14–1   *Per cent Disqualified for Military Service Selected
                  Periods, WWII–1964*

Group	WWII Ages 18–25	Korean War (July, 1950 Through July, 1953)	Aug., 1953 Through July, 1958	Aug., 1958 Through June, 1960	Aug., 1958 Through April, 1963	May, 1963 Through Dec., 1964	1964 Estimate
Those taking pre-induction examinations only[1]		32.2	38.2		46.4	52.1	55.0
All youth of draft liable age	22.7[1]	23.6[2]	26.8[2]	31.7[2]			35.2

Sources: (1) Medical Statistics Agency, Office of the Surgeon General, Department of Army; (2) Bernard D. Karpinos' "Qualification of American Youth for Military Service," Medical Statistics Division, Office of the Surgeon General, Department of the Army, 1962.

youth examined for military service. Table 14–1 shows that these rates have increased over time with the increases in the size of the relevant manpower pool.[8] The higher rejection rates for pre-inductees than for all youth are the result of two factors: (a) the average age of pre-inductees is higher than the average age of all draft-liable youth, and (b) the pre-inductees are a residual group, called upon after large numbers have entered the military.

Similar conclusions follow from an analysis of changes in the formal educational requirements for voluntary enlistments and for new officer personnel. For instance, beginning in July of 1964, the Air Force had adopted a policy of accepting only 5 per cent of its total enlistments from among non-high-school graduates. This policy was subsequently relaxed, in response to the drop off in high-quality enlistments. This drop in high quality enlistments was, at least partly, in response to the then current discussion of the possibility of eliminating the draft.

[8] The rising rejection rates are also consistent with an excess in the number of voluntary enlistments. In such a case, the services could be expected to allocate the available positions to the better-trained individuals. But, the excess voluntary supply would not explain the rising rejection rates for the draftees. Moreover, there is independent evidence that the quality of volunteers accepted for military service increases with the increases in draft quotas. For a more detailed discussion of the changes in the quality of enlistees see Harold Wool, "The Military Specialist," unpublished doctoral dissertation (Washington, D. C.: American University, June, 1965), Ch. 6.

In summary: the allocation of funds between capital and labor in defense activity is undoubtedly far from optimal. In part, this is the result of the peculiar nature of the institutional and budgetary constraints within which such allocation decisions are made. The current defense budgeting and review systems, for example, fail to provide the necessary incentives for economic efficiency in defense activity. In part, however, the deficiencies in manpower utilization may be attributable to the draft, which provides the defense establishment with labor at costs that are significantly below the real costs of its labor to the society. The low apparent costs of labor to defense seem to increase both the size and quality of the military force. But the exact cost to society of the current capital-labor mix in defense activity has yet to be estimated.

II. ALLOCATION OF RESOURCES AMONG AND WITHIN MILITARY SERVICES

Although the several services are generally assigned different missions, many of the activities performed by one service can substitute, to a greater or lesser degree, for those performed by another service. An increase in firepower, for example, can be achieved by increasing either the size of the Air Force (tactical air support), Army (ground support), Marine Corps (ground or air support), or Navy (sea or air support). Given the differences in effectiveness and costs, however, it is reasonable to assume that a given increase in firepower will be achieved at lower cost in one service (or activity) than in another. An economic increase in firepower occurs when the last unit of firepower is achieved at equal costs in all of the services (and in all activities within a service).

Is the allocation of manpower (or capital) among and within the services subject to the above constraints? In the absence of definitive measures of military manpower productivity, this question cannot, of course, be answered categorically. It can be assumed, however, that current DoD and congressional decisions on the distribution of the force, particularly among the services, are rarely made on the basis of either the relative productivity or relative costs of labor in the various services or defense activities. In fact, the review of manpower requests within the Office of the Secretary of Defense centers around single defense activities rather than alternative activities or services. And, as was pointed out in Part I, the possibilities of capital-labor substitution even within a single activity have hardly been explored.

Moreover, even the force distribution decisions, if any, that are made on the basis of relative effectiveness and relative costs are nonoptimal unless the relative costs are inclusive of the differences in cost of manpower among the services (or activities). For instance, the 1964 military pay data reveal that during the first four years of service Army enlisted personnel earned about 8.9 per cent more than Navy, about 12.2 per cent more than Air Force, and about

TABLE 14–2   Mental Grade Distribution of Initial Enlisted
              Accessions, 1964

	Percentage		
Service	Mental Groups I & II, AFQT percentile score (65–100)	Mental Group III, AFQT percentile score (31–64)	Mental Group IV,[a] AFQT percentile score (10–30)
Army	33.7	46.4	19.9
Navy	41.1	48.0	10.9
Marine Corps	37.5	53.3	9.2
Air Force	49.9	45.8	4.3

Source: *Qualitative Distribution of Military Manpower*, U. S. Army Recruiting Command, DDMP-R(M)-344, FY 1964.

[a] Army data include some individuals who scored below Mental Group IV (0–9) but were administratively accepted on the basis of psychological screening. All Army data apply to the combined distribution of both voluntary enlistees and inductees.

21.1 per cent more than Marine Corps personnel.[9] The pay differentials during the second four years of service (years five through eight) were considerably smaller; they were respectively minus 4.5, plus 4.3, and plus 10.7 per cent.

Except for the difference between the Army and Marine Corps, the higher levels of military pay for Army than for either Air Force or Navy personnel are principally the result of the higher turnover rates and the concomitant reduction in the length of time required to achieve higher grades in the Army than in either of the other two military services. Since the higher losses from the Army occur mainly at the point of first reenlistment, the smaller differences in military pay in latter years are understandable.[10]

Moreover, the higher Army incomes are earned by lower-quality personnel than those in the other services, as is apparent from the figures recorded in Table 14–2. These figures summarize the results of the mental examinations given

[9] It must be noted that the differences in earnings between Army and Navy or Army and Air Force could be partly reduced by including among the earnings the current values of military training. But, the values that are relevant for inclusion among the earnings are those that are associated with general rather than specific training, that is, with that fraction of training that contributes to higher earnings in subsequent civilian employment. Recent survey data indicate that a large majority of individuals do not enter comparable civilian occupations. See, for example, Harold Wool, "The Military Specialist," *op. cit.*, Table XL. My own work shows that veterans' earnings are no higher, and indeed are often lower, than the earnings of non-veterans of like age and formal education. This suggests that military training is useful primarily in military service.

[10] The difference between the Army and Marine Corps is principally one of organizational philosophy. The Marines are more concerned with preserving a highly pyramidal grade structure.

to those entering military service. Note that the scores on such examinations are highly correlated with education. For example, the average percentile score for non-grade-school graduates (zero through seven years of education) has been estimated at 15.7, that for high-school graduates at 54.7, and that for college graduates at 76.2.

It is apparent from both the income data and from the qualitative data recorded in Table 14–2 that manpower costs, exclusive of training,[11] are highest in the Army. In addition, the current compensatory pay differentials for Army personnel understate the differences in pay required to make Army service as attractive as, for example, service in the Air Force. This proposition is obvious from the differences in the services' ability to retain personnel beyond their initial service obligation. In FY 1964, for example, the first-term reenlistment rate for Army personnel was 15.1 per cent. The corresponding rates for Air Force, Navy, and Marine Corps were 29.5, 22.5 and 14.4 per cent.

Since average manpower costs are obviously highest in the Army, the Army should have the greatest incentive to substitute capital for labor. Further, to the extent that the Department of Defense can substitute among the services, it has an incentive to shift resources from the Army to the other services. Both of these propositions follow from the fact that, because of higher labor costs in the Army, optimal allocation of resources in defense requires a higher capital-labor ratio and less defense activity in the Army than would have been the case without these differences in labor costs. It is not clear that the Army tended more toward substituting capital for labor than has any other service. Nor is there any evidence that the Department of Defense has considered the differences in cost of labor among the military services.

III. ALLOCATION OF RESOURCES AMONG DIFFERENT KINDS OF LABOR

Under the condition of an operable draft the services can, of course, acquire almost any quantity and quality of men deemed necessary for national defense. But, as indicated earlier, the high-quality men are generally underutilized during the first term of service. The draft cannot, of course, assure the retention of such personnel beyond their initial service obligation. This objective can only be achieved by voluntary means.

Although it is recognized that the choice between a military and civilian career is influenced by many factors, the proposition that pay can, and should, be used to increase the retention of highly skilled personnel is widely accepted. Witness, for example, the increasing use of specialty pay for personnel in critically

[11] The formal training costs per man seem to be lower in the Army than in either the Air Force or the Navy; however, due to the higher turnover in the Army, the training costs per effective man are probably higher there than in either of the other two services.

short military specialties. Yet many problems in the area of pay remain. These residual problems in pay, and the concomitant problems in manpower utilization, derive from the application of a philosophy of pay that is still largely paternalistic and egalitarian. This is apparent from three distinct characteristics of military pay: (1) a large fraction of military pay is deferred until the individual has retired from the military force; (2) an even larger fraction is provided in allowances and in noncash form; and, especially, (3) insufficient pay differentiation exists among subgroups with different levels of skill. Each of these three characteristics has an impact on the size and quality of the military force. They are examined in Sections A, B, and C, respectively.

A. The Military Nondisability Retirement System

Military personnel retiring at the completion of twenty years of service receive retirement pay equal to 50 per cent of their basic pay at the time of their retirement. Retirement benefits for those retiring after twenty years of service are increased at the rate of 2.5 per cent of basic pay per year of additional service until they reach a maximum of 75 per cent of basic pay. Formally, all contributions necessary to provide retirement benefits are made by the government.[12]

In addition to retirement benefits, military personnel are fully covered under the Federal Old Age Survivors and Disability Insurance System. Formally, contributions to this system are shared equally by the service member and the government.

Since military personnel retire from active service while they are relatively young (the average age of retirement for enlisted personnel is 39, and that for officers is 45), they may be assumed to establish new careers for themselves subsequent to their retirement from service. Depending on their subsequent civilian employment, they may add to their final retirement benefits during their second careers; however, even if they do not, the average enlisted man who reaches retirement eligibility will retire in his twenty-first year of service as an E-6 or E-7. Even if he retires as an E-6 he will receive, under current pay rates, about $2,250 annually, beginning at about age 39 until his presumed death at 73. If he survives to age 62 (his wife being 60), he will receive, in addition, social security payments estimated at $1,561 per year.

The average officer currently retires as a major or lieutenant colonel after about twenty two years of service. Even if he retires as a major, he will receive, under current pay rates, about $4,825 annually, beginning at age 45 until his

---

[12] It is obviously only formally true that all contributions are made by the government; for it may be assumed that retirement benefits are viewed by service personnel as part of their compensation. In such a case, military personnel are accepting lower current earnings in exchange for a future earnings stream. The difference between that which a person accepts in current earnings with a future retirement stream and current earnings without future retirement benefits may be viewed as his contribution toward his future retirement stream.

presumed death at age 73. If he survives to age 62, he will receive in social security payments an additional $2,232 per year.

It is clear that the size and character of retirement pay will have a significant impact on the utilization of personnel and on the pattern of personnel losses from the military services. First, the nonvested aspect of military retirement benefits produces differences in the current value of total military income among subgroups of the military force; total income is higher for those who prefer to save a large fraction of their current earnings. The military services are, consequently, relatively more attractive to large savers than to others.

More important is the fact that the value of such benefits is small at the initial stages of an individual's career, thus providing little incentive for remaining in service after the initial military obligation has been fulfilled. They provide even less incentive, of course, at the point of initial entry into service.[13] Subsequently, after about eight years of service, such benefits provide too much incentive for remaining until retirement eligibility (twenty years), at which point they encourage a significant fraction of active duty personnel to retire from service.

Moreover, for a given year of service, the value of retirement benefits is relatively lower for personnel in high-skilled (personnel in whom the services have invested heavily) than for those in low-skilled occupations. This disparity comes about by linking the retirement benefits to the amount of basic pay alone rather than to basic plus specialty pay at the time of retirement. Since basic pay is largely a function of length of service, the more highly-skilled individuals will receive a smaller fraction of their total income in deferred payments. They will, therefore, have a shorter time span in which these benefits provide an incentive to remain in the military. Consequently, the retirement system contributes toward the current differential incentive for those in whom the services have invested little money—those in low-skilled occupations—to remain in the military until retirement eligibility. Since, in addition, the alternative civilian employment and earnings opportunities favor the higher-skilled by more than the differences in total military compensation, the higher-skilled will also have a greater incentive to leave the military as soon as they reach retirement eligibility.

The differential impact of the retirement system among groups classified by length of service is supported by the reenlistment behavior of both enlisted

[13] Three separate factors contribute to the low value of retirement benefits at the initial stages of the military career. The first, of course, is the fact that these retirement benefits are in the far future and are, therefore, discounted to the present at some subjective positive discount rate. The second factor centers around the probability of remaining in service long enough to collect such benefits. This probability is positively related to length of time already served. The third factor deals with variations in the subjective discount rate with age. It is reasonable to assume that the younger the individual (the point of initial entry into the military), the higher his discount rate. This assumption is supported by recent Navy and Air Force studies that show discount rates to be negatively related to age. In part, the variations of discount rates with age may be explained by parallel differences in market borrowing rates.

and officer personnel. For example, the unadjusted first-term reenlistment rate for FY 1965 was 21.5 per cent, whereas the corresponding rate for career personnel was 87.0 per cent. Separate data for the second and subsequent reenlistments show continuously rising reenlistment rates until they approach 100 per cent at about the third reenlistment point.

A similar pattern is found in the loss data for FY 1965 (and for previous years) classified by length of service. These data are presented as percentages of the total number reaching a given year of service. They show, for example, that less than 16 per cent of those who completed eight years of service fail to reenlist between then and the twenty-year point; however, retirements at the twenty-year point (the first year of eligibility) exceed 50 per cent of the eligibles. Losses from the officer population follow a similar pattern.[14]

The effect of the retirement system on military manpower utilization may also be illustrated with its unique impact on career patterns, particularly on those of officer personnel. Perhaps more than in any civilian industry, military specialties vary in their requirements for youth and vigor. At one extreme are the requirements for the combat soldier, platoon leader, or fighter pilot; and at the other extreme are the physical requirements for communications experts or other specialists, for clerical and administrative personnel, and for economists. It is generally assumed that the peak age, for purposes of productivity, varies among occupations, depending on their requirements for, among other things, physical vigor. Indeed, it is for this reason that the fighter pilot has a relatively short career as a fighter pilot.

It is unreasonable to assume, however, that all fighter pilots will subsequently be, for example, efficient administrators or supply officers. Yet this is what most of them become after they stop flying. Undoubtedly, this and other examples of a lack of specialization in the military are at least partly the result of the nonvested aspect of the current retirement benefits. Under this system, the services feel obligated to design career patterns so as to enable them to retain individuals until retirement eligibility.

B. The Composition of Military Pay

Depending on such factors as occupation, firm, industry, and union membership, civilian employees will receive larger or smaller amounts of their total earnings in the form of fringe benefits. In no other employment situation,

---

[14] But the recent trend of increasing basic pay on an annual basis may be expected to reduce the number of voluntary retirements before the thirty-year point. Under this condition, an individual who chooses to retire after twenty rather than twenty-one (or more) years of service loses annually, in addition to the 2.5 per cent of current pay, 100 per cent of the pay raise. Consequently, annual pay increases can be expected to discourage early retirements. For a more detailed discussion of the impact of changes in military pay on retention patterns see my paper, "Secular and Cross-Sectional Changes in Military and Civil-Service Pay," unpublished manuscript (Washington, D.C.: Bureau of The Budget, June, 1966), pp. 9–11, 20–25, 37.

however, will individuals receive their compensation in so many components, or in so complex a form as they will in military service.

Of particular interest here is the extremely large fraction of military compensation (about 50 per cent) that is provided in nontaxable allowances and in noncash form. This aspect of military pay is of interest because it may be expected to have a significant impact on both the cost and effectiveness of a given military force. Consider the cost first.

A pay package that has many unrationed income-in-kind items of pay may be expected to have a lower value on the average than one that consists entirely of an equal amount of cash. This is true because the former package controls, *in part*, the individual's pattern of consumption. Cash, on the other hand, may be spent by the individual on the goods and services he most prefers. Consequently, in order for the two pay packages to be equally attractive, the one with the income-in-kind components would almost certainly have to be more costly to the government than would payment in cash.[15]

The last proposition is valid even when no individual consumes, on the aggregate, more than a normal quantity of the goods and services that are provided in-kind. But the increase in cost of such a pay system will also result, because the very provision of the noncash items encourages greater consumption of such goods and services than would otherwise be the case. An illustration is the goods and services, such as medical services for dependents of military personnel, that are provided free of charge to the servicemen.[16] Given the low costs of added consumption of such services, the "average" individual has an incentive to expand his consumption of them until the last units consumed, in this case the last visit to the doctor, has near zero value to him. But the costs of providing these additional services are not at, or near, zero. Similar reasoning suggests that military personnel will tend to eat larger than normal quantities of food.

The final factor contributing to the increased cost of the military pay package is that the noncash form of pay encourages a disproportionate number of unusually heavy consumers of such goods and services to join or remain in the military, thereby further increasing the average level of consumption of such

[15] There are at least a couple of exceptions to this proposition, but neither of these seems to be relevant when total government income and expenditures are considered. The first relates to the nontaxable aspect of income-in-kind. If the value of such an item is greater than the nontaxable price, although smaller than the taxable cash equivalent, the individual would obviously prefer the item to the taxable (cash) equivalent. But in this case, the government would be able to increase the taxable cash equivalent by the amount of taxes it would receive from individuals. The second exception applies to situations in which, because of economies of scale, the military establishment can provide these goods and services at significantly lower than market prices. It is, however, doubtful whether there are greater economies of scale in the military than in the civilian sector of the economy.

[16] Although the cash prices to the individual are zero, his costs in waiting may discourage him from consuming these services below a certain positive value. Nevertheless, the military family probably consumes more of such services than does a civilian family of comparable size and income.

goods and services and the concomitant costs of military compensation. The last factor increases, of course, the value as well as the cost of military compensation. However, this particular increase in the value of compensation is likely to reduce rather than increase the efficiency of military manpower utilization. This is true because the noncash items of pay produce differences in military compensation that are related to the dependency status rather than to the military skills of individuals. The military services are, therefore, more attractive to married personnel and large families than to single personnel and small families. Similar considerations apply to the nontaxable allowances.

The differential incentive among dependency status groups to remain in military service may be illustrated with the income and retention data for FY 1964. Although these data pertain to Navy enlisted personnel only, additional evidence suggests that the patterns of income and retention differentials revealed here are equally applicable to the enlisted men and officers in other military services. These data show that military compensation during the first four years of service is about 38 per cent greater for married than for single personnel. Married personnel with additional dependents receive, on the average, an additional 17 per cent. The earnings differentials during the second term of service (years five through eight) are somewhat smaller. They are, respectively, 34 and 44 per cent.

The situation of family men receiving higher earnings than single men of like age, education, and occupation is not paralleled in the civilian sector of the economy.[17] Since military life offers greater hardship for married than for single personnel, however, it might be argued that the military earnings differentials are a necessary compensatory device. But even if the higher earnings of married personnel are *compensatory*, they increase the cost of military manpower utilization; for, under this system, identical services are obtained from single and married men at considerably different levels of remuneration. It would obviously be less costly to obtain such services, to the extent possible, from single men.

Moreover, if the differences in military earnings among dependency status groups were only compensatory in nature, married and single personnel could be expected to have identical incentives for military careers. Instead, we observe significantly higher reenlistment rates for married than for single men. For instance, during FY 1964, the first-term reenlistment rate for married personnel was about 61.0 per cent greater than that for single men. The rate for married personnel with additional dependents was about 135 per cent greater than that for single men. This differential suggests that the higher earnings of married personnel are significantly in excess of those necessary to offset the differences in hardship.

---

[17] Strictly speaking, civilian earnings are also higher for those with, than for those without, dependents. But such earnings are related to dependency status only to the extent that those with dependents tend to have lower levels of unemployment or to work more hours per week than do those without dependents. Such differences are, therefore, related to output. Military differentials, on the other hand, are unrelated to differences in output.

The pattern of income differences described above is clearly the result of a philosophy of pay that calls for the remuneration of individuals on the basis of their needs rather than on the basis of their contribution to national defense. Unfortunately, the implementation of this philosophy lowers the level of defense; for the resultant levels of pay are more attractive to the needy than to those possessing the skills required for national defense.

C. Compensatory and Qualitative Military Pay Differentials

Military pay, like civilian pay, is positively correlated with length of on-the-job experience; however, the increases in military pay with length of service differ in character from those in the civilian sector. The differences arising from the draft, the retirement system, and the allowances or noncash items of pay have been discussed in Sections A and B above. This section examines several residual differences between the military and civilian pay structures.

In addition to the differences in pay with length of service, military pay, like its civilian counterpart, varies with the conditions of work. Specifically, military pay varies with the differences in the degree of risk or hardship associated with particular military assignments. But in this dimension, too, the two sectors differ both in philosophy and method of determining the magnitude of such *compensatory* differentials. Consequently, they may be expected to have different effects on the respective labor forces.

One difference between the two sectors may be illustrated with the data presented in Part II above. The evidence presented there suggested that the conditions of service differ among the services. And although the levels of compensation show similar variations, the observed differences in pay are obviously not sufficient to make the several services equally attractive. Moreover, the differences in pay among the services are not the result of a generally recognized need for interservice differentials. On the contrary, the ruling philosophy here is one of "equal pay for equal work," independent of the conditions of work. Consequently, military pay is explicitly compensatory for differences in duty assignments within a service (sea vs. shore duty, for example) but has no explicit differentials for the differences in conditions among the services.

From the point of view of force management, it must be recognized that compensatory differentials are useful and effective only to the extent that they can influence behavior. Thus, since the decision to enter or to remain in a particular service is a voluntary one, differential pay among the services could be used to offset the current differences in the services' ability to attract or retain personnel. On the other hand, specific duties within a service are often assigned on a nonvoluntary basis. Special-duty pay will, therefore, often have a relatively small potential for correcting manning imbalances.

The point to be made is not, of course, that the specific duties do not modify the conditions of service. Obviously, these conditions are different for service on land, on a surface ship, in a submarine, in the air, in a foreign country, and so forth. But sea-duty pay, for example, cannot increase the number of men for sea duty if the specific assignments (sea vs. shore) are made on a nonvoluntary basis. Sea-duty pay can, of course, increase the number of men available for service in the Navy as a whole, but only imperfectly through its effect on total Navy pay. That is, Navy pay can be used to increase the attractiveness of the Navy.

Moreover, to the extent that specific duty assignments are voluntary, it must be recognized that special-duty items of pay do not operate in a vacuum but in conjunction with other elements of pay and nonmonetary conditions of service. Thus, if boatswains mates or stewards spend more time at sea than electronic technicians, other things being equal, boatswains mates would require more pay than technicians. But other things are rarely equal, particularly when the alternative civilian income and employment opportunities are included. And indeed, paying boatswains mates more (increasing sea-duty pay) might be expected to widen the differential in reenlistment rates in favor of boatswains mates, where greater turnover might be desirable.

Similar considerations apply to the proposed (Navy) use of a new item of pay called "responsibility pay." This measure has been approved by Congress but has thus far failed to secure overall DoD support. In the Navy proposal, responsibility pay is to be awarded to officer personnel when they command vessels at sea, independent of the quality of performance or the current willingness of officers to assume command responsibilities.

In fact, there is a substantial surplus of officers willing and qualified to take on command assignments. This surplus suggests that the levels of pay (monetary or nonmonetary, current or future pay) are already higher for command than for other duties. Responsibility pay is therefore unnecessary to increase the availability of personnel for command duties. If, on the other hand, the Navy wishes to increase overall officer retention, additional nonresponsibility pay seems more suited for this task than does responsibility pay.

To the extent, therefore, that the decision to join a particular service or type of defense activity is a voluntary one, compensatory differentials intended to equate the attractiveness of the several services or activities must be viewed in conjunction with the levels of total military pay. Given the greater risk, hardship, or responsibility associated with particular activities, total pay is either sufficient or not sufficient to attract and retain the desired quantity and quality of men. This is in fact the philosophy and method that is used to determine the need for and the size of the civilian differentials.

The net effect of establishing the magnitudes of a variety of pay items independent of one another is a pattern of differences in total military compensation that is largely responsible for the current undesirable pattern of losses from the military. Thus, unlike that in the civilian sector, total military compensation shows relatively little variation among groups classified by such qualitative characteristics as education, age (for a given length of service), and civilian occupation.[18]

Estimates (1964), for example, of enlisted men's (Navy) pay reveal that the average level of pay during the first four years of service is only about 5 per cent greater for those with at least some college education (thirteen years or more) than for those with at most a grade-school education (eight years or less). The corresponding difference in basic pay alone is only somewhat greater, about 8 per cent. The comparable differences during the second four years of service are about 5.8 per cent in total pay but only 5 per cent in basic pay alone. The small difference in second-term total pay occurs notwithstanding the inclusion of proficiency pay in the estimates of total pay. This phenomenon points out the difficulty of establishing skill differentials in a pay system that is composed of many pay elements, each having been established independently of the others.

The patterns of military pay across levels of education differ from those observed in the civilian sector in two respects. First, full-time civilian earnings for the age group that corresponds to that of the first-term population (median age of about 19) are about 40 per cent lower for grade-school graduates than for high-school graduates. Those with some college education earn about 10 per cent more than high-school graduates. Second, the civilian pay differentials that are correlated with education increase rather than diminish with age (or with length of service).[19]

Given the differences in the two patterns of remuneration it is not surprising to observe significantly higher retention rates for those with lower than for those with higher levels of civilian education. For example, an analysis of Navy (FY 1964) first-term reenlistment rates reveals that within each mental group separately reenlistment rates for those with less than eight years of education are about double those for high-school graduates.

There are currently no comparable data for the other services. Nor are there any reenlistment data based on education for second or subsequent reenlistments. But reenlistment data classified by occupation reveal that the lower retention rates for the highly skilled groups persist at least through the second reenlistment. The data for the officer population suggest that officer losses parallel

---

[18] The major exceptions to this finding relate to the break between officers and enlisted men and, within the former, to the break between medical and dental specialists and all other officers. In both of these cases, the differences in military earnings parallel differences in age at entry and in education or civilian specialty. But, unlike the officer, an enlisted man with a college degree will receive about the same level of military pay as one with only a grade-school education. Similarly, with the exception noted above, within the officer population, differences in pay will rarely be related to differences in civilian experience or education.

[19] The estimates of civilian earnings for first-term personnel were derived from DoD surveys and from the 1 in 1000 sample of the 1960 U. S. Census of Population. For a discussion of the relationship between civilian educational differentials and age, see Gary S. Becker, *Human Capital* (New York: Columbia University Press, 1964).

those of the enlisted population. Since the more highly skilled groups are also the ones in whom the military have invested heavily, in both formal and on-the-job training, such losses are extremely costly to the defense establishment.

IV. SUMMARY AND CONCLUSIONS

This chapter attempts to evaluate the impact of the institutional or budgetary constraints on military manpower utilization. Although many of the factors discussed here are equally present in other government activities, there are at least three that are unique to the military establishment. These are:

1. No other sector can acquire part of its manpower at below market clearing prices (the draft).

2. No other sector demands that its personnel enter almost exclusively at the bottom rung of a highly structured promotion ladder.

3. No other sector, including the Soviet military establishment, has a compensation system that is as paternalistic and egalitarian as the US military system.

These three factors are not, of course, independent of the institutional or budgetary constraints. Each of them inhibits the efficient use of military manpower. Although the draft assures high-quality recruits, it cannot assure the retention of such personnel beyond the initial term of service.[20] Moreover, the draft undoubtedly contributes to a greater use of manpower than would be the case if the services had to pay market clearing prices for labor. This is shown most clearly in the case of higher-quality labor, which is underutilized during the first term and lost to the services, in disproportionate measure, at the completion of the initial obligation.

Since personnel replacement takes place only at the bottom rung of the ladder, the cycle is merely repeated. Consequently, situations often arise in which highly complex equipment is managed and supported on a continuous basis by the less able men and by those with costly formal training but without sufficient on-the-job experience.

Aside from the necessary modifications in the military pay structure, manpower utilization could be significantly improved by allowing personnel to enter the military at the middle and higher rungs of the promotion ladder. This lateral entry would involve not only substituting civilian for military personnel but also admitting into the military, at middle or higher ranks, personnel who have

---

[20] The draft is able to assure high-quality men to all the services combined but not to each service individually. It has not, for example, succeeded in equalizing the quality among the services; for even if legal constraints prevent the Air Force from accepting only high-quality personnel, thereby increasing the average quality of the Army intake, the differential quality will show up after the completion of the first two years of service.

acquired their training and are practicing similar skills in the civilian sector of the economy. In this connection, it is worth noting that there are many in the civilian economy who have acquired their training and experience in the military sector but who are discouraged, through loss of grade and bonus, from reentering the military after having tried their hand at a civilian job.[21]

The loss and gain patterns described above are not, of course, independent on the military compensation system. Moreover, the relationship between compensation and retention patterns is well recognized by the Department of Defense. As Secretary McNamara has stated before the House Armed Services Committee, "When the initial commitment of 2, 3, or 4 years has been completed, the services must compete, unaided, for these men against the attractions of civilian employment. Therefore, the real test of the effectiveness of the compensation system is its ability to achieve the second objective—the retention of sufficient numbers of qualified personnel."[22] The compensation system has been unable to achieve this objective partly because the complex military pay system almost prevents the development of rational skill differentials. Currently, any skill differentials are superimposed on differentials that pull in the opposite direction.

BIBLIOGRAPHY

1. Becker, Gary S., *Human Capital*. New York: Columbia University Press, 1964.

2. ———, "Investment in Human Capital: A Theoretical Analysis." *The Journal of Political Economy*, LXX (Supplement, October, 1962), pp. 9–49.

3. Enthoven, Alain C., *Supply and Demand, and Military Pay*, P-1186. The RAND Corporation, September, 1957.

4. ———, *Mathematics of Military Pay*, P-1100. The RAND Corporation, November, 1957.

5. Gilman, Harry J., "The Supply of Labor to The Military: A Cross-Sectional Analysis of First-Term Reenlistment Rates in Fiscal Year 1964." Unpublished manuscript in the files of the Office of the Assistant Secretary of Defense for Manpower.

[21] In fact, two of the services have, in recent years, discouraged and often refused to reenlist individuals prior to discharge unless such individuals had decided to reenlist many months prior to expiration of their initial term of service. Undoubtedly, early reenlistments or commitments to reenlist reduce uncertainty and improve the services' ability to estimate their requirements for new entrants. It is doubtful, however, whether these gains offset the costs of acquiring and training (both formally and on-the-job) the new personnel. It is also doubtful whether such policies would have been implemented in the presence of more stringent constraints on manpower utilization.

[22] U. S. Congress, House Committee on Armed Services, House of Representatives, 89th Congress, 1st sess. (June, 1965), Hearings on Military Pay Bills, p. 2538.

6. ——, "Secular and Cross-Sectional Changes in Military and Civil-Service Pay," unpublished manuscript (Washington, D.C.: Bureau of The Budget, June, 1966), pp. 9–11, 20–25, 37.

7. Hitch, Charles J., and Ronald M., McKean, *The Economics of Defense in the Nuclear Age.* Cambridge: Harvard University Press, 1960.

8. Mincer, Jacob, "On-the-Job Training: Costs, Returns and Some Implications." *The Journal of Political Economy*, LXX (Supplement, October, 1962), pp. 50–73.

9. Smith, Lt. Col. Gorman C., "Occupational Pay Differentials for Military Technicians." Unpublished Ph.D. dissertation. New York: Columbia University, 1965.

10. U. S. Congress, House Committee on Armed Services, 89th Cong., 1st. sess., Hearings on Military Pay Bills.

11. Wool, Harold, "The Military Specialist, Specialized Requirements and Resources of the Armed Forces," unpublished Ph.D. dissertation. Washington, D. C.: American University, 1965.

3

SPECIAL DEFENSE PROBLEMS

T. K. GLENNAN, JR.
The RAND Corporation

The author is currently an economist with The RAND Corporation, specializing in questions of research-and-development management. During 1965 he was The RAND Corporation's representative to the Air Force Systems Command Headquarters at Andrews Air Force Base, Maryland. From 1961 until 1964, Mr. Glennan participated in studies on research-and-development management, including the use of prototypes in aircraft development, the structure of the development-planning process, and questions concerning the relationship between government and the aerospace industry.

Mr. Glennan holds a B.S. in electrical engineering from Swarthmore College and a M.S. from MIT in industrial management. He has done graduate work in economics at Stanford and is in the process of preparing a thesis on the determinants of research and development costs.

15

Research and Development

The development of the atomic bomb during World War II signified a radical change in the importance of technology to national security. Although the atomic bomb had only a small role to play in that war, recognition of the disaster that might have befallen us had our enemies developed the bomb first, together with the beginnings of thought about the implications of this new magnitude of firepower for future conflicts, raised technology to new heights of importance in the minds of government and military leaders. They imagined that in future wars victory would go not to the nation with superiority in materiel, location, or military leadership but to nations possessing superior technology. Our subsequent confrontation with another nuclear power, the U.S.S.R., and our general preoccupation with large nuclear conflicts strengthened these feelings. Mirroring this concern was the rise of spending for military research and development (R&D) from half a billion dollars in 1945 to more than six and one-half billion in 1966.

The increase in importance of R&D activities has naturally led to attempts to develop efficient management practices for the conduct of R&D projects. A number of factors made such attempts difficult. Most important perhaps was the uniqueness of the R&D process. The civilian sectors of the economy had not had extensive experience with the purposeful conduct of R&D projects, particularly with the extremes of technological advance and development speed required by the military. Thus the civilian sector provided few standards to guide the individuals responsible for establishing management policies for R&D. A more fundamental problem was the uniqueness of each R&D project. R&D is a creative process and thus difficult or impossible to generalize upon. Management procedures require such generalizations; thus the search for useful procedures has been a frustrating one. Finally, in setting up such procedures, there had been a tendency to seek efficiency in the individual project in order to minimize the resources (or time) required to achieve a technical objective. Frequently the problem of achieving efficiency in the entire collection of R&D projects has been ignored. It has often been assumed that a collection of projects, each of which is efficiently run, will lead to the efficient achievement of total R&D objectives. As shall be seen, this is not the case.

In spite of these difficulties, generalizations must be made, organizations and procedures established, and measures of effectiveness developed. Any group of organizations responsible for the magnitude of resources associated with R&D requires such guidance. This chapter will suggest a group of objectives for the military R&D programs, consider the structure of the present program, and indicate some of the problems found in meeting these objectives.

Note: Any views expressed in this paper are those of the author. They should not be interpreted as reflecting the views of The RAND Corporation or the official or policy of any of its government or private research sponsors.

OBJECTIVES FOR THE MILITARY R&D PROGRAM

The military research-and-development program must provide the United States with the capability to produce weapons that are needed or may be needed to support the needs of national security. At any point in time, the total R&D program encompasses efforts to improve existing forces, develop specific new equipment, and explore technologies that may be useful to future forces. More specifically, the objectives of the program can be viewed as:

1. To carry on the development of weapons systems required to meet the foreseeable military needs of our armed forces.

2. To expand the technological alternatives available to meet future needs of national security.

3. To provide (along with nonmilitary research) a basis for understanding the implications of technological activities of our enemies.

4. To provide technological inputs to the planning process of the military services.

THE DEPARTMENT OF DEFENSE PROGRAM STRUCTURE FOR R&D

The program which is designed to meet these objectives is divided into six categories. The categories are defined as:[1]

I. Research

Research includes all effort directed toward increased knowledge of natural phenomena and environment and toward solutions to problems in physical, behavioral, and social sciences having no clear, direct military application. By definition, "Research" includes all basic research in addition to applied research directed toward expanding knowledge in various scientific areas. It does not include efforts to prove the feasibility of solutions to problems of immediate military importance or time-oriented investigations and developments.

II. Exploratory Development

This includes all efforts to resolve specific military problems short of major development projects. These efforts may vary from fundamental applied

---

[1] These definitions follow closely those advanced by Robert S. McNamara in the 1964 Defense Appropriation Hearings, *Hearings Before A Subcommittee of the Committee on Appropriations House of Representatives*, 88th Congress, 1st Session, Part 1, Secretary of Defense, pp. 163–172.

research to sophisticated experimental hardware, study, programming, and planning efforts. The dominant characteristic of this category of effort is that it is pointed toward specific military problem areas, with a view toward developing and evaluating the feasibility and practicability of proposed solutions and determining their parameters.

III. Advanced Development

Advanced Development includes all projects that have moved into development of hardware for experimental or operational tests. Advanced Development is characterized by line-item projects, normally involving hardware designed for test or experimentation, as opposed to that designed and engineered for eventual service use.

IV. Engineering Development

Engineering Development includes development programs being engineered for service use but not yet approved for production or operation. This area is characterized by major line-item projects.

V. Operational-Systems Development

This area includes research-and-development effort directed toward developing, engineering and testing systems, support programs, vehicles, and weapons that have been approved for production and service use.

VI. Management and Support

This category includes research-and-development effort directed toward support of installations or operations required for general research-and-development use. It includes test ranges, military construction, maintenance of laboratories, operations, and maintenance of test aircraft and ships.

Several general observations can be made about the nature of these categories. If the management-and-support area is omitted and Engineering and Operational-systems development is treated as being nearly synonymous from the point of view of development objectives, the degree to which the work carried on in each category can be related to a specific system or system concept increases from Category I to Category V. The size of the average project in each category similarly increases from Category I to Category V. As a corollary to this, the degree of control and review exercised by higher headquarters or the Office of the Secretary of Defense (OSD) increases from Research to Systems Development.

In principle, the work done in Exploratory Development and Research provides the technological base for future systems as well as much of the information required by defense planners and intelligence experts. The Engineering and Operational-systems Development includes the efforts to meet immediate and near-future equipment needs of the services. The Advanced Development activities represent a bridging of the gap between the technology efforts of Exploratory Development and the systems-oriented efforts of Categories IV and V. Because of this responsibility, Advanced Development should be a key area in the present funding structure. It is the first stage in the evolution of a system from its technological origin to its final form at which the needs of the military are formally and realistically brought together with available and potential technological capabilities. The prototype hardware that is built is intended to be a concrete example of a military subsystem. The technologies demonstrated in this fashion are intended to be the "building blocks" used in the development of operational systems.

This procedure sounds quite neat and appropriate. Technological possibilities initially exposed in Research activities are explored in Exploratory Development. As a result of such explorations, and as a result of looking forward to future military needs, specific parts of the technological base are chosen for exploitation in Advanced Development. The nearly developed subsystems coming out of Advanced Development are engineered into a weapons system in Engineering or Operational-Systems Development programs. At each step the cost of the projects increases; but presumably the quality of the information upon which the project decisions are made improves and the risk of technical error decreases. Unfortunately, the orderly process pictured here frequently fails to appear. An unanticipated military threat may arise, and a system must be rushed into development before all of the technology can be proven in Advanced Development. A program such as the X-15, with objectives appropriate to Research or Exploratory Development, may cost so much that it is placed in Advanced Development where control from higher headquarters can be more easily exercised. A program may enter into systems development, but an unanticipated technological problem can force basic experimental work to be undertaken in order to obtain a solution. Although such events frequently take place, the principle behind the categories is sound and in any case represents the policy of the present DoD leadership.

After recognizing the varied characteristics of the programs called Advanced Developments, it is possible to define a series of subcategories of Advanced Development that are used by a number of people in order to clarify their thinking. These categories vary from person to person but generally are of the following sort:

1. *Programs that represent the exploitation of promising technologies.* These programs are, in reality, exploratory in nature; however, they are judged to require a level of funding larger than that which the management methods of exploratory development are designed to handle. Composite materials, for example, are judged to have great promise for obtaining required structural

strength at reduced structural weight;[2] however, much basic work on the drawing of filaments, the placing of filaments in matrices, and the design of structures using composite materials must be accomplished. As a result, many tasks have been brought together in the Advanced Development category where they can be managed collectively.

Exploratory Development is funded essentially at a level of effort. A decision to push one area very hard, as in the case of composite materials, requires a sharp increase in funding. If the program were left in Exploratory Development, a distortion of the total Exploratory Development program would result, since funds would have to be taken away from other portions of the program. Thus, some programs with objectives typical of Exploratory Development are found in the Advanced Development area.

2. *Experimental Systems.* Certain projects with Research or Exploratory Development aims require very expensive experimental hardware. Notable examples of such projects are the X-15 high-speed test aircraft and the Manned Orbiting Laboratory (MOL). Because their cost may reach several hundred million dollars, these projects require extensive management control normally alien to Research and Exploratory Development.

3. *Subsystem or component technical development.* These activities provide the "building blocks" for future systems. Models of prototypes of components or subsystems are fabricated for experimental test.

It should be noted that some feel that an orderly progression of technology through the Exploratory and Advanced Development stage to incorporation in systems is inappropriate and ineffective. They argue that the efforts to develop technology require a focus such as that imposed by the need to produce a system. The requirement to build a system "pulls" technology along to meet this requirement with the result being that efforts are focused upon a relatively few areas that are judged to provide the potential for significant improvements in military capabilities.

Supporters of this point of view argue that such an approach tends to reduce the amount of waste effort in the technology area by focusing only upon those areas in which there exists a consensus that significant breakthroughs are possible and required. Moreover, the schedules inherent in a systems-development project provide discipline to the technologist, preventing him from simply following a personal interest in exploring a technical area.

Although there have been no public advocates of this position in recent years, supporters of such a stand would probably advocate the elimination of most formal Advanced Development projects and some Exploratory Development projects in favor of defining systems that would require the use of the results of such projects. The actual work would be done as a part of the systems project.

[2] M. L. Yaffee, "Composite Materials Offer Vast Potential for Structure," *Aviation Week*, Vol 82, No 18, May 3, 1965, p. 38.

Perhaps the last major project in which such an approach was followed was the B-70. The technological results of this program are very impressive[3] and have found their way into many other military and civilian programs. Moreover, it is quite likely that without the impetus supplied by a systems effort with high performance requirements, many of these advances would not have been made. Their value would not have been perceived by the planners of the Exploratory and Advanced Development efforts.

But this program also shows most of the shortcomings of such a means of advancing technology. The requirement for the aircraft was ultimately deemed to be invalid. The program, subject to many reorientations because of questions about the value of the system, slipped badly in time and escalated in cost. Although a steady management effort would certainly have improved the time and cost performance, slippage and cost escalation would still have occurred. The result was an expenditure of approximately 1.5 billion dollars for technology, a substantial fraction of which went to what in retrospect is wasted effort toward coordinating subsystems development, integrating logistics and training considerations into the design, and laying out a production capability.

Experience such as that with the B-70 led the Director of Defense Research and Engineering (DDR&E) to issue a directive which established the project definition phase (PDP), now known as contract definition. This directive, in its latest version, defines six prerequisites which must be met before a major engineering or operational-systems development project can be initiated.[4] The prerequisites are:

1. Primarily engineering rather than experimental effort is required, and the technology needed is sufficiently in hand.

2. The mission and performance envelopes are defined.

3. The best technical approaches have been selected.

4. A thorough trade-off analysis has been made.

5. The cost effectiveness of the proposed item has been determined to be favorable in relationship to the cost effectiveness of competing items on a DoD-wide basis.

6. Cost and schedule estimates are credible and acceptable.

These prerequisites would tend to inhibit the premature initiation of a project like the B-70 today. It would not prevent the development of the technology inherent in the B-70 if the planners of the Exploratory and Advanced

---

[3] *Laboratory for Progress*, a resource of the technological achievements of the XB-70 and their application throughout the industrial complex of the U.S.A. North American Aviation Co., 1964.

[4] Department of Defense Directive 3200.9 dated July 1, 1965, Initiation of Engineering and Operational Systems Development.

Development program deemed such developments necessary and could make a reasonable case for such activities. This places a heavy responsibility on these planners. Naturally, if the value of quickly achieving a systems capability is very high, the contract definition procedures can be waived by DDR&E.

THE ENVIRONMENT IN WHICH MILITARY R&D IS CONDUCTED

The dominant characteristic of the environment in which developments are conducted is uncertainty. There is uncertainty about the future detailed objectives of our military forces, about the future effectiveness of these forces, and about the alternative means available for achieving these objectives. These uncertainties are external to the R&D programs. There remain many internal uncertainties. Will a particular technological approach to a development work as predicted? Will the components integrate together without serious interference? Will the subsystems be sufficiently reliable to permit the achievement of mission objectives? These are critical uncertainties, and much of the literature on project management concentrates on the problems of how to effectively cope with these uncertainties. The external uncertainties under consideration here are the ones which remain even if the project meets all of its technical objectives. In essence, these are the uncertainties about both the nature of the military "requirement" and the choice of the military system that will most effectively meet the requirement.

The most important reason for the dominant role played by uncertainties is the long lead-time required for the development of military systems. Military systems typically require from five to ten years to go from early concept to useful operational capability. The lifetime of the system may be from five to fifteen years. Thus the effectiveness of a system depends upon events which are at least five and perhaps fifteen to twenty years in the future. The effectiveness depends in part upon decisions that our enemies themselves have not yet made. The result is that system planners seek systems that are dominant—that remain effective in the face of almost anything an enemy can do. Alternatively, they may seek a simple extension of present capabilities, the so-called "higher-further-faster" school of planning, on the assumption that such a system is bound to be better.

Not only is there uncertainty as to the nature of the threat that must be faced, but there is uncertainty as to the precise policy military power must support. During the mid-1950's, for example, our concern was so dominated by the threat of a nuclear confrontation with the U.S.S.R. that we hardly considered questions having to do with more limited conflicts. The military services in large part shared this preoccupation, but those that did not failed to get policy support in other areas from the national authorities. This type of uncertainty as to policy cannot be resolved by simply setting up better policy-making organizations. Future policy will reflect the requirements of future alignments among the nations of the world as well as their military and economic capabilities. Moreover, this policy will depend in part upon our capabilities—thus, among other things, upon our future military systems. All of these remain uncertain.

Another source of uncertainty external to a particular systems development is the potential emergence of new technologies to provide alternative means of achieving a military end. A notable example of this type of uncertainty was reflected in the fate of the Air Force's cruise-missile program. Both the Snark and the Navaho cruise missiles found themselves overtaken by the ballistic missile; and both programs were cancelled before any useful operational capability was achieved.

The important quality of these external uncertainties is that very little can be done to reduce them. It is true that improved intelligence and a better policy-making apparatus might improve the situation, but the fact remains that the importance and effectiveness of a new military system depends critically upon decisions that will not be made or even considered for five or ten years. The implication of this situation is that the total development program of the military should provide a number of capabilities sufficient to meet all reasonable needs, not just the needs viewed as most probable. The program should have elements designed to hedge against uncertainties of the sort we have discussed. A partial solution to this problem may be the production of systems with sufficient flexibility to meet a variety of contingencies.

The hedging can be accomplished in a variety of ways. It is possible to develop a variety of different systems. Considerable expense would be involved, but the Air Force, at least, conducted its developments in this way in the 1950's. Now the cost seems prohibitive, however, and the best alternative would seem to be an active Advanced Development program. As the threat is more clearly perceived, parts of the Advanced Development program may be brought together into systems. There is no doubt that a system is more than merely a collection of subsystems. Considerable work is required to engineer a system, and frequently new approaches to one or another subsystem are required. Consequently, hedging against the uncertainties of the future using Advanced, and to some extent Exploratory, Development puts a premium upon the planning of Advanced Development projects so that subsystems technologies are available at the proper times to fit together into a system. Moreover, sufficient understanding should exist to allow adjustment to the subsystem performance during the systems-development activities.

Summarizing the discussion to this point, we have made three observations:

1. The objectives of the military R&D program have several dimensions. These include the provision of information to decision makers and the provision of insurance against unexpected enemy developments as well as the more commonly considered development of military equipment.

2. The present structure of development activities, as implied by the Research, Exploratory, Development, Advanced Development, and Engineering and Systems Development funding categories, is designed to provide an orderly progression of technology from concept into use. The procedures are supposed to match the magnitude of the financial risk to the magnitude of the technological risk; larger resource expenditures being associated with smaller technical risks.

3. The objectives of the future military forces together with the threat that they will face are uncertain and will remain so.

   With these observations in mind, several questions can be posed about the effectiveness of the military R&D program. For example:

1. What is the proper balance between funding categories, and how stable should this balance be?

2. What qualities of the present DoD organization tend to enhance or reduce the effectiveness of the R&D effort?

3. Can guidelines be developed for structuring military research organizations.

THE DISTRIBUTION OF RESOURCES AMONG TYPES OF R&D EFFORT

The problem of choosing the allocation of resources among types of R&D activities is a difficult one. There are many who would maintain that basic research is not receiving sufficient support because of the tremendous quantity of resources allocated to development activities. Others would maintain that too much effort is expended in Research and Exploratory Development where it is "wasted" on projects having no military significance. Instead, they argue, more effort should be placed on the systems-development area, so that there will be a focusing of our technological activities. In any short-run situation there is little chance of choosing the winner of this argument. A few observations can be made, however.

The size of the systems-development effort will be determined by the degree to which newly developed equipment will improve our military effectiveness combined with a determination of the value of such improvements in effectiveness. We would expect the amount of systems-development effort to be high when either a new technology giving a large increase of military effectiveness emerges or when a new threat is felt to exist. Historically, new technology and new threats do not appear continuously. There have been two major technological "revolutions" in the last twenty years, the development of nuclear and hydrogen weapons and the development of the ballistic missile. There have been perhaps three major threats perceived in this time period. The first two are associated with the achievement by the Soviets of the technological breakthroughs noted above. The third is the recognition that a strong nuclear force would not deter a more limited type of aggression such as that in Vietnam.

The consequences of the noncontinuous appearance of threats and technology is that considerable fluctuation should be expected in the size of the systems-development budget over time; thus it should be expected that the proportion of the total R&D budget that goes into systems development will fluctuate. When there is not a dominant technological development or a clear new threat, our uncertainty about the future increases. Not only are we unclear about which direction to move, but we suspect that our enemies are equally undecided. Thus, at the time when the amount of systems development falls off, there should be increased effort to hedge against these uncertainties. There should be a tendency for Advanced and Exploratory Development to increase when systems development decreases.

The determinants of the quantity of resources allocated to Research and Exploratory Development are somewhat different. These types of efforts are the sources of information on potential technological breakthroughs and provide insight into our enemies' technological programs. In these programs greater stability would be expected. There would be an attempt to cover all possible technologies, with a particular focus on those in which advances would appear to lead to significant increases in military capabilities.

The actual patterns of funding for the past three years are shown in Table 15.1. Unfortunately, the categories of development activity applied here have only recently been adopted; thus lengthy historical data are not easily assembled. These data show a small trend away from systems development (53.8 per cent of total DoD, R&D effort for FY 1964 to 47.1 per cent in FY 1966) and toward Exploratory and Advanced Development (25.8 per cent of total DoD, R&D effort in FY 1964 to 30.1 per cent in FY 1966). If the figures went back to 1960, this trend would no doubt be even more apparent. The trend in part reflects the growth in uncertainty mentioned above, but more importantly it reflects the influence of a group of decision makers in OSD who have forced the change in research and development procedures typified by DoD Directive 3200.9.

Another interesting phenomenon is shown in these figures. The Advanced Development activities comprise a relatively small proportion of the total R&D program. Indeed, if one program, the Air Force's Manned Orbiting Laboratory (MOL), were eliminated from the FY 1966 figures, the percentage of the total R&D effort expended in Advanced Development would remain relatively constant at 9 to 9.5 per cent. Although it is possible that this is an appropriate level of effort, there are some reasons to believe that the effort here may be low. This possibility is considered in the next question: What is the impact of DoD organization on the effectiveness of the R&D program?

TABLE 15–1   Research, Development, Test, and Engineering Program Funding (Millions of Dollars)

	Research	Exploratory Development	Advanced Development	Engineering and Operational Systems Development	Management and Support
Air Force					
1964	84.5	305.0	396.5	2184.7	654.6
1965	93.4	318.4	310.4	1845.8	637.9
1966	102.9	315.9	478.7	1610.5	668.7
Army					
1964	81.5	243.0	80.2	847.5	170.4
1965	91.4	237.7	111.1	714.7	221.4
1966	91.8	253.6	125.6	752.7	240.6
Navy					
1964	136.3	343.6	134.6	577.9	206.0
1965	124.5	338.3	150.6	566.5	185.8
1966	137.6	342.1	150.6	615.1	154.9
Advanced Research Projects Agency (ARPA)					
1964	46.0*	225.0*			
1965	44.7	227.3			
1966	47.0	230.0			

* 1964 ARPA Research shown as 17 per cent of total ARPA Budget (1965 is 16.4 per cent; 1966 is 17 per cent) since breakdown is not given in hearings.

TABLE 15–1 **Research, Development, Test, and Engineering Program Funding (Millions of Dollars) (continued)**

	Research	Exploratory Development	Advanced Development	Engineering and Operational Systems Development	Management and Support
TOTAL					
1964	348.3	1116.6	611.3	3610.1	1031.0
1965	354.0	1121.7	572.1	3127.0	1045.1
1966	379.3	1141.6	754.9	2978.3	1064.2
Activity as Proportion of Total					
1964	5.2	16.7	9.1	53.8	15.4
1965	5.7	18.0	9.2	50.4	16.8
1966	6.0	18.1	12.0	47.1	16.8

Source: U. S. Congress, subcommittee of the House Committee on Appropriations (Washington: GPO, 1964 and 1965), Hearings on Department of Defense Appropriations, 1965 and 1966.

Note—1964 and 1965 figures are those presented in 1965 and 1966 Hearings, respectively. 1966 figure is the budget request shown in 1966 Hearings.

THE IMPACT OF DoD ORGANIZATION ON R&D EFFORT[5]

In the military services, Exploratory Development activities are almost wholly the responsibility of in-house laboratories. Systems development, on the other hand, is handled by a development or materiel command or bureau whose primary responsibility is planning and management rather than actual engineering. In the Air Force, Exploratory Development is the responsibility of the Research and Technology Division (RTD) of the Air Force Systems Command (AFSC). There are seven laboratories that, with several other specialized organizations, make up RTD.[6] Each of these laboratories has responsibility for a portion of the Exploratory Development funds.

Within AFSC there are four "product" divisions, the Ballistic, Space, Aeronautical, and Electronic Systems Divisions (BSD, SSD, ASD, and ESD respectively). Each of these divisions has a group of system-project offices (SPO's) having responsibility for the management of the Engineering and Operational Systems Developments assigned to the division. The present SPO system is the culmination of a long evolutionary process in management procedures designed to direct and maintain control over the development of the increasingly complex systems used by the Air Force.

These procedures are very detailed. They are designed to increase the probability that the developed system will appear on time, work as specified, and adhere to the originally estimated cost. They require careful specification of the detailed goals of the development. In the latest group of projects in which they have been used, they have performed reasonably well. Indeed, they have performed very well by the historical standards of the Air Force. They have been used, however, on the type of program that has gone through contract definition and thus, presumably, is based upon technology that is well in hand. This was frequently not the case in Air Force projects of the 1950's, so comparisons of today's project performance with those of five to ten years ago may be a bit spurious. Nevertheless, the product divisions are end-use oriented and have a highly developed set of procedures designed to effectively translate technology into operational systems. The Research and Technology Division is far more concerned with science and technology. RTD was formed in 1962 in order to improve the quality of the Air Force laboratory effort. The work of these laboratories had frequently been dominated by the requirements of systems developments. As a result, little creative, new work was being done, and there was considerable dissatisfaction in the scientific community with the quality of the

[5] The observations in this section are based largely on Air Force procedures since this is the source of the author's experience.

[6] There is additional laboratory work conducted in biology and medicine at the Aerospace Medical Division (AMD) of AFSC.

labs. RTD has devoted a great deal of effort to improving the laboratory activities. Its very formation freed the laboratories from much activity directly in support of systems development. In addition, procurement procedures were modified, improved planning procedures instituted, and personnel policies revised. The effects of these changes will not be seen clearly for some years, but it is clear that much effort has been expended in considering the nature of Exploratory Development tasks and the procedures that promise to improve the performance of these tasks.

Thus, in the spectrum of development activities, from Exploratory to Operational Systems Development, both extremes have received considerable attention. The same cannot be said for Advanced Development. On either extreme of the development spectrum, the objectives of the performing organization can be translated into fairly straightforward criteria. In the case of systems development the criterion is the degree to which plans are fulfilled, and the objective is to develop an organization and procedures to enhance the capability of delivering a product according to the original plans.[7] In the case of exploratory development, the criterion is the quality of the technical work, and the objective is to improve it. In the middle of the spectrum; criteria are more difficult to establish. On the one hand, the objective is to explore new technologies and accomplish novel, technical work. On the other hand, the size of the average project is such that firm management control is required.

The solution adopted by the Air Force is to divide the Advanced Development tasks into two groups. One group is considered to have many of the attributes of systems. The projects are large and complex and are judged to require systems management. These are assigned to the various systems divisions and are managed with many of the same procedures as Operational Systems Developments. The other group of tasks, which tend to be smaller and to have more diffuse objectives, are assigned to laboratories for management.

The result of having a program made up of so many diverse elements is that no single set of procedures can cover the program. Indeed within AFSC there have been only a few instructions giving general guidance in the planning and conduct of Advanced Developments, although there are now several manuals nearing completion which have relevance to this type of activity.

Although the absence of detailed formal procedures and instructions can be viewed as giving a desirable freedom to program planners, it can also lead to attempts by planners to avoid using this category of development because of a lack of guidance and appreciation of its role in the total development process. It may also be true that a lack of appreciation of the objectives of Advanced Development programs causes programs to be included in this funding category that properly belong in other categories.

---

[7] This is the criterion that has seemed to dominate most of the procedures. Given the nature of the external uncertainties discussed earlier, it seems clear that it should not be the only criterion. There must also be an effective means of changing the original plans if necessary.

There is another difficulty associated with Advanced Development projects. In order to obtain better control over these activities, each major project has a separate program element in the program budget. Occasionally a group of projects having similar objectives are lumped together to form a single element. To obtain such an element, a program change proposal (PCP) must be submitted through USAF Headquarters to OSD. There must be approval of the PCP before funds can be obtained. Seeking such approval takes both time and effort. Moreover, the review process may tend to eliminate projects with payoffs far in the future or having high technical risks. In other words, the procedure for obtaining approvals for Advanced Development projects may result in a conservative program.

The situation is complicated further for Advanced Development projects that are closely tied to proposed systems. There frequently appears to be a reluctance to initiate advanced development on components if the division feels that a program for a development of the total system has a chance of approval. The divisions prefer to develop a total system rather than a single subsystem for later integration into a program. Their orientation is toward delivering products to the operational forces, and they frequently view work on a single part of a system coupled with a delay on the definition of the entire system as slowing down their efforts to meet their objectives. Again, the effect is to reduce the number of projects in Advanced Development.

In summary, then, there are three reasons to expect that within the Air Force there may be a bias tending to reduce the number of Advanced Development projects.

1. There are few standard procedures to guide the formulation and management of such programs.

2. The review and approval process required to establish a project may deter the proposal of some desirable projects or result in the rejection of some which are proposed and should be initiated.

3. The preference of the managers of some of the programs is to wait and do most of the work as a part of the system development.

These reasons should not be viewed as simple organizational "cussedness." They reflect the very real problems of this particular type of development program, the combination of relatively great technical uncertainties with relatively large resource requirements.

SOME GUIDELINES FOR STRUCTURING MILITARY-RESEARCH ORGANIZATIONS

A discussion of more positive guidance for structuring military R&D organizations can begin with the introduction of two concepts that are useful in thinking about Research, Exploratory, Advanced and Systems Development. In crude terms, it seems possible to break these activities into two categories: *requirements-pull* and *technology-push* efforts.

Requirements-pull efforts are those projects that are undertaken to fulfill needs clearly recognized by a large segment of the total organization, the DoD. The organization recognizes a need and perhaps even an operational means for meeting this need. They then turn to the R&D organization and tell them to do what is necessary to fulfill this requirement or need. In passing, it should be noted that this is the "comfortable" way for the entire organization to proceed. It gives the appearance that the organization knows where it is going and is able to direct its R&D resources toward efficiently fulfilling these needs.

On the other hand, it must be recognized that "needs" (and our ability to meet them as expressed in operational concepts) frequently do not become clear until scientific breakthroughs, often unexpected, are made. Our historical experience with nuclear weapons, rocketry, and numerous less spectacular areas supports this observation. As a result of this realization, there is support for many activities that might be called technology-push activities, with the hope that some breakthrough will provide the potential for new capabilities that will in turn lead to a recognition of new ways to meet needs. Naturally, requirements-pull efforts are likely to follow technology-push efforts in helping to achieve the potential revealed by the latter.

One of the problems with technology-push types of projects is that they demand faith on the part of people outside the project. The payoffs are not obvious. Resources spent in this fashion have to compete with the seemingly more attractive opportunities in requirements-pull areas, where needs have been recognized. Organizations do not find it comfortable to support such activities.

After one has worked with these concepts for awhile, at least in the terms already discussed, they seem to break down. Instead, the distinction should probably be who perceived the requirement or need. It is possible to find someone who can perceive a usefulness for almost any project—someone who can suggest some conceptual requirement that the project is working toward. Thus it is possible to say that all efforts are requirements-pull efforts, at least beyond the very early research stage. But the concepts of requirements-pull and technology-push are appealing and seem relevant to experience. To remove this ambiguity, the terms are redefined. Technology-push efforts are those efforts where the research personnel determine the type of research efforts that will contribute to needs as they, the researchers, perceive them. Requirements-pull efforts are those in which the needs are perceived by persons external to the research efforts; the research is initiated by planners and operationally oriented organizations. Phrased in this manner, the distinction between technology-push and requirements-pull efforts is seen to lie largely in the level of decision making: If the decisions are made at the top of the organization, they are clearly requirements-pull efforts; if they are made at the bottom, by the individual researchers, they are technology-push. There is a vast middle ground between the top and the bottom, and clearly the distinction is not perfect. However, the breakdown is still useful in discussing the distinctions between Research, Exploratory, Advanced, and Operational Systems Development activities.

Considering first the Advanced Development category of activities, there continues to be a distinction between projects such as the MOL (which are included solely because their size is such that they are placed by top decision makers in a development category where they are subject to line-item control) and projects that appear because they represent a logical step between raw technology and full-scale product development. Projects such as MOL will be ignored. The bulk of the remaining Advanced Developments represents attempts to advance particular components of full systems to a point where there can be rational decisions on the development of full systems. These efforts are undertaken with a fairly clear view of the final system requirement which they may ultimately help to fulfill. These efforts are quite clearly requirements-pull efforts, and quite rightly the decisions on them are made at a fairly high level.

In contrast, the basic-research program is certainly a technology-push effort. Here the initiative is taken by the labs themselves, and most projects begin through the initiative of the individual researcher. These researchers do not act in a vacuum. They know the mission of the military service for which they work and in most cases probably attempt intuitively to relate their activities to the missions of that service. Because the end use of activities in this area is so obscure, attempts are not often made to evaluate the work on the basis of its immediate contribution to the military but its professional merit. The key to the success of these activities is not proper project selection but proper personnel selection and an ability to convey informally and in broad terms the basic needs of the military service to the lab staff. (It should be noted that the success of Bell Lab's research activities can be attributed to attracting good people *and* to the fact that the mission of the lab is a clear one: to exploit technology that is likely to improve communications.[8])

When we turn to the Exploratory Development activities, we can immediately see a problem. These activities are midway between efforts that would generally be considered requirements-pull and those considered technology-push. Thus procedures appropriate to one or the other of these types of activities will not be universally applicable to Exploratory Development. The people required to obtain really useful results must be capable of the same independent judgment as the basic researcher, whereas, on the other hand, the output of the lab must have a high degree of relevancy to the military's immediate problems. The key to success in this area is clearly in the personnel and most particularly the lab director. He is the person who, as a professional researcher, can provide the critical support of the researcher, and at the same time, through his knowledge of military needs, he can guide the researcher's work into useful channels.

[8] Richard Nelson, P-1845-RC, "The Link Between Science and Invention: The Case of the Transistor."

This meeting of technology-push and requirement-pull efforts within a single organization makes for considerable difficulties in setting up organizational objectives. Yet it is important to have such organizations. They provide the transition of ideas from one stage to the other, which would be a very difficult process if technology-push efforts were the responsibility of essentially one set of organizations and requirements-pull efforts were carried on by another set. To gain insight into proper goals for organizations in the Exploratory Development area, the more polar cases of Research and Advanced Development should again be examined.

IMPLICATION OF DIFFERENT LABORATORY RESPONSIBILITIES FOR LABORATORY STRUCTURE AND PROCEDURES

In the area of research, heavy reliance is placed upon the decisions of individual researchers; thus there is a need to attract the very best research minds. Such minds are attracted by stimulating discipline areas, outstanding colleagues, and a minimum of distracting administrative procedures. The greatest possible freedom in the use of funds should be given to the laboratory director. Probably the most important consideration here is that there be relative stability in funding levels so that the cost and administrative burdens as well as personnel conflicts associated with ups and downs in activity levels may be minimized. To promote stability and to minimize the burdens of contracting, it would seem highly desirable to emphasize the in-house work as much as possible. When there is a need for peculiar skills that are unavailable within the lab, easily arranged consulting arrangements should be available. Some small amount of contract work for use of special facilities will be necessary. In general, however, it seems desirable to make basic-research laboratories fairly self-contained.

In contrast, in the Advanced-development area considerable instability would be expected. Projects that enter into Advanced Development should pass some test of value versus cost, and there is no reason to expect that the same quantity of resources will be required each year. Moreover, there may well be times when it will be desirable to shift emphasis from the essentially option-buying activities of Advanced Development to more active exploitation of systems developments.

The type of person involved in these activities is also different. Larger teams of individuals with less independent bents are required for the detailed engineering work. These people should not be allowed to decide what they want to do, although they should have a large role in deciding how they want to do it. Finally, these efforts are aimed at demonstrating feasibility for production and in a real sense represent the transition of an idea from concept to reality. Since the reality, if it ever appears, must be manufactured, it seems desirable to have most of these developments conducted by contractors so that manufacturing problems are realistically considered. Making the Advanced Development effort primarily a contractor effort has an additional advantage. It allows the bulk of the instability in funding levels to be reflected in the activities of the contractors, who can adapt more readily than government organizations.

Exploratory Development again forms the middle ground. Although less freedom should be given the lab director here than in basic research, he certainly should not have to endure a great deal of day-to-day pressure from higher authorities. Less stability should be expected in funding than in Research, but considerable stability of in-house effort is necessary to retain high-quality personnel. There is more reason to emphasize the contract activities than in basic research, because more of the work will require specialized manufacturing and test facilities.

Yet, as has been noted, in Exploratory Development there remains a very important need for the individual initiative inherent in technology-push efforts, so that really high quality personnel must be attracted and retained. Thus the same qualities of freedom from unnecessary administrative burdens, relative freedom of choice of projects, and intelligent leadership are required here as in basic research. The question is how to achieve these ends and indeed to what degree have they thus far been achieved.

The following suggestions may be considered:

1. The various types of R&D activities require vastly different types of personnel and leadership as well as different degrees of in-house/contractor participation. Combining the Research, Exploratory Development, and Advanced Development activities in one laboratory is likely to lead to great difficulties in establishing laboratory procedures and obtaining good laboratory leadership.

2. The qualities desired in the lab director differ between basic Research and Exploratory Development. In Research the need is for professional judgment. In Exploratory Development there is a need for a (rare) combination of professional and mission judgment. This probably suggests that civilian scientists are appropriate leaders for the basic research labs. In the labs responsible for Exploratory Development either military or *career* civil servants are likely to possess both the required capabilities; civilian scientists drawn from outside the government are likely to lack the necessary insight into military missions.

3. Both Research and Exploratory Development labs would benefit by reducing administrative burdens associated with contracting. In Research this appears to be most usefully accomplished by making the labs largely in-house activities. In the Exploratory Development labs, contracting procedures should be highly attuned to research requirements: emphasizing speed, a minimum of paperwork, and a maximum of individual-buyer initiative.

4. The need for quality personnel has been emphasized. One of the factors that will prove important to a researcher is his image of the difficulties that he will have in selling his projects. If people fairly far above him and the lab director have to be "sold," the prospects will appear forbidding indeed. An important factor to him will be the degree to which the lab director can unilaterally determine the utilization of funds.

5. Finally, within the Exploratory Development most management from higher headquarters should be by review. On-line management delays and disrupts work and, given the relatively small amounts involved per project, is likely to cause more harm than good. The lab director should be given great authority and each year or every six months be required to render a comprehensive report.

The ideas advanced in this chapter do not provide unified, clear-cut guidance for the conduct of the military research-and-development program; rather they are intended to indicate the wide variety of considerations involved in structuring and conducting such a program. The objectives of the program are diverse, and the means for achieving these objectives are many. The importance of the structure of the organizations conducting R&D activities should be clear. There is no obvious best allocation of resources or structure of development organizations. About the best that can be hoped is that some of the concepts advanced in this chapter will prove useful in thinking about policies for military research and development.

BIBLIOGRAPHY

These sources represent an introduction to issues of military R&D policy. It should be recognized that they represent comments based on experience of the 1950's.

1. Glennan, T. K., "An Economist Looks at R&D Management," P-2819, The RAND Corporation, November, 1963.

2. ———, "Issues in the Choice of Development Policies." P-3153, The RAND Corporation, June, 1965.

3. Hitch, C. J. and R. N. McKean, *The Economics of Defense in the Nuclear Age*. Boston: Harvard University Press, 1960, pp. 243–265.

4. Kaysen, Carl, Improving the Efficiency of Military Research and Development, *Public Policy*, XII Graduate School of Public Administration, Harvard University, Boston, 1964. (See also comments on article by Cherington and Dupres.)

5. Klein, B. H., "A Radical Proposal for R&D," *Fortune*, May, 1958, pp. 112ff.

6. ———, *The Decision Making Problem in Development, The Rate and Direction of Inventive Activity*. Princeton, N. J.: Princeton University Press, 1962.

7. Knorr, K. and O. Morgenstern, "Science and Defense, Some Critical Thoughts on Military Research and Development," Policy Memorandum No. 32, Princeton, N. J.: Center of International Studies, Woodrow Wilson School of Public and International Affairs, Princeton University, February, 1965.

8. Marshak, T. A., "The Role of Project Histories in the Study of R&D," P-2850, The RAND Corporation, January, 1964.

9. Marshall, A. W. and W. H. Meckling, *Predictability of the Cost, Time, and Success of Development in The Rate and Direction of Invention Activity*. Princeton, N. J.: Princeton University Press, 1962.

10. Peck, M. J. and F. M. Scherer, *Weapons Acquisition Process: An Economic Analysis*, Boston: Division of Research, Graduate School of Business Administration, Harvard University Press, 1962.

ROLF PIEKARZ

Institute for Defense Analyses

Rolf Piekarz is an economist on the staff of the Economic and Political Studies Division at the Institute for Defense Analyses. From 1963 through 1965 Dr. Piekarz directed a study evaluating the foreign exchange savings and budget costs of alternative measures to reduce gold losses arising from Department of Defense purchases and operations abroad.

From mid-1958 through 1962 Dr. Piekarz was a staff economist at the Rand Corporation, where he did research on international trade in military equipment and on the organization of inventory management. Some of the conclusions of this research have been described in Rand RM-3188-PR, *The DSA and Military Logistics* (November, 1962) and in a paper with Dr. Howard Laitin, "Information Systems and Prices: An Experiment in Decentralization," which was presented at the Econometric Society Meetings in Pittsburgh on December 28, 1963.

Dr. Piekarz received his Ph.D. in Political Economy from The Johns Hopkins University in 1958. His dissertation, "Proportion of Foreign Trade in National Product and Economic Growth," was a study of the interaction between the expansion fo a nation's output and the increase in its trade during the course of economic development.

16

Defense Impacts
on International Payments

The traditional measures for restoring foreign payments equilibrium have been devaluation, trade restrictions, or deflation.[1] But these remedies are denied the United States by its firm commitments to fixed exchange rates, lower trade barriers, and high domestic employment. U.S. efforts to reduce dollar and gold drains are therefore restricted to administrative actions that induce marginal changes in various sectors of the economy—for example, interest equalization tax for securities of industrial nations, increased tying of aid grants, and voluntary restraints on overseas direct investment. Among these administrative actions two have been urged as major contributions to payments equilibrium: less U.S. military spending abroad and more military sales to allies.[2]

The defense sector is a prime candidate for payments remedies because it plays a prominent role in U.S. foreign trade and its activities are under strict government control. In recent years, annual Department of Defense (DoD) purchases overseas have approximated $3.0 billion— over 10 per cent of the goods and services imported by the United States.[3] Similarly, annual commercial and aid sales of military items to allied governments have been about $2.0 billion—over 5 per cent of U.S. exports of goods and services.[4]

Burdened with the additional assignment to reduce dollar outflows, defense management can no longer choose program alternatives according to which will attain the desired objective at minimum defense outlays. It has become necessary to consider also the net foreign exchange costs at different budget requirements for the various alternatives. For example, defense executives know that the cheapest way to maintain Army units in Europe is to rely completely on local procurement. Now, however, they must weigh the higher dollar drain of this solution with the defense-budget saving it affords.

This chapter describes some of the problems defense management must face in accommodating its programs to reduce the net dollar drains resulting from national security activities. It details the effects of available options on U.S. military efficiency and the balance of payments deficit. The concluding

---

* Present and former colleagues of the author will note many points which he benefited from conversation and joint assignment with them; this is particularly true of Mr. William Cox, Dr. Stephen Enke, Miss Lois Ernstoff, and Dr. Howard Laitin. Neither these colleagues nor the Institute are responsible for any of the views expressed here.

[1] For a theoretical discussion of the traditional balance of payments adjustment process, see Charles P. Kindleberger, *International Economics*, 3rd ed., (Homewood, Ill.: Richard D. Irwin, Inc., 1963), esp. pp. 217–330.

[2] For specific proposals, see: (1) U. S. Congress, House of Representatives, Special Message on the Balance of Payments, Message from the President of the United States, Document No. 141, July 18, 1963, pp. 5–6; (2) U. S. Congress, Joint Economic Committee, *1965 Joint Economic Report*, Report of the Joint Economic Committee of the Congress of the United States on the January 1965 Economic Report of the President, March 17, 1965, pp. 13–14.

[3] Appendix, Table 1, "Defense Expenditures Abroad for Goods and Services, by Major Category, 1953–64, Annually," p. 310.

[4] Appendix, Table 3, "U. S. Military Aid and Commercial Sales, by Area, 1953–64, Annually," p. 314.

section places Defense alternatives in the context of a national program to lower dollar and gold outflows.

MILITARY EFFICIENCY VS. FOREIGN EXCHANGE SAVINGS

Defense management must find that set of measures which yields a given net reduction in United States foreign indebtedness (that is, a given foreign exchange savings) at the smallest decrease in military efficiency (that is, either lower military effectiveness or higher budget costs). Their problem is to estimate and compare the extent to which military efficiency and foreign exchange savings are affected by alternative measures aimed at reducing DoD imports or raising DoD exports.[5] The relevant effects of a reduction in Defense purchases in a particular allied nation are shown in Figure 16–1.

Overseas purchases can be reduced only by transferring troops to the United States or using domestic sources for the supplies and services now consumed by U.S. forces abroad. Throughout the postwar period, purchases by and support for U.S. troops abroad have accounted for over 90 per cent of the DoD purchases of foreign goods and services.[6]

[5] The comparison of the reduction in military efficiency from various actions to obtain foreign exchange savings involves substantial personal judgment. Comparability of changes in military efficiency necessitates a uniform unit of measurement. A convenient and generally applicable yardstick would be the additional budget costs necessary to restore the previous level of combat capability or national security. Unfortunately, actions to obtain foreign exchange savings tend to introduce changes which raise difficulties in the application of such a unit of measurement. Substitutes to existing methods of accomplishing U. S. national security objectives 1) introduce important secondary effects, and 2) alter qualitative military and political factors. To illustrate, substituting additional airlift capability and prepositioning of equipment abroad for overseas deployment would increase flexibility in the use of ground forces; but it would also diminish the benefits the United States obtains from the presence of large groups of military forces in places such as Western Europe.

[6] Despite the advanced state of certain types of military technology in Europe, practically all Department of Defense equipment is developed and produced by domestically owned firms. This policy stems primarily from the desire of U. S. officials to avoid the risks of foreign interference in national military programs. These risks include: 1) disruption in delivery of spare parts or equipment because of war or political crises; and 2) the loss of national power because of failure to maintain monopolistic control over certain military technologies (for example, nuclear weapons) having high acquisition costs and long lead times.

Such risk avoidance comes at a high price. The United States must 1) allocate scarce scientific talent to duplicate technology developed elsewhere, and 2) reproduce the investment in facilities and skills required to produce this counterpart equipment.

A more thorough discussion of the autarchical influence of national security is contained in Arthur L. Miller, "Foreign Trade and the 'Security State': A Study in Conflicting National Policies," *Journal of Public Law*, 7, (March 1958), 37–96.

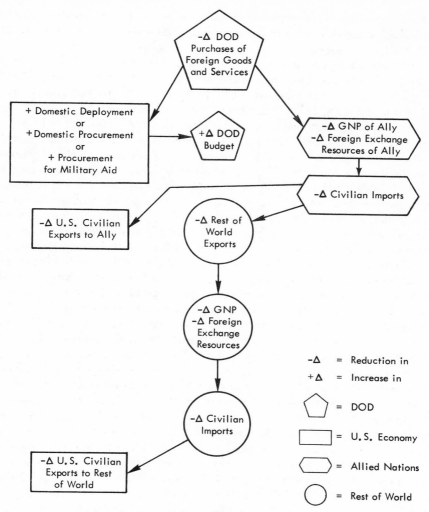

Figure 16–1   *Effects of Lower DOD Purchases Abroad*
(Unchanged Military Effectiveness)

For the activity affected by a cut in overseas spending, defense management must develop alternatives that preserve the U.S. military contribution.[7] As a result, if military imports were reduced by redeploying to the United States combat units now in an allied nation, defense officials would have to devise

[7] See testimony by Charles J. Hitch, Assistant Secretary of Defense (Comptroller), before a Subcommittee of the Senate Committee on Banking and Currency: U. S. Congress, Senate, *Balance of Payments—1965*, Part I, March 10, 1965, p. 155.

alternatives that would either maintain the current U.S. combat capability committed to the defense of that ally or raise the independent military capability of that ally.

Defense management can choose among three ways to decrease procurements in an allied nation—each alternative adding to budget costs. They can bring troops home and raise the alert status of the redeployed units to ensure their prompt return in an emergency; they can provide the ally with larger grants of military equipment or supplies to compensate for the military units transferred to the United States; or they can "stretch the pipeline" and draw on the more expensive domestic sources for the required goods and services. Suppose that an Army mechanized infantry division is to be transferred from Korea, defense could either substitute the purchase of additional equipment for prepositioning and aircraft for airlift (if necessary) or provide Korea with more arms aid to bolster the effectiveness of its forces. The first alternative requires increases either in airlift or prepositioning costs (or both); the second increases grant-aid program costs and reduces U.S. control over its arms.

The precise quantitative effects of DoD adjustments in its foreign spending are complex. The foreign exchange savings from reducing purchases in the allied nation equals the decrease in foreign currency spending *less* the value of U.S. exports lost through the spending cut. Because it decreases foreign exchange earnings and income of the host country, a reduction in defense spending lowers the imports of the host from the U.S. and from third countries. These third countries in turn lower their imports from the U.S. and from others. The total change in U.S. exports induced by the withdrawal of DoD spending in a country thus depends on two factors: (1) the share of the foreign exchange earnings from the eliminated U.S. purchases that would have been allocated to imports; and (2) the share of U.S. goods and services in the incremental imports of foreign countries. As a specific example, assume that DoD reduces its purchases from an ally (say, Korea) by $10 million and that Korea would have spent 80 per cent of these lost foreign exchange earnings on imports—15 per cent in the United States and the remainder in the rest of the world. If all other countries behaved just as Korea, the $10 million reduction in DoD foreign currency spending would lower U.S. exports by about $4 million, leaving a foreign exchange saving of about $6 million.[8] A different kind of problem attends the alternative of increasing

---

[8] Let r = proportion of a change in export earnings allocated to imports by foreign nations and p = the share of U. S. goods and services in the incremental imports of foreign nations (that is, $1 - p$ = share of the rest of the world in these incremental purchases). By assuming (1) r and p are the same for every foreign nation and (2) $r = 0$ for the U. S. (that is, U. S. import changes are not determined by changes in export earnings), the decrease in U. S. exports, $-\Delta X_{us}$, from a reduction in DoD purchases overseas, $-\Delta M_{us}$, would be

$$-\Delta X_{us} = -\Delta M_{us} \left[p \cdot r + p \cdot r \left[(1 - p) \cdot r \right] + p \cdot r \left[(1 - p) \cdot r \right]^2 + p \cdot r \left[(1 - r) \cdot r \right]^3 \right.$$

$$+ \cdots p \cdot r[(1 - p)r]^i + \cdots = -\Delta M_{us} \left[\frac{p \cdot r}{1 - (1 - p) \cdot r} \right]$$

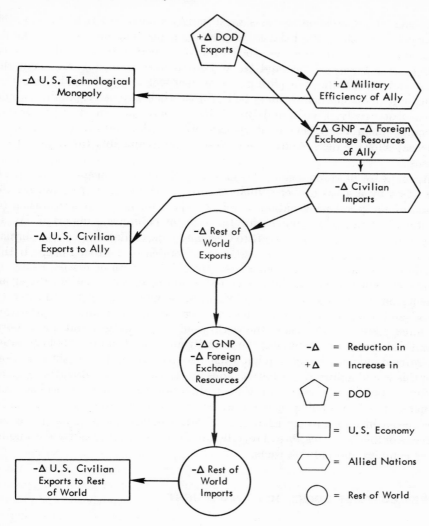

Figure 16–2   *Effects of Higher DOD Sales Abroad*

DoD sales to a particular allied nation. The relevant qualitative effects are shown in Figure 16–2.

An export sale requires a demand for a certain type of U.S. equipment by the particular allied nation and the consent of the DoD to sell this hardware. The ally's purchase, therefore, must improve its military efficiency enough to offset the risk of relying on a foreign source of supply. The sale must also result in large enough gain to compensate for the security risk in transferring certain exclusive technological capability to a particular ally. If neither offsetting factors can be counted on, officials must satisfy themselves that, on net, the improvement in the U.S. balance of payments position merits the risk. As an extreme example, these issues are central to the debate on the NATO-multi-lateral nuclear force.[9] France and Great Britain have been dubious about the strategic deterrent value of acquiring U.S. nuclear technological capability in this fashion, but West German leaders believe that their defense capability would benefit substantially. French and British leaders have also questioned whether the improvement in NATO military capability and cohesiveness adequately compensates for the risks of advancing West German capability to handle nuclear weapons.[10]

An increase in commercial sales of U.S. military equipment abroad tends to be offset by a gross loss of civilian exports. A DoD export sale reflects the decision of the purchasing nation to rely on the United States rather than on domestic or third-nation sources for the type of equipment imported. As an example, U.S. sales of F-104 aircraft to Germany reflect a decision by the German Defense Ministry that a U.S. aircraft was preferable to a French one.[11] If this sale was not made by the United States, the allied government would have to purchase a comparable item from a domestic source or third nation. Procuring the item from a domestic source would result in an increase in aggregate domestic demand and a higher level of foreign exchange resources. Direct imports from the United States and the rest of the world would increase, as would U.S. exports to the third countries. Obtaining the items from a third nation would increase the aggregate demand and foreign exchange resources of this third nation. Again this would induce U.S. exports. Thus, in the case of the F-104, the German decision to obtain a U.S. rather than a domestic or French tactical aircraft eliminated the U.S. civilian exports which would have flowed from a similar order placed in Germany or France. In short, DoD decisions either to reduce purchases or increase sales abroad reverberate throughout the free-world economy in very complex and indirect ways.

BUDGET COSTS OF DOMESTIC PROCUREMENT

Most goods and services procured overseas by the DoD are either unavailable or unreasonably expensive in the U.S. The best evidence that foreign purchases by DoD are based on the substantial superiority of certain foreign products and resources is the relatively small decrease in U.S. military purchases

[9] Henry A. Kissinger, "NATO's Nuclear Dilemma," *The Reporter*, 28 (March 28, 1963), pp. 22–37.

[10] Wilfrid L. Kohl, "Nuclear Sharing in NATO and the Multilateral Force," *Political Science Quarterly*, LXXX (March 1965), 88–109.

[11] Some of the factors involved in the German choice of the F-104 were discussed in selected issues of *Aviation Week and Space Technology* during 1958 and 1959.

abroad that resulted when DoD accepted a price penalty of up to 50 per cent to encourage the substitution of domestic for foreign supply sources between 1961 and 1963. This allowance reduced the $1.5 billion annual procurement overseas by defense agencies by about $185 million, or 12 per cent, at an average additional budget cost of about 30 per cent.[12]

This competitive advantage of foreign goods and services stems mainly from the large share of semi-skilled and unskilled foreign labor in these procurements. Much of the contractual services by military units and most purchases by self-supporting enterprises (for example, post exchanges, clubs, and so on) involve the direct hire of foreign labor. Even disregarding transportation and dislocation costs, U.S. hourly wage rates for semi- and unskilled workers are about twice as high as Western European scales—about $2.50 per hour in the U.S. compared to $1.25 per hour in France and Germany in 1963. The differentials would be even greater for countries like Japan and Vietnam. On the other hand, there probably is little difference between productivity of U.S. semi- and unskilled labor and that of foreign labor working with the same mix of capital and management.

Moreover, many goods and services purchased by the military abroad are either unique or have distinct locational advantages. For example, the high expense of shipping and storing perishable foodstuff makes obtaining them locally more economical than shipping from the U.S. Since U.S. installations must conform to peculiar local building codes and characteristics of public utilities, it is cheaper to rely on local contractors than to teach and transport American workers. Dispersion and temporary deployment of U.S. forces in certain communities make local housing cheaper than constructing permanent military installations. Dependence on local sources of entertainment and tourism during leisure hours certainly is necessary to maintain troop morale.

Finally, the waiving of trade barriers to personnel and to certain organizational purchases abroad either lowers the price or increases the availability of foreign products. For example, a large share of petroleum products consumed by U.S. forces abroad (over $200 million annually) is purchased from foreign sources for two reasons: the substantially lower delivered price of the foreign product, and the absence of import restrictions on military petroleum purchases for overseas use. Waiving of tariffs and Federal taxes on purchases for consumption abroad of items such as cars, perfume, alcoholic beverages, and so on, in many instances lowers the foreign price of these items substantially below U.S. prices, thereby making the foreign product more competitive with a comparable American product.

[12] For a more detailed statement, see testimony by Charles J. Hitch, Assistant Secretary of Defense (Comptroller) in *Outlook for United States Balance of Payments*, Hearings before the Subcommittee on International Exchange and Payments of the Joint Economic Committee, December 12, 13, and 14, 1962, pp. 49–60.

BUDGET COSTS OF BRINGING TROOPS HOME

Redeployment of troops to the United States as a payments remedy is restricted to limited-war forces.[13] To compensate for the removal of these forces from potential combat areas, it is necessary either to increase military aid or airlift capability and prepositioning equipment.

Redeployment of forces that are required overseas to offset some technological shortcomings would, however, be a questionable venture.[14] Developing new technology tends not only to be expensive but also to involve a long gestation period and uncertain outcome. These factors are evident in the development of ICBM's as successors to strategic aircraft and in present efforts to devise space satellites to supercede earth-based warning systems. ICBM's sharply reduced United States dependence on foreign base locations for strategic systems, but their development and production cost billions of dollars and required about seven years. Such a large expenditure of time and resources can be justified only by vital strategic and political considerations, not by a $100 million or even a $200 million saving in annual foreign currency spending.

Increased Military Assistance

Increased military assistance is a potential substitute for the U.S. presence only if the ally in question is among the less developed countries in Asia, South America, or Africa.[15] Inadequate economic potential bars the pro-

---

[13] Stationing a large proportion of the limited war forces overseas, rather than at home, raises their effectiveness in a number of ways. Sometimes, as in Viet Nam, the presence of these forces is necessary to resist successfully local Communist aggression. In other areas, like Western Europe, the presence of U. S. troops stems from the U. S. commitment to provide on call a predetermined number of troops to an alliance in order to counter certain military threats. In turn, the effectiveness of these commitments to nations thousands of miles distant from the United States depends heavily on the existence of large logistics installations located on foreign soil (as in Japan and France).

[14] Overseas deployment also compensates for the limitations in the state of the technological art. Placing the DEW line in Canada instead of the United States increases the warning time against potential air and missile attack. B-52 tanker bases and Polaris submarine tenders in Europe raise the efficiency and lower the vulnerability with which these weapons may be used.

[15] The economic rationale of existing military aid grants stresses the efficient use of U. S. military resources rather than foreign exchange savings. Military aid sales, combined with larger and more effective allied military forces, substantially lower the cost or raise the effectiveness of U. S. commitments to protect recipient nations against Communist aggression. The lower cost results because it is more expensive for the U. S. to increase the size of its military manpower, and to maintain and supply them overseas, than for allies to expand their military manpower with U. S. assistance. Not only do American servicemen receive higher pay

duction of modern weapons because the nation either lacks a high level of technological capability or cannot afford the large sums required. Scarce foreign exchange resources place substantial foreign purchases beyond reach without disruptive changes in the economy.[16]

Nevertheless, even for a less developed country, additional military assistance may be a questionable solution. A more suitable alternative may be additional economic rather than military aid, and further, a decrease in U.S. military presence may create unacceptable risks to the U.S. national security position.

Military aid, because it supplements the foreign exchange resources and the economic capability of the recipient, is actually a form of economic aid. As an example, instead of more arms aid, the U.S. could provide larger undesignated dollar grants. A less developed ally could apply these or existing foreign exchange resources to acquiring modern arms from a European source. Similar substitutions would be feasible for additional U.S. grants of agricultural products, raw materials, or industrial goods.

The relative efficiency of emphasizing military rather than economic aid depends largely on the desirability of tying the recipient nation to American military equipment. Emphasis on military aid permits a less developed nation to rely solely on the technology of a single industrial power, like the United States, thereby substantially easing problems of training, resupply, and coordination of tactics and strategy. This gain in efficiency is particularly important if extensive resources are necessary to counter Communist threats or if the United States forces participate in military operations jointly with local troops.

On the other hand, benefits from additional military aid may be counterbalanced by certain risks. The recipient nation could use the equipment to undermine U.S. national security objectives. Because the United States has only limited control over equipment transferred to an ally, situations may arise in which the aid is applied to purposes other than those intended. For example,

---

than do soldiers in foreign armies, but each American serviceman represents a greater loss of output to his civilian economy than does the foreign serviceman because of substantially lower labor productivity abroad. In addition, it is less costly to maintain a foreign solider in his home country than for the U. S. to ship supplies and establish maintenance operations many thousands of miles from the U. S. Military aid improves the effectiveness of the U. S. commitment because it signals U. S. willingness to aid in the defense of an allied nation.

For a more complete analysis, see Charles Wolfe, *Foreign Aid, Theory and Practice in Southern Asia* (Princeton: Princeton University Press, 1960), pp. 284–95, 317–78.

[16] For the most part, our industrially advanced allies have the economic and technological wherewithal to expand their military forces and to purchase, either domestically or abroad, the required equipment. Their manpower also has the skills to operate and maintain advanced military technology. These factors explain the decline of U. S. military aid to OECD nations from a level of $2 to $3 billion per annum in the early 1950's to about $.75 billion in 1963— most of the military aid in 1963 being allocated to Turkey and Spain. (Appendix, Table 3, "U. S. Military Aid and Commercial Sales, by Area, 1953–64, Annually," p. 314.

it may be used in combat against another state friendly to the United States, as in the Pakistan-India clash over Kashmir during 1965;[17] or a regime unfriendly to the United States may acquire the equipment through a revolution, as in Iraq during 1958. There is also some risk that a reduction of U.S. troop strength in an allied nation will be interpreted as reluctance to commit resources for defense against Communist aggression or subversion.

Airlift and Prepositioning

Additional airlift capability and prepositioning equipment can, by cutting the time needed to get troops into a foreign combat area, be an effective, if expensive, substitute for overseas deployment. For example, with airlift transport of troops and prepositioning equipment in a combat ready state, the Army can deploy units from the United States to a combat theater in Western Europe in fifteen to thirty days. This should be compared with the weeks to months needed to move the same units by boat, and the week or so necessary to move troops from European bases to nearby combat zones.

If some period of strategic warning is allowed, airlift combined with overseas prepositioning of equipment offers some advantages to deployment abroad. Flexibility is an important one. Basing Army units in the U.S. rather than Europe makes them more readily available for use in southeast Asia. Domestic deployment offers advantages for training troops to use different equipment and to function in different kinds of combat areas, and there would be fewer political repercussions from transferring troops from their home base to another foreign area. Another advantage is that domestic deployment would improve the efficiency of peacetime support of these Army units by shortening supply pipelines and permitting more intensive utilization of U.S.-based facilities.

However, there are some drawbacks. An overestimate of strategic warning time would make airlift operations more vulnerable to enemy interdiction than ground transport. A diminished U.S. presence would make an immediate large-scale U.S. response to attack less automatic and might thereby convince the enemy of more limited American involvement in a European conflict. Above all, the high cost of airlift and prepositioning more than offsets the foreign exchange savings of domestic deployment. For example, the procurement cost of just the materiel for a ROAD (Reorganization Objective Army Division) mechanized division to be prepositioned exceeds $200 million. Assuming an average annual foreign currency spending of $1,500 per man, the five-year reduction in overseas spending from the transfer of such a division to the United States would be about $125 million, or about 60 per cent of materiel costs.

---

[17] a) Stanley Karnoir, "Kashmir Clash Points Up Dilemma Involving U. S. Weapons Aid Abroad," *Washington Post and Times Herald* (September 13, 1965), p. 1; b) J. Anthony Lukas, Jacques Nevard, and Paul Grimes, "The Kashmir War: How It Happened," *New York Times* (October 12, 1965), pp. 1, 22.

EXPANSION OF U.S. MILITARY EXPORTS

Efforts to expand military exports must be limited largely to industrial allies. Only these nations have sufficient economic resources (national output and foreign exchange resources) and large enough defense programs to represent potentially important markets for modern military technology. Compare, for example, the French, British, and German annual defense expenditures of approximately $4 to $5 billion each with the $1 billion spent by all Latin American nations in 1963 and the $.6 billion defense budget of India in 1963.[18]

A purchase from the United States shortens the long development lead time and spreads the large R&D costs over a larger number of units. These considerations can outweigh any loss of national prestige or independence that results from relying on a foreign source for some modern arms.[19] For example, Defense Minister Healey's major justification for scrapping the TSR–2 program in favor of importing the F-111 was that Britain could obtain the U.S. weapon ". . . at a price per aircraft which, even on a full-scale program, would represent less than half the estimated total of $2 billion research, development, and production cost (for an equivalent force of TSR–2's)."[20] Similarly, German officials partially defended their decision to rely on the F-104 as their major tactical aircraft by stating that this choice would enable the Federal Republic to benefit from the advanced technology embodied in the aircraft without large R&D expenditures.[21] In contrast, France has been building a capacity to develop and produce domestically almost the entire inventory of weapons needed by its military. Through this approach the French government hopes to raise the nation's standing among the world powers and to be able to pursue national goals without fear of denial or reduction of U.S. military support.

The advantages to an ally of acquiring his advanced weapons from the United States rather than from domestic or other foreign sources stem largely from three factors. Technological leadership places many U.S. weapons or

[18] *The Europa Yearbook*, Volume I (London: Europa Publications Limited, 1965).

[19] West Germany, the major U. S. customer for military equipment, has additional reasons for relying heavily on foreign equipment. In fact, the Federal Republic satisfies over 25 per cent of its military equipment requirements from foreign sources. The primary reasons for this approach are (1) the vulnerability of German defense industry to external aggression, (2) the unwillingness to disturb the high rate of expansion and employment in the civilian economy, and (3) the desire to assure the continued presence of large U. S., British, and French forces by offsetting partially their foreign exchange costs from deploying troops in Germany.

[20] Herbert J. Coleman, "TSR-2 Cancellation Brings Censure Move," *Aviation Week and Space Technology* (April 12, 1965), pp. 26.

[21] D. A. Anderton, "Germany Buys Technological Time with F-104," *Aviation Week and Space Technology* (March 7, 1960), p. 33.

equipment components in production or in a late development stage when allied nations are first realizing their need for this technology. The large size of U.S. equipment procurement relative to the needs of an ally drastically reduces the R&D component in average costs. (In fact, since DoD decisions to acquire a weapon are based solely on U.S. defense requirements, equipment could be exported economically even if sunk R&D costs were excluded in the unit price.) Moreover, a superior logistics support system, by enabling the purchasing nation to rely partly on U.S. military sources for spare parts and maintenance, lowers support costs.

Sales to allies of weapons representing advanced military technology eases the U.S. defense burden. Over time, the military technology of the Soviet Union has kept pace with the technological advancement of U.S. equipment. Effective deterrence of this growing capability requires a comparable improvement in the equipment of the industrial nations of Europe, the Commonwealth, and Japan. Introducing this equipment into their inventories improves the effectiveness of the allied military forces, which in turn reduces the requirements for U.S. forces to assist in the defense of these areas. The sale, for example, of the blueprints, production equipment, and electronic components of the HAWK surface-to-air missile to a NATO production group enables European allies to replace U.S. air defense units with their own.

These benefits must be weighed against the risk that the additional sale may prove detrimental to U.S. interests. One risk is that the equipment may be used in ways that could harm American politico-military objectives. As in Algeria under French rule and in Latin American nations, U.S. equipment has been used by unpopular regimes against local rebellions. Also, U.S. equipment has been used in conflicts between two states friendly to the United States, as in Arab and Israeli skirmishes. The other risk is that technology is transferred, giving the purchasing nation a capability to produce weapons that could weaken the U.S. There is no record where this risk has been realized by any U.S. military exports in the postwar period; but British sales of jet engines to the Soviet Union soon after World War II are considered a case in point.[22]

EFFECTS OF DOD ACTIONS ON U.S. CIVILIAN EXPORTS

The export loss from a reduction in defense purchases from or increased sales to any ally represents the effects of a cumulative decline in exports and imports among all nations. A reduction in U.S. military purchases from an ally tends to lower that country's imports in three principal ways: (1) by de-

---

[22] "British Jet Stirs Queries on Soviet," *New York Times* (September 12, 1950), p. 49.

creasing aggregate demand and, therefore, income and prices;[23] (2) by drawing down foreign exchange resources and thereby influencing government monetary, fiscal, and trade policies;[24] and (3) by decreasing the need for resources that would otherwise be imported to produce the goods that would have been purchased.[25]

These influences of U.S. military purchases on a country's imports are no different from those of other exports by that country. In fact, one can assume that U.S. defense spending affects a country's total imports just as its export of civilian goods and services does. Certainly the gross foreign exchange earnings are the same. In industrial countries, where changes in aggregate demand are an important determinant of imports, U.S. military purchases tend to involve either expenditures by troops which resemble tourist expenditures or purchases of local supplies and maintenance services that would be exported or transferred to export industries. In less developed countries, which have strong central government regulation of imports because of foreign exchange shortages, the main determinant of imports is foreign exchange earnings.

Initially, then, a reduction in defense purchases lowers the imports of the allied nation, say Korea, from the United States and from the rest of the world. Mathematically, the geographical distribution of this reaction may be represented as

$$(-\Delta M_K)_2 = [b_{K.us} + \sum_{i=1}^{n} b_{K.i}]r_K(-\Delta X_K)_1 \qquad (b \geq 0, r \geq 0) \qquad (1)$$

[23] Withdrawal of U. S. military purchases in a country tends to decrease the monetary demand for goods and services, and therefore, the utilization of resources in that country. Given an initial stock of resources, this diminished claim on the resources lowers their earnings. This decline in demand could also affect the prices of the resources and the goods and services they produce. The decrease in income depresses the community's demand for goods and services, including products from the rest of the world. A decrease in the prices of domestically produced goods and services would, everything else remaining the same, result in some substitution of domestic products for foreign products.

[24] Lower Department of Defense spending in the local economy decreases the foreign exchange resources of that country. Most nations prefer to limit the dependence on untied bank reserves to compensate for diminished foreign exchange earnings that are held as extra central bank reserves. Hence many governments discourage their nationals' drawing on central bank reserves for imports or investment abroad. Measures which governments take include lowering effective demand, tightening trade barriers, or increasing controls on investments abroad. The influence of U. S. military spending in stimulating such government actions obviously depends on the extent DoD purchases contribute to the international reserve assests of the nation.

[25] A large share of the domestic product of other nations has a substantial import content. This characteristic is especially true of products and services requiring substantial raw material inputs. Where DoD purchases abroad involve these types of products, declines of U. S. military spending can decrease imports needed to produce the goods and services purchased by our forces.

where

$-\Delta M$ = decline in a country's imports,

b = share of one country in the reduced imports of another,

r = decline in a country's total imports induced by a unit decline in its exports,

$-\Delta X$ = the decline in a country's export earnings (from a reduction in DoD purchases or civilian sales).

Subscripts

K = Korea,

us = United States,

i = an exporting country belonging to the rest of the world,

j = an importing country belonging to the rest of the world,

1, 2, ... = a time period.

In the next period, these lower exports spur a further contraction in the exports of the allied nation Korea, the United States, and the rest of the world. For each country in the rest of the world, one then finds

$$(\Delta M_j)_3 = [b_{j.us} + b_{jK} + \sum_{i=1}^{n-1} b_{ji}]r_j(-\Delta X_j)_2 \qquad (i \neq j)\ (b \geq 0, r \geq 0) \quad (2)$$

Since net of shipping costs, the decline in any country's exports, is identical to the decline in other countries' purchases from it, one can derive from the above relationships

$$(-\Delta X_{us})_3 = b_{K.us}\cdot r_K\cdot(-\Delta X_K)_2 + \sum_{j=1}^{n} b_{j.us}\cdot r_j\cdot(-\Delta X_j)_2 \qquad (3a)$$

$$(-\Delta X_K)_3 = b_{us.K}\cdot r_{us}\cdot(-\Delta X_{us})_2 + \sum_{j=1}^{n} b_{j.K}\cdot r_j\cdot(-\Delta X_j)_2 \qquad (3b)^{26}$$

$$(-\Delta X_i)_3 = b_{us.i}\cdot r_{us}\cdot(-\Delta X_{us})_2 + b_{K.i}\cdot r_K(-\Delta X_K)_2 + \sum_{j=1}^{n-1} b_{ji}\cdot r_j\cdot(-\Delta X_j)_2{}^{26}$$

$$(j \neq i) \quad (3c)$$

[26] Since in this representation the influence of the reduction in U. S. military purchases does not affect imports of the U. S. or the rest of the world until period 3, $(-\Delta X_K)_2 = 0$. For succeeding periods, however, $-\Delta X_K > 0$.

Continued decline in the exports of the United States, Korea, and the rest of the world will act to lower further the export earnings of these countries in future periods.[27]

A necessary condition for a reduction in defense purchases in an allied nation to yield a finite decline in world trade is $r < 1$ to predominate among the major trading nations. Trade among the industrial nations accounts for over 60 per cent of world trade; trade between industrial nations and less developed countries accounts for another 30 per cent. For most less developed countries, $r \approx 1.0$. With $r > 1$ for most wealthier nations, there would be a tendency for

$$[(-\Delta X_{us}) + (-\Delta X_K) + \sum_{i=1}^{n}(-\Delta X_i)]_{t+1}$$

$$< [(-\Delta X_{us}) + (-\Delta X_K) + \sum_{i=1}^{n}(-\Delta X_i)]_t$$

that is, the decrease in world exports in each period would tend to be greater than the decline in the previous period. Fortunately, $r < 1.0$ for nearly all industrial nations.[28]

In fact, for the United States $r \approx 0.0$. Generally accepted estimates place the U.S. marginal propensity to import for major income changes at about 0.03 or 0.04.[29] Since exporting tends to be marginal in total U.S. economic

---

[27] The final decline in world trade, U. S. exports, and the export earnings of the allied country would then be as follows:

$$(-\Delta X_w) = \sum_{t=1}^{m}(-\Delta X_{us})_t + \sum_{t=1}^{m}(-\Delta X_K)_t + \sum_{t=1}^{m}\sum_{i=1}^{n}(-\Delta X_i)_t,$$

where $-\Delta X_w$ = total decline in world trade;

$$\sum_{t=1}^{m}(-\Delta X_{us}) = b_{K.us} \cdot r_K \sum_{t=1}^{m}(-\Delta X_K)_t + \sum_{t=1}^{m}\left[\sum_{j=1}^{n} b_{j.us} \cdot r_j(-\Delta X_j)\right]_t;$$

$$\sum_{t=1}^{m}(-\Delta X_K) = (-\Delta X_K)_1 + b_{us.K} \cdot r_{us} \sum_{t=1}^{m}(-\Delta X_{us})_t + \sum_{t=1}^{m}\left[\sum_{j=1}^{n} b_{j.K} \cdot r_j(-\Delta X_j)\right]_t.$$

These results can be estimated by means of a simultaneous equation model where there is an equation for each country N relating

$$\Delta X_N = \sum_{j=1}^{n} b_{j.N} \cdot r_j \cdot (\Delta X_j)$$

[28] Alternative estimates of r are presented by the following two studies: a) Walter S. Salant and Beatrice N. Vaccara, *Import Liberalization and Equipment*, Effects of Unilateral Reductions in United States Import Barriers, (Washington, D. C.: The Brookings Institution, 1961), pp. 149–79; b) W. Whitney Hicks, "Estimating Foreign Exchange Costs of Untied Aid," *Southern Economic Journal*, 30 (October 1963), 168–74.

[29] Walter S. Salant, *et al.*, *The United States Balance of Payments in 1968* (Washington, D. C.: The Brookings Institution, 1963), pp. 56, 59.

activity—about $30 billion of exports in a GNP (Gross National Product) of over $630 billion in 1964—small changes in exports may have even a smaller impact on imports. On the other hand, the U.S. economy is large relative to the economies of all other free-world nations—about 60 per cent of the free world's goods and services are produced by the U.S.—and U.S. imports are an important share of free world trade. The miniscule value of r for the U.S. thus becomes a central factor in holding down the loss of U.S. exports and the decline in world trade that might result from any reduction of defense purchases in an allied nation.

THE ROLE OF DEFENSE IN ADJUSTING THE NATIONAL
BALANCE OF PAYMENTS

Given U.S. military commitments and programs, opportunities for foreign exchange savings through changes in defense procedures depend on past similar attempts to reduce the payments deficits. Political considerations aside, the question of whether military or civilian alternatives are more efficient revolves about the comparative sacrifice of U.S. welfare that each implies for a given level of foreign exchange earnings.

Contribution of Defense

Compared to other sectors of the economy, defense has made an impressive contribution in reducing the balance of payments deficit. Data on DoD expenditures overseas in Appendix Table 1 show that foreign currency purchases have declined from about $3.2 billion in the 1957–59 period to about $2.9 billion in 1964—about a 10 per cent drop for a six year period.[30] This cutback was achieved with no important decline either in U.S. combat strength or commitments to assist in the defense of allies. These data indicate that purchases of materials and supplies declined by about $300 million while other outlays were held constant. Appendix Table 2 suggests that OEEC Europe and Canada account for the bulk of the lower foreign purchases.[31]

This achievement looms large considering the sharp rise in foreign prices, the rise in U.S. military pay, and the performance of other current account purchases abroad. For example, during 1961–64, wage levels in France rose by about 27 per cent, in Germany by about 30 per cent, and in Japan by about 33 per cent; at the same time, U.S. wages rose 13 per cent.[32] Similarly, the pay

[30] Appendix, Table 1, "Defense Expenditures Abroad for Goods and Services, by Major Category, 1953–64, Annually," p. 310.

[31] Appendix, Table 2, "Defense Expenditures Abroad for Goods and Services, by Major Country, 1953–63, Annually," p. 312.

[32] International Monetary Fund, *International Financial Statistics*, Vol. 18 (April 1965).

of the U.S. military increased by about 15 per cent between 1958 and 1964.[33]
In contrast to the defense sector, civilian commodity imports grew by about
one-third from 1957 to 1964; moreover, U.S. tourist spending increased by about
60 per cent during this period.[34]

A few key defense measures have played a central role in reducing foreign
currency spending. Defense has allowed an additional outlay of up to 50 per cent
for domestic sources competing with foreign sources. This lowered DoD foreign
purchases of material and supplies by about $200 million. Changes in logistics
operations, which reduced employment of foreign nationals by about 35,000
between 1962 and 1964, probably reduced foreign currency spending by another
$90 million.[35] Improvements of post exchange facilities and savings programs
contributed heavily to holding down personnel spending in the local economy.
The reductions in foreign currency spending permitted by the technological
breakthrough in strategic offensive and defense forces (which diminished reliance
on foreign bases) were just adequate to offset the rise in foreign prices.

While civilian exports grew by about 50 per cent between the 1957–59
period and 1964, annual U.S. commercial military sales increased by about 125
per cent. (Appendix Table 3 shows a rise from about $325 million annually in
1957–59 to over $760 million in 1964.[36]) These data indicate that the growth in
DoD sales stemmed solely from the increase in purchases by OEEC nations—
predominantly by the Federal Republic of Germany, according to congressional
testimony. The bulk of West Germany's purchases result from its decision to
lean heavily on foreign military technology, though the agreement to offset
U.S. military spending there probably had some effect.

Thus, reductions in overseas spending and increases in military sales amount
to about $750 million during the 1958–64 period. The foreign exchange savings
from these actions depend on the export loss associated with them. If 40–50
per cent of this $750 million results in lost exports, measures taken by the
Department of Defense reduced the balance of payments deficit by $375 to $450
million.

Cost of Defense Contributions

Achievements in deficit reduction, however, must be measured on
the larger scale of the total U.S. domestic economy. Some defense contributions
involve a large loss in U.S. domestic welfare per dollar of foreign exchange

[33] Department of Defense, *Military Compensation Progression*—December 12, 1964.

[34] a) For import data, see, *International Financial Statistics*, April 1965, p. 35; b) For data
on U. S. tourism, see Etienne H. Miller, "Foreign Travel Payments Hit New High in 1964,"
Survey of Current Business, 45 (June 1965), 25–29.

[35] See testimony by C. J. Hitch, Assistant Secretary of Defense (Comptroller), *Balance
of Payments—1965*, Hearings before a Subcommittee of the Senate Committee on Banking and
Currency, Part 1, pp. 154–61.

[36] Appendix, Table 3, "U. S. Military Aid and Commercial Sales, by Area, 1953–64,
Annually," p. 314.

savings and a discriminatory tax on certain military expenditures. For example, by allowing up to an additional 50 per cent outlay for domestic rather than foreign goods and services, the government sacrifices $0.50 of services that would be used for the benefit of U.S. citizens in order to obtain a $1.00 improvement in the balance of payments (exclusive of export losses). This $0.50 of additional defense expenditures comes, after all, from other government programs or from private citizens (through higher taxes or lower transfer payments). The criterion for military purchases then amounts to a sacrifice of up to $500 million in U.S. welfare to gain a $1 billion gain in exports or decline in imports. If the U.S. is prepared to make this kind of sacrifice in domestic welfare, numerous nondefense alternatives become candidates for achieving reductions in spending or increases in sales abroad: for example, taxes on U.S. tourism, subsidies for foreign tourists, excise tax rebates on exports, or discriminatory sales taxes on foreign products.

In a national program inducing marginal changes in various sectors, the relative efficiency of defense actions can be determined only by comparing the national sacrifice implied by each alternative. For example, defense reduced overseas procurement by $200 million at the expense of a $60 million budget increase. This amounts to achieving a $1 billion reduction in tourist expenditures overseas by imposing a $150 tax on each $1000 of spending abroad,[37] or obtaining a $1 billion increase in exports by offering firms a $300 subsidy per $1000 increase in their export sales. A devaluation which reduced real GNP by $600 million while achieving a $2 billion increase in exports or decrease in imports would be another equivalent.

However, all these alternatives, including defense actions, really represent a selective application of the traditional measures of general devaluation or discriminatory trade practices. They still require members of the society either to pay a higher price for foreign products or domestic substitutes, or to receive less income from foreign sales. In all these special actions, the burden is carried by the entire society, though the onus may be placed on a particular activity.

BIBLIOGRAPHY

1. Bandera, N. N., "Tied Loans and International Payments Problems," *Oxford Economic Papers* (July, 1965), 17, 299–308.

2. Hansen, Alvin, *The Dollar and the International Monetary System.* New York: McGraw-Hill Book Co., 1965.

3. Lederer, Walther, *The Balance of Foreign Transactions; Problems of Definition and Measurement,* Special Papers in International Economics, No. 5. Princeton: Princeton University, 1963.

[37] On average, per capita expenditures abroad by tourists amount to about $1,000.

4. Meade, James E., *The Balance of Payments*. London: Oxford University Press, 1951.

5. Salant, Walter S. *et al.*, *The United States Balance of Payments in 1968*. Washington: The Brookings Institution, 1963.

6. Shepler, Cora E., "United States Defense Expenditures Abroad," *Survey of Current Business*, (January, 1962), 42, 14–16.

7. Spencer, Daniel L., "An External Military Presence, Technological Transfer, and Structural Change," *Kyklos* (Fasc 3, 1965), 18, 451–474.

8. U. S. Congress, Joint Economic Committee, *Factors Affecting the United States Balance of Payments*. Compilation of Studies Prepared for the Subcommittee on International Exchange and Payments, 87th Congress, 2d Session. Washington: U. S. Government Printing Office, 1962.

9. Wolf, Charles, *Foreign Aid: Theory and Practice in Southern Asia*. Princeton: Princeton University, 1960.

APPENDIX TABLE 1   Defense Expenditures Abroad for Goods and Services, by Major Category, 1953–64, Annually[1]

(Millions of dollars)

	1953	1954	1955	1956	1957	1958	1959	1960	1961[2]	1962[2]	1963[2]	1964[2,3]
Total....................	2,615	2,642	2,901	2,949	3,216	3,435	3,107	3,048	3,099	2,963	3,071	2,905
Expenditures by troops, civilian personnel, post exchanges, etc.	864	846	862	861	881	890	888	873	781	772	803	849
Foreign expenditures for construction....	301	275	313	369	372	321	215	175	158	122	101	80
Contributions to the NATO multilateral construction program.	91	69	84	68	65	81	58	117	105	35	88	62
Contractual services..........	454	370	412	481	640	772	765	774	884	914	969	1,038
Offshore procurement under military assistance programs.	326	595	640	515	371	212	150	141	206	191	227	176
Purchases of equipment........	71	70	37	42	55	49	39	44	61	67	76	91
Purchases of other materials and supplies	508	417	553	613	832	1,110	992	924	905	963	807	609

Note: The data on defense expenditures abroad for goods and services represent expenditures by the Department of Defense and other U. S. Government agencies in dollars and in foreign currencies, including foreign currencies acquired by the Government as a counterpart to foreign grants, as payments on loans and other credits, and as proceeds from sales of agricultural products, excess property, and other goods and services. The data do not include expenditures in deutsche marks contributed by the Federal Republic of Germany as Allied support payments, or expenditures in yen received from the Government of Japan as contributions to the support of U. S. forces stationed there.

"Expenditures by troops, civilian personnel, post exchanges, etc." represent purchases of foreign goods and services by U. S. military and civilian personnel and their dependents stationed abroad; expenditures by Navy personnel on shore leave; outlays in Panama by U. S. personnel and their outlet stores located in the Panama Canal zone; the direct hire of foreign nationals; and the foreign disbursements of the post exchanges, Navy stores, clubs, and similar organizations which service authorized personnel.

"Foreign expenditures for construction" are comprised of payments to foreign contractors for construction abroad; direct outlays for foreign goods and services used in construction programs; and the foreign costs of U. S. firms under contract with the military agencies.

(Footnotes continued)

"Contractual services" represent the foreign cost of travel, transportation, rent, communications, utilities, repair, and other contractual expenses for troop support and the operation and maintenance of installations abroad. Supplies and materials furnished by contractors in connection with such services are included. Payments to foreign governments for employment of foreign nationals under "indirect hire" arrangements are also included.

"Offshore procurement under military assistance programs" includes purchases of foreign supplies and equipment under military assistance program contracts, offshore procurement under the Lisbon agreement, and foreign expenditures under the weapons production program and the mutual weapons development program. Other military assistance program expenditures for goods and services are included in the other categories. In some cases the supplies and equipment bought abroad and ultimately transferred as aid to foreign countries cannot be separately identified at the time of purchase from other items bought by the military forces. Grants of cash to foreign countries are not included since they do not represent military purchases of goods and services. Detail may not add to total because of rounding.

[1] *Balance of Payments Statistical Supplement*, U. S. Department of Commerce, Office of Business Economics, 1963, p. 148.

[2] Data for the years 1961–1964 are given in fiscal years and were obtained from DoD sources, however it is roughly comparable to that prepared by the Department of Commerce on a calendar year basis.

[3] Preliminary.

APPENDIX TABLE 2   Defense Expenditures Abroad for Goods and Services, by Major Country, 1953–63, Annually[1]

(Millions of dollars)

	1953	1954	1955	1956	1957	1958	1959	1960	1961	1962	1963
Total..............	2,615	2,642	2,901	2,949	3,216	3,435	3,107	3,048	2,954	3,044	2,897
Western Europe............	1,209	1,474	1,702	1,675	1,838	1,865	1,670	1,629	1,519	1,619	1,496
Austria.............	27	27	23	4	4	5	12	6	6	5	4
Belgium-Luxembourg......	58	33	64	42	31	55	26	28	12	16	12
Denmark.............	20	22	31[2]	38[2]	34[2]	40[2]	49[2]	50[2]	36	33	42
France.............	410	519	585	425	396	371	300	274	287	267	242
Germany.............	239	237	291	345	479	660	664	642	630	739	679
Greece.............	3	15	25	31	20	15	14	19	17	19	26
Iceland.............	15	18	14	15	12	17	15	14	14	13	11
Ireland.............	(x)	(x)	(x)	1	2	3	4	3	11	11	3
Italy-Trieste.............	104	178	170	153	166	117	117	106	84	106	86
Netherlands.............	37	35	35	39	41	38	30	37	28	33	28
Norway.............	9	15	21	15	14	17	19	17	13	15	14
Portugal.............	2	4	6	10	9	8	4	6	7	5	4
Spain.............	1	5	21	57	87	92	76	64	53	51	48
Sweden.............	1	3	2	3	3	3	2	2	2	3	2
Switzerland.............	39	10	10	10	9	15	9	9	6	5	8
Turkey.............	11	18	30	43	36	45	35	60	61	63	54
United Kingdom.............	232	329	370	430	488	360	289	286	224	196	183
Yugoslavia.............	1	5	3	12	4	3	4	2	4	3	4
Other countries.............	—	(x)	(x)	2	3	1	1	2	19	36	49
Canada.............	204	194	218	259	288	443	431	379	340	308	278

	1953	1954	1955	1956	1957	1958	1959	1960	1961	1962	1963
Latin American republics	53	45	43	46	56	63	48	59	57	76	79
All other countries	1,149	929	938	969	1,034	1,064	958	979	1,047	1,051	1,044
Aruba and Curacao	33	29	55	60	78	97	57	60	63	53	51
Azores	6	8	7	9	6	10	7	7	7	6	5
Bahrein	29	28	26	25	46	49	39	36	43	39	35
Bermuda	7	6	8	11	10	12	14	13	14	14	14
Cambodia, Laos, and Vietnam	1	1	1	1	2	4	7	6	10	31	50
Ethiopia-Eritrea	1	1	2	3	3	4	4	3	5	6	5
Iran	2	5	3	3	5	7	8	8	8	—³	—³
Japan	771	570	502	499	465	418	381	405	388	383	365
Korea	62	44	62	37	58	88	94	90	107	96	85
Libya	17	10	8	9	10	12	9	7	7	7	7
Morocco	55	48	46	42	47	34	27	26	21	18	15
Pakistan	—	—	1	4	13	18	18	12	9	5	5
Philippines	40	39	46	50	57	53	47	43	43	45	45
Ryukyu Islands	51	47	53	61	68	64	63	77	94	88	94
Saudi Arabia	28	35	38	49	40	43	44	42	45	44	43
Taiwan	8	9	15	14	12	19	26	25	22	21	18
Thailand	1	1	1	2	5	5	7	5	8	29	25
Trinidad	2	2	2	3	5	8	4	12	20	17	21
Other countries	35	46	62	87	104	119	102	104	133	149	161

¹ Balance of Payments Statistical Supplement, U. S. Department of Commerce, Office of Business Economics, 1963, p. 149. Data for 1962–63 are available from the Department of Commerce.

² Includes Greenland.

³ Included in "Other Countries."

Details may not add to total because of rounding (x)—less than $500,000.

APPENDIX TABLE 3   U.S. Military Aid and Commercial Sales, by Area, 1953–64, Annually

(Millions of dollars)

	Exports: Military Aid[1]							Exports: Commercial Sales[2]						
	All Areas	Europe OEEC.	Other Europe	Canada	Latin America Republics	All other countries	Inter-nat'l Institutions	All Areas	Europe OEEC.	Other Europe	Canada	Latin America Republics	All other countries	Inter-nat'l Institutions
1953	4,176	3,360	—	3	36	783	—	192	21	—	114	12	45	—
54	3,362	2,266	—	(x)	49	1,047	—	182	22	—	110	11	39	—
55	2,588	1,682	—	—	33	873	—	200	33	—	90	13	64	(x)
56	2,567	1,853	—	—	60	654	—	161	48	—	51	14	48	5
57	2,418	1,518	—	—	69	831	—	375	236	—	38	12	84	1
58	2,286	1,304	—	—	74	908	—	300	173	—	34	19	73	(x)
59	1,974	1,221	—	—	63	690	—	302	181	—	30	12	79	6
60	1,765	913	—	—	72	780	—	335	221	—	35	19	54	24
61	1,465	611	—	9	128	717	—	406	270	—	38	17	57	13
62	1,539	626	—	—	81	832	—	656	538	—	26	16	63	11
63	1,482	753	—	—	55	674	—	657	543	—	18	17	70	1
64	³	—	—	—	—	³	—	762	618	—	34	17	92	

(x)–Less than $500,000.

[1] U. S. Balance of Payments, line 2. 1953–1960, *Balance of Payments Statistical Supplement,* U. S. Department of Commerce, Office of Business Economics, 1963, pp. 120–25. 1961–1964, *Survey of Current Business,* U. S. Department of Commerce, Office of Business Economics, Volume 45, Number 6, June 1965.

[2] U. S. Balance of Payments, line 9. 1953–1964.

[3] Data are not available.

MURRAY L. WEIDENBAUM

Washington University

Murray L. Weidenbaum is Associate Professor of Economics at Washington University and Director of the NASA Economic Research Project. Previously he served as Senior Economist at the Stanford Research Institute and as Corporate Economist for The Boeing Company.

He is the author of several monographs and numerous articles on the economic impact of government, especially defense, expenditures. These include *Federal Bugeting: The Choice of Government Programs* (1964), *The Military Market in the United States* (1963), and articles in the *Journal of Finance, National Tax Journal, Public Finance,* and the *Quarterly Review of Economics and Business.*

Mr. Weidenbaum received his Ph.D. in Economics at Princeton University in 1958, where he was a Banbury Fellow from 1952 to 1954. He has served as adviser or consultant to a number of public organizations, including the U. S. Departments of Labor and State, the Washington State Department of Commerce and Economic Development, and the Congressional Joint Economic Committee. In 1964, he was Executive Secretary of the President's Committee on the Economic Impact of Defense and Disarmament.

17

Defense Expenditures

and the Domestic Economy

National-security expenditures—primarily the outlays of the Department of Defense (DoD) and the National Aeronautics and Space Administration (NASA)—exercise a limited but often catalytic role in the American economy. Using aggregate types of comparisons as a first approximation, defense and space spending appears to be of marginal importance in the economy: It accounts for less than one-tenth of the Gross National Product (GNP) and for a slightly smaller portion of the labor force. From a geographic viewpoint, most states and metropolitan areas are slightly affected by the economic impacts of these national-security programs; only a handful depend on them for as much as a third of their employment.

A similar situation prevails in the industrial economy. Most large industries—food, clothing, textiles, lumber, furniture, automobiles, mining, construction, machinery, retail and wholesale trade, and service establishments—find the military market to be a relatively small one for them. Even among the biggest defense contractors (the companies receiving the largest amounts of contract awards from DoD and NASA) the majority look to civilian markets for the bulk of their sales.

Nevertheless, because of the unusual nature of the resources devoted to defense and space programs, the American economy is affected in several important ways. The following is a sampling of these impacts:

1. Defense/space programs utilize a major share of the scientific and engineering talent in the United States; this tremendous demand may have created more than a little of its own supply, and that for the rest of the economy as well.

2. Defense/space programs receive the bulk of all the goods and services purchased by the federal government; in creating this vast market for private industry, these programs have also served as the instrument for expanding the direct role of the federal government in the American economy as a purchaser and consumer of goods and services.

3. Because of the specialized nature of defense/space purchases—primarily high-technology weapon and space systems—a relatively few durable-goods industries provide most of these needs. In turn, these industries have become the leading growth industries in the nation and the regions in which they cluster among the fastest growing areas.

4. The expansion of defense/space programs also signifies that an increasing share of the national economy is independent of the level, or of changes in the level, of private consumption and investment; these government programs are independent of forces producing fluctuations in the private sector of the economy because they respond to a different set of demands.

Some statistical perspectives may be helpful in understanding the nature of the role played by defense and space programs in the national economy.

SOME AGGREGATE COMPARISONS

Until comparatively recently, expenditures for national security were a very minor factor in total economic activity. In the half century prior to 1930, such outlays normally equaled less than 1 per cent of the Gross National Product, except for the World War I period. From 1931 to 1939 military outlays averaged 1.3 per cent of GNP. World War II, of course, raised security programs to what appears to be a relatively permanent high level. Presently, purchases by DoD and NASA are $57 billion or 9.7 per cent of the total output of the nation. The proportion was even higher during World War II (peak of 48 per cent) and the Korean War (peak of 12 per cent).

An alternate measure of the economic impact of defense/space activity is the portion of the work force devoted to this activity. Figures for 1963 reveal that 6.7 million workers were in defense-related employment, representing 9.4 per cent of total United States employment. A little over half were employed directly by the federal government, either in the Armed Forces or in defense-related work in federal agencies. The remainder were in defense-related employment in private industry, working for prime defense contractors, subcontractors, or firms providing materials and services to contractors.

The current level of military demand reflects an extended period of cold war, interspersed by incidents leading to limited conflicts, such as Korea and Vietnam, and temporary thaws and defense cutbacks, such as in 1957–58 and in 1963–64. An abrupt change in the nature of the external environment, and in the country's reaction to it, would cause another major shift from the present proportion of a little less than one-tenth of the nation's resources being devoted to armaments and related security programs. (See Table 17–1). Clearly, the

TABLE 17–1   Measures of the Economic Impact of Defense Space
Programs Data for 1963

GNP Comparisons (dollar amounts in billions)	
Gross national product	$585.1
Purchases of good and services for national defense	$56.7
National defense as per cent of GNP	9.7%
Employment Comparisons (in millions)	
Total U. S. employment	71.5
Estimated defense-related employment	6.7
Defense employment as per cent of total	9.4%

Source: U. S. Departments of Commerce and Labor.

level and composition of national-security demands are relatively independent of influences in the private economy. Defense and space spending does not regularly act as a stabilizer to counter swings in private consumption or investment, but neither does it necessarily move in parallel with the private economy to accentuate such destabilizing swings.

The impact of defense and space spending on the economy depends on many factors other than the level and rate of change of such spending. Heavy reliance on deficit financing during World War II, in contrast to the tax financing of the Korean War, produced different results on consumer income and spending and, thus, different economic stabilization problems. Variations in tax structures to finance any given level of expenditures are likely to influence the impact of defense and space outlays. Also, consumer and business expectations may differ from one period to another. Finally, the availability of resources also affects the timing and extent of the impact on prices, production, and economic growth.[1]

BUDGETARY IMPLICATIONS

Military and space spending dominates the federal budget. From the viewpoint of economic activity, these programs account for over 85 per cent of all federal purchases of goods and services. In real terms (when the dollar figures are adjusted to eliminate changes resulting from inflation) virtually all the increase in the absolute amount of federal purchases during the past two decades has been accounted for by defense and space programs. In the aggregate, purchases of all other federal government agencies are at about the same level as in 1940. The large increases in federal civilian spending have been transfer payments and grants, which do not show up directly in GNP. Thus, the rise in the federal share of GNP from 6.2 per cent in 1940 to 10.3 per cent in 1964 has been accounted for entirely by defense/space expenditures. On this basis, it can be seen that these security-related expenditures have served, intentionally or otherwise, as the means for expanding the position of the federal government as a purchaser and consumer of goods and services.

The rather unique composition of military and space requirements affords useful insights into the nature of the resources required to meet these needs and of the resultant geographical and industrial distribution of these resources. As seen in Table 17–2, capital outlays—which roughly correspond to plant and equipment expenditures in the private economy—receive 47 per cent of the funds. This is in striking contrast to other sectors of the economy, such as con-

---

[1] Arthur E. Burns, "Military Expenditures, Economic Growth, and Stability," in U. S. Congress, Joint Economic Committee, *Federal Expenditure Policy for Economic Growth and Stability* (Washington: GPO, 1957), p. 509; M. L. Weidenbaum, "The Timing of the Economic Impact of Government Spending," *National Tax Journal* (March, 1959), pp. 79–85.

TABLE 17–2   Composition of Defense/Space Expenditures, Fiscal
Year 1964

	Billions of Dollars	*Per Cent*
Capital Outlays		
Procurement of Weapon Systems:		
Department of Defense	15.4	26.4
Research and Development:		
Department of Defense	7.0	
NASA	3.3	
Subtotal	10.3	17.7
Construction:		
Department of Defense	1.3	
NASA	.4	
Subtotal	1.7	2.9
Total Capital Outlays	27.4	(47.0)
Operating Expenses:		
Department of Defense	30.5	
NASA	.5	
Total Operating Expenses	31.0	53.0
Grand Total	58.4	100.0

Source: The Budget in Brief Fiscal Year 1966.

sumer purchases of goods and services. Consumer spending on durables (including residential housing) accounts for only 21 per cent of total personal-consumption expenditures plus housing. The volume of such hard goods or capital items produced for DoD and NASA is currently almost half as large as the total production of new plant and equipment for the private sector of the economy.

Within the capital-outlays segment, the concentration on research and development (R&D)—38 per cent of capital outlays—is noteworthy. These R&D disbursements of DoD and NASA, in turn, finance about three-fifths of all the R&D performed in the United States. They also represent the major element in the rising trend of R&D in the United States in recent years, far surpassing in dollar significance the increase in R&D funds supplied by all other sources, including private industry, colleges and universities, and other nonprofit institutions.

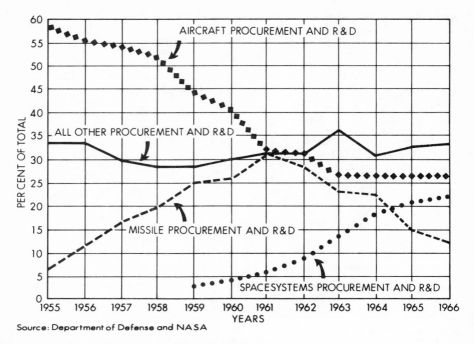

Source: Department of Defense and NASA

Figure 17–1   *Changing Composition of Defense/Space*
                  Procurement and R&D Fiscal Years
                  1955–66

Reflecting the tremendous input of science and technology, the composition of the capital goods acquired by defense and space programs has changed substantially and frequently in the period since World War II. As shown in Figure 17–1, aircraft has gone through a cycle of decline and now expansion as well as through a shift in emphasis from strategic bombers to tactical fighters and transports. With the advent of the Intercontinental Ballistic missile (ICBM), missile procurement rose sharply. With the completion of much of the second generation of this type of weapon, such as Minuteman and Polaris, a decline has set in. Space systems—although still in the research stage—have expanded greatly, the bulk being accounted for by Project Apollo and other NASA programs. It should be recognized that the civilian space-exploration program, although it uses much of the same types of resources, results from a different set of national requirements. An expansion in defense outlays resulting from a limited war might have a neutral or even adverse effect on NASA funding; a cutback in military outlays resulting from arms control or disarmament agreements might lead to expanding NASA activities.

THE INDUSTRIAL BASE

The composition of the firms and industries supplying goods and services to DoD and NASA is determined in large measure by the changing nature of the requirements of these agencies. For example, during the period July 1950–June 1953, the time of peak procurement of Army ordnance equipment for the Korean conflict, General Motors, a major producer of tanks and trucks, was the number-one military contractor based on size of orders received. It had fallen to nineteenth position by fiscal year 1964. Aerospace companies, such as Lockheed, Boeing, and North American, provide the bulk of the aircraft, missile, and space systems that now dominate DoD and NASA requirements.

The Industries Involved

Table 17–3 shows the current industrial distribution of the firms holding the largest value of military and space prime contracts. It is apparent that only a relatively few hard-goods producing industries account for the bulk of these contracts: aircraft, electronics, motor vehicles, petroleum refining, chemicals, rubber, and construction, in that order. A far greater variety of companies and industries, of course, participates at the subcontractor and supplier level. The funds for materials and parts reach many other industries in the form of subcontracts. This subcontracting does much to modify the concentration. Major Department of Defense prime contractors subcontract approximately half of all the contracts they receive, about 40 per cent of this amount going to small business firms. Data on NASA's subcontracts for 1964 show that of the 1,923 different subcontractors, 76 per cent were small business firms; they received 24 per cent of the subcontract dollars.

The extent of dependence on defense and space work varies widely among industries. It is estimated that 98 per cent of ordnance production is consumed by defense, 90 per cent of aerospace, 60 per cent of shipbuilding, and 35 per cent of electrical equipment. In contrast, the proportion is less than 5 per cent for many important industries, including food, apparel, leather, lumber and wood, wholesale and retail trade, services, finance, and construction.

A relatively few large corporations receive the bulk of the defense-contract awards. In fiscal year 1964, the one hundred companies receiving the largest dollar volume of military prime contracts accounted for 73 per cent of the Department of Defense's total. The top one hundred companies accounted for 91 per cent of NASA's prime contracts.

Concentration of economic activity is a long-standing and pervasive attribute of the American economy. By way of perspective, the 139 largest manufacturing corporations accounted for 46.5 per cent of the assets of all manu-

TABLE 17–3   Defense/Space Contract Awards, by Industry 1964
              (percentages)

Industry*	Standard Industrial Classification (SIC Code)	Dept. of Defense	NASA	Total
Aircraft	372	42.1	9.9	52.0
Electronics	481, 482			
	361, 365			
	366	22.8	2.3	25.1
Motor Vehicles	371	3.6	0.7	4.3
Petroleum Refining	291	3.6	—	3.6
Rubber	301	2.3	0.5	2.8
Construction	15, 16	1.8	0.4	2.2
Chemicals	281, 289	2.1	0.1	2.2
Education and Nonprofit Organizations	822, 892	1.4	0.6	2.0
Ship- & Boatbuilding	373	1.9	—	1.9
Instruments	381, 383	0.8	0.5	1.3
Air Transportation	451, 458	0.8	—	0.8
Primary Metals	331, 333	0.4	0.1	0.5
Engine Turbines	351	0.3	—	0.3
Industrial Machinery	355, 356	0.2	0.1	0.3
Business Services	739	0.26	**	0.3
Toy Amusement and Sporting Goods	394	0.2	**	0.2
Railroad Equipment	374	0.1	—	0.2
Total		84.5%	15.5%	100.0%

* Companies are classified according to their primary area of business. This may not coincide with the categories in which they do the bulk of their defense/space work.

* * Less than 1/10 of 1%.

Sources: Listings of SIC codes were taken from S.E.C., *Directory of Listed Companies, 1963*, Dun and Bradstreet, *Million Dollar Directory*, and Aerospace Industry Association reports. Data on Defense contracts were obtained from Department of Defense, *100 Companies and Their Subsidiary Corporations Listed According to Net Value of Military Prime Contract Awards*, for NASA contractors from NASA Annual Procurement Report, Fiscal Year 1964.

facturing corporations in 1931. Likewise, the eight largest firms in 1954 accounted for a third or more of the total shipments in 108 of 164 manufacturing industries for which data were available.

Defense contracts have been concentrated in a relatively few companies for some time. In World War II the one hundred largest contractors ranked by dollar volume of contract awards accounted for 67 per cent of the value of all military contracts, and among these the top twenty-five companies had 46 per cent. In their study of the weapons-acquisition process, Merton J. Peck and Frederic M. Scherer concluded that ". . . the weapons business is apparently less concentrated than the most highly concentrated of American industries such as automobiles and aluminum. It is still, however, competition among the few."[2]

The extent of dependence on defense work varies widely among major contractors. Of the thirty-five largest such contractors in 1964, defense-space sales represented over 75 per cent of the total company sales in the case of nine of these firms, from 50 to 74 per cent in seven firms, and less than half in the case of nineteen of the thirty-five.

Specialized Resources

Another aspect of the industrial impact of defense and space programs is the specialized nature of the resources used by the supplying companies. In contrast with the situation during World War II, and even with that during the Korean conflict, a far greater share of the work is currently being performed in highly specialized facilities that have been specifically built for the purpose, often at the initiative of DoD or NASA, which still may retain title to the factories and the equipment therein. In 1941, less than one-half of the total material needs of warfare consisted of special-purpose equipment. Most of this was material that could be produced by converting ordinary peacetime facilities. Currently, the great bulk of the material needs of defense and space programs consists of specialized equipment that is produced in special facilities built for the purpose.

Moreover, many of the companies involved in the aerospace and electronics industries were set up for, and so much of their experience is limited to, the design and production of military weapon systems and related aerospace vehicles. As a consequence of the technical requirements of defense and space work, these companies have tremendous numbers of scientists and engineers, compared with the more commercially-oriented industries. The typical company or division of a company specializing in defense and space work hires four or five times more scientists and engineers than the most technically-oriented commercial company to support the same volume of sales. For a typical company producing aerospace systems, engineers and related technical personnel no longer constitute merely a single important but limited department. They may exceed in actual numbers the total of factory or "blue collar" employment. In large measure, these companies have become primarily aggregations of R&D resources.

Aircraft and missile companies alone employ more scientists and engineers on research and development work than does the combined total of the chemical, drug, petroleum, motor-vehicle, rubber, and machinery industries. It has been estimated that about 52 per cent of all the scientists and engineers doing R&D work in American industry are engaged on projects funded either by DoD or NASA.

---

[2] Merton J. Peck and Frederic M. Scherer, *The Weapons Acquisition Process* (Boston: Graduate School of Business Administration, Harvard University, 1962), p. 118.

The defense and space programs, however, act as more than sources of demand for scientists, engineers, and other technical employees. Both directly and indirectly, they serve to increase the supply of such personnel. The direct means include university fellowships, aid to research funding, and training programs. The more indirect influence on the supply of scientists and engineers is the creation of a favorable labor market for them, by means of increasing pay rates and employment opportunities.

In addition, there has been a significant movement from defense employment to the private economy. Numerous veterans of the Armed Forces are now using skills, such as those in the field of electronics, that were acquired in the military service (over 16 per cent of enlisted-personnel separations from the Armed Services during the period 1957–63 were trained in electronic skills). An example of the movement of defense-industry personnel to civilian work occurred as the result of the Dyna-Soar cancellation: Two-thirds of the laid-off employees found jobs in nondefense fields.[3]

REGIONAL IMPACTS

The concentration of military and space production in certain industries and companies has been accompanied by a high degree of geographic concentration. The tendency of individual regions to specialize in supplying different types of military equipment is shown in Table 17–4. Firms in the East North Central states supplied over 73 per cent of the tanks and related automotive equipment ordered by DoD in 1964; the Pacific Coast states supplied 51 per cent of missile and space systems; and the Middle Atlantic states furnished 35 per cent of electronics and communication equipment.

Thus certain states and communities, because of their relatively high degree of dependence upon specific categories of defense work, are especially affected by shifts in size and types of DoD and NASA programs. In fiscal year 1964, the ten states receiving the largest dollar volume of DoD and NASA contracts accounted for 68 per cent of the total.

Subcontracting affects a significant geographic redistribution of the contract dollars. Although records of DoD's subcontract distribution are not available, a look at NASA's subcontracts gives an indication of the effects. A sample of first-tier NASA subcontracts shows that 68 per cent were awarded to companies in states other than those in which the prime contractors were located; many of these states do not participate in NASA activities at the prime-contract level at all. The lack of comprehensive data on subcontracting is a major handicap in analyzing the industrial and geographic impacts of DoD and NASA spending (efforts to fill this gap are now underway, however).

[3] Robert Brandwein, "The Dyna-Soar Contract Cancellation—A Statistical Summary," *University of Washington Business Review* (October, 1965).

Dollar procurement by state fluctuates from year to year. An illustration is the case of Missouri, whose military prime-contract dollars increased 53 per cent from fiscal year 1963 to 1964, moving the state from the tenth highest state to the third. At the same time Ohio fell to eighth from third, with a 28 per cent decrease in dollar volume.

Three key factors underlie the geographic shift and concentration or dispersion of defense procurement: the product mix or the kind of product being purchased, the upward or downward trend of a few large individual projects, and the kind of industries located within each state and their ability to compete for military business.

In some states large amounts of defense/space work represent comparatively small portions of total employment and payrolls because of the broad industrial base. This factor cushions the impact of defense/space programs. Certain states and communities, because of their relatively high degree of dependence on defense and space work, are especially affected by shifts in these programs. One indication of the magnitude of this dependence is the portion of the state's personal income derived from military payrolls and from wages and salaries of defense workers in private industry. Six states depend directly on defense and space work for at least 10 per cent of personal income—Virginia, Utah, Washington, California, Alaska, and Hawaii. For all other states, the proportion is less than 10 per cent.

Within various states, the concentration is far greater; important examples are such metropolitan areas as Washington, D.C., Boston, Wichita, Cape Kennedy, Los Angeles, Seattle, and Huntsville, Alabama.

Much of the income generated directly by defense expenditure in a given region is spent locally on retail goods, services, housing, and other consumer items. This creates additional income, business investment, and, thus, employment. This induced employment should be added to direct employment, swelling the local effect of defense expenditure. A study of Los Angeles estimated the combined effect at 43.5 per cent of total employment. Estimates for the Seattle-Tacoma, Washington, area show a similar relationship—42 per cent of total employment could be related to defense and space expenditures.[4]

The tendency of defense and space programs to cluster in a relatively few areas, and in a pattern different from that of American industry generally, is of fairly recent origin. In World War II, the distribution of Defense contracts more or less followed the then prevailing pattern of manufacturing activity. The major industrial states—Michigan, New York, Pennsylvania, Ohio, and Indiana—ranked high in prime-contract awards.

As long as automotive and conventional-ordnance products were a substantial part of defense procurement, the capabilities of established manu-

[4] Charles Tiebout, "The Regional Impact of Defense Expenditures: Its Measurement and Problems of Adjustment," in U. S. Congress, Senate Committee on Labor and Public Welfare, *Nation's Manpower Revolution*, Part 7 (Washington: GPO, 1963), pp. 2516–23.

TABLE 17-4   *Allocation of Defense Contracts by Category and Region (Fiscal Year 1964)*

Program and Area	Millions	Per Cent
Aircraft	$6,167	100.0%
New England	774	12.5
Middle Atlantic	841	13.6
East North Central	765	12.4
West North Central	1,369	22.2
South Atlantic	515	8.4
South Central	736	11.9
Mountain	32	0.5
Pacific	1,132	18.4
Alaska and Hawaii	3	0.1
Missile and Space Systems	$5,807	100.0%
New England	468	8.1
Middle Atlantic	557	9.6
East North Central	205	3.5
West North Central	182	3.1
South Atlantic	593	10.2
South Central	186	3.2
Mountain	650	11.2
Pacific	2,966	51.1
Alaska and Hawaii	*	**
Ships	$1,529	100.0%
New England	275	18.0
Middle Atlantic	320	20.9
East North Central	94	6.2
West North Central	2	0.1
South Atlantic	486	31.8
South Central	82	5.3
Mountain	1	0.1
Pacific	269	17.6
Alaska and Hawaii	*	**
Tank-Automotive	$ 779	100.0%
New England	4	0.4
Middle Atlantic	36	4.7
East North Central	573	73.5
West North Central	9	1.2
South Atlantic	55	7.0
South Central	29	3.8
Mountain	1	0.2
Pacific	72	9.2
Alaska and Hawaii	*	**

TABLE 17–4   Allocation of Defense Contracts by Category and
Region (Fiscal Year 1964) (continued)

Program and Area	Millions	Per Cent
Weapons	$ 213	100.0%
New England	44	20.7
Middle Atlantic	71	33.3
East North Central	34	16.0
West North Central	11	5.1
South Atlantic	10	4.9
South Central	9	4.4
Mountain	1	0.3
Pacific	33	15.3
Alaska and Hawaii	0	0.0
Ammunition	$ 672	100.0%
New England	67	9.9
Middle Atlantic	86	12.8
East North Central	141	21.0
West North Central	114	17.0
South Atlantic	46	6.9
South Central	104	15.5
Mountain	7	1.0
Pacific	107	15.9
Alaska and Hawaii	0	0.0
Electronics and communication equipment	$3,012	100.0%
New England	285	9.5
Middle Atlantic	1,065	35.4
East North Central	318	10.5
West North Central	114	3.8
South Atlantic	385	12.8
South Central	140	4.6
Mountain	94	3.1
Pacific	581	19.3
Alaska and Hawaii	30	1.0

* = Less than $500,000
* * = Less than one-twentieth of one per cent.

Source: U. S. Department of Defense.

facturing firms were drawn upon. Korea marked the beginning of the change. With the increasing role of aircraft, missiles, electronics, and space systems, newer firms became of greater importance, and they tended to locate in the newer industrial states of California, Texas, Washington, or in rejuvenated New England states. The dominance of California is even more striking at the present time, and Washington State, another center of aerospace activity, also appears high on the list of defense/space industrial activity.

TECHNOLOGICAL FALLOUT AND OTHER LONG-TERM EFFECTS

The impacts of defense and space expenditures on the economy manifest themselves in various ways. The incomes of government and private-industry employees working on these programs show up directly in personal income and are also reflected in the Gross National Product. The investment outlays by government contractors also are reported in GNP. In addition, as the recipients of defense-related income respend the proceeds for various types of consumer and investment items, further effects are felt of an induced nature (so-called multiplier and accelerator effects). The multiplier effect of government purchases from private industry has been estimated in the neighborhood of 1.3. Of some interest also is the further estimate that a billion dollars of such public outlay would generate additional federal tax revenues of about 488 million dollars, state and local revenues of 30 million dollars, and would reduce unemployment-insurance costs by 160 million dollars.[5] Thus the net budgetary costs of defense and space programs would appear to be rather less than the gross or clearly visible expenditures.

There is yet another aspect of the economic impact of defense/space programs that may be more illusive and controversial, but possibly of greater significance in the long run. This feature is the "spillover," "fallout," or transfer of defense and space technology to other areas of the economy. There is no simple method of measuring the dollar impacts on the economy of national-security spending for research and development.

From the point of view of investment in the private sector, four main effects have been identified:[6]

(1) The emergence of the new technologies, such as electronics, is stimulating investment in new industries.

(2) These technologies are enabling existing industries to develop a new range of equipment, instruments, and materials that are replacing, improving, or extending old types of production. Computing machines, control devices, and synthetic chemicals are examples of private investment's being so induced to create new facilities or modify old factories and production equipment.

(3) The tools and materials created by the new technologies make possible economies of production in other industries, calling forth new investment to

[5] Daniel Suits, "Econometric Analysis of Disarmament Impacts," in *Disarmament and the Economy,* ed. Emile Benoit and Kenneth Boulding (New York: Harper & Row, Publishers, 1963), p. 104.

[6] George H. Hildebrand and Norman V. Breckner, "The Impacts of National Security Expenditure Upon the Stability and Growth of the American Economy," in U. S. Congress, Joint Economic Committee, *Federal Expenditure Policy for Economic Growth and Stability* (Washington: GPO, 1957), p. 536.

finance cost-saving innovations and increased output. Examples include computers and record-keeping equipment in the office and automatic controls for factories and railroads.

(4) Induced investment results from changes in the location of industry made possible by the new technologies.

Attempts to quantify these effects of defense/space technology have yielded extremely limited results. One detailed survey resulted in an impressive catalogue of the various types of technology which have had effects on the civilian economy (see Table 17–5). But no comprehensive quantification was available.[7]

A more limited survey of large aerospace companies reported that, other than the few firms selling equipment to the airlines, the large defense suppliers obtain only 1 or 2 per cent of their sales from products based on their defense/space work that are sold in commercial markets. The list of abandoned commercial ventures is long, ranging from stainless-steel caskets to powered wheelbarrows to garbage-reduction machinery.[8]

Reasons offered for the inability of the large, specialized defense/space companies to utilize their resources in commercial endeavors include their lack of marketing capability and their inability to produce large numbers of items at low unit prices. These weaknesses are not necessarily handicaps in defense and space work. For example, the lack of commercial marketing capability of these firms results from their preoccupation with meeting the rigorous technical requirements of the government customers. Their inability to produce large volumes at low cost also reflects their unique capability to design small numbers of large-scale systems of great technical complexity.

Nevertheless, additional undertakings continue, particularly attempts to transfer advanced technology to government and industrial areas rather than to consumer markets that require so many of the capabilities found in such short supply by defense/space contracts. More recent attempts include an automatic parcel-sorting system for a railway terminal, the conversion of jet airplane engines to pumping gas and generating electricity for public utilities, and computerized systems to maintain inventory records for retail firms.

NASA, through its technology-utilization program, has been attempting to accelerate the flow of space technology to business firms that can apply it to commercial goods and services. Universities and research institutes are cooperating in order to serve as a transmission belt between government and industrial defense laboratories and commercial industry.[9]

---

[7] John G. Welles *et al.*, *The Commercial Application of Missile/Space Technology*, (Denver: University of Denver, Denver Research Institute, September, 1963).

[8] Murray L. Weidenbaum, "Adjusting to a Defense Cutback: Public Policy Toward Business," *Quarterly Review of Economics and Business* (Spring, 1964), pp. 7–14.

[9] National Aeronautics and Space Administration, Technology Utilization Program; Charles Kimball, "The Relationship Between Economic Growth and the Transfer of Technology," in *1963 Proceedings of the National Association of Business Economists* (1963), pp. 80–90.

TABLE 17–5   Tabulation by Type and Degree of Identified Missile/Space Contribution

Area of Technology	Dominant Types of Identified Contribution					Apparent Degree of Contribution		
	Stimulation of Research	Development of New Processes and Techniques	Improvement of Existing Products	Development of New Products	Cost Reduction	Strong	Moderate	Slight
(1)	(2)	(3)	(4)	(5)	(6)	(7)	(8)	(9)
Instrumentation								
Resistance Strain Gages	X		X	X			X	
Infrared Instrumentation					X		X	
Pressure Measuring Equipment	X			X			X	
Temperature Measuring Equipment			X	X			X	
Instrumentation Amplifiers			X					X
Electronic Components								
Semiconductors	X		X	X	X		X	
Microsystems Electronics	X				X	X		
Thermoelectric Refrigeration			X		X			X
Connectors, Cables, and Printed Circuits			X		X		X	
Display Systems				X			X	
Control Systems								
Inertial Guidance	X			X		X		
Electronic Computer Systems	X		X		X		X	
Power Sources								
Solar Cells	X					X		
Energy Conversion	X						X	
Fuel Cells	X						X	
Magnetogydrodynamics	X					X		

TABLE 17–5 Tabulation by Type and Degree of Identified Missile/Space Contribution (continued)

Area of Technology	Dominant Types of Identified Contribution					Apparent Degree of Contribution		
	Stimulation of Research	Development of New Processes and Techniques	Improvement of Existing Products	Development of New Products	Cost Reduction	Strong	Moderate	Slight
(1)	(2)	(3)	(4)	(5)	(6)	(7)	(8)	(9)
Propulsion								
Cryogenics	X				X		X	
Fluid Transfer Systems			X		X		X	
Fabrication								
Filament Winding	X	X				X		
Chemical Milling	X	X				X		
High Energy Forming	X	X				X		
Solid State Bonding	X	X				X		
Materials								
Refractory Metals	X					X		
Maraging Steels	X							X
Physical Metallurgy	X							
Superalloys	X							X
Epoxy Resins				X			X	X
Medical Technology	X	X		X				X
Telemetry and Communications	X		X				X	
Management Control Systems		X				X		

Source: Denver Research Institute.

ECONOMIC CONSTRAINTS ON DEFENSE/SPACE SPENDING

The question has been raised as to how much national-security spending the economy can afford; the companion concern is that short-run considerations may impair the long-term capability of the economy to support a large and sometimes expanding array of national-security programs.

There is no simple or generally agreed-on method to measure the "burden" of defense and space programs on the economy, much less, the economic ceiling, if any, that exists on such programs.

Using the GNP comparison, the portion of our national resources devoted to armaments has tended to diminish rather than increase in recent years, from 10.5 per cent in 1957 to 8.4 per cent in 1964. During much of that period, considerable unutilized or underutilized capacity existed in the economy, far more than was generally desired. Inflation has not been particularly troublesome in recent years; the wholesale price index has fluctuated within the narrow range of 99.0 to 100.7 from 1957 to 1964 (base of 1957–59 = 100).

As to the concern over budgetary deficits, the major increases in federal spending in recent years have occurred in the domestic civilian area, particularly in education, welfare, and health programs. The balance-of-payments problem continues; however, the impact of national-security programs here is not in terms of its total but of the allocation between domestic and overseas outlays. In this connection, NASA programs have little impact on the balance of payments, and DoD has taken numerous steps to reduce its adverse influence on U.S. international accounts.

The real cost to society of allocating productive resources to defense and space programs may be that these resources are unavailable for other purposes. Yet, such resources may not be entirely diverted from other uses in practice. Some or all of the resources so used might have remained unemployed but for the expansion of defense or space activities. On the other hand, if there is any such sacrifice in a given time period, and if the loss is in investment, additional sacrifices will accrue in subsequent time periods as society foregoes the returns on the foregone investment.

Even where resources utilized by defense and space programs are diverted from other sectors, the value of the resultant output does not necessarily measure the value of the output diverted from the civilian sectors. For example, when resources shift from comparatively low-valued products such as agriculture to high-valued products such as space-exploration systems, the portion of GNP utilized by the defense program exceeds in value the output yielded by the private sector; thus a net increase may occur in the level of economic output.

Such structural shifts are a characteristic of the development of the American economy and a manifestation of its relatively rapid growth pattern.[10]

There still may be an important opportunity cost involved in some of the highly specialized resources required by DoD and NASA. The most striking case may be that of R&D, where over half of all the work performed in private industry is financed by these two agencies. Those who decry private affluence amid public poverty may reflect on the allocation of one of our most vital resources, science and technology.

Overall, available analyses of the "burden" of defense/space expenditures have generally concluded that, if necessary for military or political reasons, the American economy could handle, with a minimum of dislocation or hardship, a far higher level of such spending than has been experienced in recent years. Studies or statements of this type have been made by such diverse groups as the Committee for Economic Development, the National Planning Association, a panel of the United States Arms Control and Disarmament Agency, and a group of outstanding university and research economists appearing before the Joint Economic Committee of the Congress. But many such analyses also concluded that the long-term growth and prosperity of the United States do not require even the current level of national-security spending.[11]

Thus, economic constraints do not appear to be an important limitation on the level of defense or space spending—directly. Indirectly, and essentially through the federal budgetary process, financial constraints have restricted (and are likely to continue to restrict) the portion of the nation's resources devoted to these purposes. This reflects the fact that government appropriations for these items are not made in isolation but result from the interplay of many conflicting requirements and demands, including those of numerous other federal programs and of taxpayers who wish to reduce the portion of their incomes taken by the federal government.

The nation's experience testifies to the ability of the economy to adjust successfully to major reductions in national-security spending. Demobilization after World War II was extremely rapid, and no sizable unemployment problem developed. Between June, 1945, and June, 1946, over 9 million men were released from the armed forces, about three times the present total of military personnel. Between 1945 and 1946, national defense purchases of goods and services were reduced by 75 per cent. This reduction was equivalent to more than 25 per cent of the GNP in 1945, about three times the present proportion of GNP that is represented by defense/space spending. The accumulation of savings due to wartime scarcity and the large pent-up demand for durable goods contributed to the ease of the postwar transition.

[10] Burns, op. cit., pp. 512–13.

[11] Murray L. Weidenbaum, "Costs of Alternative Military Strategies," in National Security, Political, Military and Economic Strategies in the Decade Ahead, ed. David Abshire and Richard Allen (New York: Frederick A. Praeger, Inc., 1963), p. 792.

The end of the Korean conflict involved a much smaller reduction in defense spending, which in turn started from a much lower peak than that at the end of World War II. Tax reductions helped to maintain aggregate consumer income and spending. The level-off in the total of defense and space spending in 1963–64 was accompanied by a decline in the national unemployment rate, clearly indicating the capability of the American economy to adjust rapidly at least to moderate changes in defense or space expenditures.

Numerous studies of the economic impact of arms control and disarmament have concluded that the United States is capable of making the necessary economic adjustment to fundamental reductions in the level of national-security expenditures; the limitations are considered to be mainly in the political sphere—the willingness of the nation to take measures of sufficient magnitude and promptness to utilize the resources that would be released in such an eventuality.[12]

IMPACT OF ECONOMIC ENVIRONMENT ON MILITARY DECISION MAKING

Over the years numerous local pressures have arisen to require the Department of Defense to take account of the impact on the economy of its decisions on such military matters as choice of weapon systems contractors, location and retention of bases, and so forth. The official position has been that these substantive decisions will be made on the basis of meeting military requirements in the most efficient manner, without limitation regarding the effects on individual employees, companies, and communities.

In accord with this philosophy, a number of limited actions have been taken to assist in the economic adjustments to changes in the level or pattern of defense spending. For example, in major curtailments, such as those involving the closing of ninety-five installations announced in October, 1964, the Department of Defense guarantees another job opportunity to every permanent employee whose job has been abolished. Where possible, it offers alternative choices of location to those whose jobs have been transferred.

There is much less that the military establishment can do to assist employees of its contractors. Under cost-type contracts, separation or retirement expenses can be allowable costs as can, in some instances, the costs of training and job-related education.

The Department of Defense maintains a special office whose task it is to help communities adversely affected by base closings or contract terminations.

---

[12] See Emile Benoit and Kenneth Boulding, eds., *Disarmament and the Economy* (New York, Harper & Row, Publishers, 1963); U. S. Arms Control and Disarmament Agency, *Economic Impacts of Disarmament* (1962); United Nations, Department of Economic Social Affairs, Economic and Social Consequences of Disarmament, 1963, *Report of the Committee on the Economic Impact of Defense and Disarmament* (July, 1965).

This Office of Economic Adjustment visits these communities and provides ideas and advice. It often serves as a focal point for community efforts to launch industrial-development programs.

Government officials on numerous occasions have stated that there is no public obligation to maintain any given defense contractor. Consistent with this, however, the federal government does a number of things that are deemed appropriate for a large, responsible customer. One such action is to give the specialized military suppliers the maximum feasible advance information concerning the future defense markets. The newest such program of the Department of Defense was a series of industry "briefing sessions" held early in 1965. The President's Committee on the Economic Impact of Defense and Disarmament recently recommended that maximum advance notice of cancellations and cutbacks of defense contracts be given to the contractors and localities involved, so that they can properly plan to cope with the situation.

Both the Department of Defense and NASA revised their procurement regulations in 1964 to state clearly that companies may charge to their defense or space contracts an allocable share of the costs of generalized long-range management planning, including planning for the possibility of economic dislocation or fundamental alterations in the company's present markets.

All these and related government programs are designed to alleviate the side effects of military-program actions rather than to influence them. To the extent that they are successful, these ameliorative-type programs should reduce local political pressure on defense decision making.

MAJOR STATISTICAL SOURCES

1. U. S. Congress, Joint Economic Committee, *Background Material on Economic Aspects of Military Procurement and Supply*, 1964. Washington: GPO, April, 1965.

2. National Aeronautics and Space Administration, *NASA Annual Procurement Report Fiscal Year 1964*. Washington: GPO, 1965.

3. National Science Foundation, *Federal Funds for Research Development, and Other Scientific Activities, Fiscal Years 1962, 1963, and 1964*, NSF 64-11, 1964.

4. Office of the Secretary of Defense, *Military Prime Contracts Awards and Subcontract Payments*. Washington: July–December, 1964.

5. Arms Control and Disarmament Agency, *The Economic and Social Consequences of Disarmament*. Washington: GPO, June, 1964.

6. Department of Defense, *Military Prime Contract Awards by Region and State, Fiscal Years 1962, 1963, 1964*, August 3, 1965.

7. Department of Labor, *Manpower Report of the President and a Report on Manpower Requirement, Resources, Utilization and Training*. Washington: GPO, March, 1965.

SELECTED BIBLIOGRAPHY

1. Roger Bolton, Ed., *Defense and Disarmament, The Economics of Transition.* Englewood Cliffs, N.J.: Prentice-Hall, Inc., 1966.

2. Peck, Merton J., and Frederic M. Scherer, *The Weapons Acquisition Process.* Boston: Division of Research, Graduate School of Business Administration, Harvard University, 1962.

3. U. S. Congress, Senate Committee on Labor and Public Welfare, *Convertibility of Space and Defense Resources to Civilian Needs,* Vol. 2 of Selected Readings in Employment and Manpower. Washington: GPO, 1964.

4. U. S. Congress, Joint Economic Committee, Section VIII, "Federal Expenditures for National Security," in *Federal Expenditure Policy for Economic Growth and Stability.* Washington: GPO, November 5, 1957.

5. U. S. Council of Economic Advisers, *Report of the Committee on the Economic Impact of Defense and Disarmament.* Washington: GPO, July, 1965.

6. Weidenbaum, Murray L., "Costs of Alternative Military Strategies," in *National Security, Political, Military and Economic Strategies in the Decade Ahead,* ed. David Abshire and Richard Allen. New York: Frederick A. Praeger, Inc., 1963.

7. ———, "Measures of the Impact of Defense and Space Programs," *Proceedings of the 1965 Annual Meeting, The Business and Economics Section, American Statistical Association.*

8. ———, "The Impact of Military Procurement on American Industry," in *Planning and Forecasting in the Defense Industries,* ed. J. A. Stockfisch. Belmont, California: Wadsworth Publishing Company, 1962.

MARTIN J. BAILEY

Institute for Defense Analyses

Martin J. Bailey received his Ph.D. from the Johns Hopkins
University in March, 1956. A member of the faculty of the
Economics Department of The University of Chicago, from 1955
to 1965, Professor Bailey taught courses in public finance and
macroeconomics. His *National Income and the Price Level*, a
graduate textbook and treatise in macroeconomics, was published in 1962; he is the author of twenty articles on a variety of
topics in theoretical and applied economics. His published
articles in the field of public finance include such topics as the
criteria for social choice, the criteria for investment decisions, the
social cost of inflationary finance, and the impact of the capital-
gains tax. In 1963, he joined the staff of the Institute for Defense
Analyses, on leave from The University of Chicago, and in 1965
the change became permanent. At the Institute his work has
included a study of the use of the market mechanism as a management tool within the Department of Defense. This work led to his
chapter in this book.

18

Defense Decentralization
Through Internal Prices

INTRODUCTION

This essay* is concerned with the roles that internal prices and shadow prices play and potentially can play in the defense economic organization. More broadly, it is concerned with the contribution that formal decentralization of decision making can make to better defense planning and resource use. Whether such decentralization will lead to optimum decisions has already been the subject of extensive analysis, particularly in the context of the large business firm.[1]

Some elements of the problem in the defense context were spelled out by C. J. Hitch and R. N. McKean, in *The Economics of Defense in the Nuclear Age*, who emphasized the essential role of individual incentives and motivations for the effective functioning of any decentralized arrangement.[2] Norman V. Breckner, after a detailed review of characteristics and problems of military "buyer-seller" arrangements, expressed skepticism about the effectiveness of these arrangements; he emphasized the difficulty of achieving genuine delegation of discretionary authority to lower levels while maintaining effective performance standards.[3]

Although many of these issues are still unresolved, it is clear that even a well-designed decentralized organization may fail to achieve an optimum and can conceivably do worse than a centralized organization. But the detailed knowledge and ingenuity available at the lower levels of management and the possibilities for strong incentives to good performance in a decentralized organization suggest that there is much to be gained from careful study of this type of organization and from careful attention to the conditions necessary for its effective functioning.

INCENTIVES IN THE MILITARY ECONOMY

Although there are genuine difficulties connected with quantifying performance in arranging meaningful incentives in the defense establishment, as was emphasized by Hitch and McKean and by Breckner, the problem is more

* The author is a Staff Economist at the Institute for Defense Analyses. His present and former colleagues there will note many points at which he benefitted from conversations and joint assignments with them; this is particularly true of Stanley Besen, John Cross, Br. General Sidney Giffin (Ret., USAF), John Haldi, William Niskanen, and Wade Sewell. Neither these colleagues nor the Institute is responsible for any of the views expressed here, however; they are the author's own opinions.

[1] See Jack Hirschleifer, "On the Economics of Transfer Pricing," *Journal of Business*, XIX (1956), p. 172; and "Economics of the Divisionalized Firm," *ibid.*, XX (1957), p. 96.

[2] C. J. Hitch and R. N. McKean, *The Economics of Defense in the Nuclear Age* (Cambridge: Harvard University Press, 1960), pp. 221–39.

[3] Norman V. Breckner, "Government Efficiency and the Military 'Buyer-Seller' Device," *Journal of Political Economy*, LXVIII (1960), p. 469.

tractable than it may appear at first glance. It constitutes a general problem for government organizations and for the entire military organization and should be addressed at this level first before being considered at the lower level of quasi-commercial operations and other decentralizing devices.

In the private sector, the economics of the decentralized multidivision firm are much simplified by the availability of the firm's profits as a standard of performance, which with proper care can be translated into corresponding standards for the separate divisions. The division manager then faces comparatively clear incentives, and for most purposes his motives need not be considered as distinct from the profit motive for his division and his firm. The government in general and the defense establishment in particular are more nearly comparable to an entire economy than to a multidivision firm, however, because their utility or objective function(s) reflect multidimensional goods rather than a unidimensional quantity, profits. Similarly, each suborganization serves multiple objectives, not readily reduced to a single number like profits. Accordingly a more general economics than the economics of the firm applies to the problem of incentives and efficiency.

At the same time, in the context of the general problem of efficiency in government, some unique aspects of the defense organization greatly simplify its corresponding problem. The President has clear-cut authority in the defense and foreign-policy fields, well beyond his powers elsewhere. Therefore it is particularly easy to define what the national utility or objective function in this area is: If he elects to assert his leadership, to a good first approximation the national objectives in defense and foreign policy are what the President chooses to make them. Of course, the checks and balances system assures that Congress also plays a role in determining these objectives; but this system is weaker here than anywhere else. Moreover, the concentration of authority in this area largely removes the complications of distribution-of-income that apply to discussions of policy and welfare in the rest of the economy; in this respect a firmly led defense establishment resembles a Robinson Crusoe economy more than it does the private sector of the U.S. economy.

In this Robinson Crusoe economy the military services use their own resources and those contracted from the private sector to produce military capabilities; the array of actual and potential military capabilities that they can develop at various budget levels is the production function. If he weighs alternatives carefully and has a clear-cut national value function in mind, the President (with his advisors) will seek to maximize the value function for military capabilities in the manner of Robinson Crusoe and will choose a budget level consistent with the appropriate marginal conditions vis-à-vis nonmilitary goods. This maximization requires that conditions for efficiency in production itself be satisfied, that is, that the marginal products of all resources contributing to a given type of capability be proportional to their costs; and it requires that the marginal rate of substitution between capabilities, in the value function, be equal to the ratio of their marginal costs.

More concretely, the President must consider the possible threats to the nation's vital interests that might require the use of military force. He is advised by the members of the National Security Council, specifically by the Departments of State and Defense and the Central Intelligence Agency, both with respect to the threats and with respect to possible national responses to them. The military services, with their specialized knowledge on the side of alternative capabilities, can inform him of the force requirements and associated costs for different general strategies and for alternative national objectives in the use of military force. The President then decides which threats to take seriously and which national objectives to plan for, as a basis for force-structure planning. To the extent that he makes his decisions clear, they become the basis for detailed contingency and war planning and establish criteria for performance throughout the defense establishment.

The broad outlines of this process are highlighted by the contrast between defense policy under the Eisenhower Administration and under the Kennedy-Johnson Administration. Under the earlier Administration, because of Eisenhower's philosophy of office, the evaluation of threats and possible responses was left largely to the military services and to Congress. Each service was free to formulate hypothetical threats and national responses, which, predictably, involved a preponderant role for that service, and to seek support for its views in the press and in Congress. The President's role was primarily to determine the overall size of the defense budget and to a lesser extent to allocate it among the services. The details of the force structure were worked out in a bargaining process in Congress and in the Joint Chiefs of Staff, without any assurance that the different parts of the force structure were based on a single, consistent view of threats and responses. For a variety of reasons this process resulted in a heavy emphasis on a capability to wage thermonuclear war directly against the Soviet Union and in a sharp deemphasis of the capability to wage limited wars with nonnuclear weapons. Given that the process developed this way, the Secretary of State almost of necessity enunciated a policy of "massive retaliation" as our response to any serious provocation. The direction of policy changed sharply under the Kennedy Administration, and the manner in which defense policy was formulated also changed. The President resolved to have the capability to respond to limited provocations with limited forces and objectives, that is, to build up the nonnuclear military forces and the means to deploy them rapidly, and through Secretary McNamara asserted his power to direct defense policy in detail. The post-1960 situation therefore fits the model of the Crusoe economy much better than did the earlier situation, which can be described as more nearly resembling a free enterprise economy.

Each of the military services is responsible for a limited, specialized set of military capabilities, partly complementary to and partly substitutable for those provided by the other services. As is the case with other organizations, a natural goal for each service is to enhance its own importance and size, which among other things means having as large a budget as possible. If this were the only implication, a possible mode of decentralization would be that suggested by Abba Lerner—to give each service a specific fixed budget, which in turn would be broken down among theater commanders, and so forth. But quite apart from the problem of externalities, the glaring omission from this proposal is any mention of how to determine the objectives of the organization, how to assure that the intended objectives are pursued, and how to measure performance.[4]

In the Eisenhower period, when as noted above the services were comparatively free to set their own objectives, the Air Force and Navy placed heavy emphasis on a nuclear-war capability and went as far as they could toward putting the Army out of business. In general it can be expected that the natural service bias will be toward new, high-performance, spectacular weapons and toward weapons and front-line forces in general, at the expense of less spectacular capabilities such as maintenance facilities, logistic and deployment systems, and so forth. The bias for a new system is reversed, however, if the type of expertise required to operate it is sharply distinct from that which it replaces, so that its adoption forces the top command officers in a service to declare themselves obsolescent and to replace themselves by younger officers with the new specialization. Celebrated examples involving this problem have been the replacement of the battleship by the carrier and the replacement of the manned long-range bomber by the ballistic missile; the latter instance was further complicated by a more-than-equalizing pay differential for active pilots.

An important factor that tends to mitigate difficulties in monitoring the performance of the military services is that many of the activities and systems of one service are at least partly substitutable for those of another. Tactical air forces are operated by the Air Force, the Navy, and the Marine Corps, and even to a limited extent by the Army; and in some tasks these forces serve the same objective as does artillery. Deployment capability can be provided by air transport, operated by the Air Force, by sea transport, operated by the Navy, and by forward stockpiling in the theater of potential use, operated by the service whose equipment is stockpiled. Long-range ballistic missiles are in the weapons inventory of the Air Force and of the Navy; these missiles currently are replacing long-range bombers. Because of the competition among substitutable systems, any temptation for a service to try to enlarge its budget by carrying performance requirements to expensive excess or by understating the capabilities of its systems will be tempered by the prospect that a *reduction* in its budget might result instead and that its systems might be partly replaced by those of another service. Whether decision making is centralized or decentralized, careful analysis and comparison of alternative systems by the decision maker will provide the most reliable incentives for high performance by the services. Nevertheless, each of the

---

[4] Hitch and McKean, *op. cit.*, pp. 222–24, quote extensively from Lerner's unpublished paper and discuss the problems involved in Lerner's proposal, with primary emphasis on that of externalities.

services, including the suborganizations, possesses a considerable degree of monopoly, so that a significant incentive and control problem remains.

The problem is further complicated by the complementarity between systems, such as combat forces and the lift systems that deploy them. The tendency of a service to skimp on deployment capability in its own budget, if it is permitted to do so, is reversed if the capability is provided by another service. In this latter case the cost would appear primarily to cause a reduction in the supplying service's combat forces, through the competition for funds, rather than in the forces to be deployed; that is, the deployment capability would appear to be virtually free to the using service, and it will state its demands accordingly. For example, the Army has sought and obtained a very large airlift program but has made little attempt to adopt a substantial program of forward stockpiling. In the private sector such a choice is made only in the case of products of extremely high value relative to bulk or weight; only a small proportion of the Army's equipment is in this class.

These considerations indicate the wisdom of those who drafted the U.S. Constitution in providing for the direction of foreign policy and defense policy more nearly in the manner of a Crusoe economy than in that of a free enterprise economy. In its most important characteristics, in other words, the defense establishment must be a centralized organization, and decentralization must proceed cautiously if it is to produce beneficial rather than harmful results. That it *can* produce beneficial results in other establishments is well established and is sometimes even accepted; the concern here is with the practical implementation. A certain amount of direct supervision of the choice between weapons systems and of the provision for their deployment, support, and reserve supplies is necessary for the pursuit of a rational set of national objectives. The question, then, is how to obtain the benefits of decentralization in some areas—that is, how to channel the crosscurrents of incentives to constructive ends.

Decentralized decision making is clearly inappropriate wherever personal and parochial interests frequently conflict with the rational pursuit of national objectives, as has been the case in major weapons choices such as that between the battleship and the carrier. The narrow view is inappropriate in the allocation of resources among the major military capabilities, in strategic choices with political implications (for example, in the choice between winning an engagement by deploying a modest force quickly or by deploying a larger force slowly), and the determination of strategic objectives and constraints. Therefore the decisions that the President and his advisers can appropriately delegate to the services and their suborganizations will involve less important, unglamorous matters of the resource-management variety—those that ought not to take up the time of key people at the levels of the Joint Chiefs of Staff and higher. These areas include strategic mobility, logistics, and routine supply—functions already subject to a limited degree of decentralized decision making in routine peacetime operations, under revolving-fund arrangements.

APPROPRIATE ROLES FOR INDUSTRIAL FUNDS AND
INTERNAL PRICES

The principal formal device by which a measure of decentralized decision making is now accomplished is that of revolving funds, involving buyer-seller arrangements internal to the defense establishment. The intended purpose of these funds is to encourage efficient choices by the military units and organizations using their services and to encourage good management of the activities included in the funds. Given this purpose, an essential feature of their operation is that their purchases of goods and services are charged against their receipts, and not directly against line-item budgetary appropriations; the funds' managers have full discretion regarding such purchases, provided they are necessary for carrying out stated missions assigned to the funds. Moreover, although the receipts of the industrial funds come from line-item appropriations for specific purposes, the responsible officers may have some discretion concerning which fund, if any, will provide the relevant services: for example, a line-item for procurement of aircraft spare parts or for a weapon can be used in part to cover transportation of the item to the point of delivery, and the responsible officer may select air, sea, or land transport.

Where an officer may use a portion of the appropriation for his program in whatever way best furthers its purpose, he can achieve efficiencies by using his detailed knowledge and by exercising ingenuity; such efficiencies would be lost if the detailed line-item appropriations left no room for discretion. Similarly, revolving-fund managers can use their indicated discretion to achieve efficiencies that would be lost without it. That is, for these funds to serve their indicated purposes, Congress and the Administration must delegate some of their authority over appropriations; they must, in part, decentralize.

The revolving-fund organizations in the defense establishment currently have revenues of about $9 billion annually, and they are credited with capital assets of about the same figure. These figures omit important resources employed by these organizations: The current account omits depreciation and the pay and allowances of military personnel, and the capital account omits major equipment and facilities, such as transport aircraft, ships, and military bases. If these items were included in a conventional way, these organizations would account for more than 20 per cent of defense resource use. The more interesting and important of these are the industrial funds, especially the Military Air Transport Service (MATS) and the Military Sea Transport Service (MSTS), because they manage most of the nation's strategic-deployment capability (other than troop airlift, most of which is owned and operated by the private commercial airlines).

There is little direct evidence available on the effectiveness of these funds in their stated mission to induce cost consciousness and responsible resource use.

The amount of discretion available to fund managers and to their direct customers varies from case to case and is difficult to determine. In the case of Naval ship-yards, cost reduction by their managers is virtually impossible, because Congress sets their work-force levels and other inputs by law; but the ship commanders and type commanders who use these yards for repairs have fixed repair budgets and, therefore, a definite incentive to pay close attention to relative priorities.[5] In the case of military air and sea transport, the industrial-fund managers have ample discretion regarding those resource inputs for which they are charged—fuel, spare parts, and private contractor maintenance and other services—but little or none with regard to military personnel, equipment, and base facilities. (These are determined primarily by the contingency planning and programming proc-esses, in which the industrial funds play little role.) Whether the direct customers have discretion in the use of transport is uncertain; they would have virtually none if they strictly followed the rules relating to airlift eligibility. Some mis-allocation is evident in the data on military freight flights inbound to the U.S., which operate at less than one-third of their capacity on the average, apparently because of the Military Air Transport Industrial Fund practice of average-cost pricing.[6] These examples suggest that the revolving funds are only partly success-ful in achieving their intended objectives and that they could be improved upon substantially even in their strictly peacetime operating role.

Moreover, the considerations set out in the preceding section indicate that there is no need to confine the scope of these funds to routine peacetime oper-ations. Much greater potential for improved resource allocation exists in the programming of transport aircraft, ships, and stockpiled emergency-reserve (prepositioned) goods, with respect to which the existing incentive structure is far from ideal. That central decision making could correct the effects of these antieconomic incentives is certainly true, but the attempt to do so imposes heavy additional strains on overloaded information channels and on overworked leadership, whose ability to deal with problems of this kind is inevitably limited. Any of these strains that can efficiently be thrown off by judicious correction of the incentive structure are "good riddance"; effective leadership and reliable, relevant information, like other goods, are not free.

Two elements are essential for efficiency in the programming of deployment capability, logistics, and emergency reserves. First, top-level leadership must specify unambiguously the areas of the world and the deployment speeds for which the system will be designed. Second, the costs of alternative systems must be allocated to the military services in a proper (marginal cost pricing) relation-ship to their respective requirements and must be felt by the services to be

---

[5] John Haldi, "Internal Markets as a Means to Greater Efficiency in the Defense Depart-ment," IDA Internal Note N-77 (September, 1963). This regrettably unpublished paper analyzes the Naval Shipyard case in detail, after a useful survey of the theoretical and practical issues in decentralized decision making in the military context.

[6] These data, and the pertinent analysis, were developed by Stanley Besen.

equivalent in effect to costs normally included in their own budgets. The capabilities demanded of these systems are usually easy to verify and measure, compared to those of weapons, because they can be tested and exercised routinely under conditions accurately simulating those of wartime emergency—and sometimes are tested perforce when an international crisis arises that stops short of war. The one vital characteristic that is untested without war is vulnerability to enemy action; to audit this aspect of system performance in relation to requirements, the central monitor would have to use analytical methods like those used for weapons.

The following observations may be made about incentives in a system in which each service must account for its deployment and supply capability and must charge this capability to its own budget.

The partial competition among the services implies that any reduction that a service can achieve in the cost of providing specified force-deployment capabilities will tend to increase the quantity demanded of that service's combat forces, both because of an income effect and a substitution effect in the choices of the central decision makers. If this prospect is clear and adequately communicated to the military service, there will be a powerful incentive to seek the least-cost deployment and supply system. Moreover, the comparative absence of personal and parochial interests in one such system versus another implies that if staff officers in each service are assigned a definite responsibility to program minimum-cost arrangements for their services, they will address this task loyally and possibly even enthusiastically, as they typically have their less pleasant tasks.

Deployment, logistics, and supply have constituted an area uniquely well suited for decentralized decision making, provided that a more appropriate incentive structure is effected. Other areas in which the same considerations apply include communications and services, which by and large are already covered by revolving-fund enterprise arrangements in their peacetime operations. Again, an extension to force-structure programming (that is, to capital budgeting) for these areas appears feasible and appropriate, although the sums of money involved are comparatively small.

It should also be noted in passing that nonmarket prices, or shadow prices, enter into Defense decision making in at least one other context, namely contract-letting in depressed areas. Wage offsets for depressed areas, in the determination of the lowest bidder for a Defense contract, would be a step toward rationalization of resource use at the national level if the offsets correctly measure the discrepancy between the defense cost and the social cost of labor in these areas. Inasmuch as the offset, when granted, is always 100 per cent of the wage bill, there is reason to doubt that the procedure is a step in the right direction; but it will be impossible to determine until a reliable method is found to measure the discrepancy.

In an analogous example, the costs of nuclear materials fabricated into weapon warheads appear in the AEC budget, not the Defense budget, and until recently could be regarded by the military services as a free good. In late 1964, however, the Comptroller of the Defense Department took tentative steps to require the services to treat nuclear-materials costs as practically equivalent to other costs; a nuclear-materials charge unrelated to any line item in the regular annual Defense budget may eventually appear in program budgets for weapons systems and in program-change proposals. This procedure involves no change in the degree of centralization of decision making but is simply a step toward rationalization within Defense at the national level.

In summary, the programming of airlift, sealift, and prepositioning of equipment and supplies is the most tractable area in which a step toward adopting the characteristics of a free enterprise economy rather than those of a Crusoe economy in the defense establishment appears substantially worthwhile. This step would involve expanding the functions of present industrial funds from mere peacetime operations (and operations planning) to programming their portion of the force structure, that is, to military capital-budgeting. A necessary change in the incentive structure to make this step a constructive one is the institution of charges in each service's budget for its share of the capital costs involved (with equal offsets for the services in whose line-item budgets these costs appear). Each industrial fund would be responsible for calculating the marginal costs and budget shares involved, as it now does for the out-of-pocket costs of peacetime operations. All competing and complementary systems in the strategic-lift and supply area should be treated in parallel fashion, to avoid undesirable incentives due to externalities.

The suggested system appears in outline in Figure 18–1. It differs from the present method in several key respects. First, the air-transport fund and the sea-transport fund enter into the programming process by determining the capacities necessary to satisfy specific time-phased requirements for the array of contingencies. Second, the air-transport fund and the sea-transport fund determine the marginal cost of satisfying each detailed requirement and quote them back to contingency officers whose task is to minimize costs. Third, the group of contingency-logistics planning officers is directed specifically to do the arithmetic of finding the least-cost way to satisfy the time-phased requirements submitted by the unified commands, using the shadow prices offered by the air-transport fund, by the sea-transport fund, and by the service manager of prepositioning.[7] Fourth, the costs associated with Army forces in all contingencies, for airlift and sealift as well as "prepositioning", would be attributed to the Army

---

[7] These officers would appropriately be in the general staffs of their respective services. Although the officer assigned to a particular contingency would concern himself primarily with the requirements of the theater in which his contingency occurs, he must also consider the requirements of other commands and theaters in that same contingency and their inter-actions. Consequently, he is logically situated in the general staff rather than in an operating command.

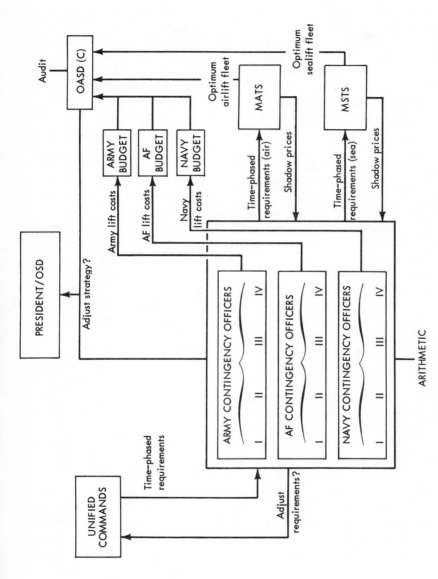

Figure 18–1   *Decentralized Optimization System*

347

budget, and similarly for the other services. *This is a key feature of the necessary incentive structure*. Although the line-item budget might be submitted to Congress in exactly the same form as it is now, the program budgets and program-change proposals would have entries in the respective service portions to represent their claims on the other services' resources; this could be in the nonadditive, shadow-charge form of nuclear-materials charges.

The essential condition is that the guidelines from the Secretary, and the general tone of Defense policy, make it clear that Army claims on Air Force resources would be treated as essentially the same as Army claims on Army resources (and vice versa), when the total budget of each service is being determined.

Some further elements of this or any alternative approach to cost minimization are worth noting. On completion of the minimization, the national response to some threat may be found to be unexpectedly costless, because the force structure and deployment capability required for other contingencies is more than ample to provide for this one in all respects. In this case those responsible for optimization can and should inform high authority, with the query whether a larger programmed response, being costless, might not be preferred. Moreover, some national response may be unexpectedly costly, dominating the others in its requirements, and the query might be raised as to whether a less vigorous response, given the cost saving, would be acceptable. It would also be appropriate to direct such queries to the unified commands with regard to detailed requirements; it may be that some could be expanded cheaply, whereas expansion of others would be especially costly, so that some reshuffling might reduce costs without reducing military effectiveness. In a totally centralized system such queries would originate uniquely from the central optimizing office; in a decentralized system they would in large part originate from the contingency officers, who would be attempting either to reduce the charges against their own service budgets or to increase the capabilities assigned to their respective contingencies. (The operational responsibilities would be the same in either type of system.)

A more decentralized system requires that the air-transport fund and the sea-transport fund engage in detailed program costing and in finding the least-cost system to satisfy the requirements transmitted to them; and it requires that they translate these costs into shadow prices. These demands necessitate additional staffing and a methodology with which they are unfamiliar. This system also requires that each service staff be responsible for finding the least-cost mode for meeting their service-deployment requirements in specified contingencies, using shadow prices supplied by the air-transport fund and the sea-transport fund and their own prepositioning programs. The novelty is that the officers involved would have a clearly stated responsibility to minimize costs for meeting specified requirements. Although only straightforward arithmetic is involved in this activity, their training, experience, and professional doctrines have scarcely prepared them for it. In principle, however, these changes could be effected by directive, because they involve no fundamental change in defense organization.

AN EXAMPLE OF PRICE- AND FORCE-STRUCTURE DETERMINATION FOR AIRLIFT

Following the discussion in Section II, it is supposed that the President selects a definite set of threats, military responses, and military goals as a basis for overall planning of the force structure. Following this selection, suppose that the unified commands and the general staffs of the services work out detailed force requirements and deployment schedules to conform to the indicated responses and goals. Logistics-planning officers in each service would then have the responsibility to minimize deployment costs for meeting these schedules for their service; each theater or contingency could be regarded as a *separate* task, because the interactions would be reflected in the price structure and would not, per se, concern them. These officers would choose between alternative deployment modes strictly on the basis of price; assurance of performance, including appropriate measures to limit vulnerability, would be the concern of each revolving-fund organization and of the monitor who "audits" it. (Because prepositioning involves distinct materiel for each service, it could continue to be managed without revolving-fund arrangements within each service; but a service manager for 'prepositioning' would have to perform the same substantive economic functions as would the air-transport and sea-transport industrial funds.)

Possibly after several rounds of minimization and recalculation the market for deployment capabilities will clear, each officer having minimized deployment cost for his contingency for his service at the final prices set by the transport industrial funds (and by the 'prepositioning' manager). Each industrial fund will have chosen a least-cost fleet to satisfy the final set of delivery capabilities demanded of it and will have based its unit prices for delivery of equipment and materiel on the associated incremental costs.

An example of the demands for military air transport, using hypothetical numbers, will help to illustrate some of the foregoing points. Suppose that the President has decided to base planning on two alternative possibilities of war, which will be called situation S_1 and situation S_2, in widely separated theaters involving a very sophisticated enemy in the first case and a much less sophisticated enemy in the second. Suppose that as a result of the different opposing forces the equipment and materiel that the contingency-logistics officers decided could most economically be moved by air are comparatively dense in the first situation and comparatively bulky in the second, according to the following requirements schedule for the early deployment period.

	W (Weight, STON)	A (Bulk, ft²)
S_1	3200	74,000
S_2	2400	80,000

Suppose further that two aircraft, the $C1$ and the $C2$, can be used to satisfy these requirements, with the following capabilities and costs:

	Cabin Load	Cabin Area	System Cost
$C1$	20	800	2×10^6
$C2$	40	800	3×10^6

Study of the requirements matrix reveals that the weight requirement W_1 of the first situation and the bulk requirement A_2 of the second dominate the other two requirements, in the sense that a fleet that can carry W_1 and A_2 can necessarily carry W_2 and A_1 and, indeed, could carry more of the latter two requirements without strain. Therefore in the final solution W_1 and A_2 will have positive shadow prices and W_2 and A_1 zero shadow prices, a situation that would apply wherever the same dominance relations held.

A least-cost fleet will just barely be able to handle these dominant requirements, giving the relations (based on the above table of capabilities)

$$W_1 = 20N_1 + 40N_2$$

$$A_2 = 800(N_1 + N_2)$$

where N_1 and N_2 are the numbers procured of the $C1$ and $C2$, respectively. These equations imply the general solution

$$N_1 = \frac{40A_2 - 800W_1}{16000}$$

$$N_2 = \frac{800W_1 - 20A_2}{16000}$$

with the particular solution for the specified requirements $N_1 = 40$ and $N_2 = 60$. The cost is given by the general relation

$$\text{Cost} = \$(2N_1 + 3N_2) \times 10^6$$

$$= \$(50W_1 + 1.25A_2) \times 10^3$$

with the particular value for these requirements of \$260 million. The cost equation tells us that additional tons programmed for the first situation cost \$50,000 per ton (regardless of their bulk) and that additional bulk in the second situation costs \$1250 per square foot (regardless of weight).

These are the shadow prices previously referred to; the charges attributable to each military service would be given by this equation also: \$50,000 per ton required by that service for the first situation, regardless of bulk, and $1250 per square foot required by that service for the second situation, regardless of weight.

If the staff officer of a military service found that he had some range of possible prepositioning options, all involving separate prepositioning for the two theaters, the pressure of the above cost relationships would lead him to use a dollars-per-pound cutoff for prepositioning for the first situation and a dollars-per-square-foot cutoff for prepositioning for the second. In other words, he would tend to emphasize prepositioning of very bulky equipment to a greater extent in the second situation than in the first and to emphasize prepositioning of very heavy dense equipment to a greater extent in the first situation than in the second. Such tendencies would lead to greater balance in the requirements for airlift, that is, to less bulk redundancy in the first situation and to less weight redundancy in the second, and so to greater efficiency in fleet utilization. This is an example illustrating the potential efficiency gains obtainable from decentralized decision making, with appropriate incentives, over and above the prospective gains from achieving the right overall mix of airlift, sealift, and prepositioning.

The task of the air-transport industrial fund is more complex than this example would make it seem, because each situation has many relevant subperiods of the peak deployment period, because there are many types of cargo and many types of aircraft, because the air-transport system operates under widely varying conditions and marginal costs in different parts of the world, and, not least, because it must anticipate its performance capabilities under emergency and combat conditions. This type of problem has been found tractable in many past instances, however, through the use of linear or almost-linear programming.[8] The principles involved are straightforward and well tested.

CONCLUDING REMARKS

The sketchy evidence available at present suggests that industrial funds and revolving funds generally make at most a modest contribution to efficiency in resource use in the defense establishment. It does encourage the belief, however, that military officers respond in a constructive way to whatever incentives toward efficiency these funds create. And the budget quantity that they would include if the funds were extended to programming or capital budgeting for their present activities is large even by defense standards.

[8] The first such application to the air-transport problem was in a classified study completed at the RAND Corporation in 1962 by William Niskanen and Donald Fort; a more recent and more elaborate application was in a classified study completed by IDA in 1965 by John Cross and this author. Cross also developed refinements of linear-programming theory and with Wade Sewell wrote a careful statement, in unpublished papers, of the relationship of the shadow prices of the linear program to the contingency requirements in the context of a decentralized organization.

An essential feature of the suggested arrangement is that staff officers responsible for planning many aspects of deployment operations would also be responsible for minimization of costs. The distinguishing characteristic of a centralized organization is the complete separation of the persons responsible for budgeting and resource allocation from those responsible for operations. Although the defense establishment is superficially decentralized in many aspects of its management, even at the lower levels there is a typical tendency for a superior officer to insist that junior officers responsible for operations pass their "requirements" upward for reconciliation with the subbudget for which the superior officer is responsible. Indeed, present law and regulations virtually require it. The superior usually lacks the detailed knowledge with which to determine priorities at the operating level, however, and must cut back on the requests coming up in a way that is bound to have considerable arbitrary elements. By contrast, he is likely to have a good appraisal of the contribution of additional funds to overall effectiveness in the operating areas under his jurisdiction, or at least he would have if he limited his attention to sharpening this appraisal. Therefore, if the superior gave the junior officer the relevant unit prices and told him to state requirements not to exceed a certain budget size and if he rewarded unusually good performance with an increased guideline budget, a substantial gain in efficiency could almost certainly be attained.

These types of organizational arrangements can play a constructive role in almost any aspect of military planning and operations in peacetime, including planning for potential war. It is hard to see how they could do so in actual emergency conditions, when the length of any future major war, even nonnuclear, is likely to be short relative to the length of the budget cycle; such a war is likely to be fought mainly with the military resources and plans available at the time of outbreak. But the decisions having the largest effect on the outcome may well be those that are made before war breaks out, in the planning and programming process. Here the contribution of improved incentives and organization could be substantial.

BIBLIOGRAPHY

1. Breckner, Norman V., "Government Efficiency and the Military 'Buyer-Seller' Device," *Journal of Political Economy*, LXVIII, 1960, p. 469.

2. Haldi, John, "Internal Markets as a Means to Greater Efficiency in the Defense Department," IDA Internal Note N-77, September, 1963.

3. Hirschleifer, Jack, "On the Economics of Transfer Pricing," *Journal of Business*, XIX, 1956, p. 172; and "Economics of the Divisionalized Firm," *ibid.*, XX, 1957, p. 96.

4. Hitch, C. J., and R. N. McKean, *The Economics of Defense in the Nuclear Age*. Boston: Harvard University Press, 1960.

A. W. MARSHALL

The RAND Corporation

Andrew W. Marshall has been a member of The RAND Corporation Economics Department since 1949. During this time he has concerned himself with many aspects of RAND systems analysis studies, both substantive and methodological. Both in the mid-fifties and recently he has been involved in studies relating to NATO.

19

NATO Defense Planning: The Political

and Bureaucratic Constraints

INTRODUCTION

Since the late fifties concern has increased over the size and balance of the military effort contributed by the European NATO Allies of the United States. This concern is sometimes expressed in assertions that the Allies are not contributing their share of the defense of Europe. Some assert that their contributions do not complement the U.S. forces as much as they could.

This concern is not a new one. When the United States began to rebuild its forces in Western Europe during the Korean War, many felt that this need only be temporary. It was hoped that after Europe had fully recovered economically and militarily, the European countries together could defend themselves. The major U.S. contribution was to be through its strategic nuclear forces. Today one hears it said that Europe has recovered its economic strength and former power. Some now argue that Europe should do more for its own defense; others argue that NATO institutions should reflect the new situation. The general argument is that since the Europeans have recovered their political and military strength; arrangements made when they were weaker are no longer satisfactory.

In fact, European economic recovery occurred by the early fifties, and current European feelings of economic strength result not so much from recovery but from the substantial growth rates and general prosperity enjoyed during most of the last ten or fifteen years. European countries have become very self-confident about future economic stability and growth. However, the major European countries have not actually recovered their earlier military and political power. In fact, one could easily argue that the capabilities of our European Allies for self-defense was better in the mid-fifties than it is now. Europe is richer, but not stronger.

The lack of strength results partly from the limited capabilities for the production and development of atomic weapons and other technologically advanced weapons systems. But there are many other causes of European military weakness and consequent political weakness. Military weakness is not attributable to a lack of resources devoted to military expenditure, even though European countries could spend more on defense. In fact, the 12 European NATO Allies have increased their military expenditures approximately 50 per cent since 1961, and are now spending almost $20 billion a year on defense. Although international comparisons are always difficult to make, it is hard to believe that the equivalent cost to the Soviets of that portion of their forces relevant to a European war is more than $20 billion.

One way to compare Soviet and Western European military expenditure is to estimate the likely cost of the current Soviet military program using typical Western European costs. This is not easy. As compared to U.S. budgetary

Note: Any views expressed in this paper are those of the author. They should not be interpreted as reflecting the views of The RAND Corporation or the official opinion or policy of any of its governmental or private research sponsors.

practices the Soviets understate their expenditures, including military R&D and some military expenditures in other parts of their state budget. The NATO Allies defense budgets may be slightly inflated due to the inclusion of duties and taxes on foreign equipment, taxes on gasoline, and so on. Nonetheless a rough comparison can be made.

The published Soviet military budget has been running about $15 billion per year at nominal exchange rates. Some military expenditures are hidden in other parts of the budget, and Soviet pay scales for military personnel are considerably below Western European levels. Adjusting these two major differences might produce estimates of total Soviet military expenditures in the range of $25 to $30 billion. However, the Soviets are investing considerable amounts in intercontinental strategic forces, in air defense for non-European regions of their country, major military installations and forces for the land and sea defense of the Soviet Far East. At least one-third of the Soviet equivalent expenditures are accounted for by these parts of their programs. No one could assert with confidence that the forces the European NATO Allies currently buy for $20 billion could defend Western Europe, whether or not atomic weapons were used, against the forces currently available to the Soviets for an attack on Western Europe.

Thus Western Europe has not recovered its former military strength; indeed it is quite weak militarily speaking. The United States must still provide most of the effective defense of Western Europe even though the Western Europeans are spending almost $20 billion a year. The remainder of this paper will suggest why the Western European Allies obtain so little capability to defend themselves for the money they spend.

SOME REASONS WHY

No explanations of why countries allocate their military budget as they do or why certain force postures result can be complete. The explanations which follow clearly are not. For example, they do not discuss the effect of the U.S. commitment to defend Western Europe upon the incentives of the European Allies to defend themselves. The U.S. commitment has probably, on balance, reduced European efforts for self-defense below what they would otherwise be.

The explanations suggested here stress certain factors which are seldom emphasized sufficiently in discussions of NATO's military problems or considered in proposals for improving NATO's military posture. Of primary importance is the fact that ultimate decisions as to budgetary allocations among military services, missions, weapons procurement programs, and so on, are made in the several countries. This means that there are at least twelve separate decision centers that in aggregate determine each year the gradual evolution of the military forces. Moreover, in each country many separate forces bear upon the

TABLE 19-1   *Estimated Defense Expenditures of NATO Countries,*
              Ranked by Size, 1964–65* (Millions of Dollars)

Country	Defense Expenditure	Cumulative Percentage
United States	50,450	71.2
United Kingdom	5,596	79.1
Germany	5,054	86.2
France	4,270	92.2
Italy	1,741	94.7
Canada	1,413	96.7
Netherlands	725	97.7
Belgium	504	98.4
Turkey	322	98.9
Norway	269	99.3
Denmark	238	99.6
Greece	210	99.9
Portugal	72	100.0
Luxembourg	8	100.00
Total	70,872	

* Institute for Strategic Studies, *The Military Balance, 1964–65*.

relevant decisions. The separate military services of each country, national munitions industries, and many other government ministries, in addition to the ministries of defense, are interested parties. Finally, the various bureaucratic elements and political groups within a given country affect the decisions of its government about procurement of weapons, the supply of military manpower, its length of service, and so on, that ultimately determine the effectiveness of the forces that country provides to NATO. Too often the bureaucratic, economic, and social factors that so strongly influence individual countrys' behavior are lumped loosely under the rubric "political" without further differentiation or analysis. Some factors are perhaps largely political in that they reflect either specific internal political issues or are related to the external political ambitions of particular nations. But a great number of them are political in only a secondary way and reflect the bureaucratic and economic interests of groups within a country and/or its government.[1]

Readers will notice that the military effort of each country, following the NATO tradition, is measured (at least initially) in terms of its total military budget. For NATO planning purposes, of course, not all a country's military

[1] See the testimony of Professor Richard E. Neustadt before the subcommittee on National Security and International Operations of the Committee on Government operations, U. S. Senate, 89th Congress, June 29–July 27, 1965, pp. 125–28.

forces can be assumed available for the defense of Western Europe. Only NATO committed forces are available almost immediately. Most countries have other forces, some of which would become available to the NATO commanders with specified delays, and are included in certain NATO plans. These two categories of forces do not include all the forces of all countries. Nonetheless it is argued that in a major war all forces of all NATO countries are potentially available; thus in discussing the contribution of each country it is appropriate to deal with their total military effort. However, all of the additional forces would not necessarily make a substantial contribution to the Alliance, even if they became available.

Included in Table 19–1 are data on military expenditures for the years 1964–65 of all NATO countries, except Iceland, which has no military forces. The data in this table suggest the important aspects of the military effort of each country. Moreover, as can easily be seen, U.S. military expenditures represent approximately 70 per cent of total Alliance expenditures, and those of Germany, France, and the United Kingdom represent nearly 75 per cent of the remaining expenditures. Hence, determining how Germany, France, and the U.K. spend their budgets is most important to an assessment of the Allies contribution to their self defense. Of course, it is precisely these three, former great world powers who are most likely for historical reasons to be tempted, or pushed by internal political, bureaucratic, and economic groups, to sacrifice Alliance strength to "national" objectives.

1. Diversion of Resources to National Rather than Alliance Use

Of the three major European alliance partners, Germany, France, and U.K., only Germany devotes almost all its military effort to agreed Alliance forces and objectives. All German forces are committed to NATO, and their general balance and organization conform to NATO plans. This is not true of either the French or British defense effort.

In the case of France, the Force de Dissuasion now occupies at least one-quarter of the total expenditure, although a better estimate might be approximately one-third. This could increase in the future, since there is no guarantee that current program cost estimates can be met. Indirect costs of this program are also likely to be high. A substantial portion of the French Navy is involved in the preparation and support of the Pacific H-Bomb Test Program. Other parts of the Navy are being reorganized into a force for use in future French military interventions in Africa, should these be required by events there.

There has already been some stretchout in the program for re-equipping the five Army divisions that are the portion of the French ground forces appropriate for use in a major European war. The remainder of the French ground forces are being reformed into home defense units with lighter weapons and trained for organized guerrilla warfare, should France be invaded. All this is undertaken as part of the difficult transition and phase-down of the French Army after the end of the Algerian War. Substantial reductions in the Army, especially the Officer Corps, would have been difficult in any case, but have been made even more difficult by the reduction required to free resources for the program to equip the nuclear forces.

From the viewpoint of the Alliance, the Force de Dissuasion is not a very productive investment for French military resources. The Alliance is not short on strategic nuclear forces, relative to other military forces. French defenders of this program use a variety of political and prestige arguments to support its acquisition. They also argue that their nuclear program and the other new technology that must be developed for the Force de Dissuasion will have a strong modernizing effect on French industry. Some argue the military effectiveness of the Force de Dissuasion. However, the sort of military force the French now have and are planning for the future is not necessarily the most militarily effective nuclear force medium sized countries, such as France, could produce. There is too much emulation of the U.S. and U.S.S.R. programs. This may result in part from an attempt of a medium-sized country to acquire forces like those of the super powers, and hence acquire the prestige of having "modern" weapons. The French acquisition of the relevant weapon systems is about a decade behind the date of acquisition of similar weapons by the United States, however. If the Soviet Union is bound to optimize its active defense weaponry against American forces, Soviet defenses will tend to have a ten-year lead on French offensive forces. Thus, if some sort of anti-ballistic missile system can be perfected, the French will consistently be procuring forces which will have difficulty penetrating to targets in the Soviet Union. It is doubtful whether the Force de Dissuasion as currently planned is a good investment, except perhaps for French prestige purposes. There probably are Darwinian niches that forces produced by countries the size of France could occupy in the arena of nuclear strategic forces, but neither the French nor the British have tried so far to produce forces of the required subtlety of design. The pursuit of numerous other objectives in these programs has perhaps obscured the way to more effective military forces.

The low productivity of the British nuclear force as far as the Alliance is concerned is not the only drain on the British defense budget that limits their capabilities to assist in the defense of Western Europe. About one-third of all British military forces are devoted to the protection of British and Western interests in the area east of Suez. These forces are not readily deployable to Europe even in time of crisis. When combined with the low productivity and diversion of substantial portions of the French military expenditure to non-Alliance purposes, almost half of the $10 billion expended each year by these two countries may be largely nonproductive of forces useful or readily available for the defense of Europe.

From a wider, and in particular a U.S. point of view, these diversions are not all net loss. The British defense of its interest east of Suez is in the general interest of the other NATO Allies, especially the United States. But the question is why the European members of NATO contribute so little to the defense of Western Europe, since they spend almost $20 billion per year for defense. Part of the suggested answer is that: 1) Some of the effort is devoted to non-European defense; 2) Some expenditure is for forces that relate more to national prestige than to the defense of Europe, at least within the framework of the NATO Alliance.

Diversion of resources to forces that have low priority from an Alliance point of view is not confined to the major countries. One example will suffice. The greatest shortage within the Alliance is of ground forces, adequately equipped, trained and available to the major NATO commanders in reasonable time. The Alliance is not *over*supplied with naval forces, but comparatively speaking it has been *under*supplied with effective ground forces. Nonetheless, essentially all the European Alliance members support navies. These navies on the average probably absorb between 10 and 20 per cent of the yearly military budgets. Navies are capital intensive enterprises as compared with ground forces and have been more affected by the steeply rising cost of modern military equipment. A technically efficient and effective Navy, requires periodic investments in new ships and new equipment. For most European countries this is increasingly difficult to afford. A number of the European countries are unable, within their current military budgets, to support both the yearly operating expenses and modernization programs for their present navies. They have a choice among a current-sized but technically obsolescent navy, a smaller but more modern navy, or more ground forces and a smaller navy. These are hard choices, especially the latter. Therefore, there is a tendency for navies to survive from year to year with declining effectiveness for the job to be done (at least in their Alliance role) using their accustomed 10–20 per cent of the national military budget. In many Western European countries there is a long naval tradition, and it is not easy politically and bureaucratically to reduce expenditures in this area.

2. Diseconomies of Scale

Overhead and other costs are high in the European military establishments because of the small scale of the separate national military programs. Within the expenditure of $20 billion, overhead costs are likely to be higher than one would expect, if only because of the large number of separate ministries of defense, and other overhead operations that each European government supports in its military establishment. The $20 billion must support 12 ministries of defense, 12 general staffs, a large number of military academies, training schools, training commands, and so on. The NATO Alliance and the required staffing of its military command structure, the general operation of the NATO machinery, may also add substantially to the overhead costs of the national military establishments.

In addition, for most types of support and maintenance operations significant economies of scale are possible. The support and logistics systems for the military forces of NATO are largely run nationally and suffer accordingly. Major savings are potentially available through combined or pooled arrangements. Some attempts have been made to run combined logistics operations, but these have not been entirely successful. Some bilateral U.S.–German logistics support operations, however, seem to be going well. For all European NATO countries other than the three largest—Germany, France, and the United Kingdom—the problems of providing adequate logistic support systems for air and naval forces are particularly acute. For example, countries such as Belgium, Denmark, Norway, if they were flying the same types of aircraft, might possibly operate a pooled maintenance system at about half the present cost of their three separate systems.

The question remains why, for example, an operation like SAS can suceed while similar arrangements usually fail in the defense area. National governments do not entirely want to pool their efforts, perhaps partly because independent capabilities for defense are involved in the notion of national sovereignty. Also, the military services of the separate countries all wish as much control as possible over procurement decisions about major weapons systems and to control national support and maintenance facilities. The pursuit of these objectives prevents the effective standardization of equipment and the use of pooled support and maintenance systems.

There has been no study of why it has been impossible to attain within the NATO Alliance the substantial cost-savings major improvements in the operation of support and logistics systems would make available. One can only speculate as to the forces within the nations that prevent effective cooperation on joint programs.

3. High Cost Production of Weapons

Until recently it was settled British policy to equip British forces with British-designed and British-produced weapons. It is probable that over the last ten or fifteen years the cost of this policy has been substantial. The British have often developed major weapon systems which they hoped would be exported to other NATO countries. These sales, plus their own planned procurement, could have led to a large enough production run to reduce significantly average cost per item. Research and development costs of new weapons are large and form a substantial part of the total program cost of developing and producing such weapons. The number of any such weapons the British themselves are likely to want is small, because of the relatively high unit costs of modern weapons, and because the British forces do not need very large numbers of these weapons. Potential savings from additional sales to other countries could be very substantial. They would allow high R&D costs to be prorated over a larger number of production units. The potential savings that might be expected from wider sales may be indicated by the following statement in a British newspaper in January of 1963: "If Britain could produce the P-1154 for NATO, for whose need it is perfect, the price would drop by half." However, the British have increasingly been disappointed in the sales of their weapons. In the early fifties, during the initial build up of NATO forces, the U.S. financed the purchase of British weapons by several of the NATO allies. U.S. weapons production was largely devoted to the rapid build up of U.S. forces and the Korean War. During most of the fifties, however, the U.S. Military Aid programs supplied a great deal of U.S. equipment to the European Allies and there was a declining market for British weapons. In recent years, some European countries have developed their own weapons, others have participated in production consortiums for the production of certain U.S. designed weapons, and the U.S. gold flow problem has led to vigorous attempts by the United States to sell U.S. weapons to its NATO Allies.

The problem of the high cost of weapons has been aggravated by the fact that the British aircraft industry has been an overlarge, declining industry. The British government has given contracts to aircraft firms to keep them alive, continued R&D although it became clear that the weapon design was unlikely to be sold or used, continually put off the day when employment in the industry would be reduced from its current level of 250,000 to 260,000, to a reasonable level of 150,000 employees. British airlines and the British military services have paid the price of the government's policy of maintaining a large British aircraft industry competing across the whole spectrum of aerospace technologies.[2]

As in other aspects of military policy, just as the British relinquish a position, the French adopt it. The French are now attempting to supply their forces with French-designed and produced equipment. The French have designed new tanks for their ground forces, and with few exceptions have been buying only French aircraft. On the average, the cost of the French equipment is probably above U.S. costs; partly because of small production runs. However, with respect to aircraft, they have been more successful than the British in producing technically good aircraft at reasonable prices. In contrast to the British, the French aircraft industry has been growing in the post-war years. Efficiency is more readily attainable in growing than in declining industries.

There has been a revival of European munitions production in the last decade. It is doubtful if European countries can produce military equipment for lower prices than similar equipment from the United States. As one would expect, price is not the only element in European procurement decisions. Moreover, European weapon designs in many cases may be better than U.S. designs of similar weapons, and in some cases will cost less. The potential gains from some form of coordinated production to take advantage of economies of scale have long been discussed within NATO. Very elaborate arrangements, in fact, have been set up within the NATO institutional framework to work towards co-

---

[2] For an unofficial, but informed, view of the situation see *The Economist*, December 18, 1965, pp. 1293–95.

ordinated production. This has included an Armaments Committee, which coordinates the activities of a complex network of interlacing agencies, including the production, logistics, and infrastructure section of the international staff, the military committee, the standing group, and mixed working groups appointed for the specific weapons under discussion as possible items for coordinated production. What has been envisaged is a NATO system which can either coordinate the process of specifying weapons requirements through to the design and prototype construction stage of development or organize the production of weapons already developed. This institutionalized NATO system for coordinated production has not worked very well, since few weapons have in fact survived this process and been produced in quantity.[3]

European production consortiums, which have so far produced weapons of American design, have emerged instead. The five weapons systems produced by such arrangement are: the Hawk Air Defense Missile, the Sidewinder Air-to-Air Missile, the Bullpup Air-to-Surface Missile, the Mark 44 Anti-Submarine Torpedo, the F-104G Fighter Bomber Aircraft. As Vandevanter points out, it is easier to form such consortiums than to put a design through the regular NATO machinery for coordinated production, since in the consortium only those who really will take part in actual procurement and production are parties to the agreement. But of primary interest is that these consortiums produce U.S. weapons at prices (which generally include no write-off of U.S. R&D expenditure) that are substantially higher than prices of these weapons if obtained directly from the United States. Of course European production conserves foreign exchange for the countries involved, and also accords other payoffs to the governments of these countries and various interest groups within them. For example, several years ago when various European countries wanted to produce missiles or more advanced aircraft types, they lacked the technological know-how. Through participation in a consortium producing these types of weapons, they introduced much more modern production technologies into their munitions and other technical industries, and brought them abreast of more advanced U.S. production technology.

Thus each participating country bargains within the consortium for its share of the production contracts, partly to upgrade the technological competency of its industries, partly to minimize foreign exchange requirements within the consortium as well as vis-à-vis the United States, partly to satisfy the desires of particular manufacturers to obtain contracts to produce specific components, and so on. The ability of a country to recoup through taxes a part of the military procurement cost from domestic manufacturers may be another reason to let contracts at home rather than with foreign manufacturers—despite more favor-

[3] For excellent study of this system and the operation of the production consortiums as well as suggestions for future Alliance undertakings in this area, see the study by Brigadier General E. Vandevanter, Jr., USAF (Ret.), *Coordinated Weapons Production in NATO: A Study of Alliance Processes*, RM-4169-PR, The RAND Corporation, November, 1964.

able prices from the latter. Moreover, even though European countries have enjoyed full employment for a long time, they probably have wanted to use production contracts to further various economic or development programs within their countries.

In any case, bargaining to maximize the satisfaction of multiple objectives of the participating countries complicates arrangements for overall direction and control of the consortium effort and for sharing out the production among the countries. This has significantly raised the prices at which these weapons have been produced, even though the United States, in all cases, has entirely absorbed the R&D expenditures. To quote from Vandevanter:

Experts almost universally agree that articles produced by international syndicates have cost more than they would have if produced under national auspices. As to just how much more, calculations and estimates run from 15 per cent to 30 per cent, depending largely on the project. Some reasons for higher cost can best be demonstrated by a quick summary of the F-104G program. . . .

Complications and uneconomical restrictions were built into the enterprise from the beginning. First, each of the four European countries insisted on having its own final assembly line, where one facility would have sufficed. Then, three countries are assembling their own engines and manufacturing their own electronic systems. These requirements, which serve only the countries' prestige, not only are dissipating the savings that might be expected to accrue from mass production, but they also vastly complicated the management of accessories and sub-assembly. . . .

One of the factors that run up the cost of common production is the "quota" system. Each country has been given the privilege of manufacturing a guaranteed portion of the entire output. Presumably, these quotas were established in proportion to the number of aircraft bought by each country, but, reportedly, Germany's slice of the production contracts, particularly in air frames, is smaller than such a pro rata share.

Under the quota system, negotiating sub-contracts became a complex task. More than five hundred contractors were involved. First, the four participating countries had to decide which would have the privilege of manufacturing a given part. Selections often were influenced as much by the necessity to keep quotas balanced, as they were by price consideration. The winning country would then choose the commercial company to negotiate with its American counterpart for licensing rights, technical assistance, initial supplies, etc. Because of the complexity of these negotiations the United States Government frequently became involved against its will. At times the Pentagon would have to intercede to persuade American manufacturers to reopen facilities already closed out in order to furnish parts needed to prime the European assembly line.[4]

There is no published study comparing across the board the prices at which U.S. and European countries procure major items of military equipment. The European countries purchase some items from the United States at U.S. prices (which often do not cover full write-off of all U.S. costs, for example, R&D), purchase some items from consortiums producing weapons of U.S. design, and purchase some items of European design and manufacture. One can only guess

[4] *Op. cit.*, pp. 49–52.

how much on the average European NATO Allies pay for major equipment as compared with U.S. prices—10 to 20 per cent might be a reasonable guess.

4. Under-Investment in New Equipment and Stocks

Not only do many of the European countries pay generally higher prices for weapons, but they devote a significantly smaller proportion of their total budget to these items than does the United States. This of course cannot fail to have a significant influence upon the effectiveness of their forces. How did this budgetary pattern come about?

Parenthetically, this pattern of under-investment in equipment and operational stocks as compared to manpower and operating costs is most typical of the medium and smaller-sized European NATO Allies. It does not hold for the German military budget. Germany has been building up its military forces since the mid-fifties and investing substantial resources in equipment for these forces. Also Germany, to offset American balance of payments problems, has agreed to purchase each year substantial quantities of American equipment. France was under-investing in equipment until quite recently, although for the 1966 and future budgets it expects to invest almost half its yearly budget in new equipment and R&D. However, most of this is going into the French Force de Dissuasion. There have been stretchouts in the previously planned programs for the re-equipping of the five divisional units and supporting tactical air forces forming the French intervention forces.[5]

Otherwise this pattern of overexpenditure in military manpower has come about partly for historical reasons. During the fifties much equipment of the European NATO Allies was either supplied under U.S. military aid programs or supported by U.S. funded procurement schemes. During this period, the budgetary expenditures of these countries could be devoted mostly to manpower costs and the costs of training and day-to-day operations. But in the late fifties, American military aid to Western European countries essentially ended. There is now only some minimal aid to Greece and Turkey. Thus, many European NATO countries have entered the sixties with patterns of budgetary expenditure appropriate to a time when substantial U.S. military aid existed.

---

[5] Jean Planchais, *Le Monde*, October 21, 1965: "Finally, the Army sees itself getting farther away from the day it will get the five divisions promised by the long-range plan: 377 million (Francs) in old program authorizations disappear. The construction of tanks in particular will be slower than planned: 100 to 110 per year instead of 15 per month. Not until 1968 will production reach its peak. A thirty-ton tank costs two to three million francs. Its price can only go up. And when the last divisions are supplied—with a delay of a year or two—won't they begin to be outdated at the time when there are thoughts of equipping the ground forces with tactical atomic weapons? The same is true for tactical helicopters, the price for which per unit has by now reached that of a jet fighter ten years ago."

It is not easy to change these patterns quickly. European military budgets have risen in the past several years and a gradual shift toward more investment in equipment is perhaps under way. But re-equipping with new weaponry will be very costly. Nations have been able to postpone many of the hard decisions by delaying re-equipment and modernization decisions, by living a little longer with obsolescing weapons. These decisions cannot be put off indefinitely. The governments of these countries must determine future budgetary allocations with many conflicting pressures from the national military services, the NATO military commanders, national industrial interests, and so on.

For example, although these countries are now supporting more men under arms, and more units in operation, than they can effectively support over the long term given likely military budgets, they have been unable to reach the force goals of the major NATO commanders. The European NATO countries have been trying to meet these goals. Defense budgets for the European NATO countries as a whole have risen about 50 per cent between 1960 and 1965. But costs, both of manpower and equipment, have been rising quite rapidly. There has been some shift in the percentage of the budget devoted to the purchase of equipment and operational stocks, but not enough to offset the reduction in U.S. Military Aid Programs and the increased unit cost of equipment. The attempt to come as close as possible to the major NATO commanders' goals has given priority to maintaining or increasing the number of military units, and the numbers of men under arms. Consequently, qualitative aspects of their forces have been slighted, including modernization of their equipment buildup to agreed levels of operational stocks, and formation of support units.

Moreover, the European NATO nations are now experiencing the effects of the increased birth rates immediately following World War II. The amount of manpower available each year for military service has increased significantly from what it was in the fifties. Many of the European NATO countries have long traditions of universal military training. This demographic bulge has forced upon these systems of universal military training more manpower than they can afford to train and equip. This has very likely reinforced the decision of many of these countries to delay the re-equipment and modernization of the equipment of their military forces. Many countries are reluctant to modify these universal military training systems, sometimes for internal political reasons.

One way to accommodate the increased size of the yearly inflow of manpower, within current budgets and authorized size of forces has been to reduce the length of military service. France has this particular problem. In mid-1965, the French changed their military service law in order to excuse from military service many more men than formerly possible. The French plan to reduce significantly the number of men they take each year, rejecting an alternative proposal that they retain the more democratic, earlier law, and reduce the training period to one year. The French have also reduced the training and equipment costs per man by diverting a substantial portion of the manpower conscripted each year into a home defense force. These can be trained more quickly and cheaply for their role in local defense and guerrilla warfare within France. Other NATO European Allies might consider similar changes in their laws and use of military manpower.

In any case, many European countries, given their universal military conscription laws and the current large manpower classes feel forced to continue their current budgetary patterns. But they are unlikely to be able to do so indefinitely. The long-run result will be over-large-peacetime-forces, manned by troops with limited training, equipped with obsolescent equipment. The operation of these systems of universal conscription, with attendant short training periods, produces large numbers of reserve military personnel that are limited in their ability to use modern military equipment. And, in any case, equipment of reserve units will be limited and even more obsolescent than that of operational units.

Hence the operation of these universal military training systems is very wasteful and very costly. The expense of training the men is largely wasted since their active period of service is so short. Their usefulness as reserves is doubtful, both because of equipment shortages and, perhaps, also because of the changed nature of modern war. Countries with this problem must find some way to reduce the manpower taken each year so that, within a reduced proportion of the budget, training periods can be long enough for adequate training with modern weapons. Enough budgetary elbow-room must be found to allow the modernization of equipment and the build up of adequate operational stocks.

IMPLICATIONS

Military force postures change slowly over time. They are the result of a sequence of past procurement and military policy decisions. The same patterns of behavior tend to continue year to year, determining budgetary allocations, weapons procurement, military manpower policy, training practices, and so on. The contribution of the European NATO countries toward their own self-defense is decisively influenced and constrained by the national objectives of the individual countries and the patterns of behavior discussed above. These countries are not now, nor will they be in the near future, nearly able to defend themselves against potential maximum levels of Soviet and Warsaw Pact aggression. Given annual expenditures of nearly $20 billion, their contributions to their own self-defense is well below what it could be. However, the limits on their past ability to produce forces adequate for their collective self-defense are unlikely to change rapidly in the future. Many of the causes are built into the European situation: the division of effective decisionmaking among the twelve nations; the attendant high overhead costs of their military establishment; the political and economic forces within each of the nations which lead to the failure of coordinated production and logistic support operations; the historical attachments to universal military training programs.

Altering NATO strategic guidance or changing a few paragraphs in supposed key NATO documents will do little about these factors that largely determine the performance of these countries in supplying military forces. Nevertheless, most suggestions for curing the ills of NATO seem to be based precisely on such changes in agreed NATO strategy or in the upper level NATO administrative or bureaucratic structure. The real problems reside within the countries; limiting their ability to produce appropriate and effective forces.

The military forces of the European countries are now, in fact, probably too large, given current and probable future budget levels, to be supported as efficient units. The defense contribution of the NATO countries to the Alliance would probably be improved if forces were smaller, if universal military training laws were changed (where this is required to allow longer periods of training), if increased budgetary appropriations for equipment were undertaken at the expense of manpower costs. Attempts at regional pooling of supply, logistics and support operations, and the encouragement of *ad hoc* coalitions of those Alliance members that have a genuine common interest in specific ventures would all be useful.

In some cases increased financial contributions to Alliance-wide efforts, such as infrastructure projects, might be obtained through the reduction of forces in some countries and could benefit the Alliance. For example, Italian forces, if kept on Italian soil, are badly placed geographically with respect to the most likely military contingencies. Italy might give increased support to infrastructure projects and reduce its forces. Through changes in the infrastructure burden sharing formula, and compensating reductions in active military forces in some of the NATO countries, a shift of resources within the Alliance is possible that would help support active forces in geographic areas where they are most needed. The United States and its European NATO Allies probably have more to gain by improvements in the efficiency with which the $20 billion is used than they have through attempts (in any case likely to be fruitless) to increase European military expenditures.

Better defense management within the countries would help, as it would at all levels within the NATO Alliance. Standard cost-effectiveness studies, however, do not usually deal with military problems in a way that will produce solutions to the kinds of problems discussed above. They may show where the biggest payoffs are, however. Practical suggestions for improvements can only be made on the basis of detailed knowledge of the forces, mostly within the individual countries, that now shape the evolution of military posture and policy. Although many of the hypotheses put forward in this chapter describe tendencies, habits, conditions, that some will call deplorable; the objective of the chapter is not to deplore, but to describe in part, how NATO force posture results from the decisions of the governments of the constituent countries, and to describe some of the reasons why the result is so often so far from what seems in principle attainable.

BIBLIOGRAPHY

1. The Institute for Strategic Studies, *The Military Balance*. (Issued yearly; first issue covers 1961–62, most recent 1965–66). London.

2. Ismay, Lord, *NATO, The First Five Years*. Paris: North Atlantic Treaty Organization, 1955.

3. Neustadt, Richard E., Testimony Before Subcommittee on Government Operations. U. S. Senate, 89th Congress, June 29–July 27, 1965, pp. 125–28.

4. Olson, Richard E. Jr. and Richard Zeckhouser, *An Economic Theory of Alliance*, RM-4297-ISA. The RAND Corporation, 1965.

5. Stikker, Dirk U., *Men of Responsibility*. New York: Harper & Row, Publishers, 1966.

6. Vandevanter, Brigadier General E., Jr., USAF (Ret.), *Coordinated Weapons Production in NATO: A Study of Alliance Processes*, RM-4169-PR. The RAND Corporation, 1964.

7. Vandevanter, Brigadier General E., Jr., USAF (Ret.), *Studies on NATO: An Anatomy of Integration*, RM-5006-PR. The RAND Corporation, 1966.

CHARLES WOLF, JR.

The RAND Corporation

Dr. Wolf's experience includes: Chief of Program Planning in the Technical Cooperation Administration (1953–54); member of the Subcommittee of the President's Committee to Study the U.S. Military Assistance Program (1959); consultant for the Agency for International Development (1961–   ); and consultant for the Asian Productivity Organization in Tokyo (1963–   ). He is also a lecturer in the Department of Economics at the University of California at Los Angeles.

The author's most recent publications are: *United States Policy and the Third World: Problems and Analysis* (Little, Brown, 1966); *Foreign Aid: Theory and Practice in Southern Asia* (Princeton, 1960); *Capital Formation and Foreign Investment in Underdeveloped Areas* (co-authored with S. C. Sufrin); (Syracuse, 1955, 1958); "Foreign Aid Reconsidered" (1961); "Defense and Development in Less-Developed Countries" (1962); "Some Applications of Operations Research to Economic Development" (1963); "Insurgency and Counterinsurgency- New Myths and Old Realities" (1965); "National Priorities and Development Strategies in Southeast Asia" (1965).

20

Military-

Assistance Programs

1. INTRODUCTION

Military assistance, which is administered by the Defense Department, is part of the foreign-aid program of the United States. Like other parts, military aid is an important instrument of American foreign policy. Of course, other programs of the Defense Department besides military aid are also closely related to American foreign policy, and these relationships extend beyond Clausewitz' maxim that war is foreign policy carried on by other means. It is, for example, evident that the size, deployment, and operational readiness of strategic as well as general-purpose forces are important tools that can be used in the conduct of foreign policy, especially in crisis and near-crisis situations, quite apart from the actual conduct of war.

Nevertheless, the Military-Aid Program (MAP) is imbedded in foreign policy to an extent that distinguishes it from most other activities managed by the Department of Defense. One indication of this difference is the legislative requirement that military-aid programs for each recipient country must be approved by the Secretary of State. Furthermore, passage of each year's military-assistance authorization and appropriation by the Congress requires prior consideration by the Foreign Relations and Foreign Affairs Committees of the Senate and House respectively, rather than the Armed Services Committees.

As an instrument of foreign policy, military assistance involves the provision of equipment and training to the military forces of certain countries for a variety of objectives. The principal objective is to strengthen the military capabilities of recipient countries for meeting specific threats that the United States and the recipient agree are important to forestall. (The fact that some of these capabilities may be used by the recipients for purposes other than those intended by the U.S.—for example, to threaten noncommunist neighboring countries in, say, Greece and Turkey, or India and Pakistan—is a possible side effect that can be both awkward and damaging to the U.S.). In addition, MAP is sometimes provided with other objectives in view: to improve the capacity of local military establishments to engage in nation-building, "civic-action" activities that contribute to economic development; to build local facilities and installations that U.S. forces, as well as the recipient country's own forces, might use under some circumstances; and to induce a recipient country to provide base rights, or other facilities or access, desired by the U.S.

2. BACKGROUND AND ORIGINS

American military assistance in the post-World War II period was begun with special programs of aid to the Philippines in 1946, Greece and Turkey in 1947, and China in 1948. Each of these programs was addressed to special

Note: Any views expressed in this paper are those of the author. They should not be interpreted as reflecting the views of The RAND Corporation or the official opinion or policy of any of its government or private research sponsors.

problems and situations in the recipient countries under separate authorizing legislation. In 1949, passage of the Mutual Defense Assistance Act (MDA) provided a single enabling act for all military-aid programs and formally asserted their common basis in a foreign policy, one of whose instruments was "the furnishing of military assistance essential to enable the United States and other nations dedicated to the purposes and principles of the United Nations to participate effectively in arrangements for individual and collective defense."[1]

At its inception, the principal geographic focus of the Mutual Defense Assistance Program (MDAP) was Europe, and timing of the program was determined by the need to provide tangible support for the North Atlantic Treaty, signed on April 4, 1949. In turn, the impetus behind NATO came from the increasing evidence afforded by events in Czechoslovakia, Greece, Germany, and Turkey of a rising temperature in the European cold war and of the unanticipated possibility of military conflict in Europe.

Following the Korean War, the geographic emphasis of military assistance gradually shifted from Europe to Asia, for two principal reasons: economic recovery and progress in Western Europe enabled the NATO countries (except for Greece and Turkey) increasingly to finance their own defense efforts; and the relative seriousness of threats in the Asian area increased with the consolidation of communist power on the mainland. Notwithstanding this geographic shift, the role of military aid in supporting alliances in which the U.S. participated (CENTO and SEATO, as well as NATO), remained prominent. In addition, the program became a principal means of supporting bilateral security arrangements with Korea, Nationalist China, and Japan. In some cases military assistance was also extended to the "unaligned" countries such as India, Indonesia, and Egypt. Although there are currently military-aid programs in more than fifty countries, a large percentage of the MAP funds are concentrated in certain key Allied countries on the periphery of the Soviet Union and Communist China.

Since the beginning of the program, annual appropriations for MAP[2] have averaged around $1.4 billion, excluding the period from 1951 to 1954 when the program underwent a substantial, temporary increase due to the Korean War. In recent years, annual appropriations have declined to about $1 billion. The annual appropriations are summarized in Table 20–1.

The amounts shown in Table 20–1 mainly represent military end-items. They also include expenditures for the Military Assistance Training Program

[1] The Mutual Defense Assistance Act of 1949, in *Documents on American Foreign Relations*, 1949, p. 626. For a discussion of the early history and background of military assistance in the postwar period, see William Adams Brown, Jr., and Redvers Opie, *American Foreign Assistance* (Washington: The Brookings Institution, 1953); *The Military Assistance Program*, Department of State, publication 3563 (Washington: 1949); and Charles Wolf, Jr., *Foreign Aid: Theory and Practice in Southern Asia* (Princeton: Princeton University Press, 1960).

[2] In fiscal year 1954, the Mutual Defense Assistance Program became the Military Assistance Program.

TABLE 20–1   *Annual Appropriations for U.S. Military Assistance,*
              Fiscal Years 1950–1966

Year	Appropriations (in billions of dollars)
1950	1.3
1951	5.2
1952	5.7
1953	4.2
1954	3.2
1955	1.2
1956	1.0
1957	2.0
1958	1.3
1959	1.5
1960	1.3
1961	1.8
1962	1.6
1963	1.3
1964	1.0
1965	1.1
1966	1.2

(MATP), under which officers and enlisted men from the armed forces of recipient countries are trained in U.S. service schools. The number of students annually trained under the MATP is currently about 15,000, at an annual cost of about $70 million.

At the present (1966) appropriation levels, MAP is less than 2 per cent of the regular budget of the Department of Defense and less than 5 per cent of the amount appropriated for U.S. general-purpose forces. The amounts shown in Table 20–1 exclude military equipment that is sold on a cash or credit basis to foreign countries able to pay for such equipment. In recent years, such sales, particularly to Western Europe, have been an important offset to U.S. military expenditures abroad in easing the U.S. balance-of-payments deficit.

The MAP appropriations shown in Table 20–1 also exclude U.S. assistance provided to support the government budgets of certain countries whose defense expenditures exceed their capacity to pay. Such "supporting assistance" is considered a separate category of economic aid, rather than military assistance, because it takes the form of consumers' or producers' goods that are sold on local commercial markets with the proceeds used to support the recipient's budget. Supporting assistance, which is administered by the Agency for International Development (AID), is currently running at an annual rate of about $400 million, excluding assistance to Vietnam.

3. PLANNING AND PROGRAMMING

Planning of U.S. military assistance is based on comprehensive guidance from the Department of Defense (DoD) in coordination with the Department of State and AID. The administrator of AID is responsible for coordinating MAP with economic aid; unresolved differences between DoD and AID are referred to the Secretary of State and the President.

DoD guidance for MAP sets forth U.S. policy objectives and dollar guidelines for future planning for each country and also specifies the military tasks that warrant emphasis in AID programming. Within this framework, the planning of five-year military-assistance programs on a regional and country-by-country basis also depends on military-requirements planning as visualized by the Joint Chiefs of Staff (JCS).[3]

On the basis of the JCS force goals and base requirements as well as the country dollar guidelines, the Military Assistance Advisory Groups (MAAG's) prepare and submit their proposed five-year military equipment and training plan for the forces of the recipient countries. MAAG plans are initially submitted to the Unified Commander and include both the dollar costs of equipment programmed under MAP and the total estimated local defense-budget costs with which the dollar programs are associated. Total defense costs are subdivided into those to be financed by the country itself and those for which foreign support is to be contributed, either from U.S. supporting-assistance funds (under economic aid), from the sale of U.S. surplus agricultural commodities (under the Agricultural Trade and Development Act, PL 480), or from other countries. The MAAG submissions also indicate what shortfalls in the JCS goals, if any, will result under the planned program and whether these shortfalls are considered to be acceptable or unacceptable in relation to U.S. objectives and to anticipated threats. In turn, the MAAG submissions are reviewed by the Unified Commander, who then approves, modifies, cuts, or reschedules (for example, by stretching out the planned MAP deliveries). As finally modified and approved by the Unified Commander, the regional programs are then submitted to the Department of Defense.

Submissions from the Unified Commanders are reproduced and distributed by DoD as the basis for inter-agency review. Within the Defense Department, the review of MAP plans is supposed to assure "that a dollar spent on military

---

[3] The guidelines contain both a firm MAP figure that applies to end-item deliveries for the immediately following year and a target dollar figure for each of the next five years. For a further discussion of programming and planning procedures, see *Information and Guidance on Military Assistance*, Directorate of Military Assistance, United States Air Force, 9th Ed. (Washington: 1965); and Amos A. Jordan, Jr., *Foreign Aid and the Defense of Southeast Asia* (New York: Frederick A. Praeger, Inc., 1962), pp. 40–70.

assistance . . . is as necessary as a dollar spent for the United States military establishment."[4] To achieve this aim, the legislation instructs the President to "establish procedures for programming and budgeting so that programs of military assistance come into direct competition for financial support with other activities and programs of the Department of Defense."[5] This provision, which relates mainly to the important question of the trade-offs between MAP-supported forces and U.S. general-purpose forces, has turned out to be considerably harder to implement than it was to formulate, as will be elaborated below.

In addition to the program review within the Defense Department, interagency review provides an opportunity to consider various policy issues that may be raised by the submissions from the field: for example, the important but often implicit political aspects of the programs; the significance of program shortfalls; needs and sources for financing local costs, and other relationships between military- and economic-aid programs. Following the interagency review, the programs are submitted to the administrator of AID in his role as foreign-aid coordinator and then to the Budget Bureau. The Budget Bureau submission requests an allotment to implement the operating program for the current fiscal year as well as approval of the basic estimates underlying the plan for the next five years, in order to permit preparation of the congressional presentation to go forward. After action by the Budget Bureau and further DoD consultation with the Unified Commanders and the MAAG's, program revisions are made so that the current program can be approved for execution and congressional presentation of the next year's program can be completed.

Underlying these planning and programming procedures are some of the major issues affecting MAP: for example, program objectives; the determination of force goals; economic impact; allocations among countries. As a point of departure for considering these issues, there will be a brief examination of the views expressed by a number of Presidential reports on military and economic aid that have been made since inception of the programs.[6]

4. PRESIDENTIAL REPORTS ON FOREIGN AID

In the past decade and a half, there have been seven Presidential committees organized to investigate and report on various aspects of U.S.

---

[4] The quotation is from Section 504b of the Foreign Assistance Act of 1963 as amended. See U. S. Congress, Senate Committee on Foreign Relations and House Committee on Foreign Affairs, *Legislation on Foreign Relations* (Washington: GPO, 1965), p. 27.

[5] *Ibid.*

[6] In addition to the Presidential reports cited below, some of these broad issues are also dealt with in Paul H. Nitze, "The Policy Background of Military Assistance," in *International Stability and Progress.* (New York: The American Assembly, 1957); Edgar S. Furniss, Jr., *Some Perspectives on American Military Assistance* (Princeton: Center for International Studies, Princeton University, 1957); Jordan, *op. cit.*; and Wolf, *op. cit.*, especially pp. 249–55.

foreign-assistance programs. Several of these reports were addressed principally to economic-aid programs. But virtually all of them presented views and conclusions on some of the basic questions that arise in planning and programming military assistance as an instrument of foreign policy: for example, the objectives behind military aid; the balance between military and economic aid; the role of force in meeting various threats facing the less-developed "third world"; and the bearing of MAP-supported forces on overall U.S. national-security policy.[7] Of the seven committee reports, three were directly concerned with military assistance: the Fairless Committee in 1957, the Draper Committee in 1959, and the Clay Committee in 1963. Nevertheless, virtually all the others also have relevant points to make and important issues to raise concerning military aid.

All the reports were completed after the Korean War began and were markedly influenced by that conflict. As noted earlier, expansion of military assistance to place primary emphasis on the less-developed countries of Asia was a direct consequence of the threat signaled by Korea. Just as the triumph of communism in China was interpreted as showing that military force was not sufficient to meet the communist threat in less-developed countries, so the Korean experience—in a country whose record of economic development between 1945 and 1950 had been impressive—was viewed as showing that economic development was not sufficient to meet aggressive communist military threats. Nevertheless, the Presidential reports usually viewed economic development rather than military force as the primary answer to the threat of internal subversion, with military aid and MAP-supported forces and alliances considered to be mainly directed toward meeting threats of overt aggression.

The reports that were directly concerned with military assistance generally

---

[7] The seven reports comprise over six hundred pages of text, supported by several thousand pages of memoranda and staff studies. In chronological order, the seven reports, with the names of the committee chairmen (or Presidential adviser) are as follows:

(1) *Report to the President on Foreign Economic Policies* (Washington: November, 1959), Gordon Gray;

(2) *Partners in Progress*, A Report to the President by the International Development Advisory Board (Washington: March, 1951), Nelson Rockefeller;

(3) *Report to the President and the Congress*, Commission on Foreign Economic Policy (Washington: January, 1954), Clarence Randall;

(4) *Report to the President by the President's Citizen Advisers on the Mutual Security Program* (Washington: March, 1957), Benjamin Fairless;

(5) *A New Emphasis on Economic Development Abroad*, A report to the President of the United States, The International Development Advisory Board (Washington: March, 1957), Eric Johnston;

(6) *Composite Report of the President's Committee to Study the United States Military Assistance Program* (Washington: August, 1959), William Draper;

(7) *Report to the President of the United States from the Committee to Strengthen the Free World: Scope and Distribution of United States Military and Economic Assistance Programs* (Washington: March, 1963), Lucius Clay.

arrived at a favorable evaluation of the program. Thus, the Draper Committee's evaluation of MAP led to the conclusion

> . . . the dollar expenditures for military assistance have made a greater contribution to United States security than an equivalent amount expended on the United States military establishment.[8]

A similar conclusion was expressed in the Clay report:

> Dollar for dollar these (MAP) programs contribute more to the security of the free world than corresponding expenditures in our defense appropriations.[9]

Secretary of Defense McNamara has reiterated the same point many times in recent years and has drawn one of the logical implications from it:

> On the basis of value received, it would be better to cut the appropriations for the Defense Department than to slash . . . military aid.[10]

In fact, the further logical inference follows that it would be efficient to *reduce* Defense Department appropriations in order to *increase* military-aid expenditures if, in fact, the "dollar for dollar" conclusion reached by Draper and reiterated by Clay and McNamara is to be taken literally.[11]

In addition to these views on payoffs from military aid, several of the Presidential committees considered explicitly the appropriate balance between military- and economic-assistance programs, notably in the Fairless, Draper, and Clay reports. With the exception of the Draper report, virtually all displayed more enthusiasm for the economic, developmental aspects of foreign aid than for military assistance, on the grounds that they represent the more positive, progressive, "nation-building" ingredients of American foreign policy. Most of the Presidential committees, except the Draper group, either favored maintaining the existing balance between military and economic aid or changing the balance in favor of economic aid. Thus, the Clay report, notwithstanding its previously cited view about the high payoffs from MAP, recommended a relatively greater reduction in military programs than in economic programs.

[8] Draper, *op. cit.*, p. 145.

[9] Clay, *op. cit.*, p. 5.

[10] Hearings before the House Foreign Affairs Committee, April 8, 1963, referred to in *The New York Times*, April 9, 1963.

[11] One might argue that *average* returns from MAP may exceed average returns from DoD expenditures, although the *marginal* dollars expended on each program (or the marginal million dollars) yield approximately equivalent returns. This logical argument requires that the functional relationship between U. S. expenditures and national security be sharply different for military-aid expenditures and other DoD expenditures, with MAP subject to much more rapidly diminishing marginal returns than, for example, expenditures on U. S. general-purpose forces. This requirement is, however, not implied by the quotations from the Draper and Clay reports referred to in the text above.

Nevertheless, from an analytical standpoint, the Draper report probably showed a more sophisticated understanding of the issues involved in the question of military-economic aid balance than did the other reports. Thus, Draper stated that it was inappropriate to specify any precise percentage rule-of-thumb governing the "mix" between military and economic aid. Instead,

. . . the vital consideration is whether the needs of comparable importance have been met in all categories of aid. The pattern of this relationship, the internal "mix," is necessarily built, and varies greatly, country by country.[12]

Although there are obvious and often serious difficulties in determining exactly what "comparable importance" means in specific cases, this basic conclusion was sound and sensible. Marginal allocations of military and economic aid should be judged, however roughly, in terms of whether the effects they seem likely to accomplish appear to be of equivalent "importance" from the standpoint of U.S. objectives. Where an additional million dollar's worth of military aid accomplishes more (or less) than the same amount of economic aid, the entire aid program would benefit from a marginal transfer of funds between the two aid categories, that is, from the less productive to the more productive. Unfortunately, the obvious merit of this dictum is weakened in practice by the difficulty of assessing the relatively incommensurable, as well as uncertain, types of "importance" for U.S. foreign policy that are connected with the two types of aid.

Although the reports are an interesting and rich source of information and hypotheses, it should be evident from this abbreviated account that the opinions expressed on military problems and programs were quite heterogeneous. Not only do some reports conflict with others, but occasionally a single report conflicts with itself. It is indeed questionable whether any of the Presidential reports revealed an understanding of the complex interplay between military problems and programs, on the one hand, and economic and political problems and programs on the other, in the process of nation-building and reconciling change with reasonable stability in the third world. In large measure, the problem was viewed in most of the Presidential reports as one requiring military forces to deter Korea-type aggression and socioeconomic development programs to deal with internal subversive threats. The reports largely ignored the important connections between external communist military pressures and internal guerrilla terrorism and warfare. Nor did they recognize adequately the numbers and types of military forces and capabilities that are often required to protect borders, control infiltration, carry out extensive civic-action programs in rural areas, respond effectively to incipient guerrilla violence, and contain the spread of larger-scale guerrilla operations. Finally, there was hardly more than a hint of the relationships between development programs and military programs, the one seeking to reduce the causes and sources of internal grievances and resent-

[12] Draper, *op. cit.*, p. 156.

ments, the other to restrain both the internal tensions that may be intensified during the process of economic development and the external efforts that may be made to exploit these tensions. The Presidential foreign-aid reports ignored such questions as the extent to which military programs conflict with and drain resources away from development programs and the extent to which military programs may be complementary to economic-development programs.

5. ANALYTICAL ISSUES AND RESEARCH PROBLEMS

The foregoing discussion has suggested some of the complex questions surrounding military-assistance programs as an instrument of American foreign policy managed by the Department of Defense. Some of these questions can be considered as strictly military questions, and some are more deeply imbedded in political and/or economic considerations, both in the United States and abroad. One way of examining these questions is to divide them among three related but separable allocation problems affecting MAP:

(1) allocation of a given MAP budget within a single country;
(2) allocation of MAP among countries (or, alternatively, among regions or Unified Commands);
(3) allocations of U. S. government funds as between MAP and other programs.

There follows a brief discussion of some of the analytical questions that arise under each of these categories.

(1) MAP Allocations within a Country

As noted earlier, the determination of force goals by the JCS for recipient countries is perhaps the most fundamental part of the problem and process of arriving at MAP allocations within a country. From the U.S. point of view, analysis of this problem requires examination of the sorts of military contingencies with which the U.S. is concerned. Should the recipient country's forces be designed with a view to fighting conventional, Korea-type wars, and if so what level of effectiveness should be sought (for example, in terms of holding out for some time period until help arrives, inflicting casualties or damage on the aggressor's forces, counterattacking, and so forth)? Or should the forces be designed instead to prevent or meet various types and scales of insurgencies, or "wars of national liberation," that might arise and, indeed, may be more likely to arise than overt aggression? Or should the forces rather be designed to contribute to a possible collective-security unit consisting of forces from several countries that might operate within the recipient country or elsewhere, for example, in Vietnam or the Dominican Republic?

As one answer to these difficult questions, it is sometimes argued that forces should be designed for the largest plausible contingency, since the smaller cases will thereby be automatically included. But it seems fairly evident that the optimal force structure for a big, and perhaps unlikely, Korea-type war may diverge substantially from the optimal force structure for other kinds and locations of conflict. Where a serious budget constraint exists, achieving a better capability for one contingency usually will be at the expense of improved effectiveness in others.

For example, if Asian forces are designed for meeting major conventional aggressions by China or North Vietnam or North Korea, or Latin American forces are designed for "hemispheric defense," their capabilities for deterring or meeting insurgent threats may be considerably less for a given budget than if they were specifically designed for these lower-level threats. A capability to prevent or deter insurgent threats may require a highly developed intelligence system, expanded engineering and medical units for "civic action," and an enlargement of paramilitary and police, rather than conventionally armed and trained military units. A capability to wage effective counterinsurgency warfare —a "war-fighting" capability—may require forces with a high degree of surface mobility, airlift, and aerial reconnaissance. On the other hand, forces to meet a major conventional aggression are likely to stress *not* these capabilities but armor, firepower, fighter aircraft, and air defense instead. Thus, the requirements in an insurgency context for both deterrence and "war-fighting" capabilities are likely to differ sharply from the requirements for deterring or meeting large-scale conventional aggression. Hence, where resources are constrained as they typically are, choices must be made. A decision to base force structures on one set of contingencies is likely to mean reduced capabilities for other contingencies.

Even if these questions can be answered from the viewpoint of the U.S., it should be evident that allocating MAP among alternative force and equipment postures within a given country also depends on the objectives of the recipient itself. In turn, the country's own objectives may stem from views about the nature of the relevant and important contingencies that are very different from the views of the U.S. That the contingencies with which the U.S. is principally concerned may diverge sharply from those with which Greece and Turkey, or India and Pakistan, are principally concerned is both obvious and frequently overlooked. This frequent, if not typical, circumstance might be taken explicitly into account in formulating intracountry MAP allocations for forces and systems: for example, forces might be deliberately designed so as to limit capabilities for fighting wars against the "wrong" adversaries. Barrier defense systems and forces that could be *less* readily deployed for offensive purposes might be preferred to other forces because of a reduced capacity for mischief that they would entail.

Sometimes, too, a country may desire a particular set of force goals less because of an explicit concern for specified contingencies than because of the relative influence and political leverage of a particular service or ministry within the country's own government structure, or for other political reasons. And the U.S. may or may not endorse this state of affairs. Thus, political considerations may often be paramount in determining MAP allocations within a country, as well as among countries, as will be discussed below.

Finally, allocation of MAP among alternative forces within a country may also be affected by the extent to which variations in force structure may have significantly different economic side effects. For example, MAP allocations to military infrastructure (airfields, communications networks, port facilities, and so forth) or to various technical-training programs may be considered preferable to other possible uses of military funds because of the beneficial effects on economic development and nation-building.[13] In many of the less-developed countries this nation-building, modernizing role of the military may be relatively important because of the limited capacity of other institutions to perform these functions. Thus, in a number of Latin American countries, the effect of military training in upgrading the quality of human resources for the civilian economy is often significant, ranging from basic literacy to middle-level technical skills and to organizational and management skills. And in a number of countries, military infrastructure can contribute not only to improved force mobility but to civilian economic development as well. Force structures and MAP allocations can, at the margin, be based on these economic side effects with considerable developmental benefits as a result.

(2) MAP Allocations among Countries

Allocation among countries or regions from a given global MAP budget involves a series of both interesting and relatively intractable considerations. One fundamental consideration is the relative "worth," or "value," of the particular country in question compared with other countries, from the U.S. point of view. Parts of this question (for example, the military dimensions of a country's value to the United States), can be viewed in terms of alternative or opportunity costs and perhaps crudely quantified.[14] Thus the question can be asked what the effect would be of a "loss" of country X, on the costs of defending another country, Y, whose defense the U.S. is concerned with. The answer provides an upper bound to this aspect of military "value."[15] Sometimes (but rarely and decreasingly) the "value" of a country to the U.S. may depend on a particular base right, facility, or access that the country in question provides to the U.S. In such cases, MAP allocations may be partly considered in terms of the "rental" costs of access to such real estate. But despite these examples, most of the relevant dimensions of "value" depend on considerations that require a heavy dose of judgment and intuition rather than quantitative analysis.

---

[13] For a discussion of research on this problem, see Charles Wolf, Jr., "Defense and Development in Less-Developed Countries," *Operations Research* (November–December, 1962). See also p. 384 below.

[14] For some views on this problem, see the author's paper, "Some Aspects of the 'Value' of Less-Developed Countries to the United States," *World Politics* (July, 1963).

[15] See *ibid.*, pp. 625–29.

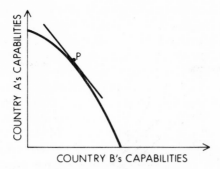

Figure 20–1   *Physical Productivity of Military Aid in Two Countries*

A model for intercountry allocations of MAP can be formulated in the following terms:

(1) The military capabilities which MAP "buys" (for example, equipment, forces, facilities) can, subject to certain constraints and exceptions, be considered as an approximation for the "outputs" resulting from these aid resources.[16]

(2) U.S. objectives can be viewed as indicating the relative "importance" to the U.S. of the various country capabilities that a given MAP budget can buy. Subject to the previously noted constraints, "importance" will depend on the value or worth of the countries in question, the threats that face them, their relative capacity and willingness to meet these threats on their own, the relative likelihood that they might misuse such incremental capabilities, and several other considerations as well.

(3) The costs of buying military capabilities, and thus the physical "productivity" of MAP in different recipient countries, will differ. The result is a trade-off relationship that shows the various combinations of capabilities in, say, Countries A and B, that can be bought with a given MAP budget.

The following curves describe in a rough way these "productivity" and "importance" (preference) considerations. Figure 20–1 shows the trade-offs between spending *a given budget* on military capabilities in Country A and Country B. The curve is concave for the usual reasons, though if economies of scale were important the curve could be convex. As drawn, Figure 20–1 shows that A's effectiveness for equal cost is higher than B's. Figure 20–2 shows two different "importance" or preference functions, U and U', comparing the value to the U.S. of capabilities in A and B. According to the first function U (reflected in the contours U_1, U_2), incremental capabilities in B are more highly valued than capabilities in A, for most of the relevant range. According to the second

---

[16] The constraints may include the base "rental" case referred to earlier, a minimum amount required for political reasons to support a particular regime, and so forth.

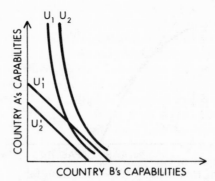

Figure 20–2   *Alternative U.S. Preference Functions for*
Capabilities in Two Countries

function, U' (reflected by contours U'_1, U'_2) capabilities in A and B are of approximately equal value to the U.S. It should be evident that the greater the extent to which capabilities in one country can (politically as well as physically) be deployed to the other country in the event of need, the closer will the preference map approximate to a series of 45° lines (for example, the U' function). With deployability, and with the substitution rates shown in Figure 20–1, it is also evident that capabilities receiving MAP allocations in (A) will be larger than in (B), as suggested by the point P—the point of tangency between the 45° U' function of Figure 20–2 and the transformation curve of Figure 20–1.

The model, though highly idealized, suggests some of the relevant considerations affecting intercountry allocations.

(3) Allocations between MAP and other U.S. Programs

At a still higher level of optimization (and, one might add, of relative intractability) a question arises as to the desirable size of MAP compared to other government programs. Here the most relevant alternatives probably arise in comparing allocations between MAP, on the one hand, and U.S. general-purpose forces (GPF), on the other. In dealing with this difficult question, it is necessary to know the costs and effectiveness of both MAP-supported forces and the potentially (and partially) substitutable U.S. GPF. Relatively high U.S. manpower costs often give the MAP-supported forces an apparently strong advantage; however, this advantage must be combined with several other sorts of considerations before arriving at a judgment. Clearly, the relative reliability of general-purpose forces, as well as their availability for use in multiple contingencies rather than just in contingencies within a single recipient country, will affect and may overbalance the usual cost-effectiveness comparison.

Moreover, the two alternatives—MAP-supported forces and GPF—are only partial substitutes, although the partial substitutability is likely to occur at the margins of both allocations, which is where the choice matters. It is primarily with respect to this choice between GPF and MAP-supported forces that the previously noted legislative requirement applies, namely "that programs of military assistance (should) come into direct competition for financial support with other activities and programs of the Department of Defense.[17]

In addition to the choice between MAP and U.S. GPF, the principal program that is sometimes viewed as a partial alternative to MAP is economic aid. Consideration of this problem immediately leads to some of the most important and, at the same time, intractable questions mentioned so far. In particular, the question arises of the political effects of both military aid and economic aid from the standpoint of achieving outcomes in the third world that are congenial to the U.S. The arguments and counterarguments on this matter are well known. Thus, in assessing economic aid, it is sometimes argued, and with considerable justification, that economic development is likely to be an acutely *destabilizing* force in the third world, carrying with it the danger of fomenting revolution that can be organized or manipulated by communism. On the other hand, there is the well-known association between levels of economic development and political democratization in the *long run*, from which it can be argued that the U.S. has a national interest in higher income levels for the less-developed countries.[18]

Similarly, views on the political effects of military aid are almost equally diverse. On the one hand, there is the view that military aid has the effect of strengthening the relative power of the military in contrast to civilian institutions, thereby tending to weaken democratic institutions and to stimulate military *coups* and dictatorships. On the other hand, there is the view that the process of reconciling major social and economic change with tolerable political stability in the third world requires that instruments of coercion and constraint (to which military aid contributes) be combined with instruments of development and reform. Moreover, according to this view there is no convincing empirical basis for the argument that military programs increase the probability of military dictatorships.[19]

---

[17] See footnote 4 of this chapter.

[18] For an illustration of these conflicting views, see, for example, Mancur Olson, Jr., "Rapid Growth as a Destabilizing Force," *Journal of Economic History* (December, 1963); and Everett E. Hagen, "A Framework for Analyzing Economic and Political Change," in *Development of the Emerging Countries*, ed. Robert Asher (Washington: The Brookings Institution, 1962).

[19] For these contrasting views see, for example, Edwin Lieuwen, *Arms and Politics in Latin America* (New York: Frederick A. Praeger, 1961), Chapter 1; and the same author's *Generals versus Presidents: Neomilitarism in Latin America* (New York: Frederick A. Praeger, 1964); Lyle N. McAllister, "Changing Concepts of the Role of the Military in Latin America," *The Annals of the American Academy of Political and Social Science* (July, 1965); and Charles Wolf, Jr., "The Political Effects of Military Programs: Some Indications from Latin America," *ORBIS* (Winter, 1965).

Notwithstanding the issue of allocation *between* military and economic programs, it is also important to keep in mind that there are several respects in which the two sets of programs complement rather than conflict with one another. Thus, economic-development programs can raise the effectiveness of military programs by increasing the resource base on which local defense budgets can draw, raising educational and literacy levels, and adding to the stock of technological skills that the military can use. On the other hand, for economic development to move forward, it is essential that adequate security be maintained and that the expectations of savers, investors, and workers be strengthened so that security will be maintained in the future. Consequently, military and paramilitary programs that control internal subversion and improve law and order are essential for effective development programs.

Moreover, as noted earlier, military programs can also contribute to development by adding joint civil-military infrastructure, by technological transfer and training that raises the quality of human resources, and, in some cases, by providing a wider market for domestic production of goods and services, including, but not confined to, military equipment. In some cases, the stimulus provided by reliable military demand may enable domestic producers to realize economies of larger-scale operation that permit a lowering of costs and prices and result eventually in access to new *civilian* markets as well. Although other methods of stimulating effective demand may often be preferable, where there are important security reasons for maintaining substantial military forces and programs, the potential economic benefits that can be derived from such demand should not be overlooked.

Each of the three successively higher levels of allocative decision—whether made implicitly or explicitly—involves important questions on which better information and analysis are needed. Some of this work is underway in the government, in private research institutions, and in the universities; much more remains to be done. Yet too much should not be expected. In a period in which defense activities and programs are becoming ever more closely related to political objectives and constraints, MAP is clearly one of the most politically-charged activities of the Defense Department. A major task of analytical work on MAP is thus to make sure that these nonmilitary objectives and constraints are taken properly into account—a task that is easier to identify than to carry out.

BIBLIOGRAPHY

1. Brown, William Adams, Jr. and Opie, Redvers, *American Foreign Assistance*. Washington, D. C.: The Brookings Institution, 1953.

2. Furniss, Edgar S., Jr., *Some Perspectives on American Military Assistance*. Princeton: Center for International Studies, Princeton University, 1957.

3. Jordan, Amos A., Jr., *Foreign Aid and the Defense of Southeast Asia*. New York: Frederick A. Praeger, 1962.

4. Lieuwen, Edwin, *Arms and Politics in Latin America*. New York: Frederick A. Praeger, 1961.

———, *Generals versus Presidents: Neomilitarism in Latin America*. New York: Frederick A. Praeger, 1964.

5. McAllister, Lyle N., "Changing Concepts of the Role of the Military in Latin America," *The Annals of the American Academy of Political and Social Science* July, 1965.

6. Nitze, Paul H., "The Policy Background of Military Assistance," in *International Stability and Progress*. New York: The American Assembly, 1957.

7. United States Air Force, *Information and Guidance on Military Assistance* (9th ed.) Washington, D. C.: GPO, 1965.

8. United States Government, Committee to Strengthen the Free World, *Report to the President: Scope and Distribution of United States Military and Economic Assistance Programs*. Washington, D. C.: GPO, 1963.

9. United States Government, *Composite Report of the President's Committee to Study the United States Military Assistance Program*, Volumes I and II. Washington, D. C.: GPO, 1959.

10. Wolf, Charles, Jr., "Defense and Development in Less-Developed Countries," *Operations Research*, November, 1962.

11. ———, *Foreign Aid: Theory and Practice in Southern Asia*. Princeton: Princeton University Press, 1960.

12. ———, "The Political Effects of Military Programs: Some Indications from Latin America," *ORBIS*, Winter, 1965.